D1595354

THE AUTOBIOGRAPHIES
OF NOAH WEBSTER

The following Collection consists of Essays and Fugitiv Peeces, ritten at various times, and on different occasions, az wil appeer by their dates and subjects. Many of them were dictated at the moment, by the impulse of impressions made by important political events, and abound with a correspondent warmth of expression. This freedom of language wil be excused by the friends of the revolution and of good guvernment, who wil recollect the sensations they hav experienced, amidst the anrky and distraction which succeeded the cloze of the war. On such occasions a riter wil naturally giv himself up to hiz feelings, and hiz manner of *riting* will flow from hiz manner of *thinking*.

Noah Webster
Hartford, June, 1790

The Autobiographies of Noah Webster

FROM THE LETTERS AND ESSAYS, MEMOIR, AND DIARY

EDITED WITH AN INTRODUCTION
BY RICHARD M. ROLLINS

UNIVERSITY OF SOUTH CAROLINA PRESS

Copyright © University of South Carolina 1989

Published in Columbia, South Carolina, by the
University of South Carolina Press

First Edition

Manufactured in United States of America

Library of Congress Cataloging-in-Publication Data

Gift 3/05

Webster, Noah, 1758–1843.
  The autobiographies of Noah Webster : from the letters and essays,
  memoir, and diary / edited with an introduction by Richard M.
  Rollins.
     p. cm.
  Bibliography: p.
  Includes index.
  ISBN 0-87249-574-4
  1. Webster, Noah, 1758–1843. 2. Lexicographers—United States—
Biography. 3. Educators—United States—Biography. I. Rollins,
Richard M. II. Title.
PE64.W5A3   1989
428'.0924—dc19
  [B]   88-37956
                                                                          CIP

DEDICATION

Respectfully Dedicated to the Memory of
Richard Lee Featherstone (1920–1986)
David Arthur Lett (1951–1987)

And to
Donald Arthur Rollins, Sr.
Barbara Irene Hunt Rollins
Jane Virginia Birdsey Lett
Marion Ellsworth Lett
Jane Scott Featherstone

CONTENTS

LIST OF ILLUSTRATIONS

Portrait in Miniature.
William Verstille, 1788. *Litchfield Historical Society, Litchfield, Connecticut.*

PREFACE

The objective of this collection of writings is to combine in one volume all the works of an autobiographical nature written by Noah Webster and to present them to the reader in a comprehensible form. It is not the purpose of the volume to present a full biography of the life of Noah Webster or a detailed historical accounting of all the events that Noah Webster participated in during his long and active life, but to provide these autobiographical essays for future biographers, historians, literary critics, and anyone else with an interest in the life of an important yet somewhat neglected figure.

It is also the objective of this collection to present the letters, essays, memoir, and diary in a form that is, as faithfully as possible, exactly like the original. A few words about editorial method are thus in order. In all three categories—letters, autobiography, diary—the original punctuation and spelling has been retained. Far be it from a twentieth-century scholar to correct the orthography of America's most accomplished lexicographer.

Contractions, abbreviations, superscripts, footnotes, ampersands, dashes, spaces, salutations and complimentary closes, and paragraphing have all been retained as they were written. Places and dates have been retained; any additions are for the benefit of the reader and have been added within brackets.

Capitalization has not been changed, but in those instances where it is difficult to tell if Webster intended an uppercase or a lowercase letter, modern usage has prevailed. It is not possible to reproduce Webster's handwriting—which remained bold and firm until the very end of his life—but an effort has been made in all cases to present an accurate, readable text with as much of the original flavor as possible. The single consistent alteration is the presentation of the eighteenth-century *S*, which was printed often as a lowercase *f*, as an *S*. The notation *sic* has been inserted in brackets when an obvious error might be mistaken for a typographical error.

Headings have been composed for each document, with the reader of the volume in mind. The item is described, dated, briefly explained, and placed in proper context. The explanation is designed to give the reader just enough information about the document and its context to make it comprehensible. Its location and any previous printings have been noted.

Much more could be written about many of the documents, and entire books have already examined many of the events that Webster was associated with or in which he participated. Each item has been chosen solely for its content, and its significance in the context of other issues will be left for others to estimate. A short bibliographical citation will give the reader whose interest is sparked by a document an idea of where to begin further reading. Footnotes have been added to identify the people and events mentioned in each document.

The introductory essay, "The Three Faces of Noah Webster," is an attempt to suggest an understanding of the way Webster wrote about himself in three different types of writing and to address the issue of how each type of writing shaped what he wrote, as well as how Webster perceived himself and presented his life at different times and under different circumstances. Textual notes have been used wherever possible so that the reader will not have to refer to notes at the end. This essay is not a definitive statement but is meant to suggest as much as possible about what I have gleaned from ten years of familiarity with Noah Webster's writing. That others might see different patterns is to the benefit of all who seek to understand those who have gone before us and who have shaped the world we live in.

Many people have given their time and thoughts to help this project reach conclusion. Richard M. Buck of the New York Public Library and Patricia Bodak Stark of the Sterling Memorial Library at Yale University have been helpful in my work at their facilities, as have the staffs of the New-York Historical Society, the Historical Society of Pennsylvania, the Manuscript Division of the Library of Congress, the Bienecke Rare Book and Manuscript Library, the Pierpont Morgan Library, and the Connecticut Historical Society. I would also like to thank Jeanine Head of the Edison Institute at the Henry Ford Museum, the staff members of the Eastern National Park and Monument Association, the National Portrait Gallery, and the Litchfield Historical Society for their help in locating the portraits of Webster and securing their publication.

Over the course of the years that it took to complete this project many individuals gave freely of their time and expertise in reading and discussing it. If many of their insights and ideas show up here, I am grateful for them, and sorry that I cannot recall exactly who has given each to me. I thank them all for their help. Mauricio Mazon, Tom Williams, and Jay Martin read several versions and commented frequently. Jane Scott Featherstone read my essay many times and helped greatly with its structure and flow. Her help over the years added much to the manuscript, and any segments of good writing are directly attributable to her help. Dawn and Stan Hecker helped with the "Memoir" at a crucial time. Warren Slesinger's interest and inquisitiveness provided much of the motivation needed to complete this effort. Any errors or misjudgments, of course, are my own.

November 22, 1987   Richard M. Rollins
                                       Redondo Beach, California

CHRONOLOGY OF THE LIFE OF NOAH WEBSTER

1758. October 16. Born in West Hartford, Connecticut, son of Noah and Mercy Steele Webster.

1774. September. Entered Yale College.

1778. September. Graduated from Yale.

1779–80. Taught school in Hartford and West Hartford.

1780–81. Studied law in Litchfield.

1781. April. Admitted to the bar.
July-October. Taught school in Sharon, Connecticut. Began work on Speller.

1782-83. Taught school in Goshen, New York.

1783. Spring. Returned to Hartford, practiced law and worked on Speller.
October. Published Speller as part I of *The Grammatical Institute of the English Language*.

1784. January 1. Began keeping diary.
March. Published Grammar as part II of *The Grammatical Institute of the English Language*.

1785. February. Published Reader as part III of *The Grammatical Institute of the English Language*.
March. Published *Sketches of American Policy*.

1785-86. Toured country lecturing about the need for an American Language.

1786. December. Moved to Philadelphia; taught school.

1787. May-September. Constitutional Convention.
October. Wrote and published *An Examination into the Leading Principles of the Constitution*.
November. Moved to New York; editor of the *American Magazine*.

1789. May. Published *Dissertations on the English Language*.
October 26. Married Rebecca Greenleaf.

1790. July. Published *Collection of Essays and Fugitiv Writings*.
August 4. Birth of first child, Emily Scholton.

1791. October. Published *The Prompter*.

1793. February 5. Birth of second child, Frances Juliana.

	August. Moved to New York to become editor of the *American Minerva*.
1794.	May 15. End of first phase of the diary.
1797.	April 6. Birth of third child, Harriet.
1798.	April 1. Moved to New Haven. Began second phase of the diary.
1799.	January 7. Birth of fourth child, Mary.
	December. Published *A Brief History of Epidemic and Pestilential Diseases*.
1800.	Began work on dictionary.
1801.	September 15. Birth of fifth child, William Greenleaf.
1803.	December 21. Birth of sixth child, Eliza.
1806.	February. Published *Compendious Dictionary*.
	November 20. Birth of seventh child, Henry Bradford, who died shortly after.
1808.	Conversion to evangelical Protestantism.
	April 2. Birth of eighth child, Louisa.
1812.	September. Moved to Amherst, Massachusetts.
1820.	September 18. Last entry in diary.
1822.	Summer. Moved to New Haven.
1823.	September. Received LL.D. from Yale.
1824-25.	Research trip to England and France.
1825.	January. Completed dictionary in Cambridge, England.
1827.	Speller revised and republished as *An Elementary Spelling Book*.
1828.	November. Published *An American Dictionary of the English Language*.
1830.	December. Traveled to Washington to lobby for copyright laws.
1832(?).	Began "Memoir of Noah Webster, LL.D."
	August. Published *History of the United States*.
1833.	September. Published edition of Holy Bible.
1841.	March. Published second edition of *An American Dictionary*.
1843.	May. Published *Collection of Papers* . . . .
	May 28. Died in New Haven.

I. THE THREE FACES
OF NOAH WEBSTER

Pastel Portrait.
James Sharples, between 1793 and 1801. *Independence National
Historical Park Collection.*

1. INTRODUCTION

"I wish to enjoy life, but books and business will ever be my principal pleasure. I must write," Noah Webster wrote to George Washington in 1785; "it is a happiness I cannot sacrifice."[1] These words written by a young, nearly unknown New England author were prophetic. Between 1783 and his death in 1843, Noah Webster spent a large part of his life seated at a desk with pen in hand, scratching out an incredible number of books, essays, and letters on a wide variety of topics. He was probably the most prolific writer in America, corresponding with hundreds of people including Washington, John Adams, Thomas Jefferson, James Madison, Benjamin Rush, Benjamin Franklin, Alexander Hamilton, Oliver Wolcott, Timothy Pickering, Daniel Webster, Andrew Jackson, and virtually every other significant individual in the early republic. Hundreds of letters remain in two major and several minor collections.[2] He wrote on politics, geography, religion, economics, government, medicine, zoology, climatology, astronomy, agriculture, commerce, linguistics, and nearly every other subject of interest in his day. A bibliography of his writings runs over 600 pages.[3] For Webster, writing was an essential part of life. In it he found his very identity as a human being, both for his family, friends, and the public as well as for himself. As an entrepreneur he managed to support himself and his family from 1798 to 1843 primarily by writing and publishing, a feat rare in the early nineteenth century. And through the act of writing Noah Webster sought to reach out and shape the world in which he lived, for himself and for the rest of his countrymen. His Speller, a revolutionary broadside, sought to instill patriotic and nationalistic values in all American children.[4] His dictionary, a cultural landmark and an achievement of historic proportions, attempted to restore the deferential world order he believed was crumbling and to shape American minds in the image of evangelical Protestantism.[5]

Born on a small family farm near Hartford, Connecticut, in 1758, Noah Webster lived a long and extraordinarily active life. By the force of his own energy and intellect, Webster emerged from obscurity to become a significant figure in American cultural life. By the time of his death in 1843 his name was known across the nation. He had joined the pantheon of American founding fathers. Along with Washington, Madison, Franklin, and Jefferson, the name "Webster" stood for educational excellence and achievement of the highest order, and today is synonymous throughout the English-speaking world with correct spelling and authoritative definitions. In his chosen fields of education and the American language he is certainly the major figure before the emergence of McGuffey, who was yet another acquaintance and someone who paid tribute to his work.

Webster exhibited an interest in books and writing at an early age. As a young man he spent so much time reading that his family afterward told stories of his preferring to sit under a tree and read rather than do farm work. At Yale between 1774 and 1778 he read voraciously and joined a literary club with an emphasis on classical literature and poetry. His senior thesis detailed the tragedy of the destruction of the Alexandrine library.

The American Revolution often interrupted Webster's studies. Although he did not experience actual combat, he marched off to fight the British on two or three occasions, and his class spent one year in the small town of Glastonbury in the belief that it would be more safe from the British army than New Haven. For several years after his graduation he wandered around New England and New York teaching elementary school and trying to study law. His attempts to begin a law practice proved unsatisfactory, and in the early 1780s he turned to the writing of schoolbooks as a means of both earning his subsistence and Americanizing the educational process.

His first success came with the publication of his famous blue-backed Speller in 1783. *The Grammatical Institute of the English Language,* renamed *The American Speller* in 1787 and *The Elementary Spelling Book* in 1829, was hugely successful, eventually selling over 100,000,000 copies.[6] From the 1790s until his death he depended largely upon proceeds from the book for subsistence. He followed its initial publication with a Grammar and a Reader, neither of which was nearly so successful. The Speller is generally acknowledged as the first attempt to nationalize the American language and provide a coherent system of education. It was indeed notable for its idealism. America, according to its author, was the last, best hope of humankind, and its citizens who learned with the little blue paper-covered book must reject the corrupt political and social principles of an aged, decrepit world. Young America would become a democratic utopia if it adopted Webster's views on politics and language.

The strong ideological tone and content of the Speller's preface also marked the reams of essays, books, letters, and pamphlets he wrote in the 1780s and early 1790s. Between May 1785 and November 1786 he toured the nation from Boston to Charleston lobbying for copyright laws, meeting significant people, lecturing on the need for a national language, and drumming up business for his Speller. It was a key experience in his life. People like Washington, Franklin, Jefferson, and Madison welcomed him and praised his work, along with dozens of educators, political leaders, businessmen, and wealthy planters. His discussions resulted in one of the first calls for a stronger centralized form of government in his *Sketches of American Policy* (Hartford: Hudson and Goodwin, 1785) to combat the chaos of the Confederation. Between stops he wrote numerous essays on political, social, and economic issues, which he published as a single volume in 1790.[7] His lectures on language, outlining a need for a common orthography and pronunciation, also met with a positive reception and were later published as *Dissertations on the English Language* (Boston: Isaiah Thomas, 1789).

By 1787 Noah Webster occupied a small space in the public consciousness. His writing helped him obtain a teaching position in a school in Philadelphia during the Constitutional Convention. As his diary reveals, he met with many of the delegates and when one of them asked him to help support the new government he responded with *An Examination of the Leading Principles of the Federal Constitution* (Philadelphia: Pritchard and Hall, 1787). While in Philadelphia he met Rebecca Greenleaf, the daughter of a wealthy businessman. They married in 1789 and remained together for the rest of his life. From this time forward Webster's family affected his life and work in many ways and served as a haven from the turmoil and strains of his public life.[8]

After the Constitutional Convention, Webster decided to move to New York City to start what he felt would be the first truly national magazine of American politics and culture. The *American Magazine* failed in 1788, and Webster returned to Hartford to attempt to resume practicing law. He met with some success and enjoyed the social life of the circle of poets who are known to us as the Hartford Wits. With Joel Barlow, John Trumbull, and Timothy Dwight, among others he discussed poetry, literature, and politics and attended parties and dances. He served on the City Council and wrote a Franklinesque collection of amusing stories and witty aphorisms, *The Prompter* (1790).[9] This popular work found its way into taverns and hostelries in every state. He also wrote an abolitionist tract pointing out the negative effects of slavery on the slaveholders themselves, *Effects of Slavery, on Morals and Industry* (Hartford: Hudson and Goodwin, 1793).

A group of eminent Federalist politicians, led by Rufus King and John Jay and including Alexander Hamilton, sponsored Webster's return to New York. The city was an important point in their struggles with the emerging opposition, and they felt the need for a daily newspaper as an outlet of their views on policies and issues. Between 1794 and 1798 Noah Webster found himself in the middle of an increasingly bitter political debate. As the editor of the *American Minerva*, which became the *Commercial Advertiser* in 1797, he took part in discussions of all major issues. The French Revolution went through its most violent stages in 1793–94 and came to symbolize to the Federalists all that was chaotic, violent, and fearful in social transformation. The topic filled the papers; Webster summarized the Federalist point of view in his editorials and his pamphlet *The Revolution in France* . . . (1794).[10] The debate became hysterical, and Webster became the symbol of Federalist conservatism. He bore the brunt of virulent professional denunciations and vicious personal attacks. Exhausted by the physical labor and financially worse off than ever, he decided to retire from the fray and return to the calmness of New England in April 1798.

The public Noah Webster was not an easy person to know or to deal with. Now forty years old, he had accomplished much yet never seemed to be able to gain confidence in his place in society or to feel comfortable in the acceptance of his work. As early as 1784 he appeared as a very combative young man who was also very sensitive to every perceived or actual slight. Any criticism of his work clearly stung him. His opposers frequently accused him of being arrogant and headstrong, and even his friend Benjamin Rush told the story that, when Webster arrived in Philadelphia, Rush congratulated him on his arrival in the city of brotherly love, to which Webster replied, "Sir, you may congratulate Philadelphia on the occasion." Another of his friends in the 1780s referred to him as "the Monarch," and in every phase of his life he became engaged in protracted, often nasty, disagreements with anyone who disagreed with him over almost any topic. Even his strongest personal friendship—with former Yale classmate Joel Barlow—disintegrated during the heated political arguments of the late 1790s. The opinions of one friend seemed to sum up what many felt when he said that Webster "certainly does not want understanding, and yet there is a mixture of self-sufficiency, all-sufficiency, and at the same time insufficiency about him, which is (to me) intolerable."[11]

Morever, by 1798 Noah Webster had become convinced that humankind was evil in nature. From this followed a rejection of democracy and bitter attacks on Republican philosophies, policies, and practices. He became a spokesman for the most conservative Federalists advocating the restriction of voting rights to people over forty-five years of age and fiercely denouncing nearly every aspect of American political life in numerous essays like *A Rod for a Fool's Back*.[12]

Webster's life between 1798 and 1812 centered primarily on writing for a living. He served his community on the New Haven City Council between 1799 and 1804 and as justice of the peace between 1800 and 1810. He stood for elective office and was sent to the Connecticut legislature each year between 1800 and 1807, all the while continuing to publish, write, and work at increasing the sales of his Speller and school books. He was very active in local politics serving on numerous committees dealing with issues like improvement of schools, streets, trees, and fire laws. While in New York he had begun a study of plagues that swept many American cities in the 1790s and published *A Collection of Papers on the Subject of Bilious Fevers . . .* (1796).[13] Now he had the time and interest to use the information gathered earlier to study and analyze what he thought were the causes of the diseases, and he published his findings as *A Brief History of Epidemic and Pestilential Diseases . . .* (1799).[14] His scientific interests resulted in essays on subjects as diverse as potato farming and the decomposition of white lead paint. These were well received and highly regarded as a contribution to the advancement of knowledge on the topic. His movement away from the center of debate did not take him away from politics altogether, however, and he continued to author a stream of essays, pamphlets, and letters attacking the Republicans and denouncing their policies.

Yet the subject that interested him most after 1798 was not politics or science, but lexicography. He had thought about writing an American dictionary as early as the 1780s, and in 1800 he began in earnest. He published *A Compendious Dictionary* in 1806 as well as several grammar books and essays in lexicography and philology. He worked on his masterpiece for twenty-five years, tracing definitions and usage of words through twenty or more languages, and along the way got sidetracked into writing a long, unpublished essay on the development of human languages, as well as numerous pieces on various aspects of philology and lexicography.[15]

After 1798 Webster supported himself and his family almost entirely from the proceeds of the sale of his Speller and other school books. His daily chores were centered on work on his dictionary and in negotiating with publishers and agents and keeping track of the flow of funds. It was not an easy life, for few writers in the years before the Civil War were able to support themselves entirely through literary endeavors.[16] Many of his works were pirated and sold with no royalties; thus Webster was constantly battling his publishers and the pirates. His strategy included writing to famous and wealthy men asking for financial help in the form of subscriptions to the dictionary.

His financial situation was always insecure and in 1812 he decided to move to Amherst, Massachusetts, primarily because he believed the cost of living would be significantly less than in New Haven. He continued to write and helped found Amherst College, giving the cornerstone address at the inaugural ceremonies in 1820.[17] His political ardor did not wane: during these years he was elected to the Massachusetts legislature several times and continued to write a stream of essays, pamphlets, and letters on political subjects.[18] In 1814 he helped organize the Hartford Convention, a meeting of representatives of New England states to consider actions in response to national and international political and economic policies. He summed up the reasons for the meeting in a Fourth of July speech, later published as *An Oration, Pronounced before the Knox and Warren Branches of the Washington Benevolent Society* (1814).[19]

Webster's conversion to evangelical Protestantism in 1808 influenced everything he wrote after that date. His account of the actual conversion is covered in detail in a later section, so it will not be examined here. He had written little on religious topics early in his career, but now it became one of his central concerns. He described his conversion for the public in a pamphlet, *The Peculiar Doctrines of the Bible, Explained and Defended* (1809),[20] which became a widely read tract. In another important essay he discussed what he thought were the obscure words and other problems that prohibited the Holy Bible from being even more widely read,[21] while *Value of the Bible and Excellence of the Christian Religion . . .* (1839)[22] was intended to instruct American families on the ways in which religion could be used in the family. Webster felt that his edition of the Holy Bible (1833)[23] was the most important work of his lifetime. In it he attempted to modernize and cleanse the language of words that were obsolete or morally unacceptable so that people could read it more easily and not fear that they would be presented with words they felt were immoral and inappropriate for family usage.

In 1822 Webster moved back to New Haven and built the two-story Federal-style house that now stands in the middle of Greenfield Village and the Henry Ford Museum, in Dearborn, Michigan. Here he spent much of the final twenty-one years of his life in the second-floor study he had insulated with sand between the walls and floors. He sat at a round table in a chair with casters, moving from one lexicon to another tracing the development of words through more than twenty languages. In addition, he continued to pour forth the *Elementary Spelling Book* (1829), textbooks such as *A Manual of Useful Studies* (1839) and *Biography, for the Use of Schools* (1830), as well as the *History of the United States* (1832).[24] From his study he continued to negotiate with publishers and promote the sales of his work, a full-time job in itself. And while politics occupied fewer of his thoughts, it was still on his mind. His last significant political essay, published as "A Voice of Wisdom"[25] in 1837, denounced the contemporary political parties and praised those of the era of Washington.

Webster's most famous work, *The American Dictionary of the English Language*,[26] came off the press in 1827, though dated 1828. He had finished writing it while in England on a trip that combined a search for scholarly information with a search for an English publisher. Its publication did not meet with overwhelming success. The critical response was mixed, the sales lagged, and the publisher went bankrupt because of problems not related to the dictionary. In 1839 Webster mortgaged his home to fund a second edition, which appeared in 1841.[27]

Noah Webster's writing changed in its focus over the years, but never stopped. Just before he died he finished compiling a new collection of essays and was in the process of overseeing its publication when he caught pleurisy and died in May 1843.[28] The scope of interest and experience displayed in the essays neatly symbolized a life devoted to writing. He included many old works on topics as diverse as the French Revolution, agriculture, banking, international law, education, the Constitution, and copyright laws. He also included new, original essays on the founding of Amherst College, philology, education, the origin of the Hartford Convention, and the development of political parties in the United States. His granddaughter noted that as he lay dying on his bed he carried on a long conversation with his son concerning his works and held a copy of his Speller in his hand.

2. Personal History

Noah Webster also wrote about Noah Webster. Indeed, his own life was one of his favorite subjects. He left us autobiographical statements—his own personal history—in three distinct types of written documents. He kept a diary, he described his life in letters and essays, and he wrote a formal autobiography.

In each type of document Noah Webster turned a different face to the world. The facts of his recorded life rarely overlap or correspond in all three genres. Even when two different accounts of an event or phase in his life were recorded in the same period of time, they often differed in significant ways. And accounts of crucial events—such as his marriage or religious conversion—sometimes varied dramatically from genre to genre. In fact, in at least one instance, Webster consciously rewrote an account of a significant event when he wrote it in another form.

Moreover, the basic themes of Webster's life and his portrayal of his own ideas, beliefs, and concerns changed from form to form. A reader of his diary, knowing only the information contained therein, will develop a very different impression of its author than the reader of his autobiography. A reader of his personal letters and public essays will become familiar with a third distinct Noah Webster.

Yet the overarching resonance of the author's personality is clearly present in each type of document. The three faces of Noah Webster are three different facets of his personality. While they do differ, sometimes sharply, they are each the product of the details of his life and the special requirements of the genre in which he wrote. In his diary the author records one profile; in his letters and essays a second; in his autobiography he looks at himself directly. The three faces of Noah Webster may best be thought of as three glances in the mirror: each face reveals only part of the self and is shaped in part by the genre in which it is expressed. Each fulfills certain needs in the author's life and ignores others. They are written at different stages of life, with varying objectives in mind. When considered as a whole they reveal different aspects of the same life and character.

Each allows us to view the same subjective self writing to understand his life, to explain it to others, or to influence the lives of other
people.

Few writers have analyzed the similarities and differences between the three modes of writing about one's own personal history.
Historians, distrustful of the subjectivity involved in formal autobiography, have sought to estimate the accuracy of individual works.
They use them as primary sources in a straightforward manner while
paying little attention to the theoretical aspects of the genre. The
same could be said for historians' use of diaries and letters. Their
interest in these documents is usually related to what the specific
writer has to say about an event, and perhaps how the stated opinion or information given fits into larger historical patterns.[29]

Literary critics approach personal history from a very different
perspective. In their concentration on formal autobiography as literature they tend to ignore diaries and letters, relegating them to the
ash heap of historical documents, assigning them inferior status as
not "true" autobiography.[30]

Yet genuine differences exist between autobiographical statements written in different genres. Definitions developed by scholars
working largely on formal autobiography help clarify the ways in
which the demands of each genre shape the ways in which an author
writes about the life of the self. Two major differences are usually
cited by autobiographical critics. First, the diarist and autobiographer write from different vantage points in time. The diarist is
rooted in the immediate present. In the words of one critic, he is a
prisoner of the present. The autobiographer is reflective, looking
back over the life, usually from the vantage point of advanced years,
with the opportunity to sum up what is important and valuable in a
life already lived.[31] A second point is a correlation with the first. A
diarist is generally spontaneous, recording events, ideas, or information with little thought to the general impression created by the
words. Little consideration is given to sentence structure, symbolism, and the reader's response. The autobiographer typically com-
poses a story, a complete and unified work. Attention may be
lavished on the overall significance of the life and the patterns or

shapes of component parts. Stylistic ploys, such as metaphors, symbolism, and other manipulations of language may be used to shape the story and to impose an interpretive framework on it.[32] Letters and other types of documents are so diverse that few generalizations may be made. They can fall into the category of either autobiography or diary, or somewhere between, according to the specific document.

Each genre Noah Webster used helped shape the character of the face it revealed to the reader by providing the basic parameters within which the facts of his life were presented. In his diary Noah Webster recorded his private self: his needs, thoughts, and concerns as they surfaced in his everyday life. They show the values of the author and the perception of the self as he wanted immediately to record them. This is a private self in the sense that it existed for his eyes only and was not intended for the perusal of others. Above all, it reflects a strong desire for approval from other people, especially from significant people. Webster's sense of his own identity is weak when he begins writing; thus the diary provides a means to shape it, to prove to himself his own worth and role in life. In his letters and other essays he presented himself in the shape of a prophet, speaking first for his culture's highest ideals, then for God, to the American people, always urging them to conform to certain types of behavior. He sought approval from his contemporaries, for if they did as he wished, it would signify their approval of him. In his formal autobiography Webster presented his life as that of an exemplary figure, the public servant. Here he sought to record his life as he wished it had been lived, to seek approval from future generations of Americans yet unborn, from posterity itself.

Each self is different from the others, and each has its own quality of truth. They are three aspects of his perception of his life, its significance, and its relationship to the world in which he lived: Three forms of his personal history. When studied separately they present three different views of his life; read together they merge to present an uneven, yet consistent and fascinating, study of the inner life of an author and its outward manifestation in his own accounts of his life in three different forms of his writing.

These "three faces of Noah Webster" will attempt to make comprehensible Noah Webster's perception and presentation of his life in three genres over a span of some six decades of American life, as well as the interrelatedness of those written accounts. Along the way we shall also look at a number of fascinating side issues, such as the reasons behind his abandonment of the autobiography and why he failed to publish it.

3. THE PRIVATE SELF

In the years between 1784 and 1794, and again between 1798 and 1820, Noah Webster kept a diary. In the beginning he made entries daily; by the end of the first decade they had become sporadic and continued to be so throughout the final section. The content, tone, and essential function of the diary changed radically over its thirty-six years, as did the author's self-portrait contained within it. Indeed, the changing facts and circumstances of Webster's life combined with the requirements and framework of diary writing to shape the image of the self. In the beginning he portrayed himself privately as the rising young man in search of his personal niche in the world. In the final twenty years he appears as the detached scientific observer of the natural world.

The perspective of a diarist is immediate and highly personal: it is a daily record of the events and ideas of interest to the author. Each entry is self-contained, written shortly after the recorded event, and displays little attention to style. It is written for personal reasons and—in contrast to journals, travel narratives, historical chronicles, religious journals, annals, reminiscences, minutes, orderly books, muster rolls, captain's logs, letters, or other forms of writing—is not adapted to the needs of a potential reader through the inclusion of interpretive statements, a concern for spelling or punctuation, or thought for omissions or additions. There are, of course, diaries written consciously for publication, but those are exceptional among the more than 10,000 American diaries listed by scholarly bibliographers.[33]

In the first ten years, Webster's diary is similar in structure and content to thousands of others. He recorded the events of the day and how he felt about them, as well as other bits of information: ideas, thoughts, and aphorisms; the weather; financial and political news; agricultural and meteorological data; thoughts about his job, family, or friends; travel records; and self-examination—all as he felt appropriate.

Like other American diarists, Webster began writing in his youth. Most diarists are young, usually between sixteen and twenty-five, and Webster began his at age twenty-five. Studies of American diarists reveal that they are typically prompted by their own growing consciousness of their uniqueness, and of their individual roles in the social world. They often express the belief, reflected in their need to write down the reality of their experiences, that older people do not understand or value them. Often diarists are spurred on by the failure in their personal relationships or by a sense that moral conflicts have become unbearable. In all of these, Webster may be said to conform to the general patterns discovered by scholarly research. About two-thirds of American diarists are female, and here Webster is in the minority.[34]

Webster's diary contains an implicit interpretation of his life. Every diarist subjectively chooses what to write about and which events, feelings, thoughts, activities, and beliefs to ignore. Those choices impose a conceptualization on the writing and on the life: they reveal an assumed ordering of values and priorities. In addition, the narrative contains the author's subjective evaluation of the material record. The choice of words—their tone, phrasing, punctuation, and even the order in which they are presented—as Noah Webster certainly understood, colors the flavor of the work with the author's implicit feelings.

Webster's diaries reveal a face he turned toward himself and no one else. When read with an eye toward understanding the types of information it contains, the style of recording, the portrayal of life by the author, and the changes in these characteristics over time, they reveal a private self writing only for his own purposes. Webster was not an exceptionally introspective person, and his diary was not a place for long confessional passages full of intensive self-examination. Instead he recorded what he thought important about himself, his life, and the world in which he lived. The key to understanding the self-portrait in the diary is an analysis of what he thought important and what it says about his perception of his life.

What he wrote in his diary reflected and was shaped by his inner feelings and fits into a pattern recognizable throughout his life and traceable to his childhood. We know little of Noah Webster's earliest years. He was one of five children, born in 1758 on a small farm in what is now West Hartford, Connecticut. Of his upbringing by his parents we know almost nothing at all. According to research by various scholars, child-raising practices common in New England in the middle of the eighteenth century reduced emphasis upon direct supervision of children. They were strikingly less authoritarian than before, advising parents not to force children, physically or mentally, into strict habits of behavior. Children raised in this atmosphere often exhibited a sense of ambivalence, of no firm sense of self-identity. They typically yearned for the comfort and guidance of close parental attention, yet felt a strong need to assert their individual opinions, wishes, and rights.[35] Some historians have even suggested that the ability of the revolutionary generation to carry out their revolt may be due in part to their upbringing.[36] Parental authority ebbed, undermined by Enlightenment doctrines of individualism and the demographic pressure of large families living on small amounts of land, as in the case of the Webster family. Parents became less demanding, less involved in children's lives, and less in control of them.

Child-raising manuals in widespread use at Webster's birth allowed parents to become more aloof and encouraged them to avoid intense involvement in their children's development. Children became more self-reliant, making important, life-shaping decisions about marriage, career, family size, and even leisure. If Noah Webster's upbringing was cold and emotionless, one would expect his adult relationships, especially with his parents, to be equally distant and shallow. In fact, his mature relationships with his parents appear as natural extensions of aloof, cold child-raising practices.

With his mother he had virtually no relationship. Mercy Steele Webster was extraordinarily absent from his writing. Her name did not appear among the hundreds of meetings with individuals he recorded in the diary. He did not mention her in any of his recorded thoughts in any other type of document. The distance between son and mother in the diary was so enormous as to be unmeasurable. No letters passing between them have survived, if indeed any existed. Webster's mother appeared only twice in the autobiography, and then very briefly. She is mentioned by name only once, listed not as an important part of his life or even as an individual herself, but merely as the daughter and granddaughter of someone else. The second entry was simply that his mother, father, and family were "pious" ("Memoir," No. 3). Here again, the mother was not significant, only her religious attitude. That she was a distant, unloved, and unloving figure in Webster's written legacy is documentable. To say that she occupied a similar role in his emotional life is not documentable, but probably accurate.

His father, Noah Webster, Senior, appeared equally aloof and distant. As a small-time farmer with five children to feed, he probably allowed his wife to raise the children while he worked the farm and served as justice of the peace and deacon of his church. He was also virtually absent from the diary, but when he did appear, Webster's entries revealed much about their relationship. Direct contact between the two occurred only three times. (January 20, March 12 and 17, 1790). In each entry, the author simply stated that the father visited him. He did not mention his name, or record any details of the occasion or any related emotions. All three meetings occurred in 1790, in the *sixth year* of the work. The first two were visits by the father to the son, and on one occasion the son misspelled "visits." Less than one month after the third visit the father sold the family farm (April 14, 1790), a move that family legend links to the mortgage incurred in 1774 as a means of paying for the son's Yale education. It is logical to assume that the major topic of discussion,

probably even the major reason for the visits, was the father's request for help in paying the mortgage. In addition, while residing in
Hartford, Webster often rode or walked to his father's house. On
several of these visits he described meeting, talking to, or eating and
drinking with friends, siblings, relatives, and even strangers. He
never mentioned his father or any contact he may have had with
him. And when he left Hartford for New York (November 24, 1787)
the author noted farewells to his friends, but not his parents. The
final relevant entry in the diary mentioned that the father was visiting the city, but not the son (December 26, 1791).

This lukewarm (at best), even distant relationship was also apparent in written communications between the two. No letters from
son to father survive, if any ever existed. Three letters from father to
son all contain statements of grand principles and lofty sentiments
along with thinly veiled rebukes for not visiting often enough. He
urged the son to be virtuous, patriotic, upstanding: all were written
as if to abstract, disembodied images. No trace of personal feeling
appeared: they could be addressed to a son or a stranger. The father's attitudes were detached, aloof, depersonalized, even dehumanized.[37]

And the son's perception of the father as revealed in the autobiography reflects the impact of these conditions. The author tells us
of a shallow, idealized, but ultimately unloving, uncaring, unhelpful, and even menacing father. When he was first introduced, he
was passed over quickly, significant only as a small part of the author's paternal lineage ("Memoir," No. 2). His second appearance
was presented in neutral, emotionless terms: he was a small-time
farmer, justice, and deacon. The third appearance was an important
one: the author recalled that at age fourteen, after being "occupied
on his father's farm," he expressed a wish to go on to college. A
clash ensued: his father "hesitated to comply," but "finally consented." It is not an angry moment, but one of great distance between the two, told in formal, cold tones. The next two times the
author mentioned his father he was insignificant, even once portrayed as "the father of N.W." ("Memoir," No. 4).

The most significant and revealing portrayal of Webster's relationship with his father was an incident that occurred after the former's graduation from Yale. Completion of his degree left him in a vulnerable position, without an occupation in a nation in social turmoil. He felt lonely, insecure, afraid: "cast out upon the world, at the age of twenty, without patrons, and in the midst of a war which had disturbed all occupation; had impoverished the country; and the termination of which could not be foreseen." The author quickly linked his father to his vulnerability, then recalled a crushing rejection: his father gave him a small sum, then kicked him out, saying "take this; you must now seek your living; I can do no more for you." The author's response: anxiety and withdrawal. He fled to his room and the safety of books, to be alone and to read ("Memoir," No. 4).

Two additional incidents fit this pattern and deserve mention. Late in his life Webster wrote to his daughter concerning the naming of a grandchild. "I do not like my own name, *Noah*," he told her and advised her to name the child differently.[38] His name, of course, was the same as his father's, the man who had bestowed it upon him. When his father died in 1816, Webster built a small monument to him.[39] In every way, his relationship with his parents was distant, cold, shallow, and idealized.

A child growing up in this atmosphere could easily mature feeling that his parents, and the adult world they represented, thought little of him. With no love or esteem, no sense of importance, value, or significance forthcoming from the most significant people in his life, it would be natural for a child to look to himself for those qualities, and not to expect them from others. He would hang onto his parents, but in an unemotional, ritualized, and intellectualized way, as Noah Webster did with his.

Taught by his parents that he was of little importance, he turned this perception of himself inward, internalizing it and feeling on a deeply emotional and probably unconscious level that he was an inadequate and perhaps worthless, powerless person. He interpreted virtually everything as a form of personal rejection.

INTRODUCTION

Between 1778 and 1784 Webster wandered about New England and New York in search of his niche in American life. He failed to find it, existing mainly by teaching school, one of the lowest-paid and least-prestigious occupations in the new nation. He moved often, tried to study law, but had to return to teaching to survive. He developed romantic relationships with two young women, both of whom rejected him in favor of other men. By the autumn of 1783, he had been rejected or had failed in every endeavor, every phase of his life. He felt as though he had no family, friends, occupation, or future. In his only hopeful venture—the writing of a spelling book— he had been continually discouraged for two years by all but his closest friends. No one thought enough of it to publish it, so he ended up paying for the production costs.[40]

As a means of coming to terms with these feelings and to develop a sense of self-confidence and acceptance, Webster tried to reach out and shape his world, to transform it into something he understood, valued, and from which he in turn received positive reinforcement. To shape the world to fit his own needs, he learned to utilize culturally acceptable rhetorical devices, to write in the name of the people. Thus works like his 1783 Speller, his later textbooks, dictionaries, and moral-reform tracts sought to improve American life and drew upon his own internalized need for approval for their intensity and motivation. If others would follow his lead, this would mean he was a significant, valuable individual: it would be the love he longed for and never received.

And when his efforts to shape the world in self-rewarding ways failed, Webster often became overwhelmed by depression or withdrew from social contact, or both. Thus in 1778 he closeted himself in his room when he felt rejected by his father and had no meaningful occupation. In 1781, after three more years of constant rejection, he left New England and ended up in Goshen, New York, where "for some months" he suffered, as he recalled half a century later, "extreme depression and gloomy forebodings" ("Memoir," No. 7). In 1788, alone in New York and with his fledgling *American Magazine* (a nationalistic journal of culture, business, and politics), in financial difficulty, he wrote to his future wife:

THE PRIVATE SELF

> I sometime think of retiring from society and devoting myself to read-
> ing and contemplation, for I labor incessantly and reap very little fruit
> from my toils. I suspect I am not formed for society; and I wait only to
> be convinced that people wish to get rid of my company, and I would
> instantly leave them for better companions: the reflections of my own
> mind.[41]

Under the pressure of this sense of rejection and depression he was
willing to accept a wholly negative evaluation of himself, as if he
were totally worthless. "Mankind generally forms a just estimate of a
man's character; and I am willing to think they do so with me," he
wrote. "And if I find that they think less favorable of me than I do
myself, I submit to their opinion and consent to a separation." He
went on to reveal that this feeling of rejection and depression came
often in his life, that it had its roots deep in his private past, and that
he preferred not to face them. "You will see by the tenor of this
letter that I am in the dumps a little and will require the reason.
Why, Becca, I have been asked the question so often that it really
displeases me. To satisfy such inquiries, it would be necessary to
relate the history of my life, which you have heard before, and to
enumerate a thousand things which ought to be forgotten."[42] When
the project failed a few months later, he fled New York and public
life for the arms of his future wife. A decade later, in the midst of
bitter political battles as editor of the leading Federalist paper in
New York City, which included vicious, personal attacks on him, he
suffered exhaustion and again fled New York for New England, to
save his own sanity, he told a friend.[43] And four years later, watch-
ing the world disintegrate around him as Federalist virtue dissolved
into Republican immorality, he felt lonely, isolated, and intense
pangs of rejection. He wrote to a friend:

> Either from the structure of my mind, or from my modes of investiga-
> tion, I am led very often to differ in opinion from many of my respect-
> able fellow citizens; and difference of opinion is now a crime not easily
> overlooked or forgiven. The efforts which have been made and are
> now making to deprive me of the confidence of my fellow citizens, and
> of course of my influence, and reputation . . . render it necessary for me
> to withdraw myself from every public concern and confine my atten-
> tion to private affairs and the education of my children.[44]

Introduction

Thus Noah Webster kept his diary as a means of reassuring himself of his value as an individual. His experiences from birth to the beginning of the diary had instilled in him a sense of rejection, failure, and deep doubts about his worth to society as a human being. His youth, family relationships, education, love affairs, search for an occupation, and the Revolution had all met with little or no success. In his diary he sought compensation by charting his emergence from obscurity to regional and then national prominence. The act of writing down the almost endless names of people—especially famous figures like Franklin, Adams, and Madison—helped him attempt to achieve a sense of uniqueness and identity, of approval and significance. In his diary he recorded not only the world's growing recognition and approval of him, but his own approval of himself.

In 1784 Webster perceived himself as a little-known, relatively poor young man; by 1794 he had become a nationally famous figure. During that decade Webster carefully recorded the names of each individual he met. His engagement with society was evident in his work, his writing, and his personal life as recorded in his diary. He was energetic, outgoing, and deeply involved in the social whirl. He read poetry, discussed ideas, and was involved in politics. As his reputation grew, and his contacts with people of local, regional, and national importance increased, concern for his status and significance lessened. By the early 1790s entries had become less frequent and less informative. Now an important figure in Federalist circles, the diarist continued to note important contacts and social engagements while confining the rest of his writing to family affairs, travel, health, weather, business, and a little politics. When he moved to New York and entered the center of political debate in 1793, his diary trickled to an end. He stopped writing in early 1794, justifying his action with words revealing a sense of frustration and importance: "It is too much trouble to make *particular* remarks every day, and general ones are of little use" (April 23, 1794).

Many of the most revealing entries appear at first glance to be positive comments about himself, yet when examined closely reveal an underlying sense of insecurity, isolation, and self-doubt. The ex-

istence of numerous attractive young ladies ended up as a statement
of his lack of self-confidence:

> At home. Read a little, loitered some, had some company, and visited
> the ladies in the evening as usual. If there were but one pretty girl in
> town, a man could make a choice—but among so many! One's heart is
> pulled twenty ways at once. The greatest difficulty, however, is that
> after a man has made *his* choice, it remains for the lady *hers* [April 8,
> 1784].

Even a pleasurable moment of relaxation ended up as a reminder of
his problems:

> Amusing myself with books and with a flute. What an infinite variety
> of methods has mankind invented to render life agreeable! And what a
> wise and happy design in the organization of the human frame that the
> sound of a little hollow tube of wood should dispel in a few moments,
> or at least alleviate, the heaviest care of life! [August 10, 1784.]

The companionship of famous people served as a major source
of reassurance of the significance of the private self. As an unknown
traveler, he visited George Washington at Mount Vernon in 1785.
Two years later, Washington, a veritable god in the young republic,
took time out from his busy schedule in Philadelphia to pay his
homage to Webster in a personal visit (March 20 and November 5,
1785, May 26, 1787). The private self became a good friend of Benjamin Franklin, another internationally famous figure of godlike stature and already considered the genius of the New World, and the
two even engaged in a "visit with the ladies" together (May 28,
1787). James Madison, Tom Paine, Benjamin Rush, David Rittenhouse, John Adams, and virtually every important figure in the new
nation's public life appeared in the pages of Noah Webster's diary.
His tour in 1785–86, and especially his lectures on the need for a
national language as a bond of union, met with great public acclaim
(see especially October 19–26, 1785).

Webster's tour of the South awakened his sense of identification
as a New Englander and his personal value as an inhabitant of that
section. He found Virginians dissolute, spending time and money
frivolously on parties and dancing (December 7, 1785, February 2,
1786). Southerners need to send their children North for a sound

education, underscoring the importance and value of his work (June 2, 1785). He found southern politics riotous and potentially dangerous (October 30, 1785). Shocked by southern illiteracy, he congratulated his region, and by extension himself, on its/his superiority:

> Converse with Mr. Lloyd, a senator—a sensible man from the Eastern shore. He informs me that, great numbers of men, who acknowledge deeds before him cannot write their own names. This is the case in Maryland and Virginia. An eminent merchant in Alexandria informed me that of 50 planters in Virginia, who sold him tobacco, 4 or 5 only could write their names but [others] made a mark on the receipts. O New England! how superior are thy inhabitants in morals, literature, civility and industry. A small fall of snow and cold weather [January 6, 1786].

The author's birthday provided occasions for statements of insecurity and of affirmations of the value of the self. The effort to achieve significance and morality is paramount in 1784: "My birthday. 26 years of my life are past. I have lived long enough to be good and of some importance. Introduced to Miss S. Dwight of Springfield, a fine lady" (October 16, 1784). Three years later the concerns are identical: "My birthday. 29 years of life gone! I have been industrious—endeavored to do some good, and hope I shall be able to correct my faults and yet do some good. Put my trunk aboard for New York" (October 16, 1787).

A year later the diarist restated his concern for public approval, indicated he was aware of his need, and even revealed that he needed approval of his actions by himself:

> Mr William Young calls on me. My Birth Day. 30 years of life gone—a large portion of the ordinary age of man! I have read much, and tried to do much good, but with little advantage to myself. I will now leave writing and do more lucrative business. My moral conduct stands fair with the world, and what is more, with my own conscience. But I am a bachelor and want the happiness of a friend whose interest and feelings should be mine [October 16, 1788].

A fourth and final bit of self-examination is perhaps the most revealing entry in the entire diary. It occurred on the day of his marriage to Rebecca Greenleaf, his wife until his death fifty-three years later, and perhaps the single most important person in his life.

On this day he recorded none of the details of the event—where it occurred or who was present—nor his emotional response to it. Webster's entry on the day of his marriage neatly summed up the portrayal of his life in the early sections of the diary. The private self, lonely, full of self-doubt, yearned for a sense of direction and accomplishment, for the internal feelings usually given to a child by a parent:

> Much better. This day I became a husband. I have lived a long time a bachelor, something more than thirty-one years. But I had no person to form a plan for me in early life and direct me to a profession. I had an enterprising turn of mind, was bold, vain, inexperienced. I have made some unsuccessful attempts, but on the whole hav [*sic*] done as well as most men of my years. I begin a new profession, at a late period of life, but have some advantages of traveling and observation. I am united to an amiable woman, and if I am not happy, shall be much disappointed [October 26, 1789].

The first sentence referred to the end of the week-long bout with a mild illness, the second to events of the day, thus revealing that the existence of the private self was more immediately important to him than his new attachment to another individual, or than his new wife. The third sentence expressed his loneliness. The fourth revealed his sense of a lack of achievement and direction, and was a direct reference to his strained and distant relationship with the father who had rejected him eleven years earlier. By beginning the fourth sentence with "but," the author linked it to the third sentence, and thus indicated that his rejection by his father was the cause of his sense of loneliness. The fifth sentence perfectly mirrored his need for affirmation and his self-doubt: he recorded his belief in his intellectual ability and his feelings of inadequacy. The sixth reversed the fifth, stating his self-doubt first, then papering it over with a tentative statement of semi-self-satisfaction. With the seventh sentence the tense shifted dramatically into the present, but continued the basic theme of self-doubt and tentative self-approval. The eighth and final sentence referred to his new wife in unemotional terms and left the reader in doubt as to the precise meaning of the word "happy." Was he referring to his marriage, his profession, or his inner life in general? All in all, it is a remarkable paragraph, full of hidden emotion and self-evaluation.

The private self gradually changed over the years as the author's life shifted, yet it continued to be shaped by the limitations and demands of diary-keeping. The energy and excitement gradually disappeared after 1789. New entries on successive birthdays referred generally to the passage of time, with the author recording his fear that his life was slipping away without significant achievement (October 16, 1790, 1791, 1792, 1793). He stopped writing in 1794, at the beginning of his new career as editor and Federalist polemicist. Now surrounded with important figures like Hamilton, Rufus King, Oliver Wolcott, and other leading men, he no longer needed his diary. It ended with the comment that it was too much trouble and of little use or value (April 23, 1794).

The next four years were hectic ones. As the leading Federalist editor in New York City, Webster found himself in the middle of an increasingly bitter political world. As Federalists and Republicans fought for political power, Webster attracted a great deal of verbal abuse. He worked so hard that he became physically exhausted on more than one occasion. And as New York became increasingly Republican, he felt that his work was worth little.[45]

In 1798 Noah Webster fled the political wars of New York for the relatively calm fields of Connecticut, to save his own sanity, as he told a friend.[46] Now with much time on his hands, he returned to his diary-keeping. The contents of his entries at first glance seem in striking contrast with those he wrote in the beginning years. On closer inspection it is apparent that the evolution noticeable in the 1790s has run its full course. No further need to underscore his identity, establish his value, or find approval is apparent. Information about social and political events virtually ceases to exist. They are replaced by meteorological and agricultural notes. Webster moved to Connecticut to escape the problems of human civilization, in search of peace and tranquillity. He evidently found it among his pear trees and pea plants, for he records almost no information about his life. The self in the diary after 1789 appears isolated from the human world around him. While Webster continued to pay close attention to politics until 1840—serving in the Massachusetts and Connecticut legislatures along the way—and became active in religious reform circles after his conversion to evangelical Protestantism in 1808, he made no mention of these events in his diary.

A single passage written after 1798 can be considered self-reflective, and even it revealed the author's sense of alienation. It was an explanation of his move from New York to Connecticut and his disengagement from society, and once again revealed his inadequacy and sense of rejection:

> Removed with my family to New Haven. My attachment to the State of Connecticut, my acquaintances, my habits, which are literary and do not correspond with the hustle of commerce and the taste of people perpetually inquiring for news and making bargains; together with the cheapness of living, are among my motives for this change of residence. Take Mrs. Sloane's house, near the water [April 1, 1798].

After 1798 Webster wrote as the author of an almanac, not a diarist. For the next twenty-two years he recorded primarily the weather and crops. We see him venturing out of his garden only three times: to purchase type for a spelling book, to move his family to Amherst, and to give an address at Amherst College (1803, 1812, 1820). He was virtually a man alone, untouched by human emotions or public concerns, weighing beets and planting peas and corn: we glimpse him as if through the branches of his pear tree as he works in his orchard and garden: "May was mostly cold and wet. First eat peas June 10, first strawberries ripe at the same time, cut grass June 11th. Early apples ripe July 15. Eat green corn July 21 [1800]."

The style of writing reflected the particular qualities of the private self as they shifted and changed over the course of the years. The entries were short and to the point. No effort was made to elaborate on ideas or to detail events; and no attention was paid to grammatical structure, development of an image, or language in general. The writer did not attempt to develop a style to evoke the emotions of his reader, nor to any other aspect of literary technique. The concentration was entirely upon the event and its significance, known only to the private self.

INTRODUCTION

In the first ten years apparent nonsequiters were plentiful, yet what seems to be a random pattern of thought at first glance, under closer inspection turns out to show consistent links to subject matter. The entries cited above, for example, were all similar in their expressions of need for approval. It is no accident that his entry for January 6, 1786, cited earlier, began with a conversation with a senator, for that conversation with an important figure from a distant region showed the value of the private self to that senator. The private self gained self-esteem, approval, and gratification through the occurrence of the conversation, and that was the theme of the rest of the entry, though stated differently. On his twenty-sixth birthday the author stated his own value, which was then reinforced by the fact that he was introduced to a "fine lady." Three years later he again recorded his approval of his life, then noted his move to New York, the new center of political power. The entry on his wedding day, full of non sequiturs at first glance, was consistent in its concern for approval of the private self.

The first week was generally representative of the style of the entries in the first ten years of the diary:

January 1st 1784. Thursday at home.

2. Rode to West division; returned, and at the evening danced at Mr. Collier's.

3. P.M. rode in company with Mr. Church, Mr. J. Pratt and Mr. Coit as far as Dr. McLeans seat.

Sunday 4th. At church; heard Mr. Strong A.M. and Mr. Boardman P.M.

5. Attend town-meeting. Convened to deliberate upon the proposed act for incorporating the town with city privileges. Meeting adjourned.

6. Attend town-meeting—a committee was appointed to fix the limits of the proposed city. Adjourned till Friday, the 9th.

7. At home.

After 1798 the daily recording of facts was replaced with a style more convenient for the disengaged student of plants and the weather. Most of the entries were occasional jottings, more relaxed,

fuller in structure and slightly retrospective—looking back a few
weeks or months. Entries appeared every few months, recounting
the immediate past. The author of the following record of the first
six months of 1815, for example, was totally concerned with his
crops, and oblivious to such concerns as structure, language, syntax,
or the themes that dominated the first decade:

> Jany. 1815. Moderate till the 17th then began to be tempestuous, and
> several storms or snow followed. The last week very cold, and on the
> last day the thermometer fell to twelve degrees below cypher in Bos-
> ton. It continued to be very cold in Feby, and our harbors were closed
> with ice. Some very warm weather in March dissolved the snow, then
> followed a cold wet spring. Apple trees in Amherst began to blossom
> about May 23. I finished planting corn May 24, in fine weather.

The diary trickled to an end in 1820.

4. THE PROPHET

Most of Noah Webster's major contributions to American cultural life—especially the two most important, his Speller and the
American Dictionary—included autobiographical introductory essays
in which he related events in his own life to the project at hand. In
letters to close friends he wrote about his inner feelings and his life.
And in a miscellaneous group of items, including letters to friends,
letters to editors, a confession of participation in a rebellious incident in college, and in a circular asking for support for his work,
Webster portrayed his life in a variety of ways.

All these writings must be considered carefully. Like the diary,
the point in time at which they were written profoundly affected the
presentation; yet the author's perspective may vary from immediate
to distantly retrospective. Perhaps more important, these items were
not written in private, to be read only by the author in the seclusion
of his study. They were written for two (or more) people: the author and the intended recipient. One's personal history may be

shaped differently when presented to a future spouse than when re-called for thousands of impersonal readers.

In contrast to the diary, no single dominant pattern appeared in all these autobiographical statements. Indeed, the self-portraits they contain were almost as diverse as the moments in which they were composed. Each one must be examined by itself in its special con-text. Yet when considered overall as a group, a few interesting pat-terns do appear.

In his major public essays, written for the general American public, Noah Webster revealed a side of himself strikingly different from the diarist. Not only were the events of his life different, but his major concerns differed dramatically. His acceptance and signifi-cance as an individual were of secondary concern and usually not stated but implied, though that would be reinforced by the success of the work. Instead, he adopted a stance not unique in American culture: he was the prophet, speaking to Americans on behalf of their highest ideals, urging them to reform their world.

The prophet characteristically emphasizes the confluence of self and society, is highly critical of the status quo, yet urges his readers to greater unity in the quest for greater perfection; he does not ad-vocate social schism.[47] Like the private self, this face changed over time. In the beginning, Webster spoke as the voice of liberal nation-alism; later he became an evangelical, a self-appointed spokesman for God, interpreting the past (national and personal) and claiming the future in terms of God's will. At all points, the prophet subordi-nated the details of his own life to the story he told, and used them as a means of explaining and achieving his goals.

The prophetic self originates in a sense of cultural crisis. In re-sponse to a perceived challenge to the basic norms, values, and shared beliefs of the society, or in response to a perceived failure among the community to live up to those ideals, the prophetic American merges self and society in his own imagination. The con-fluence of the two produces a unique perspective on all elements of life: past, present, and future. The universal becomes cause for per-sonal concern, and details in the life of the individual are projected onto the stage of community life.[48] Figures such as John Winthrop,

THE PROPHET

Michael Wigglesworth, Cotton Mather, Jonathan Edwards, Frederick Douglass, and Malcolm X were concerned with personal and communal salvation.[49] Benjamin Franklin wrote to his son and all of us; Henry Adams's historical neck was our historical neck.[50]

Thus Noah Webster's sense of prophecy was thoroughly American. His first political essay, published in 1782, just four years after his father kicked him out of his house, assessed the Confederation's relationship with England in terms that could easily describe his father. He portrayed England as a haughty, tyrannical parent bent on imposing its will on a noble and virtuous child. His Speller (1783) told Americans it was their duty to attend the arts of peace as well as those of war. The Speller was composed, noted its author, "to inspire the minds of youth, with an abhorrence of vice, indolence and meanness; and with a love of virtue, industry and good manners."[51] Thirteen years later the Federalist editor revealed to his readers that his opinions were products of his Republican upbringing, that events had proved them correct for all Americans, and that opposition to the Federal administration and the Constitution were wrong in principle.[52]

Webster's 1808 conversion to evangelical Protestantism shaped the contours of the rest of his public statements. His account of the conversion, written as a letter to his brother-in-law, clearly outlined the perspective that he held for the remainder of his life.[53] The further evolution of the nation faded into secondary consideration when compared to the will of God. Webster's preface to the *American Dictionary of the English Language* (1828) neatly symbolized both the style and the transformation of the prophet. The first section was an account of the first spark of interest in dictionary-making, which came immediately after the American Revolution and linked it to nationalistic concerns. The preface ended with the dedication of the work to God. In between, the prophet carefully declared that he was not trying to unsettle the English language, but to reduce its ambiguities and to establish a firm standard of speech. He wanted to resist historical change, not encourage it:

> If the language can be improved in its regularity, so as to be more easily acquired by our own citizens, and by foreigners, and thus be

rendered a more useful instrument for the propagation of science, arts, civilization and christianity; if it can be rescued from the mischievous influence of sciolists and that dabbling spirit of innovation which is perpetually disturbing its settled usages and filling it with anomalies: if, in short, our vernacular language can be redeemed from corruptions, and our philology and literature from degradation; it would be a source of great satisfaction to me to be among the instruments of promoting these valuable objects.[54]

Five years later Webster published what he considered the most significant work of his life:[55] a new edition of the Holy Bible. He believed that the Bible was the source of all true wisdom. Like other evangelicals, he believed it was the literal word of God: if all Americans would read it, society would benefit. Yet the very obscurity of many of the words used in the 1611 King James Version, coupled with the offensiveness of many vulgar phrases, prevented use in many homes. Webster considered it his "moral duty" to remove its indelicate, even indecent, phrases. The prophet not only spoke to the people for God, but also verified that God's words were acceptable in prudent society: if not, he would censor them.

His last significant political essay, "A Voice of Wisdom" (1837), summed up the prophetic self. He looked back over his political life and portrayed himself as a lifelong adherent of the "Washington school" of political thinkers. He realized that an enormous gap existed between himself and the American people. He felt out of step, yet it was the American people who had erred, not Noah Webster. He remained the prophet.[56]

The style of expression used by the prophetic self reflected the overall perspective and contrasted sharply with the passive diarist. He was now forceful in urging compliance with his ideas. He coaxed and cajoled his reader, pointing out the correct answer to every question or outlining the proper path or procedure. The prophet always knew the truth and tried to convince others of his doctrines. He was emotional when necessary, and his sentences carried the visible mark of their origins in a sense of personal and cultural crisis: sharply put, they moved swiftly on the strength of numerous verbs and adjectives, both of which were virtually nonexistent in the diary. The prophet was primarily concerned with the cause or principles he advocated, not his own life. Personal experiences were not discussed for their own importance, but for their relevance to the issue at hand. The self was part of, yet clearly subordinate to, the higher cause he supported.

5. THE PUBLIC SERVANT

The prophet also authored a formal narrative of his life story, and the face he turned to the world in the "Memoir of Noah Webster, LL.D." differs strikingly from the self presented in the other two genres. It is a third facet of the author's self-portrait, one that adds another dimension to our understanding of him. In his clear and strong hand, Noah Webster attempted to tell the story of "N.W.," beginning with the arrival of the Webster family in the 1630s and ending abruptly in 1825. Through it all N.W. is the public servant, doing good deeds for all Americans, often to his own financial detriment.

The "Memoir" is a complex document, one that is shaped by the burden of Webster's life experiences and personal needs at every level of meaning, as well as by the limitations and opportunities of the genre of autobiography. It is not a finished essay, but a preliminary draft of a document in need of much additional information and revision before it would become publishable (and therein lies another story, which will be discussed later in this section). It can and should be analyzed from several different perspectives, all of which reveal different aspects of the author and his work, each with its own degree of significance. Its style, structure, and thematic content; the author's sense of failure and need for public approval; his essential creative impulses; his compulsion to instruct didactically people and thus correct his world; and the context of early national America—all helped shape the content, form, character, and significance of the "Memoir of Noah Webster." They contained the motivations behind the attempt to write the essay as well as the reasons for ultimately abandoning it.

INTRODUCTION

In his diary Webster sought approval of himself from himself and from the immediate environment in which he lived on a day-by-day basis; in his public writings he sought approval for his ideas from the public at large. The "Memoir" expands his search to a timeless, almost cosmic scale: he seeks approval of his entire life from the future, from history itself.

Modern American autobiography began in the early national period. Earlier efforts to represent the self in the seventeenth and eighteenth centuries—by figures such as John Winthrop, Increase Mather, Jonathan Edwards, Edward Taylor, Thomas Shepard, and Cotton Mather—were not so much examinations of the self as narratives of spiritual discovery.[57] It took the American and French revolutions to shake off the deference to religious and political authority and propel humankind's consciousness of self to the forefront of their imagination. In the process a new form of literature appeared: the autobiography, or personal history.

Early national America, according to recent scholarship, is best understood as the disintegration of one cultural system and the beginning formation of another. As royal government, mercantilism, elite domination of politics, and rural, agrarian-oriented society gave way to individualism, laissez-faire economics, the beginnings of industrialization and urbanization, and voluntary social organizations, literature emerged as a reflection of our attempt to understand what was transpiring.[58] Preoccupation with the self and historical transformation led to the development of a new form of writing, with new demands, objectives, and assumptions; a form capable of helping an individual understand one's own life, the world in which he or she lived, and the interaction of self and society.[59] Franklin's *Autobiography* stands not only as a major contribution to American letters, but as the first modern American autobiography. His discovery of himself coincides, both in historical time and in the narrative of his autobiography, with the American Revolution.[60] As James Cox has pointed out, the term "autobiography" did not appear before 1800; it was first used by Robert Southey in 1809.[61] According to Roy Pascal, what is common in the new age of autobiography is a devoted but detached concern for the intimate self, a partial yet impartial unraveling of individual uniqueness. It is a kind of wonder and awe toward the self, and an attempt to understand the individual's role in the historical phenomena of a world out of control. Personal history was not possible before the world-shattering, tradition-smashing revolutions of the late eighteenth century.[62]

The "Memoir of Noah Webster" is unsigned and written in the third-person singular. Webster never mentioned it in his voluminous correspondence: yet he is clearly the author. Throughout his life he collected copies of his works and kept copies of his correspondence and newspaper articles, often adding marginal comments in later years. He valued them highly enough to will them to his son.[63] The "Memoir" appears to draw heavily on this collection, naming specific letters and articles, and incorporating several documents into the text. In a note scrawled at the bottom of one page in the manner of an instruction to a publisher, the author reveals his identity as the subject of the work by referring to N.W.'s letter in the first person: "Here may follow my letter to Judge Dawes in manuscript and the copy printed in the Panoplist, July 1809" ("Memoir," No. 50).[64]

In order to understand its meaning and significance, an autobiography must be considered within the context of the author's life, and particularly within the stage of life in which he wrote it. By 1832, the last date mentioned in the text, and the year in which he apparently sat down to compose it, Webster had carried on a dialogue with the American people for over half a century. His books, essays, and letters had addressed virtually every concern of national importance. Indeed, he had written an enormous number of words since the 1770s, nearly all of which had been directed toward leading the nation down the true path of reform. It appeared to have had little impact: the society he saw around him in the 1830s bore no resemblance to what in the 1770s he had hoped would develop. His political and social ideas brought scorn; even the evangelical movement often seemed headed in the wrong direction. Large revival camp-meetings, spectacular gimmicks to induce conversions ("ultraist" preaching and the front-row "sinners' bench") seemed to encourage the type of disorder and undisciplined behavior he abhorred.[65]

The author of the "Memoir of Noah Webster" felt a strong sense of rejection by, and alienation from, American society. Much of his work sparked bitter controversy and personal attacks. His first important book—the 1783 Speller—touched off a year-long series of articles ridiculing his effort.[66] His essays on economics and educational reform brought additional personal abuse, and as early as the 1780s even his potential business partner criticized him and his work.[67] His advocacy of Federalist policies in the 1790s brought heaps of criticism, including the publication of such epithets as "self-exalted pedagogue" and "incurable lunatic." Throughout his years of labor on the dictionary, friends and associates constantly discouraged him: others openly mocked not only Webster's ideas but also his personality. Critics accused him of writing his own favorable reviews, selecting reviewers, and publishing work done by others under his own name.[68] The dictionary itself failed financially when the printer went bankrupt due to problems unrelated to the dictionary. His political writings also drew fire. Critics called his last significant essay, "A Voice of Wisdom" (1837), the last gasp of Federalism and even alleged that its author preferred monarchical rule to American politics.[69]

These attacks shaped Webster's feelings of rejection and estrangement from the dominant thrust of American life, and these emotions colored the essential character of the autobiographer's perspective. This paragraph, written in 1837, summarized his point of view:

> We are indeed an erring nation. Possessing more *physical* advantages for public happiness than any nation on the globe, we reject the *moral* means necessary to secure the enjoyment of prosperity, peace and harmony, in possession of these advantages. The whole soul of our nation is bent on temporal good, without a dependence on the moral and religious means of obtaining it.[70]

Estrangement from the dominant thrust of American society provided much of the character of the "Memoir"; the demands of the autobiographical genre supplied the rest. Webster was attracted by the opportunity to write his own personal story, the history of his life as he wanted it to be written. It provided a vehicle to present his "true face" to the world, as he thought it should be seen. Through the process of selecting some "facts" while ignoring others, and presenting them in certain ways, the historical autobiographer can shape and even invent the content, tenor, and meaning of his own life in subjective ways. Webster's "Memoir" was not simply a mimetic mirror of his life but an imaginative creation, not bound tightly by the restrictions of historical truth-telling and full of hopes for the future. It was an attempt to create a symbolic self, not an actual one.

A good autobiography—like those written by Franklin, Henry Adams, and Malcolm X—brings together the personal, unassimilated experiences of the writer and the shared expectations and values of the society to create an ideal persona. The autobiogaphy reveals a self that is both a sovereign entity and a member of a larger cultural unit. It is both authentic in its presentation of the self and mythological in its links to the larger norms. Arising from a consciousness that is both historical and personal, the autobiography responds to a certain inner necessity. The weight of personal and societal history, of memories and experiences, says Roy Pascal, "seems to arise from the oppression one feels that all this past experience has not been absorbed, digested into the system of one's life, that it has not been grasped and utilized."[71] The consciousness of the outcome of the present imposes itself on the past. Personal history is shaped into a form that is a mythical depiction of the self in a culturally meaningful image.

Webster fully understood that an individual's historical reputation could differ dramatically from the critical views held by his peers: he doubtless hoped to shape the opinions of his life and work that would be held by future generations, and to ensure thereby perpetual approval of his life. As early as 1801 he revealed his sensitivity to this issue and his hope that contemporary criticism would be forgotten. "I have long observed that men who explode error seldom have credit for it in their lives," he told Benjamin Rush: "But when the men are dead who are jealous of improvements which oblige them to change their opinions, and with them their prejudices are asleep, a new generation who examine the doctrines without the same prejudices will do them justice and their authors. So that you and I are to have our portion of fame when we are dead."[72]

Autobiography allows us to trace the creative impulse unique to the individual writer. That factor influences and dominates the style of the actual writing and, since personal history is an attempt to describe one's lifework, also its content. As James Olney has said, an autobiography is like "a magnifying lens, focusing and intensifying that same peculiar creative vitality that informs all the volumes of his collected works; it is the symptomatic key to all else that he did, and, naturally, to all that he was."[73]

Everything came together in the "Memoir of Noah Webster." The transformation of early national America and birth of modern autobiography; Webster's sense of failure and estrangement from American life; his need to grasp and understand the meaning of his life; the opportunity to influence future opinion of himself and his work by rewriting his personal history and that of his nation; the essential creative impulse in his life, namely, the need to impose order on everything—all merged to produce an ideal, even mythical self, not only one based on "fact," but one that incorporated documentary evidence of its truth. Its third-person perspective allowed the author to accumulate and link together his efforts to glorify his actions in a manner impossible in the first person. It cloaked the work with an air of objectivity, making it seem more realistic or accurate than a first-person work.

The face Noah Webster turned to the world in his autobiography was the one he wished had been recognized by the world; it was the image of the individual he wanted Americans to see and remember. It is the face of the public servant, struggling hard for the good of all, sacrificing his own well-being in his duty to the nation. It is selected events in his public and private lives, recounted in a particular manner and chosen for their symbolic value. Webster's autobiography fulfills perfectly George Gusdorf's notion that "every autobiography is a work of art and at the same time a work of enlightenment; it does not show us the individual seen from the outside in his visible action but the person in his inner privacy, not as he was, not as he is, but as he believes and wishes himself to be and to have been."[74]

Much is left out of the "Memoir." The difficult, numerous, often bitter public quarrels are almost completely absent. Nothing is said about the dispute over his Speller in the 1780s, attacks on his ideological writings and personality in the 1790s, or of the intense debates over his dictionary. He does not discuss the constant criticism, even ridicule, from all sides, which he endured after 1800. Moreover, throughout Webster's life he paid scrupulously close attention to business matters, maintained lengthy and detailed correspondence with publishers and booksellers over profits.[75] Virtually every move he made had a financial angle to it, and Webster kept extremely close watch over his money. It is fair to say that financial considerations provided a significant part of the motivation behind such events as the writing of his textbooks, his role as newspaper editor, and indeed many aspects of his public writings. And the need for public approval often surfaced as the need for ego gratification, another motivation downplayed and often ignored throughout the autobiography. His earliest essays, far more radical and emotional than proper for a public servant, and his conservative goals he set for future Americans also found short shrift.

The conceptual style of the "Memoir" drew upon and merged Webster's personal needs with his lifelong desire to influence American life. In this it resembled his spelling book, through which he gained public approval, financial reward, and formed the character of young people by instilling them with patriotism. In his autobiography, Webster sought to create his historical reputation by providing future Americans with an exemplary figure to model themselves after. He could achieve eternal approval and instill the values of order, deference, and morality at the same time.

The "Memoir" is written in the manner of a grand biography of a famous, respected, and even heroic public figure. By the 1830s American historians and biographers had latched onto the mode of historical biography as a weapon in their advocacy of cultural and political nationalism. In the hands of men like Jared Sparks, Mason Locke Weems, and John Marshall, the lives of George Washington, Patrick Henry, John Hancock and others became material useful not just in telling the stories of great men, but of great *Americans*. They served as vehicles for the expression of the highest ideals of the nation, and offered an opportunity to illustrate the ways in which they could be incorporated into individual lives. The events of heroic lives and, more important, the character they exhibited in the face of danger, in the line of public duty, and in their everyday behavior would inspire Americans to live in similar ways long after their deaths. Thus biography became a useful didactic mode: when Weems wrote of Washington's honesty, he sought not only to memorialize the President, but to instill certain values and behavior in his readers.[76]

Webster found this strategy most comfortable. He had in fact employed a similar tactic in all he had written during the last few decades of his life. Upset, bewildered, and repelled by the individualism, competitiveness, materialism, and increasing democratization of early national America, he had written textbooks, dictionaries, moral-reform tracts, and United States histories, and had edited the Bible. Through all he had sought to instill certain forms of social behavior in his readers.[77] Americans who read his works would learn to be courteous, deferential to their social, religious, and civil superiors, as well as less restless and less concerned with such things as material rewards and political rights.

In fact, the inspiration for his self-portrait may have come from one of his textbook projects. In 1830 Webster published *Biography, for the Use of Schools*.[78] It was a good synthesis of his other work, using biographies of the founding fathers, with heavy emphasis on their moral character and Christian devotion as models for American schoolchildren.

Writing a full-length study of the life of a single public servant would provide schoolchildren with a longer, fuller role model. Future generations might learn that individuals should strive to improve themselves through hard work, diligence, thrift, study, and moral behavior, as well as religious devotion, and to do so without agitating for or causing social unrest. Here was the perfect vehicle for instilling the virtues he cherished most: his own story, the life of an individual of outstanding character, one who had risen from obscurity to significance and had spent his entire life working to improve society without disrupting it. Through his autobiography the author could secure his future approval and again mold American lives by providing them with a model for their own lives.

Webster used a literary technique to secure his goals. Like other nineteenth-century biographers he included letters and documents written by the subject. This epistolary style, common among historians and novelists of the day, provided a procedure to lessen the distance between reader and idol: a means of helping the reader to identify with the subject and, in N.W.'s case, to heighten the impact of the model on the life of the reader. It also assured the reader of the accuracy of the work, cloaking the portrait of the subject in a veil of historical objectivity. It thus eased the reader into receptivity, without directly addressing the problem.

The structure of the "Memoir" reinforced the image of the public servant. It was divided into fifty-three units, each marked "No.," for number. In the first half of the work, each number was a separate chapter in the life of N.W. Fourteen of the numbers ran over onto a second page, and a fifteenth would have also, if the document described at the end of No. 25 had been included as intended. It covered part or all of sixty-eight pages. This system broke down only when the author attempted to describe his conversion by including an account written immediately after the event, which occurred over two decades before the writing of the "Memoir." At that point the conversion could not be contained by the structure; it was simply too powerful, too important, and forced the author to reconsider the overall development of his narrative.

The structure and tone of the sentences clearly revealed and helped define the attitude the author wished the public to embrace. The "Memoir" recorded what appears to be the almost day-by-day activity, all carefully selected and narrated to create the impression of strenuous activity, oriented toward the betterment of society, not self. Nearly every paragraph began with "N.W." as its first two let-

44

INTRODUCTION

ters or in the first clause of the topic sentence, never letting the
reader stray from concentration upon the central subject/object of
the work. The tone throughout was hushed and respectful, at times
lapsing into outright admiration and bordering upon awe. Consider, for example, the following paragraph in No. 3:

> N.W. was educated in the religious principles of the first planters of
> New England; his father, mother & most of his family relatives, pater-
> nal & maternal, being pious. He had, in his early years, no other educa-
> tion than that which a common school afforded, when rarely a book
> was used in the schools, except a spelling book, a Psalter, testament or
> Bible.

The reader would pass over this section quickly and be left with
the impression that Webster grew up as a Puritan in a Puritan family; that religion was central to his life from the beginning, and that
the man who wrote the dictionary as well as hundreds of essays and
books began with a meager education. The reader could only admire or perhaps stand in awe of such an achievement. The paragraph, however, was misleading and created several incorrect
impressions. Webster's parents, by the standards of John Webster's
generation—the original Puritans—would doubtless have been considered something less than "visible saints." They had not experienced a personal conversion, and thus lacked the essential element
in Puritan religiosity. Noah Webster, a devout evangelical, firmly
believed that the Puritan form of religion was the only "true religion." It was also the only possible means of personal and social
salvation, and for him to have forgotten—much less not known—
that his parents were uncoverted is unthinkable. Yet he chose to
ignore it, or possibly portray them incorrectly, all in favor of composing a specific image of N.W.
The second sentence in the paragraph above described a much
different form of education from that in the first sentence. Webster
spent much of his later years trying to merge church and state, not
separate them, and this sentence reflected that effort as well as his
attempt to create an ideal image. More important, linking the two
in such a fashion used the structure of the narrative to reinforce the
religiosity of the subject. Furthermore, while Webster did indeed

attend a public school as a child, the obstacles that it may have presented (if any) were considerably lessened by two years of private
preparation by tutors provided by his father.[79] And a Yale education, even one disrupted by the American Revolution, hardly constitutes a deprivation. Finally, the list of books read reinforced the
feeling of deprivation and Christian upbringing: placing the Speller
first in the list also further reinforced the significance of his Speller
as a contribution to the public welfare.

One additional point of style deserves mention. As in the diary,
the author littered his work with the names of famous Americans
and their positive comments about N.W. George Washington,
James Madison, John Jay, and numerous other figures with national
reputations were portrayed as N.W.'s companions and admirers,
thus providing the overall image with a sort of reflected verification.
This time, however, their presence in the narrative further underscored the stature of N.W., the public servant.

The thematic content of the "Memoir" was the heart of Webster's attempt to portray N.W. as the good public servant. Selection
and emphasis on symbolic events and activities created a characteris-
tic way of organizing and understanding his life, which would
simultaneously create public approval.[80] Throughout the autobiography, N.W. spent his time on projects designed to improve the
quality of life for all Americans. Special emphasis was skillfully and
subtly placed on his efforts to help those who were not members of
the privileged classes. After decades of criticizing the emergence of
popular culture and politics, Noah Webster sought to make clear his
lack of animosity toward the poor and uneducated. They were un-
equipped to make difficult decisions but still deserved, and received,
his help.

Webster, interested only in establishing his historical self as the
exemplary public servant, unknowingly coupled (but did not suc-
cessfully fuse together) the two major themes in American autobiography. He reminded us of the Franklinian success story, though
his was not so grandiose, was less materialistic, and centered more
on success in terms of achieving public approval rather than the
gathering of influence. And he ended with an Edwardsean account

of his spiritual life. Yet the two were not conceptually linked and did not smoothly join together. They were two minor themes that emerged because the form of autobiography—telling one's life story from the perspective of old age—forced them together. The personal success was the working out of the need for approval, which ran the entire course of his life. His conversion might also be understood as the final conclusion to the long struggle with his father. In the end, he accepted fatherly rule, and even became spokesman for it. Thus the needs of the private self and of the prophet interrupt the story of the public servant and even dominate it.

The two minor themes also formed two separate parts of what may be the essential American myth. Both the success and Christian stories trace the moral and religious journey from darkness to light, from imperfection to perfection. Americans embrace this sense of linear progression and celebrate heroes who rise from obscurity and adversity to success and recognition in their religious and public lives, and Webster managed to tell both in his autobiography.[81]

The story of Webster's rise to prominence occupied the first forty-two numbers. Although a descendant of one of the original planters, he began as the grandson of an undistinguished military official and the son of an ordinary farmer. His father "possessed a small farm, part of the estate of his grandfather," and served as a minor public official ("Memoir," No. 3). All in all it is a respectable but humble beginning: N.W. attended a common school and worked on the farm until age fourteen. His Yale education was less satisfying, he felt, than that afforded students before or after the war. The revolution interrupted college life, forcing the campus to close and students to disperse ("Memoir," No. 4).

N.W.'s life immediately after graduation was one of the most significant chapters in the "Memoir." In the passage already quoted at length above, he recorded his feelings: he was alone, rejected by the nation as a whole, which refused him an occupation because of the turmoil associated with the war. In his loneliness he returned to his father's house, only to be rejected again. Webster, author of thousands of pages of writing, only once recorded the conversation he had with his father at this crucial point in his life. After giving

THE PUBLIC SERVANT

N.W. a measly sum, his father said, "take this; you must now seek your living; I can do no more for you" (No. 5).

This incident allowed the autobiographer an opportunity to underscore N.W.'s moral character. It threw him into a "state of anxiety." He turned to books for relief, and read Samuel Johnson's *Rambler*, a collection of didactic essays. Johnson "produced no inconsiderable effect on his mind," inspiring him to resolve "that whatever was to be his fate in life, he would pursue a most exact course of integrity and virtue." One sentence stood out in his mind, and he determined to live his life according to Johnson's ideal: "to fear no eye, to suspect no tongue, is the great prerogative of innocence; an exemption granted only to invariable virtue." This standard was "indelibly impressed on his memory" ("Memoir," No. 5).

Young N.W. drifted in obscurity for three years, then endured a second important incident that fused his virtue and need for approval with the cause of the nation. In 1781 he fell in love, was rejected, and fled to Goshen, New York. He taught school and practiced law, neither of which seemed suitable. In Goshen he was without friends, relations, or money, and his health failed. "In this situation of things, his spirits failed and for some months, he suffered extreme depression and gloomy forebodings" ("Memoir," No. 7).

His solution echoed Franklin's and Jefferson's: merge self and society and achieve success and approval through public service. "In this state of mind, he formed the desing of composing elementary books for the instruction of children. . . ." In Goshen he began to write his famous Speller: it fused American nationalism and education, the perfect vehicle to enhance the portrayal of N.W. as the highly successful citizen, helping everyone, especially children. His Speller not only taught them to spell, but to be patriots above all else.

As the origin and nature of spelling books revealed, the themes of personal success and public service were intimately connected. The Speller launched N.W.'s public career precisely because it was the very embodiment of the ideal of serving all Americans. From 1782 until 1808, N.W.'s life was one act of public service after another. He lectured on the need for a national language, reformulated American textbooks along nationalistic lines, and agitated for copyright laws ("Memoir," Nos. 8–9). Efforts to solve the Confederation's political and economic woes included the first major call for a strong centralized form of government ("Memoir," Nos. 9–11).

Webster's need to establish his historical self was profound: he was willing to adopt the cloak of a martyr to accomplish it. N.W., noted the autobiographer, drove himself to "bad health and exhaustion" in the service of his country ("Memoir," No. 12).

As in the diary, Webster met all the major figures in American life during his lecture tour in 1785–86, and Benjamin Franklin became his friend. George Washington paid him a visit as President of the Constitutional Convention. He founded the first truly national magazine and lost money on it, entering debates on banking, penal systems, import duties, and slavery in the meantime, all in efforts to help all his countrymen. His defense of the Jay Treaty was significant enough to draw praise from Rufus King and near hysterical criticism from Thomas Jefferson, who by the 1790s had become his archenemy. Webster delighted in quoting Jefferson's attack on N.W. as the "collossus" of Federalism, more effective as polemicist than Alexander Hamilton. To Madison, Jefferson said N.W. was "a host within himself. We have only middling performances to oppose him. In truth, when he comes forward, there is nobody but yourself who can meet him" ("Memoir," No. 31). N.W.'s election to the New Haven City Council, the Connecticut Assembly, and a Justiceship of the Peace, all served as examples of success ("Memoir," Nos. 34–36).

As editor of an important and patriotic newspaper he defended national principles and played a significant role in establishing America's international safety. The great plagues in which hundreds died inspired him to undertake a scientific study of yellow fever and "pestilential disease." He wrote more essays on banking, agitated for a relief-society designed to assist the hard-working poor, and began work on his dictionaries—all in the name of the public ("Memoir," Nos. 12–44).

The second minor theme ended up dominating the life of the public servant. The Christian story appeared briefly in the beginning of the "Memoir," disappeared between Nos. 3 and 42, and then reemerged as a topic so powerful that neither the structure of the narrative nor its major theme could contain it. Nos. 43 through 50 detailed N.W.'s fall from piety into "skepticism" and his conversion to evangelical Protestantism.

The conversion dominated the end of the "Memoir" just as it shaped the last four decades of Noah Webster's life. It covered eight of the fifty-three numbers: 15 percent of the entire manuscript was devoted to a brief moment in his life. Furthermore, the narrative effectively ended with the conversion: the three additional pages recall his move to Amherst and scholarly voyage to England, neither of which add much to the essential story. Yet, as the words of the "Memoir" indicate, the conversion episode visibly and substantially altered N.W.'s private and public lives. His family relationships were transformed, as were his psychological, intellectual, social, and political lives.

The conversion experience was of such importance that he *rewrote and substantially altered* his original account of it. He sought to bring it into line with his needs and values at the time he authored the autobiography, twenty-four years after the event. In December of 1808, eight months after his conversion, he explained to his brother-in-law, Thomas Dawes, what had happened. Dawes replied, asking Webster for permission to publish the account. On February 23, 1809, Webster wrote a long theological treatise, which was published as *Peculiar Doctrines of the Gospel*.[82]

The letter to Dawes, December 20, 1808, was copied in the autobiography. Inserting it into the narrative had many advantages. It was an easy, precise, and efficient means of recounting the event. Its closeness to the event gave the narrative an attractive sense of dynamism. The incorporation of the documents gave both the autobiography as a whole, and the specific section on the event, an air of authenticity and credibility.

The account it presented described a good example of an evangelical conversion. N.W. began as a pious young man, but lost this trait in college. He indulged in the use of profanity and subscribed to a "species of skepticism." He harbored doubts about specific doctrines and viewed the Second Great Awakening as an overly emotional and fanatical movement. Yet his wife and two eldest daughters became converted, and the unity of his family life appeared threatened. Contemplation of the revival stirred his theological concern, but he could not bring himself to believe in the need for a profession of faith. His mind was constantly agitated. A traumatic, emotional conversion occurred. N.W. devoted the remainder of his life to the service of God. He believed in the "calvinistic doctrines," which are "not only true," but "the only genuine religion of the Bible" ("Memoir," No. 49).

It was an effective and moving account, merging self, family, religion, and nation into one event. However, it is not precisely the same letter he had written in 1808. Indeed, slight variations changed it to produce a different conversion. The omissions, alterations, and additions made in 1832 are significant. The author acknowledged his revisions in his introduction to the documents:

> The following is the substance of the letter, but with some additions and emmendations, made by his own hand, in 1832, stating some facts which he deemed it inexpedient to communicate at the time the letter was written ["Memoir," No. 43].

He specifically copied the date: "New Haven, December 20, 1808" ("Memoir," No. 43).

Slight alterations appeared in the account of N.W.'s religious sentiments immediately before the event, in the descriptions of the conversion itself, and in the consequence of the conversion. The first five pages of the "Memoir" version followed the original, with only minor changes in structure. Two sentences, however, were omitted. At the point at which Webster recalled almost separating from his family, he originally told Dawes that "I went so far as to apply to a friend for a seat in the Episcopal Church but never availed myself of his kindness in offering me one." Later he neglected to copy his admissions of having "short composure" while wrestling with the problem. The reasons for the first omission might include his reluctance to admit having seriously considered Episcopalian member-

ship because of his devout evangelicalism, or some other more
personal matter. In the second case, the omission effectively added
to a more positive portrayal of N.W.'s personality.

The alterations of the description of the moment of conversion
were more striking and changed an important part of the image of
N.W. in the mind of the reader. In 1809 Webster told Dawes:

> I closed my books, yielded to the influence which could not be resisted
> or mistaken, and was led by a spontaneous impulse to repentance,
> prayer, and entire submission and surrender of myself to my Maker
> and redeemer. My submission appeared to be cheerful, and was soon
> followed by that peace of mind which the world can neither give nor
> take away.[83]

In 1832 the event was far more traumatic:

> One morning, I entered my study and seated myself for writing or
> reading, when a sudden impulse upon my mind arrested me, and sub-
> dued my will. I instantly fell on my knees, confessed my sins to God,
> implored him pardon, and made my vows to him that upon that time I
> would live in entire obedience to his service. From that time, I enjoyed
> perfect tranquillity of mind; my views of religion were wholly
> changed; all my opposition to the doctrines of God's sovereignty, elec-
> tion, the agency of the spirit in regeneration, the atonement, and the
> divinity of Christ, was completely vanquished . . . ["Memoir," No. 48].

The new version cast a different light on N.W. It was a more
direct, personal, and emotional conversion than he admitted to earlier. His complete obedience to God—emotionally, psychologically,
and intellectually—stood in clearer focus. The new second paragraph spelled out his support for specific evangelical doctrines and,
combined with the first passage, portrays N.W. in the light of the
emotional characteristics of "enthusiastic" revivalism, a major point
he wanted to avoid in the earlier period. The author also omitted an
eight-sentence passage in which he described his feelings of intellectual insufficiency, regret for his life without Christ, and his ingratitude toward God. He expressed contrition for the hardness of his
heart, and his own participation in an "enormous crime, the greatest
man can commit against God, of resisting the influence of his Holy
Spirit."[84]

The changes in the end of the letter were also important. He closed the 1809 letter to Dawes with a few words on his wife's happiness over his conversion and salvation. These were omitted in the "Memoir." The copied letter breaks off, and the author adds "(Thus far the Letter)," as if to remind himself that what comes next was not written in 1808. He adds an entirely new paragraph in which a direct, personal relationship between N.W. and God is detailed, something that Webster never hinted of in his diary or letter:

> The following fact is remarkable. Not long after I had become reconciled to the doctrines of scripture, I was for some time afflicted with a local pain. I used various remedies for it without success. After being disappointed repeatedly, I resolved to supplicate ease from the only Being who is able to deliver us from troubles. I rose in the morning, retired to my study, and falling to my knees, I earnestly prayed God for relief. No sooner were my words uttered, than the pain ceased, and never returned. That this was a supernatural interposition of divine power, I do not know; but the fact I know; respecting this there can have been no deception, and the frequent recollection of this fact has had no small influence in confirming my faith through life. And it deserves to be considered, whether modern Christians, on the ground that miracles have ceased, do not go too far in denying or disbelieving the special interposition of divine power, in the ordinary course of God's moral government; and whether this is not a material difference between old testament and modern Christians ["Memoir," No. 50].

This seemingly minor or insignificant addition in fact revealed the fundamental nature of Webster's conversion and the relationship between his private needs and public views. It appeared to be a statement of personal faith, and a part of the debate common in evangelical movements over the intervention by God in human lives. It also underscored the links between Webster's emotional and intellectual lives. Here was a direct example of the Almighty's approval of N.W. God's approval had "no small influence" in "confirming" his "faith through life." The American people, having repeatedly rejected Webster's views and personally attacked him, stood corrected by God. They must obey God in order to achieve stability, thus they must also accept, and approve of, Noah Webster.

These revisions effectively altered the nature of the conversion in the reader's eyes, and in so doing, recast the character of N.W. by portraying him in a more positive light than the earlier account. They were the product of the narrator's act of looking back on the past, finding it unsuitable for his present needs, and reshaping a specific historic event to fit the demands of the immediate concern. The added emotion and frenzy underscored the culmination of the Christian journey and its authenticity. It was a bold statement of total submission to an omniscient, approving force. The incident of direct divine intervention on N.W.'s physical self added further concrete evidence of his achievement of perfection and its rewards. Its strategic placement at the end of the narrative elevated the story of N.W. to a higher plane, making him symbolic not merely of the American people, but of the continuity of all Christian tradition and culture. The lessons we might learn from the life of God's servant were important for all humankind.

The conversion (especially in its new form) also effectively transformed the essential theme of the autobiography. Beginning with No. 43, the emphasis on public service gave way to an emphasis on the workings of God. The "Memoir" is transformed from a Franklinesque secular lesson to a spiritual autobiography strongly reminiscent of those written by Puritans and Quakers in the seventeenth and eighteenth centuries.

The "Memoir of Noah Webster" ended with N.W.'s return from a trip to England in 1825, where he had finished his quarter-century work on *The American Dictionary of the English Language* (No. 53). The final publication and the account of the making of his greatest work would have been the next logical topic. Instead, Webster stopped writing. That story, from his perspective, remains unwritten.

Why did he not complete his autobiography? Why was it never published? The final answers to those questions are not provided by the author of the "Memoir." No evidence of his feelings on either point remains.

The same interaction between the facts of his life and the act of writing, which shaped this presentation of his life in the three genres, probably also prevented or hindered him from completing the manuscript. The next two topics—the dictionary and the Bible—neatly symbolized two halves of his intellectual and emotional life before and after 1808. They also sharply underscored the clash between the story he wanted to tell, his hopes for future public approval, and the reality of the central aspects of his life after 1808. Facing the task of writing about his greatest work, as the public would undoubtably see it (and in fact has seen it), and the work the author himself felt was his most important summoned feelings and emotions to the surface that Webster did not want to face and ultimately could neither comprehend nor reconcile. In the end it caused him to stop writing.

Webster's conversion transformed his life in every way. Beginning in 1781 when he began his career as educational reformer and cultural nationalist, his concerns centered on national questions. The life of the nation—its future and its past, its shortcomings and its potential—occupied a central place in his work and in his conception of his life and career. His writings, from political treatises to reform tracts, addressed national issues. They were not written wholly as an act of public service, for Webster consistently sought financial and psychic reward in everything he did, just as he did in his autobiography. Until 1808 his work centered on improving national life, even when he was bitterly critical of, and hostile to, the dominant thrust of social development.

His conversion sharply and immediately changed all that. After 1808 God occupied the center of everything Webster thought and wrote, from personal letters to national broadsides. Evangelical Protestantism replaced nationalism or patriotism as the central framework within which Webster understood himself and the world in which he lived. He now produced evangelical tracts, and his political and educational works took on a new perspective: all sought to instill evangelical, not patriotic, values in their readers. Even his dictionary, dedicated to God and filled with definitions formed in evangelical terms, placed greater emphasis on religion than on any form of patriotism or nationalism. His United States history textbooks, published at the time he wrote the autobiography, celebrated the origins of all that was good in America, not in the Declaration of Independence, in the Constitution, or in the ideals of equality, but in the lives, habits, and deferential religious ideals of the Puritan founders of New England.[85] Writing about the dictionary and the Bible thus posed a serious intellectual and emotional problem. Should he recount his motivations and a quarter-century of labor on the dictionary in terms of public service, and thereby further his chances for eternal public approval? If so, how then could he revert back to his evangelical mode to recall his religious tracts and his edition of the Bible, the most important work of his life? Or should he write about the dictionary in evangelical terms, the framework of belief he used to comprehend everything after 1808? If he chose this option, it would lessen the impact of his self-portrayal of the public servant. It would also place his edition of the Bible in a more significant spot in his narrative and open the way for him to emphasize its contribution to the world instead of the dictionary's. Yet to do so would limit his appeal to other evangelicals, and probably alienate some future Americans.

Other Christians found an answer to similar problems in America's "civil religion." They merged patriotism and Christianity to view the United States as God's chosen land, his instrument for progress and order on earth. We were the redeemed nation, they thought, and though not yet perfect, we could become so, and in the process correct the ills of the world.[86]

Federalists such as Webster commonly employed a traditional American rhetorical style—the Jeremiad—to communicate their beliefs. They bemoaned the nation's weaknesses and defects, and even appeared to find satisfaction in detailing its sins. Yet they did so only to exult ultimately in the possibilities of the future. Like Noah Webster they expressed deep concern over social change and voiced strong criticism of democracy and the seamier aspects of laissez-faire capitalism. Yet their laments ended in affirmation: if Americans kept their noses to the grindstone and obeyed their Christian teachings, all would be well.

Webster came close to this view, yet he ultimately failed to embrace it in his life or in his autobiography. He believed duty to God came before earthly concerns, and that individualism and exploitation in politics and economics contradicted Christian teaching and led inevitably to social disruption. His conservative critique of American life went too deep to be overcome; American life was the problem, not the answer. It must be totally transformed. Americans were a sinful, depraved people. "We are an erring nation," he wrote; "we deserve all our public evils." And on another occasion he noted, *"We have foresaken God, and he has foresaken us."*[87] After 1800, and especially after 1808, Webster did not embrace American democracy as God's will, but instead roundly and repeatedly rejected it. He did not castigate the people and urge them on to new democratic glories and nationalistic perfection, but railed bitterly against them and scolded them as the spokesman of an angry God. Indeed, his evangelicalism contained a strict hierarchy of values. People must first worship God and seek to glorify him. Spiritual duties and relationships took precedence over earthly matters. Men must worry first about God and their relationships to him; earthly, and thus national, problems must take second place.

All of these questions must have surfaced when Webster contemplated writing the next section of his autobiography. The *American Dictionary* certainly came next. As he sat in his study thinking about his next chapter, he probably recalled twenty-five or more years of hard work and twenty-five or more years of criticism and public ridicule. His long and bitter political battles, linked in his emotions to the criticisms of his philological work, undoubtably surfaced. It must have been a difficult moment, full of defensive anger; frustration over his inability to make others see what he knew to be true; powerful feelings of rejection by his critics, his country, and probably his parents; resentment against them all, and bitterness over his lifelong economic struggle. He had done so much for so long, yet no one seemed to appreciate it. Now he must account for those years and do so in a manner that would win acceptance and approval for all time.

Yet it could not be done. If he wrote it as the work of the public servant, it would contradict his account of his conversion: and the next subject he must face after the dictionary would be his evangelical revision of the Holy Bible (1833). If he wrote it as an evangelical work, he would contradict the main message he wanted to get across.

No solution to this dilemma acceptable to Noah Webster could be found. He put down his pen, stuffed the manuscript in a drawer, and forgot about it.

6. CONCLUSION

The "Three Faces of Noah Webster" turned to the world differ significantly. Separated in composition by time, written for various audiences, and recorded with alternative goals in mind, each self-portrait presented aspects of the author's life and feelings, his concerns and needs, which contrasted with the others. Yet each also revealed common and similar themes. In all three cases, the special circumstances and rules of each genre of writing merged with the essential facts of the author's life, both surface events and inner feelings, to shape the presentation of self.

Historical reality and literary technique produced three faces of Noah Webster. In his diary he wrote about what was important only to the private self, and thus charted his rise from obscurity to recognition in terms of the response of the world in which he lived to his private and public self. In his public essays he subordinated his self to the cause at hand, using certain selected aspects of his life in order to accomplish his goals. In his autobiography he presented his life as he wished it had been, and sought to establish his personal character and reputation for all future Americans. In all three cases he sought love and public approval, reaffirmation of his importance and usefulness to other people. All three self-portraits combine to give us the personal history of one articulate individual, an account of how he perceived himself and wanted to be seen by others.

NOTES to Section I

1. Noah Webster to George Washington, Dec. 18, 1785. Papers of Noah Webster, New York Public Library.

2. The largest collection of letters, the Papers of Noah Webster housed in the Rare Books and Manuscripts Division of the New York Public Library, fills ten large boxes. It also includes the diaries and many other documents. The second largest, the Webster Family Papers at the Sterling Memorial Library at Yale University, contains letters from all members of the Webster family. For other collections, see the footnotes in Richard M. Rollins, *The Long Journey of Noah Webster* (Philadelphia: University of Pennsylvania Press, 1980), and Harry R. Warfel, *Noah Webster: Schoolmaster to America* (New York: Macmillan Company, 1936). Additional secondary works include Horace E. Scudder, *Noah Webster,* introduction by Richard M. Rollins (New York: Chelsea House, 1981); Ervin C. Shoemaker, *Noah Webster: Pioneer of Learning* (New York: Columbia University Press, 1936); Joseph J. Ellis, *After the Revolution: Profiles of Early American Culture* (New York: W. W. Norton, 1979); Lawrence J. Friedman, *Inventors of the Promised Land* (New York: Knopf, 1975).

Webster's published letters may be found in Emily Ellsworth Fowler Ford, *Notes on the Life of Noah Webster,* 2 vols. (New York: Privately printed, 1912), and Harry R. Warfel, ed., *Letters of Noah Webster* (New York: Library Publishers, 1953).

3. Edwin H. Carpenter, Jr., ed., *A Bibliography of the Writings of Noah Webster* (New York: New York Public Library, 1958).

4. The spelling book was first published as Noah Webster, *A Grammatical Institute of the English Language . . . Part I* (Hartford: Hudson and Goodwin, 1783). For analyses of its content, see Warfel, *Noah Webster: Shoolmaster to America,* hereafter cited as *Webster;* Rollins, *Long Journey,* chap. 2. The most extensive sustained analysis is E. Jennifer Monaghan, *A Common Heritage: Noah Webster's Blue-Backed Speller* (Hamden, Conn.: Archon Books, 1983).

5. See Rollins, *Long Journey,* chap. 8.

6. For a complete listing of all editions, see Carpenter, *Bibliography.*

7. *Noah Webster, A Collection of Fugitiv Writings on Moral, Historical, Political and Literary Subjects* (Boston: J. Thomas and E. T. Andrews, 1790).

8. This is a topic too important and complex to be dealt with within an essay on Webster's autobiographical writings. For further insights, see Rollins, *Long Journey;* Warfel, *Webster;* and Monaghan, *Common Heritage.*

9. Noah Webster, *The Prompter: Or a Commentary on Common Sayings and Subjects, Which Are Full of Common Sense, the Best Sense in the World* (Hartford: Hudson and Goodwin, 1791).

10. [Noah Webster], *The Revolution in France Considered in Respect to Its Progress and Effects. By an American* (New York: George Bunce and Company, 1794).

11. Ebenezer Hazard to Jeremy Belknap, quoted in Ford, *Notes,* 1: 179.

12. Noah Webster, *A Rod for a Fool's Back* (New York: Read and Morse, [1800]).

Notes to Section I

13. Noah Webster, ed., *A Collection of Papers on the Subject of Bilious Fevers, Prevalent in the United States for a Few Years Past Compiled by Noah Webster, Jun.* (New York: Hopkins, Webb and Company, 1796).

14. Noah Webster, *A Brief History of Epidemic and Pestilential Diseases; with the Principal Phenomena of the Physical World, which Preceed and Accompany Them, and Observations Deduced from the Facts Stated*, 2 vols. (Hartford: Hudson and Goodwin, 1799).

15. Noah Webster, *A Compendious Dictionary of the English Language* (New Haven: Sidney's Press, 1806). See also the essays cited in Carpenter, *Bibliography*, sec. 4: "Philological, Didactic, and Religious Works."

16. Lawrence Buel, *New England Literary Culture: From the Revolution through Renaissance* (Cambridge: Cambridge University Press, 1986).

17. Noah Webster, ed., *A Plea for a Miserable World* ... (Boston: Ezra Lincoln, 1820).

18. See Carpenter, all sections, but especially appendix A for a chronological listing of Webster's public service in these years as well as earlier.

19. Noah Webster, *An Oration, Pronounced before the Knox and Warren Branches of the Washington Benevolent Society, at Amherst, on the Celebration of the Declaration of Independence, July 4, 1814* (Northampton, Mass.: William Butler, 1814).

20. Noah Webster, *The Peculiar Doctrines of the Gospel, Explained and Defended* [New York: J. Seymour, 1809].

21. Noah Webster, *A Brief View of Errors and Obscurities in the Common Version of the Scriptures; Addressed to the Bible Societies, Clergymen and Other Friends of Religion* [New Haven: N.p., 1834?].

22. Noah Webster, *Value of the Bible and Excellence of the Christian Religion: For the Use of Families and Schools* (New Haven: Durrie and Peck, 1834).

23. Noah Webster, ed., *The Holy Bible, Containing the Old and New Testaments, in the Common Version. With Amendments of the Language* (New Haven: Durrie and Peck, 1833).

24. Noah Webster, *A Manual of Useful Studies: For the Instruction of Young Persons of Both Sexes, in Families and Schools* (New Haven: S. Babcock, 1839); *Biography, for the Use of Schools* (New Haven: Hezekiah Howe, 1830); *History of the United States; to Which Is Prefixed a Brief Historical of Our English Ancestors, from the Dispersion of Babel, to Their Migration to America; and of the Conquest of South America* (New Haven: Durrie and Peck, 1832).

25. [Noah Webster], "A Voice of Wisdom," [New York] *Commercial Advertiser*, Nov. 20, 1837.

26. Noah Webster, *An American Dictionary of the English Language*, 2 vols. (New Haven: Hezekiah Howe, 1828).

27. Noah Webster, *An American Dictionary of the English Language; First Edition in Octavo*, 2 vols. (New Haven: By the Author, 1841).

28. Noah Webster, *A Collection of Papers on Political, Literary, and Moral Subjects* (Boston: Webster and Clark, 1843).

NOTES TO SECTION I

29. For the historians' view, see Norman S. Fiering, "Will and Intellect in the New England Mind," *William and Mary Quarterly,* 3rd series, 29 (1972): 515–58; Edmund S. Morgan, ed., "The Diary of Michael Wigglesworth," Colonial Society of Massachusetts *Publications,* No. 35 (Boston, 1951); Michael G. McGiffert, ed., *God's Plot: The Paradoxes of Puritan Piety, Being the Autobiography and Journal of Thomas Shepard* (Amherst: University of Massachusetts Press, 1972); *The Autobiography of Benjamin Franklin,* ed. L. W. Labaree, R. L. Ketcham, H. C. Boatfield, H. H. Fineman (New Haven: Yale University Press, 1964); Michael Zuckerman, "The Fabrication of Identity in Early America," *William and Mary Quarterly,* 3rd series, 24 (1977): 183–214; John A. Garraty, *The Nature of Biography* (New York: Knopf, 1957); *The Diary of Elihu Hubbard Smith,* ed. James M. Cronin (Philadelphia: American Philosophical Society, 1973); Roy N. Lokken, "The Case of the Mysterious Diary," *The Historian as Detective: Essays on Evidence,* ed. Robin Winks (New York: Harper Colophon Books, 1970); *The Diaries of George Washington,* ed. Donald Jackson, vol. 1 (Charlottesville: University of Virginia Press, 1976); *The Diary of Isaac Backus,* ed. William G. McLoughlin, vol. 1 (Providence, R.I.: Brown University Press, 1979); *Hayes: The Diary of a President; 1875–1881,* ed. T. Harry Williams.

30. For the views of literary critics, see William Spengemann's indispensable bibliographic essay in *The Forms of Autobiography: Episodes in the History of a Literary Genre* (New Haven: Yale University Press, 1980). For reasons that will be clear later in this essay, I have found the following most useful in my attempts to come to terms with Webster: Robert F. Sayre, *The Examined Self: Benjamin Franklin, Henry Adams, Henry James* (Princeton: Princeton University Press, 1964), and "Autobiography and the Making of America," *Autobiography: Essays Theoretical and Critical,* ed. James Olney (Princeton: Princeton University Press, 1980); James Olney, *Metaphors of Self: The Meaning of Autobiography* (Princeton: Princeton University Press, 1972); John Paul Eakin, *Fictions in Autobiography: Studies in the Art of Self-Invention* (Princeton: Princeton University Press, 1985); Jerome Hamilton Buckley, *The Turning Key: Autobiography of the Subjective Impulse since 1800* (Cambridge: Harvard University Press, 1984); Susanna Egan, *Patterns of Experience in Autobiography* (Chapel Hill: University of North Carolina Press, 1984); Mutlu Kanuk Blasing, *The Art of Life: Studies in American Autobiographical Literature* (Austin: University of Texas Press, 1977); G. Thomas Couser, *American Autobiography: The Prophetic Mode* (Amherst: University of Massachusetts Press, 1979); Louis Kaplan, *A Bibliography of American Autobiographies* (Madison: University of Wisconsin Press, 1961); Richard G. Lillerd, *American Life in Autobiography: A Descriptive Guide* (Stanford, Calif.: Stanford University Press, 1956); James M. Cox, "Autobiography and America," (*Aspects of Narrative,* ed. J. H. Miller (New York: Columbia University Press, 1971); and Roy Pascal, *Design and Truth in Autobiography* (Cambridge: Harvard University Press, 1960). For an analysis of recent works in literary criticism along the lines of constructionist and deconstructionist theoretical lines, see Paul Jay, "What's the Use? Critical Theory and the Study of Autobiography," *Biography* 10 (Spring 1987): 39–54.

Anthropologists and psychologists have also written significant studies: see Lewis Langness, *The Life History in Anthropological Science* (New York: Holt, Rinehart and

NOTES TO SECTION I

Winston, 1965); Murray G. Murphy, "An Approach to the Historical Study of National Character," *Context and Meaning in Cultural Anthropology,* ed. Melford E. Spiro (New York: Free Press, 1965); Bruce Mazlish, "Autobiography and Psycho-Analysis: Between Truth and Self-Deception," *Encounter;* Gordon Allport, *The Use of Personal Documents in Psychological Science* (New York: Social Science Research Council, 1942); and Erik Erikson, "Ghandi's Autobiography: The Leader as Child," *Life History and the Historical Moment* (New York: W. W. Norton, 1966).

For interdisciplinary approaches, see Albert E. Stone, "Autobiography and American Culture," *American Studies: An International Newsletter* (Winter 1972); James Olney, "Autobiography and the Cultural Moment: A Thematical, Historical, and Bibliographical Introduction," in his anthology; Robert F. Sayre, "The Proper Study—Autobiography in American Studies," *American Quarterly* 29 (Winter 1977); David Levin, "The Autobiography of Benjamin Franklin: The Puritan Experimenter in Life and Art," *In Defense of Historical Literature: Essays on American History, Autobiography, Drama and Fiction* (New York: Hill and Wang, 1967); James Cox, "Jefferson's Autobiography: Recovering Literature's Lost Ground," *Southern Review* 14 (1978); William Earle, *The Autobiographical Consciousness: A Philosophical Inquiry into Experience* (Chicago: Quadrangle Books, 1972); John William Ward, "Who Was Benjamin Franklin?" *American Scholar* 32 (Autumn 1963); Mary Carlock, "American Autobiographies, 1840–1870: A Bibliography," *Bulletin of Bibliography* 23 (May–August 1961); Patricia Spacks, "Women's Stories, Women's Selves," *Hudson Review* 30 (1977); Sacvan Bercovitch, *The Puritan Origins of the American Self* (New Haven: Yale University Press, 1975); and Arna Bontemps, "The Slave Narrative: An American Genre," *Great Slave Narratives* (Boston: Beacon Press, 1969).

31. Sayre, *The Examined Self;* Pascal, *Design and Truth;* Daniel B. Shea, Jr., *Spiritual Awakening in Early America* (Princeton: Princeton University Press, 1968); and William L. Howarth, "Some Principles of Autobiography," *New Literary History* (Winter 1974), 365–69, all discuss the problem of time and perspective.

32. Ibid. All discuss this second point also.

33. On American diaries, see William Matthews, comp., *American Diaries: An Annotated Bibliography of American Diaries Written Prior to the Year 1861* (Berkeley: University of California Press, 1945); and *American Diaries in Manuscript, 1580–1954: A Descriptive Guide* (Athens: University of Georgia Press, 1974); Harriette Merrifield Forbes, comp., *New England Diaries, 1602–1800: A Descriptive Catalogue of Diaries, Orderly Books, and Sea Journals* (Topsfield, Mass.: Perkins Press, 1923); Jane DuPree Begos, comp., *Annotated Bibliography of Published Women's Diaries* (Pound Ridge, N.Y.: Begos, 1977); and Davis Bitton, *Guide to Mormon Diaries and Autobiographies* (Provo, Utah: Brigham Young University Press, 1977).

34. Allport, *Use of Personal Documents.*

35. On childhood in eighteenth-century New England, see Constance B. Schulz, "Children and Childhood in the Eighteenth Century," in Joseph M. Hawes and N. Ray Hiner, eds., *American Childhood: A Research Guide and Historical Handbook* (Westport, Conn.: Greenwood Press, 1985); Philip J. Greven, *The Protestant Temperament: Patterns of Child-Rearing, Religious Experience, and Self in Early America* (New

62

NOTES TO SECTION I

York: New American Library, 1977); and John F. Walzer, "A Period of Ambivalence: Eighteenth-Century American Childhood," *The History of Childhood,* ed. Lloyd deMause (New York: Harper & Row, 1975), pp. 351–82.

36. Jay Fliegelman, *Prodigals and Pilgrims: The American Revolution against Patriarchal Authority, 1750–1800* (Cambridge: Cambridge University Press, 1982).

37. See several letters printed in Ford, *Notes,* vols. 1 and 2.

38. Noah Webster to Harriet Webster Fowler, Apr. 6, 1835, Warfel, *Letters of Noah Webster* (hereafter cited as *Letters,*) pp. 448–450.

39. Warfel, *Webster,* and Monaghan, *Common Heritage.*

40. Ibid.

41. Noah Webster to Rebecca Greenleaf, Jan 11, 1788, Warfel, *Letters,* p. 73.

42. Ibid.

43. Noah Webster to E. Waddington, July 6, 1798, Warfel, *Letters,* pp. 181–82.

44. Noah Webster to Stephen Twining, Jan. 22, 1802, Warfel, *Letters,* pp. 248–49.

45. See ibid., and Noah Webster to Timothy Pickering, July 17, 1978, Ford, *Notes,* 1: 465, and Warfel, *Webster.*

46. See above, fn. 43.

47. For studies of the prophetic mode of presentation of self, see Couser, *American Autobiography,* and Sacvan Bercovitch, *The American Jeremiad* (Madison: University of Wisconsin Press, 1978).

48. See Couser, *American Autobiography;* William C. Spengemann and L. R. Lunquist, "Autobiography and the American Myth," *American Quarterly* 17 (Fall 1965), 92–110; and Eleanor Wilner, *Gathering the Winds: Visionary Imagination and Radical Transformation of Self and Society* (Baltimore: Johns Hopkins University Press, 1975), for fuller analyses of prophetic autobiography.

49. Shea, *Spiritual Autobiography.*

50. Franklin, *Autobiography;* and Henry Adams, *The Education of Henry Adams,* introduction by James Truslow Adams (New York: Modern Library, 1931).

51. Webster, *A Grammatical Institute, Part I.*

52. Cox, "Autobiography and America"; Pascal, *Design and Truth.*

53. Noah Webster to Thomas Dawes, Dec. 20, 1808, Warfel, *Letters,* pp. 309–15.

54. Webster, *American Dictionary.* Also relevant here are letters to Andrew Stevenson, June 22, 1841, and to Her Majesty, Victoria, Queen of Great Britain, June 22, 1841, Papers of Noah Webster, New York Public Library, Box 1.

55. Noah Webster to Messers Morse, Feb. 24, 1834, Warfel, *Letters,* p. 433.

56. [Noah Webster], "A Voice of Wisdom," *Commercial Advertiser,* [1837].

57. Shea, *Spiritual Autobiography;* Owen C. Watkins, *The Puritan Experience: Studies in Spiritual Autobiography* (New York: Schocken Books, 1972); E. D. Lerner, "Puritanism and Spiritual Autobiography," *Hibbert Journal* 55 (1857): 373–86; and Cynthia G. Wolf, "Literary Reflections of the Puritan Character," *Journal of the History of Ideas,* 1971.

58. See Karl J. Weintraub, "Autobiography and Historical Consciousness," *Critical Inquiry* 1 (June 1979): 821–48, and *The Value of the Individual: Self and Circumstance in Autobiography* (Chicago: University of Chicago Press, 1978).

Notes to Section I

59. Cox, "Autobiography," and Pascal, *Design and Truth*.

60. Cox, "Autobiography," p. 150.

61. Ibid., p. 145.

62. Pascal, *Design and Truth*.

63. "Will of Noah Webster," June 7, 1843, Webster Family Papers, Yale University.

64. Just to be sure, I gave a copy of the "Memoir" and several letters written by Webster and housed in different archives to Bruce Greenwood, Examiner of Questioned Documents, Los Angeles Police Department. After examination he reported that the "Memoir" and the letters were all written by the same person, Noah Webster.

65. For works on the revival, see the bibliography cited in Rollins, *Long Journey*, chap. 7, n. 1.

66. For attacks on his Speller, see Carpenter, *Bibliography*, part 4, "Controversies Involving Webster."

67. Quoted in Warfel, *Webster*, 163, 234.

68. For example, see "Webster's Dictionary and Spelling Book," [New York] *Evening Post*, June 27, 1828.

69. See Carpenter, *Bibliography*, part 4.

70. *Hampshire Gazette*, May 23, 1838. For an analysis of Webster's state of mind in the 1830s, see Rollins, *Long Journey*, chap. 9.

71. Pascal, *Design and Truth*, p. 59. See also Weintraub, "Autobiography," p. 845; Howarth, "Principles"; the chapters in Olney and Gusdorf in Olney's anthology; Warner Berthoff, "Witness and Testament: Two Contemporary Classics," in Miller, *Aspects*; Richard Gilman, *Confusion of Realms* (New York: Random House, 1976); and John Mandel Barrett, "The Autobiographer's Art," *Journal of Aesthetics and Art Criticism* (Winter 1968), pp. 215–16.

72. Noah Webster to Benjamin Rush, Sept. 11, 1801, Warfel, *Letters*, p. 237.

73. Olney, *Metaphors of Self*, p. 11.

74. George Gusdorf, "Conditions and Limits of Autobiography," *Autobiography*, ed. Olney, pp. 28–48.

75. See numerous letters in the Papers of Noah Webster, Box 1, New York Public Library; Monaghan, *Common Heritage*.

76. For example, see John Marshall's biography of George Washington as well as the more famous Weems work.

77. For example, see Noah Webster, *A Manual of Useful Studies: For the Instruction of Young Persons of Both Sexes, in Families and Schools* (New Haven: S. Babcock, 1839); *Instruction and Entertaining Lessons for Youth: With Rules for Reading with Propriety, Illustrated by Examples* (New Haven: S. Babcock & Durrie and Peck, 1835).

78. Noah Webster, *Biography, for Use of Schools* (New Haven: Hezekiah Howe, 1830).

79. Warfel, *Webster*, chap. 1.

80. See Olney, *Metaphors of Self*, for other examples of this.

81. Spengemann and Lunquist, "Autobiography," p. 503.

64

NOTES TO SECTION I

82. Noah Webster, *Peculiar Doctrines of the Gospel, Explained and Defended* . . . (Hartford: J. Seymour, 1809).

83. Noah Webster to Thomas Dawes, Feb. 23, 1809, Papers of Noah Webster, New York Public Library.

84. Ibid. See also Webster, *Peculiar Doctrines.*

85. See Rollins, *Long Journey,* chap. 7.

86. Ernest R. Tuveson, *Reedemer Nation: The Idea of America's Millennial Role* (Chicago: University of Chicago Press, 1968).

87. [Hampshire] *Gazette,* May 23, 1838.

II. MISCELLANEOUS LETTERS AND ESSAYS OF NOAH WEBSTER

Oil Portrait.
James Herring, 1833. *National Portrait Gallery, Smithsonian Institution.*

1. CLASS CONFESSION, 1778

A self-explanatory confession of student rebellion at Yale in 1778. No historian of Yale has mentioned this incident. For more on Yale during the American Revolution, see Brooks Mather Kelley, Yale: A History *(New Haven: Yale University Press, 1974).*

Previously unpublished. Bieneke Rare Book and Manuscript Library, New Haven, Connecticut.

Yale College, Class of 1778
Confession of Causing a Disturbance in Chapel
Signed by 26 Students.

We, whose Names are underwritten, being members of this College, do most humbly confess, that on the Morning of the 3rd Instant we walked out of Chapel contrary to Order in a very indecent irregular Manner when two of our class were about to receive that discipline in which they justly deserved. We acknowledge this was done in Consequence of a premeditated and preconcented Combination entered into by us: and that our conduct therein cannot be rationally be viewed in any other light than that of an audacious Contempt of all the Authority of College, and a practical Countenanceing and Approving of the Crimes of others. We are truly sensible, that this our Conduct was utterly inexcusable, entirely criminal, and highly affrontive, an Example tending to the Subversion of all good Order, and the necessary Government of College. We publicly condemn ourselves for it, and confess we justly deserve a very severe punishment on account of it: we humbly ask Forgiveness of the Rev^d. President and all the other Authority of College, whom we have hereby undutifully offended. We cast ourselves on their clemency, and beg all that lenity may be escribed towards us, that is consistent with the due Government of College, publicly and sincerely promising that we will for the future carefully avoid all such like disorderly Behaviour, and endeavour to evidence the Sincerity of this Confession by a decent Deportment, and a becoming dutiful obedience to all the Authority and Order of College, while we are Members of it.

Abraham Bishop	Josiah Meigs
Joel Barlow	Ashen Miller
Aaron Buell	Giles Pettibone
Phineas Bartholomew	Daniel Reed
Ebenezer Daggett	Ebenezer Sage
Ezekiel Gilbert	Noah Swift
Thomas Cole	Zephaniah Swift
Obadiah Hotchkiss	John Thayer
William Hotch kiss	Noah Webster
_____ Jacob	John Welch
Eben^r. Johnson	Ichabod Wetmore
William Johnson	Zephaniah Willis
David Judson	Oliver Wolcott

2. INTRODUCTION TO THE "BLUE-BACK SPELLER," 1783

Originally written in 1782, this essay encapsulates much of Webster's early ideas on orthography, prosody, the need for a national language, as well as a good feeling for his strong sense of national pride. It put him at the forefront of education and nationalism, preceding efforts such as Jedidiah Morse's geography. It is an emotion-packed statement in which he merges self, language, and American history into a utopian synthesis. A classic statement of the American prophetic perspective applied to a specific subject, it was altered, rewritten, and omitted in later editions. It was still in print in 1987. For an excellent detailed study of the Speller as an educational text, and as an entrepreneurial project, see E. Jennifer

Monaghan, A Common Heritage: Noah Webster's Blue-Back
Speller *(Hamden, Conn.: Archon Books, 1983).*
  The Grammatical Institute of the English Language . . .
(Hartford: Hudson and Goodwin, 1783).

To attack deep rooted prejudices and oppose the current of
opinions, is a task of great difficulty and hazard. It commonly requires lengths of time and favourable circumstances to diffuse and
establish an sentiment among the body of people; but when a sentiment has acquired the stamp of time and the authority of general
custom, it is too firm to be shaken by the efforts of an individual:
Even errour becomes too sacred to be violated by the assaults of
innovation.

But the present period is an era of wonders; Greater changes
have been wrought, in the minds of men, in the short compass of
eight years past, than are commonly effected in a century.

Previously to the late war, America preserved the most un-
shaken attachment to Great-Britain: the king, the constitution, the
laws, the commerce, the fashions, the books and even the sentiments of Englishmen were implicitly supposed to be the best on
earth: not only their virtues and improvements, but their prejudices,
their errours, their vices and their follies were adopted by us with
avidity. But by a concurrence of those powerful causes that effect
almost instantaneous revolutions in states, the political views of
America have suffered a total change. She now sees a mixture of
profound wisdom and consummate folly in the British constitution;
a ridiculous compound of freedom and tyranny in their laws; and a
few struggles of patriotism, overpowered by the corruptions of a
wicked administration. She views the vices of that nation with abhorrence, their errours with pity, and their follies with contempt.

While the Americans stand astonished at their former delusion
and enjoy the pleasure of a final separation from their insolent sov-
ereigns, it becomes their duty to attend to the arts of peace, and
particularly to the interests of literature; to see if there be not some
errours to be corrected, some defects to be supplied, and some im-

provements to be introduced into our system of education, as well as into those of civil policy. We find Englishmen practicing upon very erroneous maxims in politics and religion; and possibly we shall find, upon careful examinations, that their methods of education are equally erroneous and defective.

The British writers remark it as one of the follies of their nations, that they have attended more to the study of ancient and foreign languages, than to the improvement of their own. The ancient Greek and Roman languages, and the modern French and Italian, have generally been made a necessary part of a polite or learned education; while a grammatical study of their own language, has, till very lately been totally neglected. This ridiculous practice has found its way to America; and so violent have been the prejudices in support of it, that the whispers of common sense, in favour of our native tongue, have been silenced amidst the clamour of pedantry in favour of Greek and Latin.

The consequence is, that few attempts have been made to reduce our language to rules, and expunge the corruptions that ignorance and caprice, unguided by any standard must necessarily introduce. It is but a short time since we have had a grammar of our own tongue, formed upon the true principles of its Saxon original. And those who have given us the most perfect systems, have confined themselves chiefly to the two last branches of grammar, Analogy and Syntax. In the two first, Orthography and Prosody, that is, in the spelling and pronunciations of words, we have no guide, or none but such as lead into innumerable errours. The want of some standard in schools has occasioned a great variety of dialects in Great-Britain and of course, in America. Every county in England, every State in America and almost every town in each State, has some peculiarities in pronunciation which are equally erroneous and disagreeable to its neighbors. And how can these distinctions be avoided? The sounds of our letters are more capricious and irregular than those of any alphabet with which we are acquainted. Several of our vowels have four or five different sounds; and the same sounds are often expressed by five, six or seven different characters. The case is much the same with our consonants: And these different sounds have no mark of distinction. How would a child or a foreigner learn the different sound of o in the words, rove, move, dove or of oo in poor, door? Or that a, ai, ei and e have precisely the same sound in the words, bare, laid, vein, there? Yet these and fifty other irregularities have passed unnoticed by authors of Spelling Books and Dictionaries.* They study the language enough to find the difficulties of it—they tell us that it is impossible to reduce it to order—that it is to be learnt only by the ear—they lament the disorder and dismiss it without a remedy. Thus the pronunciation of our language tho' the most important and difficult part of grammar, is left to parents and nurses—to ignorance and caprice—to custom, accident or nothing—Nay to something worse to coxcombs, who have a large share

---

* Not to mention small differences, I would observe that the inhabitants of New England and Virginia have a peculiar pronunciation which affords much diversion to their neighbors. On the other hand, the language in the middle States is tinctured with a variety of Irish, Scotland German dialects which are justly censured as deviations from propriety and the standards of elegant pronunciation. The truth is, *usus est Norma Loquendi*, general custom is the rule of speaking, and every deviation from this must be wrong. The dialect of one State is as ridiculous as that of another; each is authorised by local custom; and neither is supported by any superior excellence. If in New England we hear a flat drawling pronunciation, in the Southern States, we hear the words *veal, very, vulgar,* pronounced *weal, wery, wulger; wine, winter,* &c— changed to *vine, vinter; soft* becomes *saft*; and *raisins* and *wound,* contrary to all rules and propriety, are pronounced *reefins, woond.* It is the present mode at the Southward; to pronounce *u* like *yu,* as virtyue, fortyune &c. And in rapid pronounciation, these become *virchue, forchune,* as also *duty, duel,* are changed to *juty, juel.* The advocates for this pronunciation pretend, that this is the English sound of *u*; but this can not be true; because they do not give *u* the sound of *yu,* to one word originally English. It seems to arise rather from an imitation of the French, which has been a remarkable folly of the English nation; or perhaps is originated in a fondness for singularity which, has corrupted the language more than all the ignorance of the vulgar. But every innovation of this kind ought to be discountenanced.

It would be much more for the reputation of Americans to unite in destroying provincial and local distinctions, in refitting the stream of corruptions that is ever flowing from ignorance and pride, and in establishing one uniform standard of elegant pronunciations; then to blend two different languages together by applying French sound to English words, to suffer the structure of our language to be constantly changing and its beauty to be disfigured by every coxcomb. Ed. Note: Throughout this section footnotes originally written by Webster are indicated by an asterisk. Editors notes are numbered.

in directing the polite taste of pronunciation, which of course is as vicious as that of any other class of people. And while this is the case, every person will claim a right to pronounce most agreeably to his own fancy, and the language will be exposed to perpetual fluctuation.

This consideration gave rise to the following little system, which is designed to introduce uniformity and accuracy of pronunciation into common schools. It cost me much labour to form a plan that should be both simple and accurate. The one here adopted seems to unite these articles; at least so far as to prevent any material errours. A more accurate method might have been invented; but it must have been too complicated to be useful. The rules for ascertaining a just pronunciation are so simple and concise, that I flatter myself they fall within the comprehension of the most indifferent capacity. Some may possibly be too indolent to study them; and others, from a principle of self-sufficiency, may affect to despise them. The former will be modest enough neither to approve nor condemn what they deem beneath their attention; and I would inform the latter that after I have devoted nine years to the acquisition of knowledge, three or four of which were spent in studying languages, and about the same period in teaching English, I was astonished to find myself a stranger to its principal beauties and most obvious faults. Those therefore who disdain this attempt to improve our language and assist the instructors of youth must be either much more or much less acquainted with the language than I am. The criticism of those who know more, will be received with gratitude; the censure or ridicule of those who know less, will be inexcusable.

The principal part of instructors are illiterate people, and require some easy guide to the standard of pronunciation, which is nothing else but the customary pronunciation of the most accurate scholars and literary Gentlemen. Such a standard, universally used in schools, would in time, demolish those odious distinctions of provincial dialects, which are the objects of reciprocal ridicule in the United States.

In order to render the sounds of words easy and natural for children, it was necessary to alter the customary method of dividing syllables. This is done with deliberation and difference; but with full conviction that both necessity and utility demanded an alteration. Besides this, I am supported by the authority of some of the most eminent literary characters in America, and the best English Grammarians. Mr. Dilworth had endeavored to establish general and arbitrary rules for division of syllables, and has divided his tables according to them without any regard to the proper sound of words, which is the only just rule in this matter. This single circumstance has led learners into more errours in articulation,* than all other causes whatever.

As Mr. Dilworth's New Guide (which by the way, is the *oldest* and most imperfect guide we use in schools) is commonly used and his authority becomes as sacred as the traditions of the jews, or the Mahometan bible, I shall take the liberty to make some remarks on it, with the plainness that is due to truth.

It is an unerring rule in our language, that when the accent falls upon a consonant, the foregoing vowel is short, and when the accent falls upon a vowel, it is long.

The words *cluster, habit*, Mr. Dilworth divides *clu-ster, ha-bit*; according to which, a child naturally pronounces the vowel in the first syllable, long. But the vowels are all short; the accent is on the first syllable and not only so, but particularly on the consonants *s* and *b*. Here then, according to his plan of dividing syllables, the accent, which is on the first syllable, falls upon a consonant that is joined to the left. Into such monstrous absurdities was he driven by his zeal to establish general rules. In order to obviate this difficulty, he has placed a double accent thus, *clu''ster, ha''bit*. If by double

---

* "A good articulation conflicts in giving every letter in a syllable its due proportion of sound, according to the most approved custom of pronouncing it; and in making such a distinction, between the syllables, of which words are composed, that the ear shall without difficulty acknowledge their number, and perceive at once to which syllable each letter belongs. Where these points are not observed, the articulation is proportionally defective."

Sheridan on Elocution, Lect.2.

74

INTRODUCTION TO "BLUE-BACK SPELLER," 1783

accent he meant, a union of two accents, this is not true, for there
can be but one. If a double accent be meant, the sound of the consonant repeated—that is, the sound joined to the first and to the last
also, this is not true: For if fifty consonants of the same kind were
joined together, no more than one could be sounded. I appeal to
the most accurate ear, whether, in ordinary pronunciation, there be
the least difference in the sound of these words, *ha-bit, hab-bit,
habb-bbit*: And if there be not, then double accent is a term without
meaning, and the use of it is only an additional circumstance to
puzzle children. Had Mr. Dilworth attend the foregoing rule, he
could not have blundered into so gross an errour. But this is not so
surprising when we reflect that the authors of dictionaries have
made the same mistake. I do not recollect to have seen more than
one dictionary, that takes notice of the important distinction between an accented vowel and an accented consonant. Let words be
divided as they ought to be pronounced *clu-ster, hab-it, nos-tril, bishop*, and the smallest child cannot mistake a just pronunciation of
words; and the easiest and most natural way to do this, in spite of
the most venerable authority, must eternally be the best way.

Mr. Dilworth tells us that *ti* before a vowel, sounds like *si* or *sh*;
but there are so many exceptions to this rule, that it would better
have been omitted. There are several hundred words, in which *ti*
before a vowel retain their proper original sound. But they do not
sound like *si*, for then *nation, motion*, must be pronounced *na-si-on,
mo-si-on*. The proper sound of ti is that of sh. Then if we make three
syllables of these words, they will stand thus, *na-sh-on, mo-sh-on*, and
will have one syllable without any vowel and consequently without
any sound. But they are not words of three syllables and are not
considered as such, except in the old version of the psalms. However, they might be pronounced formerly, *tion, tia*, &c. are now by
universal consent pronounced in one syllable and so are written by
all the poets. In compliance with universal custom and the settled
propriety of the language, I have ventured to consider them as one
syllable, as will be observed in the 21st, 22nd, 23rd, 24th, 25th, 26th
and 27th tables.

Mr. Dilworth tells us that *b* sounds like *t* in *subtle*, and *t* like *s* in
whistle, thistle. This is so far from being true, that in those words

they have no sound at all; and in all words where *b* is not mute, it has one invariable sound. He has twelve or fifteen pages devoted to names of English, Scotch and Irish towns and boroughs. Whatever purpose these may have served in Great-Britain, they certainly are useless in America.

His Grammar, being found entirely upon the principles of the Latin language, is in fact worse than none, as it is calculated to lead into errour. The only circumstance that renders it tolerably harmless, is that it is very little used and still less understood.

In short, though his Spelling book was a great improvement upon former methods of education, yet almost every part of it was originally defective; and is rendered still more so by the improvements that have been made in our language since it was first published. But the late revolution has rendered it still more improper in America; and yet ten thousands of these books, are annually reprinted and find rapid sale, when one half of the work is totally useless and the other half defective and erroneous.

In the following work, I have begun with easy monosyllables, and proceeded to easy words of four syllables; because it seems a great errour to admit difficult words into the first lessons for children. Some of our hardest words to pronounce are monosyllables; these I have reserved till children have gone through easy words of four syllables, when they will in some measure be fitted for engaging with the more difficult tables. I have endeavoured to associate words of the same class in the same table, that persons may know where to find them and learn their true pronunciation; I have been careful to arrange them in such a manner that their sound might be represented by the smallest possible number of figures. To effect this, in some short tables I have wholly disregarded the order of the Alphabet; and in all I have paid no regard to this order, further than the first letter. Particular care has been taken to collect the words, which cannot be comprised in the rules I have laid down, being principally derived from the French or Greek, and to show their true pronunciation in a difficult column.

The names of domestic articles, animals, fruits &c. are collected for the use and pleasure of children, who are usually taught to be better acquainted with all words in the language, than with the written names of articles with which they are most familiar.

The advantage of publishing, in a work of this kind, the names of the United States, the counties in each &c. will not be disputed by any American. The accounts from several states, are yet imperfect: but care will be taken to collect, by the best means of information, such accurate accounts from the several states as to correct any errours and supply any defects, that the present imperfect and fluctuating state of geography in this country may unavoidably occasion.

In spelling and accenting, I have generally made Dr. Johnson's dictionary my guide; as in point of orthography this seems to be the most approved authority in the language. *

It will be observed, that in all the easy lessons, taken from scripture, the name of the Deity is generally omitted. The reason of this omission is important and obvious. Nothing has a greater tendency to lessen the reverence which mankind ought to have for the Supreme Being, than a careless repetition of his name upon every trifling occasion. Experience shows that a frequent thoughtless repetition of that sacred word, which, in our Spelling Books, often occurs two or three times in a line, renders the name as familiar to children as the name of their book, and they mention it with the

---

* There seems to be an inclination in some writers to alter the spelling of words, by expunging the superfluous letters. This appears to arise from the same pedantic fondness for singularity that prompts to new fashions of pronunciation. Thus they write the words favour, honour, &c. without U. But it happens unluckily that, in these words, they have dropped the wrong letter—they have omitted the letter that sounded and retained one that is silent; for the words are pronounced onur, favur. They may with the same propriety drop u in pious, virtuous, &c. and a thousand other letters. Thus e is omitted in judgement; which is the most necessary letter in the word; it being that alone which softens g. Into these and many other absurdities are people led by a rage for singularity. Our language is indeed pronounced very differently from the spelling; this is an inconvenience we regret, but cannot remedy. To attempt a progressive change, is idle; it will keep the language in perpetual fluctuation without an effectual amendment. And to attempt a total change at once, is equally idle and extravagant, as it would render the language unintelligible. We may better labour to speak our language with propriety and elegance, as we have it, than to attempt a reformation without advantage or probability of success.

same indifference. To prevent this profanation, such passages are selected from scripture, as contain some important precepts of morality and religion, in which that sacred name is seldom mentioned. Let *sacred things* be appropriated to *sacred purposes*.*

The easy dialogues, familiar phrases, stories & fables are calculated not only to entertain; but to inspire the minds of youth, with an abhorrence of vice, indolence and meanness; and with a love of virtue, industry and good manners.

The reason why no grammar is annexed to the Spelling Book is very obvious. Children commonly wear out more than one book before they are able to read, much less to study grammar; in such hands a grammar is thrown away. For this reason it is proposed to publish a grammar, founded on the true principles of our language, in a separate volume, with rules for reading, and a collection of historical and moral essays, selected from the best authors, as exercises for reading and speaking. These will make the second and third parts of this work.—This will serve as a general explanation of the outlines of this institute. The author's intention is certainly good—he wishes to render the acquisition of our language easy and the pronunciation accurate and uniform. The necessity of reforming our present method of instruction, was suggested by his own experience; and the plan here adopted, has been pursued with increasing conviction, that, if well executed, it would be extensively useful. He feels diffident of his own abilities in this arduous and delicate undertaking; but is induced, by the opinion of better judges, to hazzard an edition and submit the performance to public scrutiny. Whatever innovations are admitted into the work are warranted by reason, experience, or the authority of eminent scholars: On these the author rests the work and hopes for a favourable reception. Mankind are always startled at new things: they believe a thing right and best, because they have never suspected otherwise, or because it is the general opinion. But cus-

---

* The same objection occurs against the frequent use of the Bible as a school book. See this matter considered in the essay prefixed for the third part of this work.

tom or the run of opinion is only presumptive evidence that a thing is right and no proof at all that it is best. A person of sense must have better evidence before he believes either. Those who rail so much at new things ought to consider, that every improvement in life was once new; the reformation by Luther was once new; the Christian religion was once new; their favourite Dilworth was once a new thing; And had these and other new things never been introduced, we should all, this moment, been pagans and savages.

The author feels the danger to which he exposes himself by this publication: He forsees that some will find fault with it because they think it has merit; others, because they think it has none: Some will condemn it from motives of prejudice, some from ignorance, some perhaps from worse motives and not a few, who seldom look further than the title page, will gravely enquire with the harmless Israelite of old, *Whether any good thing can come from Nazareth?*

So much may be relied on, that whoever studies the language with half the attention the author has, will be convinced, there is room enough for amendments, in every part of Grammar.

Books of this kind have generally been ushered into the world under the patronage of great names. The author sincerely laments the necessity of this practice; and is determined to adopt it only in part. The favourable sentiments of a few Gentlemen of eminence offered to the public in another channel, will be sufficient to excite their attention to the performance: Then if it have merit, it will make its own way in the world; if it have not, the author, chuses not, by any means, to use the authority of respectable names to impose a worthless production upon his country men: He chuses rather to see it buried in universal neglect. The plan has the approbation of some principal literary characters, not only in Connecticut, but in the States of New-York, New-Jersey, and Pennsylvania.

The author wishes to promote the honour and prosperity of the confederate republics of America; and cheerfully throws his mite into the common treasure of patriotic exertions. This country must in some future time, be as distinguished by the superiority of her literary improvements, as she is already by the liberality of her civil and ecclesiastical constitutions. Europe is grown old in folly, corruption and tyranny—in other countrys laws are perverted, manners are licentious, literature is declining and human nature debased. For America in her infancy to adopt the present maxims of the old world, would be to stamp the wrinkles of decrepid age upon the bloom of youth and to plant the seeds of decay in a vigourous constitution. American glory begins to dawn at a favourable period, and under flattering circumstances. We have the experience of the whole world before our eyes; but to receive indiscriminately the maxims of government, the manners and the literary taste of Europe and make them the ground on which to build our systems in America, must soon convince us that a durable and stately edifice can never be erected upon the mouldering pillars of antiquity. It is the business of *Americans* to select the wisdom of all nations, as the basis of her contributions—to avoid their errours—to prevent the introduction of foreign vices and corruptions and check the career of her own,—to promote virtue and patriotism,—to embellish and improve the sciences,—to diffuse an uniformity and purity of *language*,—to add superior dignity to this infant Empire and to human nature.

3. Letter to George Washington, 1785

Written during his lecture tour in 1785, this letter reveals the prophet seeking approval for his work and himself from the most famous of all Americans. Webster had visited Washington at Mount Vernon in March, and had discussed his educational ideas in detail. Webster's request for endorsement of his work was rejected on the grounds that Washington was no judge of literary work.

Papers of Noah Webster, New York Public Library.

To George Washington, 1785

Baltimore—July 18th, 1785

Sir.

　If the request I am now to make should need any apology but such as will naturally be suggested by its own importance, I am sure it will find it in your candour. The favourable reception of my grammatical publications in the northern States, has induced me to offer them for sale in the Southern; and I am happy to find they meet with the approbation of those literary Gentlemen, with whom I conversed on my tour to Charleston. The performance may possibly appear, at first thought trifling; & yet as containing the rudiments of our native language, the foundation of our other scientific improvements, it doubtless ought to be considered as extremely important. If you, Sir, view it in the latter point of light & have taken the trouble to examine the general plan & execution, your name, as a patron of the Institute, would be very influential in introducing it to notice in these States. I should be very unhappy to make any request, a compliance with which would require the least sacrifice from so distinguished a character; but if it can be done, consistently with the sentiments of your heart and the delicacy of your feelings, the addition of your name, Sir, to the catalogue of patrons, will, I vainly hope, be a continuation of your public utility—& will certainly be esteemed a singular favour conferred on one who is anxious to improve the literature & advance the prosperity of this country.

I have the honour to be
Sir
with the highest respect,
your most obedient
most humble Servant,
Noah Webster

PS. I shall probably remain here till October.

81

4. LETTER TO TIMOTHY PICKERING, 1786

Webster wrote to Timothy Pickering (1745–1829; quartermaster general of the Continental Army, appointed postmaster general by Washington, secretary of state by Adams, and elected to the Senate from Massachusetts), who had read Webster's Speller and liked it. They exchanged letters while Webster toured the eastern seaboard, and met in Philadelphia. Here Webster vents the frustrations of his struggle to find a niche for himself and his Speller, and clearly reveals his perception of himself as a kind of prophet of language to the American people. He was trying to convince the various state governments to adopt his books, and to pass copyright protection legislation, and had already communicated with the Delaware legislature. Thomas Sheridan (1719–88) wrote an English dictionary, which was generally the standard guide to elocution. Robert Lowth (1710–87), bishop of London, authored an English grammar that derived language structures from Latin. For more detail concerning this trip and Webster's relationship to Washington, to Pickering, and his attitudes toward language, as well as his work with Benjamin Franklin, see Warfel, Webster, *and Rollins,* Long Journey.*

Pickering Papers. Massachusetts Historical Society.

Sir:

Before I went into Virginia I had the honour of receiving a letter from you, which I could answer in a few words only. I have now finished my business in these States, having secured the copyright of my works & introduced them into the schools. I have also read Lectures in the Principal towns in Virginia & Maryland, & tho' I most pointedly oppose Dr. Sheridan & Bishop Lowth in some particulars, I find no opposition—I convince the judgement, tho' I may not reform the practice. My success has encouraged me to proceed & I shall risque my reputation in Philadelphia New York & Boston, upon the merits & strength of my criticism. I shall make a *General* effort to deliver literature & my countrymen from the errors that fashion & ignorance are palming upon Englishmen. The question will then be, whether the Americans will give their opinions & principles as well as their purses to foreigners & be the dupes of a strolling party of players, who, educated in the school of corruption, have not professions but to make people laugh, & who, dependent on opinion, for subsistence, must conform to caprice at the expense of every principle of propriety. I must wait on the Legislature of Delaware & shall, I expect, be in Philadelphia by the tenth of February. Two circumstances will prevail against me. I am not a *foreigner*; I am a *New Englandman*. A foreigner, ushered in with letters & letters, with half my abilities, would have the whole city in his train. But let my fate be what it will, I am convinced I am right, & have had the good fortune to convince every good judge who has heard me that I proceed on true principles—they tell me that my plan will certainly succeed—& I have the honour to be with respect

> Your Most Obedient
> Most Humble Servant
> Noah Webster

Baltimore January 20th 1786

5. LETTER TO REBECCA GREENLEAF, 1788

Webster met Rebecca Greenleaf, daughter of Boston merchant and financier William Greenleaf, in Philadelphia in 1787. They fell in love immediately, and were married in September 1789. This letter, written while he was editing the American Magazine *in New York, comes after 10 years of traveling around New England and the middle states in search of an occupation. It reveals the frustrations of these years and his failure to establish himself, as well as his sense of rejection by society.*

Webster Family Papers. Yale University.

TO THE PUBLIC, 1796

New York, January 27th, 1788.

My Dear Friend:

Mr. Ingraham has furnished me with another conveyance to Boston, and I cannot neglect the opportunity of sending you a momento of the respect I have for your personal worth and the interest I feel in your happiness. Becca, I could speak of a thousand things which I cannot write, and yet I speak but little. I wish to see you every day, and yet I know not whether you would add to my happiness. I sometimes think of retiring from society and devoting myself to reading and contemplation, for I labor incessantly and reap very little fruit from my toils. I suspect I am not formed for society; and I wait only to be convinced that people wish to get rid of my company, and I would instantly leave them for better companions: the reflections of my own mind. Mankind generally form a just estimate of a man's character, and I am willing to think they do so with mine. And if I find that they think less favorable of me than I do myself, I submit to their opinion and consent to a separation.

You will see by the tenor of this letter that I am in the dumps a little and will require the reason. Why, Becca, I have been asked the question so often that it really displeases me. To satisfy such enquiries, it would be necessary to relate the history of my life, which you have heard before, and to enumerate a thousand things which ought to be forgotten.

I suspect that I have elevated my views too high, that I have mistaken my own character and ought to contract my wishes to a smaller compass. I am endeavoring to bring my mind to this state—a melancholy tale indeed! Well, I wish everybody were as good as James Greenleaf and his sister Becca. I should then be a much happier man, but as it is I will not be unhappy. I am as patient as possible, waiting for the sun to disperse the clouds that hang over the mind of your Cordial Friend and Admirer.

Noah Webster

6. TO THE PUBLIC, 1796 (BROADSIDE)

As editor of the American Minerva/Commercial Advertiser, *Webster occupied a strategic role in the development of Federalist and Republican politics. Both parties vied for the voters of New York and perceived newspapers as crucial to their success. The battles became extremely heated, and Webster found himself under attack for his editorial work, his political opinions, and even his personal demeanor.* Papers such as the New York Journal *devoted hundreds of columns to attacking Webster, calling him such names as "self-exalted pedagogue," "utter enemy of the rights and privileges of the people," "quack," and "this scribbler of a British faction, this ephemeron of literature, this petite maitre of politics." In this broadside he defends his political views as correct in all aspects, and indicates that the American people will be better off if they will simply trust and follow his advice.*

The paper had also been criticized for sloppy printing: typographical errors, excessive ink, and other problems that detracted from its readability and appearance. In an effort to solve these problems Webster had recently changed printers.

On the political battles of the 1790s, see Marshall Smelser, "The Federalist Period as an Age of Passion," American Quarterly *10 (1958): 391–419.*

The Minerva, *May 2, 1796. Reprinted in* Warfel, Letters.

To The Public

New York, May 1. 1796.

During the time which I have conducted the publication of this paper, the public mind has been much agitated with party spirit and with a variety of political events of great magnitude. Amidst contending passions and prejudices, it has been impossible to avoid censure from one party to another; and I have made it a point to act independent of all influence whatever but that of my own judgement. The complexion in the matter of the paper has been given by myself, and I alone am responsible for the tenor of the *opinions* it contains.

To the Public, 1796

In point of *facts*, my invariable rule has been to state them as I find them, and according to the best evidence obtained, without regard to any party.

I have defended the administration of the National Government, because I believe it to have been incorrupt and according to the spirit of the Constitution. I have advocated the Constitution, because, if not perfect, it is probably the best we can obtain and because experience teaches us it has secured to us our important rights and great public prosperity. I have vindicated neutrality, because there has appeared no occasion for war, but great advantages in peace. I have reprobated Democratic Clubs, because I foresaw the mischief they would produce and which they *have produced*. I have cautioned my fellow citizens against all foreign intrigues, because I was aware of the fatal dissensions they would introduce into our councils, and because I hold it proper for us to attach ourselves to no foreign nation whatever, but to respect ourselves and be in spirit and truth *Americans*.

I was born and educated in a state which is probably as republican as any on earth, a state where great *personal* independence is united with *civil* subordination to law.

My own principles are those which prevail generally in the state which gave me birth and among the northern people. They are principles of which I cannot be ashamed and which I shall continue to maintain while they *wear well*.

The extensive circulation of the paper and the respectability of the subscribers are a proof of the approbation in which the paper is held. I acknowledge it with gratitude.

The complaints of inaccuracies in the work have been numerous and too well founded. This was an evil I could not personally correct, having no knowledge of the business; but from the character of the present printer and other circumstances, I presume there will be hereafter less occasion for complaint.

From examining the principal newspapers published in the United States for more than two years, I am persuaded that these channels of information may be the instruments of great good or extensive evil, according as they are well or ill conducted. It is obvious that the falsehoods and calumny propagated by means of public papers have been the direct and principal means of all the civil dissensions which distract this country and have threatened it with civil war. This is a well ascertained fact. And what is singular, there are many people well affected to the government, and who reprobate these abusive papers, who still subscribe to them for the sake of seeing the abuse they contain, and thus lend their aid towards convulsing the government which alone protects their lives and property.

We want no other proof that our government is on the whole well administered than this: That *all public measures, when well explained and understood by the people at large, have given general satisfaction.*

First impressions on the public mind have often been unfavorable to the administration, but these impressions have been given by the opposition by means of *their* papers and in every instance have proved to be *wrong*. That is, whenever the public mind has been inflamed to discontent by false representation of facts, time, further information, and cool reflection have invariably allayed the ferment and defeated the effect of the first impressions. This is to my mind a decisive proof that there must be something wrong in *principle* in opposition. *Forever* to mistake truth and the public sentiment cannot be the effect of ignorance or want of information.

While I continue to superintend a public paper, it shall be my business to counteract all attempts to weaken or subvert our Constitution; at the same time, should malpractices appear in the administration, I shall be the first to expose them. Impartial truth has been and will continue to be my aim; and I trust, as I have the *best* sources of information, that the confidence which the public have in the authenticity of the intelligence communicated in this paper will not be forfeited.

The public will observe that I am responsible only for the *materials* of the paper; the execution of the work and the distribution are in other hands. All orders for the paper are to be addressed solely to the firm at No. 40 Pine Street.

N. Webster, Jun.

7. LETTER TO E. WADDINGTON, 1798

A subscriber had written to cancel his subscription; in his reply Webster again defends his work. Note the perspective as well as the sense of rejection.

Papers of Noah Webster, New York Public Library.

To E. Waddington, 1798

New Haven, July 6th, 1798

Sir,

The enclosed letter is returned; it does not belong to me.

The paragraph which has offended you, I think very censurable; and I know Mr. Hopkins well enough to affirm that he suffered it to be inserted without attending to the abuse it contained.

A newspaper is common property in which all parties claim a right to utter their venom; and although I should not have admitted the paragraph you complain of had I been present, yet under the most prudent management of the paper I found myself exposed to so many personal indignities from different parties that retirement was essential to my happiness, if not to my life. I found in more instances than one that my best endeavors to please those whose esteem I valued gave offence. To a gentleman of my education and standing in society this treatment became intolerable. It wounded me to the soul that the purest motives were often misinterpreted into the basest designs; the worst possible construction was put on paragraphs; articles and opinions laid to my charge which were easily known to come from other quarters; and any little mistake was laid hold of to injure my feelings, and as an excuse for exercising revenge, by discontinuing papers. A property of this kind is hardly worth the purchase, and in the collision of hostile passions in our country few men of honour and feeling can consent to take charge of public papers—they must generally be superintended by men who are callous.

The *Commercial Advertiser* is the medium through which I communicate my opinions on political and literary subjects, and its general tenor is highly agreeable to the sound part of my fellow citizens, whether natives or foreigners. Its character will continue the same, though I sometimes find in it sentiments of others not altogether agreeable to my own views of things.

Men who take offence at paragraphs which do not please them and who withdraw their subscriptions for incidental errors when the usual tenor of a paper is good are not desirable as subscribers. The candid citizen will inquire before he takes a decisive step. Your letter gives me no pain, nor can it have the least influence on my conduct.

I remain, Sir, Yours, &c.

N. Webster, Jun.

8. LETTER TO STEPHEN TWINING, 1802

*After fleeing New York for the calmer world of New Haven in
1798, Webster spent most of his time on his books, family, and local
politics and schools. He was one of the five founders who incorporated
the Connecticut Academy of Arts and Sciences in 1799, and actively
participated in its affairs. He wrote essays for the Connecticut
Academy on the history of newspapers, climatology, and racial
toleration. In this letter he declines a request to work on a research
project, giving his sense of failure as a prophet as justification.*

*Papers of Noah Webster, New York Public Library. Reprinted
in Ford, Notes.*

New Haven, Jan. 22nd 1802.

Sir,

You informed me, the other day, that the Connecticut Academy had
assigned to me the task of furnishing information, on some subject relative
to the town of New Haven. I beg you to make my acknowledgements to
the Academy for this instance of their respect, but I am under the necessity
of declining the duty.

This is the nineteenth year, since with an ardor bordering on enthusiasm, I have been engaged in some kind of service, either wholly or essen-
tially directed to the interest of my country. In this pursuit, which has not
always been guided by discretion, I have made many and great sacrifices of
my private interest, without hope or expectation of other reward than the
approbation of my fellow citizens. But amidst the turmoil of parties and
passions, even this reward is not longer to be expected. Either from the
structure of my mind, or from my modes of investigation, I am led very
often to differ in opinion from many of my respectable fellow citizens; and
differences of opinion is now a crime not easily overlooked or forgiven. The
efforts which have been made and are now making to deprive me of the
confidence of my fellow citizens, and of course of my influence, and reputation, efforts not limited to this town, render it necessary for me to withdraw myself from every public concern, and confine my attention to private
affairs and the education of my children.

TO JAMES KENT, 1804

If I should survive the enmities and illiberalities of the times, nothing would give me more pleasure than to unite with my fellow citizens in any plan or proposal for improvements of any kind. But in the present state of things, my efforts can be of little or no use; as I cannot make the sacrifices of opinion, either on matters of science or government which would probably be necessary to command confidence.

I will thank you to return by the bearer, my dissertation on the Seasons, which by a vote of the Academy I am permitted to receive, and assure the gentlemen of the Institution of my personal respect.

I am Sir, with great esteem,
Your Obedient Servant,
Noah Webster

9. LETTER TO JAMES KENT, 1804

In this letter to Kent (1763–1847), a lawyer and a member of the New York Supreme Court, Webster questions the role of Alexander Hamilton in the development of the Constitution and reviews his contribution to the climate of opinion of the 1780s. His assessment of the development of American nationalistic writing is fairly accurate, though somewhat truncated and of course both biased and self-serving. For a modern scholarly look at the same topic, see Richard B. Morris, Witness at the Creation: Hamilton, Madison, Jay and the Constitution *(New York: New American Library, 1985). See also Richard B. Bernstein,* Are We a Nation? The Making of the Constitution *(Cambridge, Mass.: Harvard University Press, 1987) and Richard Beeman, et al.,* Beyond Confederation: Origins of the Constitution and American National Identity *(Chapel Hill: University of North Carolina Press, 1987).*

Library of Congress. Printed in Warfel, Letters.

To James Kent, 1804

New Haven, October 20, 1804.

Dear Sir,

In Dr. [John Mitchell] Mason's[1] oration on the death of General Hamilton, the writer observes that "it is indubitable that the original germ" of the federal government, which we now enjoy "was in the bosom of Hamilton," and that with the express intention of retrieving public affairs by establishing an efficient government, he consented to be nominated a candidate for the legislature of the state. I could wish to know from the journals of the Assembly, or other authority, in what year he was candidate, whether he was elected and whether he made any proposition leading to the formation of the national government and what was his project. On these points I am ignorant and wish for information, as the history of the origination and formation of the present Constitution is interesting to us all and will be more so to posterity.

Mr. [Harrison Gray] Otis[2] also asserts in his eulogy that in the Convention at Annapolis in 1786, General Hamilton "first suggested the proposal of attempting a radical change in its principles." From a member of that Convention I have information that renders this doubtful. But the "Address to the People," he says, was written by General Hamilton.

It is possible, not to say probable, that erroneous opinions are entertained on this subject. That General Hamilton must have been, at an early period, impressed with the unsuitableness of the Confederation as a durable instrument of compact, there can be no question. But it is equally certain that such impressions were common to all men of intelligence and information in our country; and it is not yet ascertained that General Hamilton had more agency in originating the project of a national government of a more efficient kind or in uniting opinions on the subject than some other Gentlemen.

The best account I have of these events, collected from authentic documents or personal knowledge, is this. In February, 1783, Mr Peletiah Webster,[3] merchant of Philadelphia, who had been much consulted on subjects of finance by the New England members of Congress and some others during the whole Revolutionary War, published a pamphlet entitled *A Dissertation on the Political Union and Constitution of the Thirteen United States of North America, Which is Necessary to Their Preservation and Happiness*. This was republished the same year in Hartford, and a copy of this last impression is now before me. In this pamphlet the author attempts to prove and urges the necessity of a more efficient national government, one which shall

To James Kent, 1804

vest in Congress a power to control the several states in general concerns and to carry all their decisions into effect. The Congress, or national legislature, he proposes to have divided into two houses. This is the first proposition for a more efficient government I have ever seen, and probably was the first published. You will observe the date is anterior to the definitive treaty.

In June of the same year, 1783, General Washington, in his Circular Address to the Governors of the Several States, suggests "That it is indispensable to the happiness of the individual States, that there should be lodged somewhere a Supreme Power to regulate and govern the general concerns of the Confederated Republic without which the Union cannot be of long duration." Which I take be be a [hint] of the necessity of revising the Constitution. *

The neglect of New York and Rhode Island to comply with the measure of a general impost, the popular tumults and discontents in New England in 1783 and 4 on account of the half pay and Commutation, which menaced Connecticut with a revolution, the total loss of public credit, and the ruinous state of our commerce, induced me, tho then young in political affairs, to take up the pen. In a series of papers, published in the [Connecticut] Courant in 1783 and 4, I combated the spirit of popular discontent under the signature of "Honorious," &c.,* and in February, 1784, in a series of papers under the title of the "Policy of Connecticut," which were intended to persuade the legislature to empower Congress to lay and collect an impost, I introduced the subject by endeavoring to evince the absolute necessity of enlarging the powers of Congress, or rather of creating a supreme power adequate to the purposes of a general government.

I was much flattered by the success of my essays, for these were my first; in May following, an Act was passed authorizing Congress by levy an Impost, and [Stephen Mix Mitchell] a member of the legislature, now one of the judges of our Superior Court, was obliging enough to ascribe it more to my writings than to any other cause.

---

* That address was not the work of General Washington himself. The General gave a few sketches or heads to Colonel [David] Humphreys,[10] who wrote an Address, which did not meet the General's wishes. Judge [John] Trumbull and Mr. [Joel] Barlow of this state happened to be at Headquarters on their way to Philadelphia, and *they* wrote an Address which, with a few alterations by the General, was sent to the Governors [who wished] to see it.

To James Kent, 1804

But New York and Rhode Island, continuing to withhold from Congress the like powers and the general state of our public affairs growing worse and worse, I resumed the subject more in detail in [January, 178]5, and in that month or the next published a pamphlet, entitled *Sketches of American Policy*.[6] On reviewing the work, I find in the first parts of it many chimerical notions representing a popular government which I had imbibed from the writings of Dr. Price and Rousseau.[7] But the fourth Sketch contains my arguments for a new form of federal government and an outline of it. This pamphlet you may not be acquainted with.

In May following, that is, 1785, I went to Mount Vernon from Baltimore, where I was on a journey to Charleston, intending to sail thence down the [Chesapeak] Bay, which I afterwards did. On this visit I put into the hands of General Washington one of my *Sketches*. Mr. Madison, now Secretary of State, visited the General in the following summer and there read my pamphlet. In November following I went to Richmond to petition the Legislature of Virginia for a Copyright law, when I called on Mr. Madison, with whom I had before some acquaintance. On this occasion Mr. Madison expressed himself pleased with the pamphlet. It was in this or the following month that Mr. Madison introduced to the House of Delegates, of which he was a member, a proposition for a meeting of commissioners to devise some more effectual commercial regulations, which proposition produced the Convention at Annapolis in September, 1786. That Convention, you know, originated the Convention which framed the present Constitution.

In the summer of 1786, and before the Convention met at Annapolis, I wrote several pieces which were printed in the public papers and some of which are republished in my *Essays*,[8] in which I urged the necessity of a form of government more energetic than the Confederation. Indeed, from the summer of 1783, when the discontents in Connecticut first assumed the shape of a formal opposition to the Commutation of Half Pay, to the year 1787, I spent in the whole nearly a year in writing on the subject of our political affairs in vindication of Congress and in proving the necessity of a new federal compact. I know of no other person who took the same active part or who devoted half the time to the subject which I did. At that time, young and unknown, it was expedient to conceal my name. In Connecticut many of my writings were ascribed to Mr.—now Judge—Trumbull;[9] in Baltimore, to Judge [Samuel] Chase, &c. These facts were of little consequence to me then and they are so still, but the truth of history demands that they should be recorded. While the eyes of men are fixed on a character of great luster, they are not apt to see surrounding objects of less distinction; and military events are often ascribed to the Commander-in-Chief when they result from the plans of subordinate officers. But in the formation of our present government, many events and opinions occurred which the world are apt to overlook. The merit of it belongs to a great number of persons and not exclusively to any one. General Hamilton acted a conspicuous part in the progress of that revolution in our affairs, but I very much question whether he was the first mover of it. The Journals of the Assembly of New York, or persons still living who were intimate with him, may determine.

One fact more. In the Convention at Philadelphia in May, 1787, it was considered that the delegates from Virginia, the state which had taken the lead in the proposition for revising the Constitution, ought also to take a lead in the project of a form. Accordingly, they met by themselves and drafted a plan, which, with corrections, alterations and additions, was ultimately adopted. For this fact I have the authority of one of those delegates.

On this subject I can say or write little, and that only to a confidential friend whose virtues have long since secured my sincere attachment. To your known friendship and fidelity are the foregoing anecdotes confided; in your bosom may they rest till jealousy and malevolence shall sleep with me in the grave.

I rejoice at your elevation to the Office of Chief Justice, and long may the citizens of New York rejoice that you bear the sword of justice.

Present my affectionate regards to Mrs. Kent, in which request Mrs. Webster joins me, and be assured of [our] friendship, Dear Sir,

Your obedient Servant,

N. Webster, Jun.

10. LETTER TO THE FRIENDS OF LITERATURE, 1807

The struggle for financial survival from the proceeds of his books after 1798 was successful, but not overwhelmingly so; Noah Webster was never a rich man. He attempted to supplement his income by soliciting subscriptions to his dictionary and even donations from many wealthy and influential people during the long years of research and writing. This broadside of 1807 is a good example of his efforts and reveals his presentation of self and his work. His concept of studying the evolution of words through several languages to their origination—what he called their "radical words"—was a sound idea, which never came to a satisfactory fruition.

Papers of Noah Webster, New York Public Library. Reprinted in Warfel, Letters.

TO THE FRIENDS OF LITERATURE IN
THE UNITED STATES

New Haven, February 25, 1807

When I first contemplated the publication of an English Dictionary, my design was chiefly limited to the correction of a few palpable errors in orthography and definition, and the insertion of a great number of legitimate words and significations not found in any British work of the kind. Being led gradually and almost insensibly to investigate the origin of our own language, I was surprised to discover that this field of inquiry had never been explored with due attention and success; and that the origin and history not only of the English, but of the Greek, Latin, and other European languages are yet involved in no small degree of obscurity. The learned men on the continent of Europe—Vossius, Scaliger, and others, who diligently studied the elegant language of Greece and Italy—neglected to resort for the radical words to some of the best sources for correct knowledge, the

To the Friends of Literature, 1807

Celtic and Teutonic dialects, which, next to the Hebrew, are the purest remains of the primitive language. Hence, much of their labor was spent in vain. They wandered into the field of conjecture, venturing to substitute opinions for evidence, and their mistakes have led subsequent writers into error. Some English investigators of the subject have been more successful; but they have left not a small part of the field unexplored. In consequence of these ill-directed and imperfect researches, the English Dictionary of Johnson, the Latin Dictionary of Ainsworth," and the Greek lexicons now in use, which are deemed the highest authorities, contain material errors in the deduction of words from their originals. Were these errors a few mistakes only, "quas incuria fudit," the imperfections incident to every human production, the evil might be permitted to exist without essential injury to literature. But they are very numerous and important. In our own language the primitive senses of words are in some cases totally lost or greatly obscured, which renders the definitions imperfect; and some of its idioms are scarcely explicable without resorting to the original ideas of the words. To this ill consequence it may be added that the origin and progress of language, one of the noblest gifts of God to man, the instrument of most of his social enjoyments and all his improvements, lie covered with darkness.

This state of our language has long been lamented by men of erudition in Great Britain, tho none of them appear from their writings to have known the extent of the evil; much less has any man manifested the courage to attempt an effectual reformation.

From an examination of all the radical words in the Hebrew and a great part of those in the Celtic and Teutonic languages, I can assure the friends of learning that much new light may be thrown on this subject. The wonderful structure of language and its progress from a few simple terms expressive of natural objects, which supplied the wants or affected the sense of unlettered men, thro a series of ingenious combinations to express new ideas, growing with the growth of the human mind to its highest state of refinement, are yet to be charted and elucidated; numerous facts respecting the origin, migration, and intermixture of nations are to be unfolded or illustrated; and the common origin of all the nations of Europe and those of Asia, at least on the west of the Ganges, may be confirmed beyond the possibility of a reasonable doubt by the affinity of their languages. Equally useful are these inquiries in disentangling the difficulties of the heathen mythology, which have perplexed and confounded the ablest writers.

Having devoted some years to the investigation of this subject and made discoveries which are deemed interesting to literature, I propose to compile a complete Dictionary of the English Language, inviting to my

To the Friends of Literature, 1807

assistance the instructors of the principal seminaries of learning with whom I can most conveniently correspond. At the same time I would exhibit correct etymologies of many Greek and Latin words, which, if it should be thought advisable by good judges of the subject, might be inserted in new editions of the lexicons of those languages. A few corrections of the same kind would also be noted in the Hebrew Lexicon of Parkhurst.[12] As I make a practice of noting the affinities of other languages, a Dictionary of the German, of the Dutch, French, Spanish, and Italian languages in which these affinities are noted will be deposited in some public library for the use of future inquirers.

Having advanced far in this design and amassed a large part of the materials for its execution—materials which no other person could use to advantage—I consider it my duty, as it is my wish, to proceed to the accomplishment of the work. This is also the wish of the gentlemen of literary eminence who best know my views and the progress I have made, and who from their own knowledge of the nature of this subject are best qualified to appreciate the merit of the undertaking. Whatever differences of opinion on particular points of practice may exist among men of letters, there seems to be but one opinion of the utility and importance of my general design.

But this work has enlarged so much upon my hands that the state of my own property will not justify the prosecution of it entirely at my own expense. The incessant labor of eight or ten years, including the time already devoted to the subject, is of itself a great sacrifice; but to this are to be added the expences of a numerous family and the cost of many books. My own property is not adequate to these expenditures. Similar undertakings in Great Britain have been supported by contributions; and can there be a question whether the lovers of learning in the United States will aid by like means any design which promises to enlarge the sphere of knowledge? It is judged proper to make the experiment. There are two modes in which the friends of this undertaking may assist me: by contributions in money and by extending the use of the books which I have published for the use of schools, which would augment my own resources. The certificates and communications annexed have reference to both these modes. The contributions of individuals and of societies will be gratefully received and faithfully applied to the proposed object.

Gentlemen who receive several copies of this address are respectfully desired to give them an extensive circulation in the towns in which they reside and the vicinity, and to take such measures to promote the general object as they shall deem most expedient.

Noah Webster, Jun.

11. LETTER TO THOMAS DAWES, 1808

This is Webster's account of his conversion in a letter to his brother-in-law, Thomas Dawes (1756?–1825).

Dawes, a Boston lawyer, judge, and member of the Massachusetts Supreme Court, had written an inquiry into Webster's religious views. For a survey of the revivals of the early nineteenth century, see Stephen E. Berk, Calvinism Versus Democracy: Timothy Dwight and the Origins of American Evangelical Orthodoxy *(Hamden, Conn.: Archon Books, 1974) or the older but still informative Clifford S. Griffin,* Their Brother's Keepers: Moral Stewardship in the United States, 1815–1865 *(New Brunswick: Rutgers University Press, 1964).*

Papers of Noah Webster, New York Public Library. Printed in Ford, Notes.

New Haven Dec 20th 1808

Dear Brother,

I have received your letter of Oct. 25, with a copy of *Review of Hints on Evangelical Preaching* enclosed. I have read both the letter and the pamphlet with attention, and I trust with a sincere desire to learn the truth. The subjects of them are important; but as I differ from you and the writer of the pamphlet on several points, which may be among the fundamental and essential doctrines of christianity, I will take the liberty of communicating to you, at some length the grounds of my own faith; being "ready to give an answer to every man that asketh me a reason of the hope that is in me, and (I trust) with meekness and fear."

You inform me that you give me the pamphlet as a text only, on which you request my opinion, that you may know whether it is true, that I have lately received some impressions from above, not in the ordinary way of ratiocination—that you are no disbeliever, though you have many doubts, that you could never believe satisfactorily in the conversion by a ray of light—that the case of Col. Gardener, which you read when young, though the facts seem to be admitted, forms no ground of a general rule, and that you have thought to exercise our talents, such as we have to obtain knowledge, and honestly to abide by its dictates, is all that can be expected by our maker.

This candid avowal of your own opinions demands from me, a faithful and explicit exposition of my own, and the reasons on which they are founded. Errors are always mischievous, but never so much so as in the concerns of our immortal souls and in the relations which exist between God and ourselves.

Being educated in a religious family, under pious parents, I had, in early life some religious impressions, but being too young to understand fully the doctrines of the Christian religion and falling into vicious company at college, I lost those impressions and contracted a habit of using profane language. This habit however was not of many years duration—profaneness appeared to me then as it now does, a vice without the apology which some other vices find in human propensities, and as unworthy of a gentleman as it is improper for a christian.

I rec'd my first degree in Sept. 1778, at a time when our country was impoverished by war, and when few encouragements offered to induce young men to enter into professional employments. Having neither property nor powerful friends to aid me, and being utterly unacquainted with the world, I knew not what business to attempt nor by what way to obtain subsistence. Being set afloat in the world at the inexperienced age of 20, without a father's aid which had before supported me, my mind was embarrassed with solicitude, and overwhelmed with gloomy apprehensions. In this situation I read Johnson's Rambler, with unusual interest and with a visible effect upon my moral opinions, for when I closed the last volume, I formed a firm resolution to pursue a course of virtue through life, and to perform all moral and social duties with scrupulous exactness; a resolution which I have endeavored to maintain, though doubtless not without many failures. I now perceive that I ought to have read my Bible first, but I followed the common mode of reading, and fell into the common mistake of attending to the duties which man owes to man, before I had learned the duties which we all owe to our Creator and Redeemer.

For a number of years just past, I have been more and more impressed with the importance of regulating my conduct by the precepts of Christianity. Of the being and attributes of God I have never entertained a doubt, and my studies as well as frequent contemplations on the works of nature have led my mind to most sublime views of his character and perfections. These views produced their natural effect of inspiring my mind with the highest admiration and reverence, mingled with gratitude; and for some years past, I have rarely cast my eyes to heaven, or plucked the fruit of my garden without feeling emotions of gratitude and adoration.

Still I had doubts respecting some of the doctrines of the Christian faith, such as regeneration, election, salvation by free grace, the atonement and the divinity of Christ; these doubts served as an apology for my forbearing to make a profession of religion; for though I could never read or hear that solemn declaration of our Savior, "whosoever shall confess me before men, him will I confess before my Father who is in heaven" without some compunction and alarm; yet I endeavored to justify my neglect by a persuasion that I could not conscientiously assent to the usual confession of faith required in Calvinistic churches as the condition of admission to their communion. That is in plain terms, I sheltered myself as well as I could from the attacks of conscience for neglect of duty, under a species of scepticism and endeavored to satisfy my mind, that a profession of religion is not absolutely necessary to salvation. In this state of mind I placed great reliance on good works, or the performance of moral duties, as the means of salvation, although I cannot affirm that I wholly abandoned all dependence on the merits of a Redeemer. You may easily suppose that in this state of distraction, and indecision of opinions, I neglected many duties of piety.

About a year ago an unusual revival of religion took place in New Haven, and frequent conferences or private meetings for religious purposes, were held by pious and well disposed persons in the Congregational societies. I felt some opposition to these meetings, being apprehensive that they would by affecting the passions too strongly, introduce an enthusiasm or fanaticism which might be considered as real religion. I expressed these fears to some friends and particularly to my family, inculcating on them the importance of a *rational religion*, and the danger of being misled by the passions.

My wife, however, was friendly to these meetings and she was joined by my two eldest daughters who were among the first subjects of serious impressions. I did not forbid but rather discouraged their attendance on conferences. Finding their feelings rather wounded by this opposition, and believing that I could not conscientiously unite with them in a profession of the Calvinistic faith, I made some attempts to persuade them to join me in attending the Episcopal service and ordinances. To this they were opposed. At some times I almost determined to separate from my family, leaving them with the Congregational Society and joining myself to the Episcopal. I went so far as to apply to a friend for a seat in the Episcopal Church but never availed myself of his kindness in offering me one. In this situation my mind was extremely uneasy. A real desire of uniting myself to some church by a profession of faith, a determination not to subscribe to all the articles of the Calvinistic Creed, and an extreme reluctance against a separation from my dear family in public worship, filled my mind with unusual solicitude. On examining the creeds of the two churches however, and the conditions of admission to church communion, I found less differences than I had supposed, as to the essential doctrines of Christianity, and in a conversation with Mr. Stewart,[13] our pastor, some of my objections to our own confession of faith were removed. During this time, my mind continued to be more and more agitated, and in a manner wholly unusual and to me unaccountable. I had indeed short composure, but at all times of the day and in the midst of other occupations, I was suddenly seized with impressions, which called my mind irresistibly to religious concerns and to the awakening. These impressions induced a degree of remorse for my conduct, not of that distressing kind which often attends convictions, but something which appeared to be reproof.

These impressions I attempted to remove by reasoning with myself, and endeavoring to quiet my mind, by a persuasion, that my opposition to my family, and the awakening was not a real opposition to a *rational religion*, but to enthusiasm or *false religion*. I continued some weeks in this situation, utterly unable to quiet my own mind, and without resorting to the only source of peace and consolation. The impressions however grew stronger till at length I could not pursue my studies without frequent interruptions. My mind was suddenly arrested, without any previous circumstance of the time to draw it to this subject and as it were fastened to the awakening and upon my own conduct. I closed my books, yielded to the influence, which could not be resisted or mistaken and led by a spontaneous impulse to repentance, prayer and entire submission and surrender of myself to my maker and redeemer. My submission appeared to be cheerful and was soon followed by that peace of mind which the world can neither give nor take away.

This my dear friend, is a short but faithful narration of facts. That these impressions were not the effect of any of my own passions, nor of enthusiasm is to me evident, for I was in complete possession of all my rational powers, and that the influence was supernatural, is evident from this circumstance; it was not only independent of all volition but opposed to it. You will readily suppose that after such evidence of the direct operation of the divine spirit upon the human heart, I could no longer question or have a doubt respecting the Calvinistic and Christian doctrines of regeneration, of free grace and of the sovereignty of God. I now began to understand and relish many parts of the scriptures, which before appeared mysterious and unintelligible, or repugnant to my natural pride. For instance, I was remarkably struck with the 26th verse of John, 14th, "But the Comforter which is the Holy Ghost, whom the Father will send in my name, *he shall teach you all things, and bring all things to your rememberance, whatsoever I have said to you*"—a passage which I had often read without realising its import—in short my view of the scriptures, of religion, of the whole christian scheme of salvation, and of God's moral government, are very much changed, and my heart yields with delight and confidence to whatever appears to be the divine will.

Permit me here to remark in allusion to a passage in your letter, that I had for almost fifty years, exercised my talents such as they are, to obtain knowledge and to abide by its dictates, but without arriving at the truth, or what now appears to me to be the truth of the gospel. I am taught now the utter insufficiency of our own powers to effect a change of the heart and am persuaded that a reliance on our own talents or powers, is a fatal error, springing from natural pride and opposition to God, by which multitudes of men, especially of the more intelligent and moral part of society are deluded into ruin. I now look, my dear friend, with regret on the largest portion of the ordinary life of man, spent "without hope, and without God in the world." I am particularly affected by a sense of my ingratitude to that Being who made me, and without whose constant agency, I cannot draw a breath, who has showered upon me a profusion of temporal blessings and provided a Savior for my immortal soul. To have so long neglected the duties of piety to that Being on whom I am entirely dependent, to love whom supremely is the first duty, as well as highest happiness of rational souls, proves a degree of baseness in my heart on which I cannot think without trembling on what my condition would have been had God withdrawn the blessed influences of his spirit, the moment I manifested opposition to it, as he justly might have done, and given me over to hardness of heart and blindness of mind. I now see in full evidence, the enormous crime, the greatest, man can commit against his God, of resisting the influence of his holy *Spirit*. Every sting of conscience must be considered as a direct call from God to obey his commands; how much more then ought man to yield to those pungent and powerful convictions of sin which are unequivocally sent to chastize his disobedience and compel him to return to his Heavenly Father.

In the month of April last I made a profession of faith; in this most solemn and affecting of all transactions of my life, I was accompanied with my two eldest daughters; while I felt a degree of compunction that I had not sooner dedicated myself to God, it was with heartfelt delight, I could present myself before my Maker, and say "Here am I, with the children which thou hast given me."

Mrs. W. was confined at the time and could not be a witness of this scene, so interesting to her, as well as to us who were personally concerned, but you may easily conceive how much she was affected, the first time she met her husband and children at the Communion.

I have now, my dear Sir, given you a brief narrative of the facts which were the subject of your kind enquiries. I may perhaps in a future letter offer you my opinions on some doctrines of my religious faith; but I am not confident of the propriety of what may be deemed an obtrusion. Of your benevolence, sincerity and affection for me, I have had sufficient proof and my heart reciprocates all your kind wishes for my welfare. I have long been accustomed to consider you as the best of men, and if we have not corresponding views of Christian principles, my friendship for you will remain undiminished. Accept my sincerest love and that of my wife and daughters for yourself and Sister D. and all the family. From your affectionate brother,

Noah Webster

12. ACCOUNT OF COMPLETION OF THE DICTIONARY (COMPLETED 1825)

After twenty-five years of almost daily labor, Webster finished the research and writing phase of his greatest work while in England in 1825. In this undated fragment he describes his feelings at that moment.

Papers of Noah Webster, New York Public Library. Reprinted in Ford, Notes.

I finished writing my dictionary in January 1825 at my lodging in Cambridge, England. When I had come to the last word, I was seized with a trembling, which made it somewhat difficult to hold my pen steady for writing. The cause seems to have been the thought that I might not then live to finish the work, or the thought that I was so near the end of my labors. But I summoned strength to finish the last word, and then walking about the room, a few minutes, I recovered.

Noah Webster

13. PREFACE TO THE *American Dictionary* (dated 1828)

The introduction to Webster's greatest work discusses the origin of the work in terms of Webster's life story and explains why it took so long to complete. He also justifies his work in terms of national development. Robert Keith Leavitt, Noah's Ark: New England Yankees and the Endless Quest *(Springfield, Mass.: G. and C. Merriam Co., 1947) places Webster's work in the context of the "dictionary wars" of the period, while Joseph Friend,* The Development of American Lexicography *(Paris: Mouton, 1967) is a scholarly analysis of his work in lexicography.*

Noah Webster, An American Dictionary of the English Language *(New York: S. Converse, 1828).*

In the year 1783, just at the close of the revolution, I published an elementary book for facilitating the acquisition of our vernacular tongue, and for correcting a vicious pronunciation, which prevailed extensively among the common people of this country. Soon after the publication of that work, I believe in the following year, that learned and respectable scholar, the Rev. Dr. Goodrich[14] of Durham, one of the trustees of Yale College, suggested to me, the propriety and expediency of my compiling a dictionary, which should complete a system for the instruction of the citizens of this country in the language. At that time, I could not indulge the thought, much less the hope, of undertaking such a work; as I was neither qualified by research, nor had I the means of support, during the execution of the work as very desirable, yet it appeared to me impracticable; as I was under the necessity of devoting my time to other occupations for obtaining subsistence.

About twenty seven years ago, I began to think of attempting the compilation of a Dictionary. I was induced to this undertaking, not more by the suggestion of friends, than by my own experience of the want of such a work, while reading modern books of science. In this pursuit, I found almost insuperable difficulties, from the want of a dictionary, for explaining many new words, which recent discoveries in the physical sciences had introduced into use. To remedy this defect in part, I published my Compendious Dictionary[15] in 1806; and soon after made preparations for undertaking a larger work.

My original design did not extend to an investigation of the origin and progress of our language; much less of other languages. I limited my views to the correcting of certain errors in the best English Dictionaries, and to the supplying of words in which they are deficient. But after writing through two letters of the alphabet, I determined to change my plan. I found myself embarrassed, at every step, for want of a knowledge of the origin of words, which Johnson,[16] Bailey,[17] Junius,[18] Skinner,[19] and some other authors do not afford the means of obtaining. Then laying aside my manuscripts, and all books treating of language, except lexicons and dictionaries, I endeavored, by a diligent comparison of words, having the same or cognate radical letters, in about twenty languages, to obtain a more correct knowledge of the primary sense of original words, of the affinities between the English and many other languages, and thus to enable myself to trace words to their source.

I had not pursued this course more than three or four years, before I discovered that I had to unlearn a great deal that I had spent years in learning, and that it was necesary for me to go back to the first rudiments of a branch of erudition, which I had before cultivated, as I had supposed, with success.

I spent ten years in this comparison of radical words, and in forming a synopsis of the principal words in twenty languages, arranged in classes, under their primary elements or letters. The result has been to open what are to me new views of language, and to unfold what appear to be the genuine principles on which these languages are constructed.

After completing this synopsis, I proceeded to correct what I had written of the Dictionary, and to complete the remaining part of the work. But before I had finished it, I determined on a voyage to Europe, with the view of obtaining some books and some assistance which I wanted; of learning the real state of the pronunciation of our language in England, as well as the

PREFACE TO THE DICTIONARY, 1828

general state of philology in that country; and of attempting to bring about some agreement or coincidence of opinions, in regard to unsettled points in pronunciation and grammatical construction. In some of these objects I failed; in others, my designs were answered.

It is not only important, but in a degree necessary, that the people of this country, should have an *American Dictionary* of the English Language; for although the body of the language is the same as in England, and it is desirable to perpetuate that sameness, yet some differences must exist. Language is the expression of ideas; and if the people of one country cannot preserve an identity of ideas, they cannot retain an identity of language. Now an identity of ideas depends materially upon a sameness of things or objects with which the people of the two countries are conversant. But in no two portions of the earth, remote from each other, can such identity be found. Even physical objects must be different. But the principal differences between the people of this country and of all others, arise from different forms of government, different laws, institutions and customs. Thus the practice of hawking and hunting, the institution of heraldry, and the feudal system of England originated terms which formed, and some of which now form, a necessary part of the language of that country; but, in the United States, many of these terms are no part of our present language,—and they cannot be, for the things which they express do not exist in this country. They can be known to us only as obsolete or as foreign words. On the other hand, the institutions in this country which are new and peculiar, give rise to new terms or to new applications of old and which will not be inserted in their dictionaries, unless copied from ours. Thus the terms, *land-office; land-warrant; location of land; consociation* of churches; *regent* of a university; *intendant* of a city; *plantation, selectmen, senate, congress, assembly, escheat, &c.* are either words not belonging to the language of England, or they are applied to things in this country which do not exist in that. No person in this country will be satisfied with the English definitions of the words *congress, senate,* and *assembly, court,* &c. for although these are words used in England, yet they are applied in this country to express ideas which they do not express in that country. With our present constitutions of government, *escheat* can never have its feudal sense in the United States.

But this is not all. In many cases, the nature of our governments, and of our civil institutions, requires an appropriate language in the definition of words, even when the words express the same thing, as in England. Thus the English Dictionaries inform us that a *Justice* is one deputed by the *King* to do right by way of judgement—he is a *Lord* by his office—Justices of the peace are appointed by the *King's Commission*—language which is inaccurate in respect to this officer in the United States. So *Constitutionally* is defined by Todd or Chalmer,—*legally,* but in this country the distinction between *constitution* and *law* requires a very different definition. In the United States, a *plantation* is a very different thing from what it is in England. The word *marshal,* in this country, has one important application unknown in England or in Europe.

A great number of words in our language require to be defined in a phraseology accommodated to the condition and institutions of the people in these states, and the people of England must look to an American Dictionary for a correct understanding of such terms.

The necessity therefore of a Dictionary suited to the people of the United States is obvious; and I should suppose that this fact being admitted, there could be no difference of opinion as to the *time,* when such a work ought to be substituted for English Dictionaries.

There are many other considerations of a public nature, which serve to justify this attempt to furnish an American Work which shall be a guide to the youth of the United States. Most of these are too obvious to require illustration.

One consideration however which is dictated by my own feelings, but which I trust will meet with approbation in correspondent feelings in my fellow citizens, ought not to be passed in silence. It is this. "The chief glory of a nation," says Dr. Johnson, "arises from its authors." With this opinion deeply impressed on my mind, I have the same ambition which activated that great man when he expressed a wish to give celebrity to Bacon, to Hooker, to Milton and to Boyle.

I do not indeed expect to add celebrity to the names of *Franklin, Washington, Adams, Jay, Madison, Marshall, Ramsay,*[20] *Dwight,*[21] *Smith,*[22] *Trumbull,*[23] *Hamilton,*[24] *Belknap,*[25] *Ames,*[26] *Mason,*[27] *Kent,*[28] *Hare,*[29] *Silliman,*[30] *Cleaveland,*[31] *Walsh,*[32] *Irving,*[33] and many other Americans distinguished by their writings or by their science; but it is with pride and satisfaction, that I can place them, as authorities, on the same page with those of *Boyle, Hooker, Milton, Dryden, Addison, Ray, Milner, Cowper, Davy, Thomson,* and *Jameson.*

A life devoted to reading and to an investigation of the origin and principles of our vernacular language, and especially a particular examination of the best English writers, with a view to a comparison of their style and phraseology, with those of the best American writers, and with our colloquial usage, enables me to affirm with confidence, that the genuine English idiom is as well preserved by the unmixed English of this country, as it is by the best *English* writers. Examples to prove this fact will be found in the Introduction to this work. It is true, that many of our writers have

PREFACE TO THE DICTIONARY, 1828

neglected to cultivate taste, and the embellishments of style; but even these have written the language in its genuine *idiom*. In this respect, Franklin and Washington, whose language is their hereditary mother tongue, unsophisticated by modern grammar, present as pure models of genuine English, as Addison or Swift. But I may go farther, and affirm, with truth, that our country has produced some of the best models of composition. The style of President Smith; of the authors of the Federalist; of Mr. Ames; of Dr. Mason; of Mr. Harper; of Chancellor Kent; (the prose) of Mr. Barlow; of the legal decisions of the Supreme Court of the United States; of the reports of legal decisions in some of the particular states; and many other writings; in purity, in elegance and in technical precision, is equaled only by that of the best British authors, and surpassed by that of no English compositions of a similar kind.

The United States commenced their existence under circumstances wholly novel and unexampled in the history of nations. They commenced with civilisation, with learning, with science, with constitutions of free government, and with that best gift of God to man, the christian religion. Their population is now equal to that of England; in arts and sciences, our citizens are very little behind the most enlightened people on earth; in some respects, they have no superiors; and our language, within two centuries, will be spoken by more people in this country, than any other language on earth, except the Chinese, in Asia, and even that may not be an exception.

It has been my aim in this work, now offered to my fellow citizens, to ascertain the true principles of the language, in its orthography and structure; to purify it from some palpable errors, and reduce the number of its anomalies, thus giving it more regularity and consistency in its forms, both of words and sentences; and in this manner to furnish a standard of our vernacular tongue, which we shall not be ashamed to bequeath to *three hundred millions of people,* who are destined to occupy, and I hope, to adorn the vast territory within our jurisdiction.

If the language can be improved in regularity, so as to be more easily acquired by our own citizens, and by foreigners, and thus be rendered a more useful instrument for the propagation of science, arts, civilization and christianity; if it can be rescued from the mischievous influence of sciolists and that dabbling spirit of innovation which is perpetually disturbing its settled usages and filling it with anomalies; if, in short, our vernacular language can be redeemed from corruptions, and our philology and literature from degradation; it would be a source of great satisfaction to me to be one among the instruments of promoting these valuable objects. If this object cannot be effected, and my wishes and hopes are to be frustrated, my labor will be lost, and this work must sink into oblivion.

This Dictionary, like all others of the kind, must be left, in some degree, imperfect; for what individual is competent to trace to their source, and define in all their various applications, popular, scientific and technical, *sixty* or *seventy thousand* words! It satisfies my mind that I have done all that my health, my talents and my pecuniary means would enable me to accomplish. I present it to my fellow citizens, not with frigid indifference, but with my ardent wishes for their improvement and their happiness; and for the continued increase of the wealth, the learning, the moral and religious elevation of character, and the glory of my country.

To that great and benevolent Being, who, during the preparation of this work, has sustained a feeble constitution, amidst obstacles and toils, disappointments, infirmities and depression; who has twice borne me and my manuscripts in safety across the Atlantic, and given my strength and resolution to bring the work to a close, I would present the tribute of my most grateful acknowledgements. And if the talent which he entrusted to my care, has not been put to the most profitable use in his service, I hope it has not been "kept laid up in a napkin," and that any misapplication of it may be graciously forgiven.

New Haven, 1828.   N. Webster

14. PREFACE TO THE HOLY BIBLE, 1833

By 1833, when Webster published his edition of the Holy Bible, he was still writing from the perspective of the prophet, though very defensively and somewhat tentatively. He was still trying to shape American moral character and even daily life through the language. In a letter to a publisher, he stated that he considered this "the most important enterprise of my life. . . ."

Noah Webster, ed., The Holy Bible . . . *(New Haven: Durrie and Peck, 1833).*

Preface.

The English version of the sacred scriptures, now in general use, was first published in the year 1611, in the Reign of James I. Although the translators made many alterations in the language of former versions, yet no small part of the language is the same, as that of the versions made in the reign of Queen Elizabeth.

In the present version, the language is, in general, correct and perspicuous; the genuine popular English of Saxon origin; peculiarly adapted to the subjects; and in many passages, uniting sublimity with beautiful simplicity. In my view, the general style of the version ought not to be altered.

But in the lapse of two or three centuries, changes have taken place, which, in particular passages, impair the beauty; in others, obscure the sense, of the original languages. Some words have fallen into disuse; and the signification of others, in current popular use, is not the same now as it was when they were introduced into the version. The effect of these changes, is, that some words are not understood by common readers, who have no access to commentaries, and who will always compose a great proportion of readers; while other words, being now used in a sense different from that which they had when the translation was made, present a wrong signification or false ideas. Whenever words are understood in a sense different from that which they had when introduced, and different from that of the original languages, they do not present to the reader the *Word of God*. This circumstance is very important, even in things not the most essential; and in essential points, mistakes may be very injurious.

In my own view of this subject, a version of the scriptures for popular use, should consist of words expressing the sense which is most common, in popular usage, so that the *first ideas* suggested to the reader should be the true meaning of such words, according to the original languages. That many words in the present version, fail to do this, is certain. My principal aim is to remedy this evil.

The inaccuracies in grammar, such as *which* for *who*, *his* for *its*, *shall* for *will*, *should* for *would*, and others, are very numerous in the present version. There are also some quaint and vulgar phrases which are not relished by those who love a pure style, and which are not in accordance with the general tenor of the language. To these may be added many words and phrases, very offensive to delicacy and even to decency. In the opinion of all persons with whom I have conversed on this subject, such words and phrases ought not to be retained in the version. Language which cannot be uttered in company without a violation of decorum, or the rules of good breeding, exposes the scriptures to the scoffs of unbelievers, impairs their authority, and multiplies or confirms the enemies of our holy religion.

These considerations, with the approbation of respectable men, the friends of religion and good judges of this subject, have induced me to undertake the task of revising the language of the common version of the scriptures, and of presenting to the public an edition with such amendments, as will better express the true sense of the original languages, and remove objections to particular parts of the phraseology.

In performing this task, I have been careful to avoid unnecessary innovations, and to retain the general character of the style. The principal alterations are comprised in three classes.

1.   The substitution of words and phrases now in good use, for such as are wholly obsolete, or deemed below the dignity and solemnity of the subject.

2.   The correction of errors in grammar.

3.   The insertion of euphemisms, words and phrases which are not very offensive to delicacy, in place of such as cannot, with propriety, be uttered before a promiscuous audience.

A few errors in the translation, which are admitted on all hands to be obvious, have been corrected; and some obscure passages, illustrated. In making these amendments, I have consulted the original languages, and also several translations and commentaries. In the body of the work, my aim has been to *preserve*, but, in certain passages, more clearly to *express*, the sense of the present version.

The language of the Bible has no inconsiderable influence in forming and preserving our national language. On this account, the language of the common version ought to be correct in grammatical construction, and in the use of appropriate words. This is the more important, as men who are accustomed to read the Bible with veneration, are apt to contract a predilection for its phraseology, and thus to become attached to phrases which are quaint or obsolete. This may be a real misfortune; for the use of words and phrases, when they have ceased to be a part of the living language, and appear odd or singular, impairs the purity of the language, and is apt to create a disrelish for it in those who have not, by long practice, contracted a like predilection. It may require some effort to subdue this predilection; but it may be done, and for the sake of the rising generation, it is desirable. The language of the scriptures ought to be pure, chaste, simple and perspicuous, free from any words or phrases which may excite observation by their sin-

Preface to the Bible, 1833

gularity; and neither debased by vulgarisms, nor tricked out with the ornaments of affected elegance.

As there are diversities of tastes among men, it is not to be expected that the alterations I have made in the language of the version will please all classes of readers. Some persons will think I have done too little; others, too much. And probably the result would be the same, were a revision to be executed by any other hand, or even by the joint labors of many hands. All I can say is, that I have executed this work in the manner which, in my judgement, appeared to be the best.

To avoid giving offense to any denomination of christians, I have not knowingly made any alteration in the passages of the present version, on which the different denominations rely for the support of their particular tenets.

In this country there is no legislative power which claims to have the right to prescribe what version of the scriptures shall be used in the churches, or by the people. And as all human opinions are fallible, it is doubtless for the interest of religion that no authority should be exerted in this case, except by commendation.

At the same time, it is very important that all denominations of christians should use the same version, that in all public discourses, treatises and controversies, the passages cited as authorities should be uniform. Alterations in the popular version should not be frequent; but the changes incident to all living languages render it not merely expedient, but necessary at times to introduce such alterations as will express the true sense of the original languages, in the current language of the age. A version thus amended may require no alteration for two or three centuries to come.

In this undertaking, I subject myself to the charge of arrogance; but I am not conscious of being actuated by any improper motive. I am aware of the sensitiveness of the religious public on this subject; and of the difficulties which attend the performance. But all men whom I have consulted, if they have thought much on the subject, seem to be agreed in the opinion, that it is high time to have a revision of the common version of the scriptures; although no person appears to know how or by whom such revision is to be executed. In my own view, such revision is not merely a matter of expedience, but of moral duty; and as I have been encouraged to undertake this work, by respectable literary and religious characters, I have ventured to attempt a revision upon my own responsibility. If the work should fail to be well received, the loss will be my own, and I hope no injury will be done. I have been painfully solicitous that no error should escape me. The reasons for the principal alterations introduced, will be found in the explanatory notes.

The Bible is the chief moral cause of all that is *good*, and the best corrector of all that is *evil*, in human society; the *best* book for regulating the temporal concerns of men, and the *only book* that can serve as an infallible guide to the future felicity. With this estimate of its value, I have attempted to render the English version more useful, by correcting a few obvious errors, and removing some obscurities, with objectionable words and phrases; and my earnest prayer is, that my labors may not be wholly unsuccessful.

New Haven, September, 1833.

Note—The copy used by the compositors was the quarto Bible, prepared for the press by the late President Witherspoon,[34] and published by the late Isaac Collins, of New York. The proof-sheets were read and compared by another copy, either one published by the American Bible Society, or a copy from the authorized Edinburgh press, or other approved edition. No material differences in the copies have been discovered.

15. LETTER TO THE EDITOR OF THE *Palladium*, 1835

Webster formed his mature political and social views in the 1790s and by the 1830s the political evolution of "Jacksonian Democracy" had passed him by. He wrote many attacks on the party system, and this letter, one of a series in an ongoing discussion of politics in local newspapers, defends his views as those of an earlier generation. The letter was never published and may not have been sent. Most of those who had been Federalists in the 1790s and early 1800s felt similarly. See Linda Kerber, Federalists in Dissent: Imagery and Ideology in Jeffersonian America *(Ithaca, N.Y.: Cornell University Press, 1970).*

Papers of Noah Webster, New York Public Library. Printed in Warfel, Letters.

LETTER TO THE EDITOR, 1835

To the Editor of the Palladium

New Haven, February 17, 1835

Sir,

I shall not discuss with any person the subject of parties; this would be of no use. But to close my remarks, I will relate what I once heard from Dr. Franklin, who was distinguished by his good sense. After he was eighty years of age, he said to me, *"Sir, I have been all my life changing my opinions."* Now at seventy-six years of age I can say the same thing; I have in the course of my life been often obliged to change my opinions. I began life, as other young men do, full of confidence in my own opinions, many of which I afterwards found to be visionary and deceptive. It is possible that you, Sir, if you live many years, may find your strong confidence must yield to truths resulting from experience, truths which no arguments would *now* induce you to believe. That some of your opinions on the subject of government and some opinions that are now maintained by *both* and *by all* political parties are fallacious and deceptive is, in my own view, unquestionable. To err is the lot of humanity.

How much of the *spirit of aristocracy* I possess, must be left to the judgement of the world. It is not more, I hope, than that of many young men of this age who positively contradict the opinions and decisions of General Washington and the Supreme Court of the United States. I began life by ardently embracing republican principles; these I learned with some acquaintance with law and history in the school of Washington and of the great and worthy men who assisted in obtaining Independence, and in the formation and organization of the government.

In the most critical period of the Revolutionary War, when the British forces were attempting to cut off the communication between the eastern and southern States, when the companions of my youth were sinking into the grave by the sword or by a deadly pestilence, I offered to hazard my life to protect the liberties which *you*, Sir, now enjoy in common with others; I marched, a volunteer, to the banks of the Hudson, ill able to bear the fatigues of a soldier and glad at times to find a bed of straw in a barn or a shed. And you are not to suppose that I feel no indignation at the base ingratitude which would charge me and my companions with principles or designs unfriendly to the government of my country. Though you may not have made such charges, others have; and such charges are involved in denunciations of the party with which I have acted.

I am a farmer's son and have collected all the small portion of property which I possess by untiring efforts and labors to promote the literary improvement of my fellow citizens and to establish the freedom and tranquillity of my country. If I have any other aristocracy about me, it must be my *old age*, an aristocracy resulting from God's appointment, with a reference doubtless to the advantages which society may derive from the wisdom, prudence, and correct judgement which age only can furnish.

N. Webster

16. Letter to Emily Webster Ellsworth, 1840

In a letter to his favorite daughter, Webster writes about his sense of rejection and how he had attempted to lead Americans down the path of Federalist political ideology. In the year it was written William Henry Harrison campaigned for the Presidency, portrayed by his supporters as a man of the people because he had supposedly been born in a log cabin. It marked a significant change in campaign rhetoric and tactics; Federalists such as Washington and Adams had not actively solicited votes or campaigned as "common" men. On the development of the new style of politics, see Richard McCormick, The Second American Party System: Party Formation in the Jacksonian Era *(New York: Norton, 1966).*

Webster Family Papers. Connecticut Historical Society.

TO EMILY WEBSTER ELLSWORTH, 1840

New Haven July 3. 1840

Dear Emily.

We are in tolerable health, as your husband & son will inform you. Your mother has had an ill turn, but has again seated herself to needle work. I have been in part confined for two or three weeks, with my leg; but now there is a hope that I may recover entirely.

You urge us to visit you, but you will readily understand that your mother's attentions are soon to be called for in her own family. As for myself, I can not think of leaving home this summer; & in truth, I have little wish to visit Hartford. The opposition made in that town to some of what I believe to be my most valuable improvements in school books, & in the version of the Bible alienate my mind from my native town. I lately sent to Mr. Middell a notice of the innovation of my Testament into our public schools, with an advertisement for injection in his papers; but his words to me were he had scruples about inserting it, without an apology to the public for doing it. He wrote to me what he should say to the public—& on receiving this, I sent for the Notice & the bank bill inclosed, which he returned to me & I sent them to the Courant. The illiberality of the clergy is surprising. But I shall give them no further trouble. I have other opposers in Hartford, & my native town is to take the lead in frustrating my best efforts to serve my country & advance its moral & literary character.

But the *Log Cabin*—oh how our country is degraded, when even men of respectability resort to such means to secure an election! I struggled, in the days of Washington, to sustain good principles—but since Jefferson's principles have prostrated the popular respects for sound principles, further efforts would be useless. And I quit the contest forever.

Mrs. Edward Ellsworth & her two children are here, & Julia has more cousins than beds; but Mrs. E & her children go soon to Durham for a residence.

We sympathize with Judge Williams on account of *his* loss, which is also a serious loss to his friends & to the poor.

Our love to you all

Affectionately yours

N Webster

17. LETTER TO HENRY BARNARD, 1840

Henry Barnard (1811–1900), then secretary of the Board of School Commissioners of Connecticut, and later president of the University of Wisconsin and United States commissioner of education, had written to Webster asking for his evaluation of education in the 1840s. In reply Webster recalls the schools he went to as a child, the books he learned with, and how he tried to contribute to an improved educational system. For more on education in the early nineteenth century, see the works cited in Diane Ravitch, Revisionists Revised: A Critique of the Radical Attack on the Schools *(New York: Basic Books, 1977)*.

Barnard Papers. New-York Historical Society.

New Haven, March 10th, 1840

Mr. Barnard

Dear Sir.

You desire me to give you some information as to the mode of instruction in common schools, when I was young, or before the revolution. I believe you to be better acquainted with the methods of managing common schools at the present time than I am; & I am not able to institute a very exact comparison between the old modes & the present. From what I know of the present schools in the country, I believe the principal difference between the schools of former times & at present consists in the books & instruments used in the modern schools.

When I was young the books used were chiefly or wholly Dilworth's Spelling Books, the Psalter, Testament & Bible. No geography was studied, before the publication of Dr Morse's small books on that subject, about the year 1786 or 7.[33] No history was read, as far as my Knowledge extends, for there was no abridged history of the United States. Except the books above mentioned, no book for reading was used before the publication of the geography & history of the United States, & these led to more enlarged definitions of the country. In 1788, at the request of Dr. Morse, I wrote an account of the transactions in the United States, after the revolution; which account fills nearly twenty pages in the first volume of his Octavo editions.

Before the revolution & for some years after, no slates were used in common schools; all writing & the operations in Arithmetic were on paper. The teacher wrote the copies & gave the sums in Arithmetic; few or none of the pupils having any books as a guide. Such was the condition of the schools in which I received my early education.

The introduction of my Spelling Books, first published in 1783, produced a great change in the department of Spelling; & from the information I can gain, Spelling was taught with more care & accuracy, for twenty years or more, after that period, than it has been since the introduction of multiplied books & studies. *

No English Grammar was generally taught in common schools, when I was young, except that in Dilworth, & that to no good purpose. In short, the instruction in schools was very imperfect, in every branch; & if [I] am not mis-informed it is so to this day, in many branches. Indeed there is danger of running from one extreme to another; & instead of having two [*sic*] few books in our schools, we shall have too many.

I am, Sir, with much respect

Your friend & Obd Svrt

N Webster

18. UNDATED FRAGMENT (REFERRING TO EVENTS OF 1775)

Webster evidently wrote this as part of a Fourth of July speech to a group of young people recalling his experiences during the American Revolution. The incident involving Washington occurred on June 29, 1775. It is difficult to date the piece, but Harry Warfel, in Noah Webster: Schoolmaster to America, *says it was written when he was "an old man."*

Papers of Noah Webster, New York Public Library.

---

* The general use of my Spelling Books in the United States has had a most extensive effect in connecting the pronunciation of words, & giving uniformity to the language. Of this change, the present generation can have a very imperfect idea.

Undated Fragment

My young friends.

In the year 1775, General Washington passed through New Haven, on his way to Cambridge, in Massachusetts, to take command of the American army. He was accompanied by Gen Charles Lee,[36] who had been an officer in the British service. These gentlemen lodged in New Haven, at the house of the late Isaac Beers, & in the morning, they were invited to see a military company of students of Yale College, perform their manual exercise. They expressed their surprise & gratification at the precision with which the students performed the customary exercises then in use. This company then escorted the generals as far as Nuh (?) Bridge, & this was the first instance of that honor conferred on Gen Washington in New England. It fell to my humble lot to lead the company with music.

I was then a freshman in Yale College; & as I had the advantage of knowing the state of the country, & will mention two facts to show you how much you ought to value independence and your happy condition. So impoverished was the country, at one time, that the steward of college could not supply the necessary provisions of the table; & the students were compelled to return & spend several months at home. At one time goods were so scarce, that the farmers cut corn stalks, crushed them in cider mills & then boiled the juice down to sirup, as a substitute for sugar.

In the autumn of the year 1777, when the British army under Gen. Burgoyne was marching toward Albany, all able bodied men were summoned into the field. My father & my two brothers were in the service; I shouldered a musket & marched, a volunteer, to defend that independence which we are now assembled to celebrate, leaving at home no person but my mother & a sister to take charge of the farm.

At the close of the revolution, but before the American army was disbanded, I set myself to favor the independence of my country, by compiling books for the instruction of youth; & with one express purpose of lessening the dependence of this country on foreign supplies. As it is probable that most of you may, in some sense, be denominated my pupils, I will present to you my hopes & good wishes for you & my country, in a few lines written in the year in which the present constitution of the United States was ratified (1788).

19. UNDATED FRAGMENT (REFERRING TO EVENTS OF 1776)

Webster recounts his adventure traveling to Canada in 1776 to help his older brother Abraham (1751–1831) recover from smallpox and rejoin the Continental Army. In September 1775, under the command of Benedict Arnold, 1,100 volunteers left Massachusetts on a march to Quebec with the intention of capturing that city. They began a siege of Quebec in December and, along with troops commanded by Brigadier General Richard Montgomery, attempted to storm the garrison. They were repulsed and Montgomery was killed. Reinforcements arrived in the spring, but an army of 6,000 British regulars and volunteers under General John Burgoyne forced them to retreat toward Montreal. A disorganized group of about 500 Americans were captured outside Montreal at "The Cedars," and this is probably where Noah's brother Abraham was taken. The rest of the troops retreated across the border into New York.
Papers of Noah Webster, New York Public Library.

"Autobiographical Notes"

In the summer of 1776, my oldest brother, Abram, was a soldier in Canada, & taken prisoner at the Cedars. He was seized with the smallpox & obtained a furlow to return to his friends. He could not travel. He was obliged to resort to a cabin inhabited by a French woman, where he lay with the disease so bad that it seemed to him his flesh would leave his bones, & without friends or nurse or physician. He had nothing to sustain him but milk. He however recovered, & was able to reach home. After his health was restored, I went with him to rejoin the army. We took horses, & traveled through Bennington to Skeensborough, now Whitehall, passing the last twelve miles through a forest, by marked trees.

At that place, the head of South Bay, I found Ashbel Wells, the companion of my youth, a soldier in the troops at that place. The musketoes [*sic*] were so numerous that the soldiers could not sleep at night, except by filling their tents with smoke. I spent one night in Mr. Wells's tent in that condition.

The next night I slept in a batteau, on South Bay. When we arrived at Mount Independence, we found about half the soldiers sick with dysentery and fever, so that the very air was infected.

I returned through the woods, sleeping one night on the floor of a hospitable farmer, who had just begun to live, on a new farm. I passed through Tinmouth, to Walingford, on Otter River, where lived Mr. Jackson, who married my mother's youngest sister, Jerretha. Here I was very comfortable. My aunt was in ill health, & she took one of my horses, & rode with me to Hartford. She soon after died, by the consumption. One son of Mr. Jackson now lives in Canada.

N. Webster

20. UNDATED FRAGMENT REFERRING TO EVENTS OF 1777.

A short account of Webster's experience during the invasion of New England by British troops under the command of General John Burgoyne, ending in the Battle of Saratoga, written in the third person. Burgoyne led a force of 7,700 British, German, Canadian, and Indian troops south from Lake Champlain in June, occupying Fort Ticonderoga in New York and defeating an American force at Bennington in August. In September a series of clashes began with American forces under the command of Benedict Arnold. New England felt threatened by the approach of Burgoyne's army and sent numerous militia units, such as the one Webster marched with. British troops burned Kingston, New York, on October 16 even though Burgoyne, short of food and other supplies, had already begun negotiations toward an end to his invasion. The alarm ended when Burgoyne surrendered to General Horatio Gates on October 17.

Papers of Noah Webster, New York Public Library.

In the autumn of 1777 when Gen. Burgoyne was marching from Canada toward Albany, while terror and devastation were spread throughout the northern counties of New York, and the adjacent settlements of Vermont, Mr. Webster though exempted from Military duty, volunteered his services and marched with both his brothers under the command of his Father, all the male members of the family, toward the scene of action. The regiment to which he belonged was advancing along the east bank of the Hudson when Kingston which had been fired by a detachment from British ships, was in flames on the opposite side, and the whole country around was fleeing in consternation. Before they reached Albany, however, they were met by a courier, waving his sword in triumph, and crying out as he passed, "Burgoyne is taken, Burgoyne is taken." It was perhaps the most eventful crisis of the war. The enterprize of uniting the British forces in Canada, with those in the City of New York, by a line of posts along the Hudson, which might cut off all communication between New England and the Southern colonies, was defeated at a blow. An army of British regulars had for the first time surrendered to a body of undisciplined Continental troops, and well might every American, who had shared in the conflict, or who was hastening to meet the foe, exult in such a victory. As additional troops were no longer needed in that quarter the regiment was dismissed soon after they reached the scene of action, and Mr. Webster returned home.

21. UNDATED FRAGMENT (REFERRING TO EVENTS OF 1781).

Another short account of Webster's youth, probably written later in life, describing his school in Sharon, Connecticut, in 1781.

Papers of Noah Webster, New York Public Library. Printed in Ford, Notes.

Undated Fragment

In 1781 I kept a school in Sharon. I had in my school the children of Gilbert Livingston.[37] a refugee, & two of his connection, named Flake. I had for scholars also two sons of Mrs. Prevost, Frederick & Bartow. This lady was the widow of a half-pay British officer. She had, like others, returned to the country, while the British were in New York. Jonas Platt, son of Judge Platt of Poughkeepsie, was also one of my pupils; & after I opened a school in Goshen, Orange County, he attended the school & received what classical education he obtained. He was a most amiable youth, & afterwards became one of the judges of the Supreme Court in the state of New York. The friendship we contracted continued through life, & when I lived first in New Haven, he placed his son, in college, under my guardianship.

When I established a school in Goshen, the next year, I had under my care, the children of Mr. Wisner,[38] of Wall-Kill, among whom was the father of the two clergymen, one of whom was minister of the Old South in Boston. General Wilkins (or Mr. Wilkins) of Goshen was also my pupil, as was a brother of his. I had also under my care the children of the Rev. Mr. Kerr, one of whom, a daughter was afterward married in New York—her second husband I think was a Mr. Caldwell. At the time I resided in Sharon, Judge Hobart was residing there also.

In my school in Sharon were some of the children of John Canfield, Esq.,[39] a jurist of talent & of uncommon philanthropy. One of his daughters, Laura, my pupil was married afterward to Judge Spencer, and she became the mother of John C. Spencer, the present Secretary of State, in New York.[40]

[Marginal note:]

In Sharon, I studied French under the Rev. Mr. Tetard, a native of Geneva in Europe, who was minister of the descendents of the French Protestants, in New Rochelle—an excellent scholar & christian, who had retired to the country for safety.[41]

22. ACCOUNT OF A VISIT WITH GEORGE WASHINGTON IN 1785 (WRITTEN 1843).

This brief description of dinner with Washington during Webster's 1785 tour of Virginia was written in a book of autographs. It was described by Nathaniel Hawthorne as being written in a sturdy, awkward hand. The trip is described in Warfel, Webster, and Rollins, Long Journey.

Papers of Noah Webster, New York Public Library. Printed in Ford, Notes.

Feburary 10. 1843

When I was traveling to the South, in the year 1785 I called on General Washington at Mt. Vernon. At dinner the last course of dishes was a species of pancakes which were handed around to each guest, accompanied with a bowl of sugar and another of molasses, observing to the gentlemen present that I had enough of that in my own country. The General burst out with a loud laugh, a thing unusual with him. "Ah," said he, "there is nothing in that story about your eating molasses in New England." There was a gentleman from Maryland at the table, and the General immediately told a story, stating that during the revolution, a hogshead of molasses was stove in at the town of Westchester by the oversetting of a wagon, and a body of Maryland troops being near, the soldiers ran hastily, and saved all they could by filling their hats and caps with molasses.

NOTES to Section II

1. John Mitchell Mason (1770–1829), theologian and Professor at Union Theological Seminary.

2. Harrison Gray Otis (1756–1848), wealthy Boston lawyer and politician.

3. Pelatiah Webster (1726–1795), a distant relative, wealthy Philadelphia merchant, and early advocate of strong central government. His *A Dissertation on the Political Union and Constitution of the Thirteen United States of America* . . . (1783) was read and approved by many significant figures of the day, and probably lent Noah Webster a little extra support simply because of his name and reputation.

4. See Webster's essays in the *Connecticut Courant*, Aug. 26, Sept. 9, 23, 26, and Oct. 13 and 14, 1783, as well as Jan. 13 and Apr. 20, 1784.

5. *Connecticut Courant*, Feb. 24, 1784.

6. Noah Webster, *Sketches of American Policy* (Hartford: Hudson and Goodwin, 1785).

7. Richard Price (1723–91), a British clergyman who wrote several essays supporting American protests against British legislation. Jean-Jacques Rousseau (1712–78), French *philosophe* and strong advocate of individual and national rights. A favorite of eighteenth-century liberals.

8. Noah Webster, *A Collection of Essays and Fugitiv Writings on Moral, Historical, Political, and Literary Subjects* (Boston: J. Thomas and E. T. Andrews, 1790).

9. John Trumbull (1750–1831), a Hartford Wit, author of *The Progress of Dulness, a Satire on American Education* (1772) and *McFingal, a Swiftian Satire on British Society and Politics* (1782). Also a lawyer and, as Webster notes, a judge in Connecticut.

10. David Humphreys (1752–1818), another Hartford Wit, wealthy merchant, and ambassador to Spain between 1796 and 1801.

11. Robert Ainsworth (1660–1743), English educator and author of a Latin dictionary.

12. John Parkhurst (1701–65), English clergyman and linguist, compiled *An Hebrew and English Lexicon* (1762).

13. Moses Stuart (1780–1852) was a pastor in New Haven. He became a professor of sacred theology at Andover Seminary in 1810 and a leading student of the Old Testament.

14. Elizur Goodrich (1734–1797), clergyman, Yale trustee, father of Webster's son-in-law, and collaborator on the second version of the dictionary, Chauncey A. Goodrich (1790–1860). Author of a noted study in astronomy.

15. Noah Webster, *A Compendious Dictionary of the English Language* (New Haven: Sidney's Press, 1806).

16. *Samuel Johnson (1709–84), author of A Dictionary of the English Language (1784),* the standard work before Webster's.

Notes to Section II

17. Nathaniel Bailey (?–1742) British lexicographer and editor of *An Universal Etymological Dictionary* (1721), and important influence on Samuel Johnson's work.

18. Franciscus Junius (1589–1677), German philologist and author of several important works.

19. Stephen Skinner (1623–67), English philologist.

20. David Ramsay (1749–1815), member of the Continental Congress from South Carolina and author of one of the first histories of the new nation.

21. Timothy Dwight (1752–1817), poet and Hartford Wit: *The Conquest of Canaan* (1785) and *The Triumph of Infidelity* (1788). Author of an important travel narrative, *Travels in New England* (1821–22). President of Yale College from 1785 to 1815. Webster liked and published his early poetry and may even have helped Dwight write some of it.

22. Webster might have been thinking of two Smiths. Samuel Stanhope Smith (1750–1819), a friend who taught philosophy at Princeton and was president of the college from 1795 to 1812; and Elihu Hubbard Smith (1771–98), another Connecticut Wit who earned his living as a physician but wrote poetry and drama in his leisure time. His home became the meeting place for the Wits.

23. See n. 9 above.

24. Undoubtably Alexander Hamilton (1755–1804), secretary of the treasury under Washington and author of several very important essays on economics and politics, including several issues of *The Federalist*.

25. Jeremy Belknap (1744–98), Congregational clergyman in Boston and historian most widely known as the author of *The History of New Hampshire* (1784–92) and *American Biography* (1794–98). A founder of the Massachusetts Historical Society.

26. Fisher Ames (1758–1808), archconservative Federalist politician. Webster must have been thinking of his speeches, many of which were published.

27. See Document #9, n. 1.

28. See my n. 38 to the "Memoir."

29. Robert Hare (1781–1858), chemist and inventor, and collaborator with Silliman on numerous scientific papers.

30. Benjamin Silliman (1779–1864), professor of chemistry at Yale, wrote the first scientific account of the fall of a meteor in America. Founder of the *American Journal of Science and Arts* in 1818.

31. Parker Cleaveland (1780–1858), professor of chemistry and mineralogy at Bowdoin College. His essays on the mineralogy and geology of New England were considered a major contribution to scientific knowledge.

32. Robert Walsh (1784–1859), journalist who founded and edited the *American Review of History and Politics* in 1811–12.

33. Washington Irving (1783–1859), accomplished essayist and perhaps the first major American author, known most widely for his essays and folktales published as *The Sketch Book*.

34. John Witherspoon (1723–1794), Presbyterian minister, signer of the Declaration of Independence, and president of the College of New Jersey (1782–1794), now Princeton University.

Notes to Section II

35. Jedediah Morse (1761–1826), a good friend of Webster, often referred to as "the father of American geography," was also a leading clergyman in New England. His *Geography Made Easy* (1784) was the first American geography book widely used in schools and an important contribution to the growth of American nationalism.

36. Charles Lee (1731–82). Born in England, Lee rose to the rank of general officer during service in the British army in the colonies in the 1750s, and was wounded at Fort Ticonderoga in 1758. He became a soldier of fortune with a strong interest in eastern and southern Europe and returned to the colonies in the early 1770s where he became very interested in the cause of American independence. Appointed general by the Continental Congress in 1775, he served with Washington around Boston, defended New York in 1776, and then led the American army in the South. Captured by the British in December 1776, he was exchanged and returned to service. He was accused, and found guilty, of retreating at the Battle of Monmouth in 1778, suspended from the service, and dismissed in 1782.

37. Gilbert Livingston, son of Robert R. Livingston, powerful New York patroon, and brother of Philip Livingston.

38. Henry Wisner (1725–90) of Goshen, member of the Continental Congress who voted in favor of independence but did not become a signer because he was called to attend the New York Provincial Congress.

39. John Canfield, a lawyer in Sharon and member of the Connecticut legislature.

40. John Canfield Spencer (1788–1855), lawyer in Canandiagua and member of the U.S. House of Representatives, 1817–19; secretary of war, 1841–43; secretary of the treasury, 1843–44.

41. Rev. John Peter Tetard not only taught him French, but discussed Rousseau and other French and English political theorists with him and heavily influenced and refined Webster's early political thought.

III.   MEMOIR OF NOAH WEBSTER, LL.D.

Memoir of Noah Webster. LLD

Noah Webster, the second of the name, was a descendant from John Webster, one of the original planters of Hartford, in Connecticut. He was informed by Col George Wyllys, who was well acquainted with some of the grandsons of John Webster, that the family came from Warwickshire in England. John Webster was one of the founders of the Colony of Connecticut; and after the formation of the constitution of that Colony in 1639, he was chosen one of the magistrats, council or senate, and he continued to be re-elected and to act as a member of that council and as judge of the particular court, till the year 1655. In this year, he was chosen deputy governor, & in 1656, he was chosen Governor of the colony. In the three following years he was elected first magistrate.

In the year 1659, in consequence of a long controversy in the church, in which he opposed the rev. Mr Stone, the pastor,[*] John Webster and a number of other members of the church determined to purchase a tract of land, about forty miles north of Hartford, & remove to that, with their families. An agreement for this purpose was made at the house of one Ward, on the 18th day of April 1659. This agreement, a copy of which is on the records of Hadley, was signed by fifty nine persons, belonging to Hartford & Wethersfield, with one or two from Windsor. The first name on the list is that of John Webster, & his son Robert is also one of the signers. This company purchased the land which now contains Hadley, (written in the records Hadleigh) Amherst, South Hadley, & Granby, on the east side of the river Connecticut, & on the west side, Hatfield & a part of Williamsburg.

[*] Se Trumbull's History of Connecticut. Vol. 1. Ch. XIII.

First page of Noah Webster's autobiography.
Photograph courtesy of Yale University Library.

"Memoir of Noah Webster, LL.D."

The "Memoir" is written on sixty-three pages of writing paper. It is printed here in accordance with the principles outlined in the preface to this volume. I have inserted, as No. 27, the "affidavit" concerning Webster's conversation with Edmund Genet now in the Connecticut Historical Society Goodrich Family Papers. Webster clearly intended it to be included. The manuscript is in good condition, with the exception of chipping at the top of the first page.

Noah Webster, the second of the name, was a descendant from John Webster, one of the original planters of Hartford, in Connecticut. He was informed by Col. George Wyllys,[1] who was well acquainted with some of the grandsons of John Webster, that the family came from Warwickshire in England. John Webster[2] was one of the founders of the colony at Connecticut; and after the formation of the constitution of that colony in 1639, he was chosen one of the magistrates, council or senate, and he continued to be re-elected and to act as a member of that council and as Judge of the *particular court,* till the year 1655. In this year, he was chosen deputy governor, and in 1656, he was chosen Governor of the colony. In the three following years he was elected first Magistrate.

In the year 1659, in consequence of a long controversy in the church, in which he opposed the Rev. Mr. Stone, the pastor,* John Webster and a number of other members of the church determined to purchase a tract of land, about forty miles north of Hartford, and remove to that, with their families. An agreement for this purpose was made at the house of one Ward, on the 18th day of April 1659. This agreement, a copy of which is on the records of Hadley, was signed by *fifty-nine* persons, belonging to Hartford, and Wethersfield, with one or two from Windsor. The first name on the list is that of John Webster, and his son Robert is also one of the signers.

* See Trumbull's *History of Connecticut,* vol. 1, chap. XIII.

This company purchased the land which now contains Hadley, (written in the records Hadleigh), Amherst, South Hadley, and Granby, on the east side of the river Connecticut, and on the west side, Hatfield and part of Williamsburg.

No. 2

The Rev. John Russel, Jr., Minister of Wethersfield, and several of his congregation, formed a part of this company.

The company proceeded to the land purchased, early in the Spring, to make preparation for the removal of their families. John Webster accompanied them, but he lodged in Northampton, where he was taken sick and made his last will and testament. This will is dated June 25, 1659, and witnessed by John Russel, Jr., above named, and Eleazer Mather,[3] minister of Northampton. It is on the records of probate of the county of Hampshire, and a copy of it is in possession of the writer.

Mr. Webster recovered from the sickness, and was chosen first Judge of the Court, or Commissioner, as he is called in the records. The court consisted of John Webster, John Pynchon, and Samuel Chapin; and the sessions were alternately held in Northampton and Springfield. John Webster died in Northampton April 5, 1661.[4]

John Webster had four sons: Robert, Matthew, William, and Thomas. Matthew settled in Farmington. William settled in Hadley, where he died. Thomas settled first in Northampton; but he removed to Northfield. This town being destroyed in Philip's War, Thomas removed to Hadley, where he died.[5]

Robert Webster, sole executor of his father's will, either did not remove his family from Hartford, or if he did, he soon returned, the family having large tracts of land in this township. He died in 1676, and his will dated Hartford, May 20, 1676 is on the records of Hartford. A copy is in the possession of the writer, as is a copy of the will of his widow, Susannah, dated January 23, 1698.

By the latter will, it appears that Robert Webster's sons were John, Jonathan, Samuel, Robert, Joseph, and William. From John descended the subject of this memoir; the line of ancestors from the progenitor is the following, John, Robert, John, Daniel, Noah the father, and Noah the son.

No. 3

In the maternal line, N.W. was descended from George Steele, one of the original settlers in Hartford. His mother, Mercy Steele, was a daughter of Eliphalet Steel[e] of West Hartford, and granddaughter of Samuel Steele, who married Melatiah Bradford, granddaughter of William Bradford, the second Governor of the Plymouth Colony.

Noah Webster, the subject of this memoir, was born in West Hartford, October 16, 1758. His grandfather, Daniel Webster, was one of the early settlers of that society, and in the Spanish war of 1745, he commanded a military company. His father possessed a small farm, part of the estate of his grandfather. He was for many years a Justice of the Peace, for the town of Hartford, and Deacon of the church in West Hartford during the ministry of the Rev. Dr. Perkins.[6]

N.W. was educated in the religious principles of the first planters of New England; his father, mother, & most of his family relatives, paternal & maternal, being pious. He had, in his early years, no other education than that which a common school afforded, when rarely a book was used in the schools, except a spelling book, a psalter, testament, or Bible.

Until the fourteenth year of his age N.W. was occupied on his father's farm; and he contracted a fondness for agriculture which continued, unimpaired, during life. At fourteen years of age, he expressed a wish to obtain a collegiate education. His father, who had five children to provide for, and a small farm only, though he wished to gratify his son, hesitated to comply with his request. But he finally consented, and in the autumn of 1772 his son began the study of the classics under the Rev. Nathan Perkins, minister of the society. In the summer following he left his studies, and assisted his father on his farm. In the winter of 1773 he was in the grammar school, under Mr. Wales in the town, (now city) of Hartford but he returned and finished his preparatory studies under the tuition of Mr. Perkins. He was admitted a member of Yale College, at the commencement in September 1774. At that time, the Rev. Naphtali Daggett, Professor of Divinity, officiated as President, and continued in the performance of the duties, until the appointment of the Rev. Ezra Stiles, who entered the duties of President in the summer term, in 1778.[7]

No. 4

In April 1775 commenced the war of the Revolution, which occasioned various interruptions of the collegiate studies. In the beginning of the year 1777, the students were dismissed for a time, by reason of the difficulty of procuring provisions for the commons. In the summer following, the classes were stationed in different towns, under the care of their respective tutors. The senior class under Mr. Dwight was stationed in Wethersfield; the junior class, to which N.W. belonged, was placed in Glastonbury, under their tutor, the Rev. Joseph Buckminster, as was the sophomore class, under their tutor. The class of freshmen was stationed in Farmington. The advantages then enjoyed by the students, during the four years of college life were much inferior to those enjoyed before and since the Revolution, in the same institution.[8]

In the autumnal vacation of the year 1777, when Gen. Burgoyne, with a British army was marching from the Lake toward Albany, the father of N.W. was ordered into the service, with his company, composed of men above forty-five years of age, and called the *alarm list*, as they were to be summoned into the field only in extraordinary emergencies. On this occasion N.W. shouldered a musket, and marched a volunteer with the militia, and encountered the hardships of a soldier. He was marching northward on the east bank of the Hudson, when Kingston, on the other side, was in flames; and the regiment, under Col. Hezekiah Wyllys, was ordered to the banks of the river to fire on a British sloop of war, or advice boat, descending the river. The shot from the sloop passed over the heads of the American Troops, who received no injury. Before the regiment reached Albany, it was met by an express upon a full gallup brandishing a drawn sword exclaiming as he passed the regiment, Burgoyne is taken; Burgoyne is taken!

In the following winter, the senior class to which N.W. belonged was ordered to repair to New Haven, although the other classes were permitted to remain in the country. This gave offense, and few of the seniors obeyed the summons. N.W. remained at his father's house. This disobedience of the seniors was never punished; the affairs of the college were deranged by the war, and the administration was inefficient.

At the close of the vacation in May 1778, the students assembled under the care of Dr. Stiles, who then commenced his duties as President. In the September following, N.W. received the degree of Bachelor of Arts.

No. 5

The subject of this memoir was now cast upon the world, at the age of twenty, without property, without patrons, and in the midst of a war which had disturbed all occupations; had impoverished the country; and the termination of which could not be foreseen. He remained some time at his father's house; and while there, his father put into his hands an eight dollar bill of continental currency, then worth three or four dollars; saying to him "take this; you must now seek your living; I can do no more for you."

In this state of anxiety which his condition produced, N.W. employed his time in reading; and among other books, he read Johnson's *Rambler*.⁹ This book produced no inconsiderable effect on his mind; and he then resolved that whatever was to be his fate in life, he would pursue a most exact course of integrity and virtue. This sentence of the great moralist, "To fear no eye, to suspect no tongue, is the great prerogative of innocence; an exemption granted only to invariable virtue," was indelibly impressed on his memory.

As N.W. was under the necessity of immediate employment to obtain subsistence, not having means to enable him to prepare for professional business he took charge of a school in Glastonbury, the town in which, with his class, he had spent the summer of 1777. He continued in this school, till the spring of 1779, when he took a school in Hartford, and boarded in the family of Oliver Ellsworth, Esq., afterward Chief Justice of the United States.¹⁰ He had determined on the study of the law, and hoped to pursue his studies to some advantage with the eminent jurist. But daily occupation, and some nervous affections which affected him at this period of life, in a grand measure, frustrated his purpose.

In the severe winter of 1780 he lived in his father's family and kept a school in West Hartford. For three months he was obliged to walk daily, three quarters of a mile, and for several weeks on drifts of snow, as high as the adjoining fences.

No. 6

In the following summer, N.W. was invited to live with Jedadiah Strong, Register of Deeds in Litchfield, and assist him in the duties of his office. In pursuance of the advice of that distinguished jurist the Hon. Titus Hosmer of Middletown,¹¹ a native of West Hartford, he read law, while in Litchfield, in his own apartments. He continued in Litchfield and with a sister in Salisbury, till the spring of 1781, when he presented himself to the County Court in Litchfield, to be examined for admission to the bar. It happened that nearly twenty other young men offered themselves at the same time, and all were examined together, the same evening. To the surprise of all concerned, the gentlemen of the bar declined recommending to the court any of the candidates. Whether they thought them not qualified or whether any were alarmed at the prospect of such an addition to the bar at once, was not fully understood. But N.W. immediately went to Hartford, and offered himself for examination to the County Court in April. He was examined in Company with Chauncey Goodrich,[12] afterward Lieut. Gov. Goodrich, and both were admitted to practice.

The war was still continued; no good prospect of professional business presented itself to N.W., and he established, in the summer of 1781, a private school in Sharon, a town bordering on the state of New York. In that town resided several refugees of whig principles from the city or vicinity of New York. Among these were the family of Gilbert Livingston, and of Mrs. Prevost, who was afterwards married to Col. Burr. The children of these families were N. Webster's pupils, and among them were the two sons of Mrs. Prevost, Frederick, and Bartow. There also resided the venerable Judge Hobart of the state of New York, whose friendship N.W. enjoyed. To this place had retired also Mr. Tetard, a native of Geneva in Europe, who was the pastor of the church in New Rochelle, descendants of the protestants who fled from France on the revocation of the Edict of Nantes. This pious and learned clergyman took a small shop, which had been used by a shoemaker, and there he spent most of his time in devotion and reading. He was an accurate classical scholar, and with him N.W. commenced the study of the French language.

Among the pupils in this school in Sharon was Jonas Platt, the son of Judge Platt of Poughkeepsie. This amiable youth attended N. Webster's school, not only in Sharon, but afterward in Goshen, in Orange County. He afterward became a Judge of the Supreme Court in New York. Between the preceptor and the pupil a strong attachment took place, which lasted during life.

At the Commencement in New Haven in 1781, N.W. attended, took a part in the exercises, and received the degree of Master of Arts.

In the following winter, N.W. made an attempt to find some mercantile employment; but without success. Seeing no prospect of permanent business in Connecticut, he determined to seek business in some of the southern or western parts of the country. In the pursuance of this purpose, he crossed the Hudson, spent a day with a friend, an officer of the army then lying at Newburgh, and proceeded to Goshen, in the county of Orange. There, after encountering many difficulties, he opened a classical school, and received pupils from the most respectable families in that village and its vicinity. Here he enjoyed the advantage of receiving the pay for tuition in silver; an advantage rarely enjoyed in any business at the time.

No. 7

In this situation, he continued about a year. But his prospects of better employment were not encouraging; it was uncertain when the war would be at an end; and he knew not by what means he could find business better suited to his inclination. He had, in hours stolen from necessary occupations, acquired so much knowledge of Law, as to obtain a license to practice; but he had not made himself acquainted with the forms of proceedings, and could not enter upon the practice with advantage. In addition to these circumstances, his health was impaired by close application, and a sedentary life. He was without money and without friends to afford him any particular aid. In this situation of things, his spirits failed, and for some months, he suffered extreme depression and gloomy forebodings.

In this state of mind, he formed the design of composing elementary books for the instruction of children; and began by compiling a spelling book on a plan which he supposed to be better adapted to assist the learner, than that of Dilworth.

In the autumn of 1782, he went to Philadelphia for the purpose of gaining some advice and information which he wanted, and in obtaining laws, in New Jersey and Pennsylvania, to secure to authors the exclusive rights to their literary productions. He took letters of introduction to Mr. Duane[13] and Mr. L'Hommedieu[14] delegates in Congress from the state of New York; and by these gentlemen, he was introduced to Mr. James Madison, then a member of Congress from Virginia.

On his way to Philadelphia, he called on the Rev. Samuel S. Smith, then Professor of Theology in Princeton College, and submitted to him the manuscript of his proposed elementary books. Professor Smith approved the plan and suggested some improvements, which were adopted.

No. 8

At Trenton he called on that distinguished patriot, Governor Livingston,[15] for the purpose of inquiring of him whether it was probable a copyright law could be obtained in New Jersey. The Governor replied that he would consult the Council, then convened in that place, and would report their answer. After a few hours, the Governor informed N.W. that his own opinion was decidedly in favor of such a law, but his council gave him little encouragement to expect success in an application to the legislature for the enactment of such a law.

In Philadelphia, N.W. obtained favorable opinions respecting his protected elementary book, and hints for improvements in the plan, which determined him to prosecute his purpose. He then rode to Hartford in Connecticut when the legislature was in session, and through the agency of his excellent friend, John Canfield, Esq.,[16] of Sharon, he presented a petition to the General Assembly for a copyright law; but it was so near the close of the session, that a hearing could not be obtained.

As this is the first effort in the United States to procure a law for securing copyright to authors, and this memorial the first document ever prepared on that subject, an extract from it is here subjoined.

After describing the literary work which the author wished to have secured to him, he adds:

"To close the whole is annexed a short account of the discovery of America, the time of the first settlement of each state, with an epitomy of their respective Constitutions, as established since the revolution; which is designed to diffuse a political knowledge of this grand confederation of republics, among that class of people who have not access to more expensive means of information."

"Your memoriealist, was ambitious to promote the interest of literature, and the honor and dignity of the American empire, designs the above mentioned work for the general benefit of the youth in the United States. And in order to prevent spurious editions, and to enable your memorialist to have the books under his own correction, and especially to secure to him the pecuniary advantages of his own productions, to which he conceived himself solely entitled, your memorialist therefore humbly prays that this honorable Assembly would appoint a committee to examine into the merit of the performance, and upon their favorable report, would, by a law passed for the purpose, vest in your memorialist and his assigns the exclusive right of printing, publishing, and vending the said *American Instructor*,* in the state of Connecticut, for and during the term of thirteen years from the passing of said act, or for other such term of time, as the honorable Assembly shall, in their wisdom, see proper. And your memorialist, as is duty bound, shall ever pray.

Dated at Hartford, the 24th day of October 1782."

No. 9

N.W. then returned to Goshen, and devoted his leisure time, during the winter, to the correction, enlargement and improvement of his proposed works. In January 1783, he went to Kingston, during the session of the legislature of New York, in that place, with the purpose of presenting a memorial to that body for a copyright law; but the necessity of this was superseded by the prompt efforts of

---

* This was the title originally designed; that by the advice of Dr. Stiles, it was omitted, and that of *Grammatical Institute*, substituted.

Gen. Schuyler, who on motion obtained a bill to be passed in the Senate, which, at a subsequent session, was enacted into a law.

In the spring of 1783 N.W. left Goshen, and repaired to Hartford for the purpose of procuring the publication of his first elementary books. Here he had serious obstacles to encounter. Most persons, who were apprised of his design, considered it as visionary, and among his friends, two gentlemen only, John Trumbull[17] and Joel Barlow,[18] ventured to encourage him with the prospect of success. In addition to this discouragement, he was destitute of the means of defraying the expenses of publication; and no printer or bookseller was found to undertake the publication at his own risk. But in the most trying exigencies, his fortitude never forsook him. He received a little aid from Mr. Barlow, whose generosity far exceeded his ability; and N.W. contracted with Hudson and Goodwin his obligation although the future sales only would enable him to fulfill his engagement. But it was not a time to shrink from the execution of his design; he had confidence in its success, and took upon himself the risk.

The first elementary book was published in October 1783; the author being twenty five years of age. The success was better than he had expected; the edition of five thousand copies being exhausted during the following winter.

The second part of the work, of grammar, was published in March 1784, and the third, in January 1785.

No. 10

In the summer of 1783 commenced a popular opposition to the act of Congress which granted extra pay to the officers of the American army, to indemnify them for the losses they had incurred by being paid in a depreciated currency. This opposition was most general and violent in Connecticut. Inflammatory publications roused the people of many towns to call meetings, and discuss the subject. In these publications and discussions it was alledged that the *com-*

mutation, or five years full pay in lieu of a pension for life, was unjust that the officers of the army had not suffered more than other citizens, who were obliged to hire men for soldiers with large bounties, and who had supplied provisions and clothing for the army. To oppose this grant of Congress, the citizens, in many towns, appointed delegates for the purpose of holding a convention at Middletown. In the first meeting, there was not a majority of the towns represented; but at the second meeting, more than fifty towns, being five sevenths of the state, were represented. In this convention some resolves were proposed against the act of Congress, and against the Society of the Cincinnati. At their last meeting, they took measures by secret nomination to change the Council or Senate of the state, but without success.

In this crisis, N.W. commenced writing a series of papers with different signatures, in vindication of the act of Congress. The principal of these appeared in the *Connecticut Courant,* commencing August 26, 1783, with the signature of *Honorius.* For several months, he devoted a large portion of his time to the object of enlightening and tranquilizing the minds of his fellow citizens. The result was a degree of success which more than answered expectations. The discontent was greatly allayed; and at the election in the Spring of 1784, three fourths of the members of the house of representatives were chosen from the supporters of the government. The Middletown Convention ended in smoke. See *Connecticut Courant* August 26, 1783; Sept 2nd–9th–16th–30th; Oct. 14th–21st; December 30th 1783; January 13th–27th; Feb. 10; March 30; April 6, 1784.

NO. 11

For these labors N.W. received the thanks of Governor Trumbull and other gentlemen; and Mr. Mitchell, then a member of the Council, afterward Chief Justice of the state, coming from the statehouse one day, during the session of the legislature in May, and meeting N.W. said to him, "You Sir, have done more to appease public discontent, and produce a favorable change, than any other person."

In February, N.W. began a series of papers entitled "Policy of Connecticut." See *Courant* Feb. 24, 1784.

In January 1785 he wrote a series of papers on the claims of Connecticut to lands west of the Delaware. This was at the request of some proprietors of those claims. See *Courant* January 4, 1785.

The Congress, under the Confederation, having no power to enforce any act or resolve for raising money to supply the treasury, depended on recommendations and requisitions, addressed to the legislatures of the several states. But the danger and necessities of the war being at an end, these requisitions were partially complied with or wholly neglected. In consequence of this neglect, the debts contracted during the war were not paid nor funded; the officers and soldiers were obliged to take certificates, as evidences of their claims; as were the men who had furnished provisions of the army. These certificates gradually depreciated, till they were sold for one eighth of their nominal amount; commerce was almost annihilated; there were no manufactures, except domestic; the country was exhausted of money, taxes were oppressive; and murmurs were heard in every quarter.

N.W. now employed his pen to convince his fellow citizens of the inefficiency of the Confederation for the government of the United States, and the preservation of the union.

No. 12

Early in the winter, he wrote and published a pamphlet entitled *Sketches of American Policy* which appeared in March of that year.

In the first sketch, the author treats of the theory of government. This was written soon after reading Rousseau's *Social Contract*, from which he had imbibed many visionary ideas, which subsequent reflection and observation induced him to reject.[19]

The second sketch gives a brief view of the governments on the eastern continent.

The third sketch contrasts the condition of the United States with that of European States, in regard to the forms and principles of government.

The fourth sketch purports to describe a plan of policy for improving the advantages, and perpetuating the union of the American States. He laid it down as a fundamental principle, that there must be a supreme power at the head of the union, vested with authority to make laws that respect the United States, and to compel obedience of those laws—a supreme head having as ample power to enforce its laws, as the legislatures of the several states have to make and enforce laws, on their citizens, in matters of their own police that so long as a single state could defeat or control the measures of congress of the twelve other states, our union was but a name, and our confederation, a cobweb.[20]

In May of the year 1785 N.W. set out on a journey to South Carolina. From Baltimore, he rode to Mount Vernon, where he passed some time in Gen. Washington's hospitable mansion. He carried with him copies of the pamphlet above named, and presented one to the general. In a few weeks afterward, Mr. Madison visited Gen. Washington and while at his house, he read the pamphlet. In the autumn following, N.W. met Mr. Madison in Richmond, and the latter spoke in praise of its contents.

The ex-Chancellor Kent of New York has repeatedly said that this pamphlet contains the first distinct proposition for the formation of a new Constitution that was made or published.

NO. 13

One object of the journey to the South was to make applications to the legislatures of several states for the enactment of laws to secure authors the copyright of their writings.[21]

"Memoir of Noah Webster, LL.D."

From Mount Vernon N.W. returned to Baltimore, and in June, embarked on board of a sloop for Charleston. He had a long passage, with head winds, but arrived safe and spent a week in that city. He then returned to Baltimore; and as the legislatures of Maryland, Virginia and Delaware were not in session, he continued in Baltimore during the summer. Here he employed his time in writing remarks of the English Language. These, in imitation of Dr. Mayes [*sic*],[22] the blind Scottish philosopher, who was reading lectures on Natural Philosophy, he read publicly in Baltimore, Wilmington, Philadelphia and other principal cities, during the Spring and Summer of 1786. These lectures were afterward revised, and in the year 1789, were published in the octavo volume, with the title of *Dissertations on the English Language.*

Lectures on Language were not very interesting to a popular audience; his hearers were not numerous, but always respectable. The proceeds of tickets furnished the means of traveling; during the year 1785 and 1786 he had opportunities of becoming acquainted with many literary gentlemen, in the principal cities and towns, between Baltimore and Portsmouth in New Hampshire, and of extending his knowledge of books treating of the subject of philology.

In November 1785 N.W. made a journey to Richmond in Virginia, for the purpose of applying for a copyright law. On his way, he passed two days at Mount Vernon. One day, at the dinner table, the following incident occurred: Gen. Washington said, in the course of conversation, that he wanted a man to live with him, to act as his secretary, and as instructor to Mrs. Washington's grandchildren, by the name of Custis. He said that he had begun a letter to his correspondent in Scotland, requesting that he would recommend to him a person qualified for these purposes.

No. 14

N.W., struck with surprise that the General was about to send to Scotland for a secretary, asked him what European nations would think of this country if, after the exhibition of great talents and achievements in the war for independence, having obtained our object, we should send to Europe for secretaries, and men to teach the first rudiments of learning. The question was well received; and the General instantly replied, "What shall I do? There is no person here to be obtained for my purposes." N.W. replied he believed any northern college could furnish a person who would answer his wishes. Here the conversation at table ceased.

After dinner, walking in the hall, the General addressed him saying, "Sir, I have been thinking of what you said, in regard to a secretary. I have indeed a letter partly prepared to send to Scotland on this subject; but if you can recommend to me a person, who will answer my views, I will lay aside my letter." N.W. answered, that it was several months since he left the north; but on his return, he would endeavor to procure for him a suitable person. After N.W. left Mount Vernon, he thought to offer his own services to the General, and wrote to him to that effect; but on reconsideration, he declined to pursue the intention.

Not long after this interview, as N.W. was informed, General Lincoln made a visit to Gen. Washington; and the latter mentioning to him his want of a secretary, Gen Lincoln recommended Tobias Lear[23] of New Hampshire, who accepted the place, and acted as Gen. Washington's private Secretary, and after his election to the presidency, as his public secretary for many years.

Taking letters of introduction from Gen. Washington, Governor Harrison and others in Richmond, N.W. proceeded to that city, where the legislature was in session. There he met Mr. Madison, then a member of the house of delegates, and there he registered his books to secure the copyright.

NO. 15

At this session of the legislature of Virginia the proposition was introduced for a convention of delegates to meet at Annapolis, for the purpose of forming commercial regulations for the United States. For many years N.W. had supposed that this proposition was introduced by Mr. Madison. This was suggested to him in a letter dated New Haven, August 20, 1804. In his answer dated Washington, Oct. 12, 1804, Mr. Madison admits the fact that he made his proposition in the legislature with success; but he wrote from memory, without documents. After he had leisure to examine his papers, he wrote a letter to N.W. dated Montpelier, March 10, 1826, in which he corrects his mistake. His words are "I find reason to believe that the impression under which I made the statement was erroneous; and that the proposition, though probably growing out of efforts made by myself to convince the legislature of necessity of investing Congress with such powers, was introduced by another member more likely to have the ear of the legislature, on the occasion, than one whose long and late service in Congress might subject him to the suspicion of bias in favor of that body."

In December of the year 1785 N.W. left Richmond, returned to Baltimore, and thence went to Annapolis, and registered his books to secure the copyright, according to the law of Maryland. In February 1786 he went to Dover in the state of Delaware, where the legislature was in session. He presented a petition for a copyright law, which was granted, but on the last day of the session, and a committee was appointed to prepare a bill in the form for the next session. This was done, and the bill passed into a law.

Proceeding northward, he read his lectures on Language to numerous auditors in Wilmington, where he was introduced to Governor Dickinson, the author of the celebrated essays, entitled *The American Farmer*.[24]

No. 16

In Philadelphia, N.W. found a most benevolent and disinterested friend in Col. Timothy Pickering, whose kindness he often mentioned in subsequent periods at his life. Here he also became

acquainted with Dr. Rush,[25] whose attachment to him was manifested to him during life. He waited on Dr. Franklin, president of
the trustees of the University, and obtained permission to read his
lectures in an apartment in that building. He read one lecture in the
University Hall for the benefit of The Pennsylvania Hospital, and a
handsome sum was received. He was introduced to Mr. Rittenhouse,[26] and many other distinguished citizens. Among other ac-
quaintances made at this time, was Thomas Paine, to whom Col.
Pickering introduced him, for the purpose of seeing his model of an
iron bridge in miniature. While in this city he registered his Institute under the copyright law of Pennsylvania.

In New York N.W. read his lectures to a small audience, but
among his hearers were several members of Congress, which was
then sitting in that city. He was treated with much politeness by Dr.
Ramsay,[27] the chairman of Congress, a gentleman who, through life,
manifested a particular friendship for N.W. While in New York he
numbered the houses in the city, which amounted to three thousand
and five hundred. He then visited Albany and the cohog of the
Mohawks; then returned and visited Hartford, after an absence of
thirteen months. He then journeyed eastward, as far as Portsmouth,
and visited the principal towns in Rhode Island, reading his lectures
in the principal towns through which he passed. In Boston, a subscription was set on foot for a second reading of the last lecture,
which was geographical and political; the same which had been delivered in Philadelphia, for the benefit of the hospital. In Fanueil
Hall he had, on this occasion, a large audience.

No. 17

In the autumm of 1786, N.W. went to Philadelphia, at the request of Dr. Franklin, who wished to consult with him on a plan for
reforming the orthography of the English Language. Dr. Franklin
had, many years before, formed the scheme of a new alphabet, and
had types cast for printing his new characters, specimens of which

are seen in his works. It was the Doctor's desire that N.W. should take three types and prosecute the plan. This desire of the Doctor was somewhat embarrassing to N.W., for he was then and has ever been of the opinion that any scheme for introduction of a new alphabet, or new characters, is and will be impracticable. Nor did he think any scheme of this kind necessary for the purpose; being persuaded that the characters were used, with a few points attached to some of them, to designate different sounds, may be made to answer all essential purposes of a perfect alphabet. Accordingly he declined the Doctor's offer of the use of his types, alledging that he could not risk the expense of the undertaking, especially during the troubles of the times. The doctor treated N.W. with much politeness, and gave him free access to his library, while in the city.

During this and the following year, N.W. employed his leisure in writing short essays, on political and litarary subjects, some of which were after printed in his volume of essays.

In February 1787 he put to press the third edition of his grammar in Philadelphia.

In April of this year 1787, he accepted the place of instructor in the English department of the Episcopal Academy in that city, which was under the superintendance of the Rev. Dr. Andrews. In this employment he continued till the October following.

NO. 18

During the summer of this year, was held the Convention of delegates from the several states. which formed the present Constitution of the United States. Their deliberations were closed and the form of the Constitution published in September. On the 15th of that month, two days before the close of the proceedings, Mr. Fitzsimmons,[28] one of the delegates of Pennsylvania, wrote a note to N.W. requesting him, if he should approve of the form of the constitution, which was to be proposed to the people, to give it his support. The following is a copy of the note.

Sir.

I shall make you no apology, for addressing myself to you upon the present occasion, because you must be equally interested with me in the event, and having contributed my mite to the service of our common country, I have some right to call upon others for their assistance. I consider the present moment, as the crisis that will determine whether we are to benefit by the revolution we have obtained or whether we shall become a prey to foreign influence and domestic violence. The business of the convention is nearly at an end, and a few days will bring before the people of America the constitution prepared for their future government. That it is the best which human wisdom could devise, I mean not to assert; but I trust it will be found consistent with the principles of liberty, and calculated to unite and bring together the members of a great country. It is already too evident that there are people prepared to oppose it, even before they are acquainted with its outline, and it is as easy to foresee that if unreasonable jealousis are disseminated, its adoption may be be at least protracted. In my mind, to delay is to destroy. There are so many interests, foreign & domestic, opposed to order & good government in America, as to warrent an apprehension of their interfering, if time is given for cabal and intrigue.

It too often happens that men whose views are upright, trust to the goodness of their cause; while men of opposite views are indefatigable in misrepresenting them.

Under these opinions and from a conviction that your abilities may be eminently useful on the present occasion, I am induced to call your attention to this subject. If as a friend to your country, you can support the act of the convention, I hope you will exert yourself to that purpose. I ask it only upon that condition.

> I am Sir your most obed Servt
> Thomas Fitzsimmons

Walnut Street
15 Sept. 1787

(Document No. 7)

N. Webster, Esq.

In consequence of this application, N.W. wrote and published a pamphlet entitled "An Examination into the Leading principles of the Federal Constitution," and inscribed it to Dr. Franklin. This pamphlet was written in haste, and was not satisfactory to himself or to friends of the Constitution.

(Miscellanies Vol. 16)

After the close of the Convention, Dr. Franklin presented a copy of the Constitution to the Speaker of the House of Assembly which was read. The bells of the City were rung on the occasion.

No. 19

In convening with Dr. Franklin on the subject of the Constitution, after it was published, the Doctor said to N.W. that he had agreed to the form of the Constitution, although it had always been his opinion that the legislative body should consist of one house only. But said the Doctor, "I have been all my life changing my opinions on many subjects, in this case, I have yielded my own opinions to those of other men."

In February of this year 1787, N.W. visited the steam boat constructed by Mr. Fitch,[29] a native of East Windsor, in Connecticut. The boat had made a trip from Philadelphia to Burlington, and was then at the wharf. Mr. Fitch was an illiterate man, and poor. He made various attempts to procure aid in his design, but died without accomplishing his object.

N.W. left Philadelphia in October, and visited his friends in Hartford. He then formed the design of publishing a monthly periodical in New York, and the first number, with the title of "The American Magazine," was published in January 1788. But in the impoverished and distracted state of the country, no adequate encouragement was found, and at the close of the year, the publication was discontinued. In this undertaking a considerable pecuniary loss was incurred.

After this failure, a plan was formed to unite with Ebenezer Hazard Esq. and Mr. Francis Childs,[30] in publishing a periodical with a different title, and on a more enlarged plan; but this design also failed.

During the summer 1788, the Convention of the State of New York ratified the Constitution of the United States, and the ratification was celebrated, in the city, with great pomp and magnificence. After the celebration, the committee of arrangements requested N.W. to draw up an account of the proceedings, which was done, and the account was published in the *Daily Advertiser* August 2, 1788.

NO. 20

The winter of 1788–9, N.W. spent in Boston, superintending the publication of his *Dissertation on the English Language*. By this publication he incurred a heavy pecuniary loss.

In May 1789 N.W. returned to Hartford, and took lodgings at Mr., and afterward, Judge Trumbull's, and was occupied in the study of Law, which he determined to pursue as a profession.

In October 1789 N.W. married Rebecca Greenleaf,[31] daughter of William Greeenleaf Esq., of Boston, an amiable Lady, and well qualified to insure domestic happiness to a man sensible of her worth. But he began housekeeping with very unfavorable prospects. The county of Hartford had been recently divided; a law enlarging the jurisdiction of justices of the peace, and the incorporation of a part of the town of Hartford with city privileges and with summary jurisdiction in cases of debt, had very much diminished the profits of business. But with some business in his profession, some receipts for the copyright of his elementary books, a small amount of fees of his business as Notary Public, and the aid of his generous Brother-in-Law James Greenleaf, he was able to sustain his family for a few years.

In this year, at the request of the merchants, he wrote and published a small pamphlet on the excise law of Connecticut, a law
which was disliked by the merchants, and was soon repealed.

In 1790, N.W. prepared for the press and published a volume of
essays and fugitive pieces; but the work produced no profit.

In this year also N.W. abridged his grammar, and published it
with the title of *The Little Reader's Assistant*. In this little book, he
introduced what was called a *Federal Catechism,* or explanation of
the Constitution of the United States, and the principles of government and commerce. This was the first attempt of the kind, and
much applauded by particular persons; but the book did not continue long in use in schools.

No. 21

In the year 1790 N.W. suggested to Hudson and Goodwin,
and others the project of covering the main street in Hartford
with stones; the ground having been originally soft and in wet
weather, a mass of deep mud. This suggestion being approved,
he drew up a plan for the purpose on May 1, and a meeting of
citizens was called, and a tax of four pence on the pound to be
raised annually was voted for carrying this scheme into effect.
The tax and the prosecution of the plan were continued for several years.

In this year also N.W. published Governor Winthrop's Journal or Diary.[32] He first saw the manuscript at the house of Governor Trumbull in Lebanon, in the year 1786; and he immediately
contracted with the Governor's Secretary, John Porter Esq., afterward Controller of Public Accounts, to transcribe the manuscript,
and furnish a correct copy for publication. Mr. Porter undertook
this work for the sum of *seven pounds* lawful money (dollars at six
shillings), but after finishing the copy, he represented the labor to
have been greater than he expected, twenty shillings were added
to that price paid. Thus a manuscript which made an octavo vol-

ume of three hundred seventy pages was copied from an antiquated and difficult handwriting, for the sum of $26.66 a price which shows the scarcity and value of money in the period of distress which intervened between the peace of 1783 and the revival of business after the new Constitution had been put into operation.

A small edition only of this valuable work was published, and the whole was sold; but it afforded no profit to the Editor.

On the 22nd day of October 1790, N.W. was admitted Attorney and Counselor of Law, in the Circuit Court at Hartford, Chief Justice Jay presiding.

NO. 22

In this and following year N.W. wrote and published in *The Connecticut Courant* a number of short pieces on domestic economy and certain vices and follies, to which pieces he gave the title of *The Prompter*. These pieces were anonymous, and for a long period the author was not known to the public, nor even to his family friends. They were written in the familiar style of Dr. Franklin's Poor Richard, and were so popular, that they were republished in many newspapers in the United States, and finally a copy was published in England. In an English notice of the little book, it was said to be a very good shilling-worth publication. An edition, with considerable additions, was published in New Haven in 1803, and the original copy has been since repeatedly republished.

This little book gave origin to the "Lay Preacher," by Joseph Dennie Jun., of Walpole in New Hampshire. The following is a copy of a letter from Mr. Dennie to N. Webster, with a copy of that book.

Walpole, New Hampshire

Sept. 8, 1796

"Memoir of Noah Webster, LL.D."

Sir:

Though a stranger to your acquaintence, I am familiar with your writings. Some of them I have read for instruction, and some for delight. I have been informed by your philological and political speculations, and I have been amused by the *Prompter*. The simplicity and ease of that little volume taught me the value of the Franklin style. If there be any merit in the short essays or the "Lay Preacher," consider the author as your debtor, and flatter him by accepting his book.

I am, Sir, Your hum. Svt.

Joseph Dennie, Jun.[33]

Noah Webster ESQ.

NO. 23

In 1791 N.W. called the attention of the public to the subject of banking, by publishing an essay on the utility of banks, in the *Courant* in March of that year. In September of the same year, he discussed the subject of Penal Law.

In January 1792 N.W. commenced a series of papers, headed by the title of "Patriot," and continued it in eight numbers, published in the *Courant*. These papers were intended to show the means of improving the natural advantages of Connecticut, by the importation of goods from Europe, but these advantages have not been realized.

In December 1791 N.W. wrote and published a short address to the citizens of Hartford, for the purpose of exciting them to form a Charitable Society. The following is a copy of the address.

TO THE CITIZENS OF HARTFORD

Poverty and want, in consequence of unforeseen and unavoidable misfortunes, are the lot of great multitudes of men. Sickness, wounds, fire, shipwreck, and other calamities, from which no man is exempt, frequently and suddenly deprive whole families of property and the means of subsistence.

The laws of Connecticut require that every town shall support its own poor. But there are, in every town, more especially in Hartford, great numbers of mechanics and other laborers, who do not fall under the description of the *poor* of the town, who, notwithstanding, have no means of subsistence but their daily earnings. Many of these are honest, industrious, and frugal, with large families. While the parents are in health, they are able by their labor to feed and clothe their families, and enjoy all the necessaries, and many of the conveniences of life. But such people are as much exposed to sudden sickness and losses, as others, and more exposed to wounds which disable them for weeks or months, than people in easier circumstances. By such misfortunes, they are often reduced to want without fault of their own, and pride or modesty may prevent them from disclosing their distress and applying to the overseer of the poor for relief. Their families thus suffer, or they must contract debts for supplies, which debts afterward oppress and harass them. Instances of this kind happen every year, and within every man's observation.

To establish a fund for the relief of such people, when in distress, it is proposed to form a *Charitable Society* in Hartford, to consist of those persons who subscribe the proposal, the outlines of which are as follows:

I. Every subscriber shall pay annually on or before the first Monday of January, into the treasury of the Society, such sum as he shall think proper to give, not less than one dollar, for which sum, he shall be credited in the cash book of the society.

II. An annual meeting of the subscribers shall be held on the first Monday of January, at which shall be chosen a chairman of the Society, a clerk who shall also be a treasurer, and a Committee of Appropriations who shall direct the payment of the moneys of the Society under such regulations as they shall prescribe at their meeting, and shall also be empowered to receive donations from members of the Society or others.

III. The Committee and the Treasurer shall render an amount of receipts and expenditures, to the Society at their annual meeting.

IV. The object of the Society being to give relief to honest, industrious and frugal people especially mechanics and other laborers, who may be suddenly reduced to want; no person who is addicted to excessive drinking, idleness or other vice, by which his substance of his earnings shall be wasted, shall be entitled to any relief from this society.

V.   The Society at their first meeting form such rules and regulations, as they shall judge best calculated to answer the benevolent purposes of the institution.

See *Courant* Dec. 12, 1791

No. 24

This address did not effect the object. But on the first day of October 1792, was published by him another address on the same subject, in which additional arguments for the establishment of a Charitable Society were urged, and these were re-enforced by the recent death of two laboring men, by casualty. (See *Courant* Oct. 1, 1792. The address may be inserted.)

The consequence of this appeal, a meeting of citizens was held and a Society was formed. It was incorporated in May 1809, and now has a considerable fund. By means of these funds and annual subscriptions many distressed families have been relieved.

It may be noted that the meeting which formed the Society was held in the state house in the evening of Thanksgiving day, November 29, 1792.

May 4, 1791 N.W. circulated a petition for a lottery, to raise money for erecting a new State and Court House: the old one being too small, and in state of dilapidation. This product was not effected.

In October of the same year, he set on foot a subscription for the same object and a considerable sum was obtained; but ultimately the new house was erected chiefly by a contract with Messrs. Woodbridge and T[rum]bull for a grant of the gore, a tract of land, part of the Connecticut claims west of New York.

In March 1792 N.W. was elected a member of the Common Council of the city of Hartford.

During the year he employed much time examining the records of Hartford, to ascertain what lands on the banks of the rivers belonged to the town. He read to the town-meeting a long report on the subject.

In July 1793 N.W. wrote resolutions approving of the neutrality of the United States, according to President Washington's proclamation. These were presented to a meeting of citizens on the first of August, who agreed to them, and to send them addressed to the president.

No. 25

On the 6th of March 1792, a meeting of merchants and other gentlemen was held for the purpose of originating a bank in Hartford. The subject was discussed, and it was voted to open a subscription for such an institution, and a committee was appointed to offer it to the citizens. John Trumbull, Chauncey Goodrich, and Noah Webster, Esquire, were appointed to procure an act of incorporation. Mr. Trumbull and Mr. Goodrich drew the first sketch of a charter; but omitted to insert a section making promissory notes assignable, like bills of exchange. N.W. proposed to the gentlemen to add a section for this purpose; but they objected, alledging that repeated attempts had been made in the legislature to procure an act for their purpose without success; they therefore thought an attempt to effect the object would be fruitless. But the principal management of the business with the legislature being left with N.W., he determined to make an effort to carry the point on this occasion, and for their purpose he inserted the clause which constitutes the thirteenth Section of the charter of the Hartford Bank, copying the substance of it from the British Act of Queen Ann, which makes notes assignable, like inland bills of exchange. This project succeeded; the act of incorporation was passed without opposition; and in subsequent charters of banks in the state, a similar section has been introduced.

In May 1792, the Society for the Promotion of Freedom appointed N.W. to deliver the annual oration before the Society in May 1793, he took that occasion to write a short treatise on the subject of slavery. This was published with the Title "Effects of Slavery on Morals and Industry." See Pamphlets No. 23 Document No. 10.

No. 26

In 1793 N.W. found that his professional business, with small emoluments of his office of Notary Public, was not adequate to the support of his family; and the proceeds of the sale of his copyrights in the eastern states, were exhausted. He then began to contemplate a change of business, and for this purpose, to remove his family to some state further westward, in which he might receive aid from further sales of his copyrights. In pursuance of this design, he made a journey to New York in August, and took lodgings at Mr. Bradley's in Maiden Lane, in whose house were the French minister, Mon. Genet[34] and his suit. Sitting one day at the dinner table, with Timothy Phelps[35] of New Haven, and the French gentlemen, he heard Genet's secretary say in French "General Washington is making war on the French Nation." The secretary probably did not know that any American at table understood what he said.

N.W. communicated this declaration to Oliver Wolcott Esq., Controller of Public Accounts in Philadelphia, who communicated the fact to one of the heads of departments. It was judged that this conversation of the French man was of importance to be verified by proof; and Mr. Wolcott, by letter Sept. 12, 1793, requested N.W. to make his affidavit of the facts, and send it to Mr. Wolcott. With this request, he complied.

The following is a copy of the Affidavit:

NO. 27

The Affidavit

Noah Webster Jun of Hartford in the State of Connecticut of lawful age, testifies & says, that on or about the twenty sixth day of August last past, the deponent with Mr Timothy Phelps of New Haven, & a Mr Haxhall of Petersburgh in Virginia, dined in company with Mr Genet, the French Minister, Capt Bompard, & Mr Genet's Secretaries, at the house of Mr Bradley, in Maiden Lane, New York. After dinner, but before the Gentlemen rose from table, the deponent related the report from Boston, which had that day been circulated "that the Governor of Massachusetts had taken measures to secure a prize or two which had been sent into that port by a proscribed privateer, (socalled) for the purpose of restoring the said prizes to the owners; that in consequence of this the Commander of the Concord, frigate, had taken the prize or prizes for the benefit of the owners." When the deponent had related this story, Mr Pascal, one of Mr Genet's Secretaries, immediately replied in French "Mon. Washington fait la guerre á la nation Francaise," or in words to that effect; to which Mr Genet & Capt Bompard both assented saying Yes. Mr Genet proceeded & said that the Executive of the United States was under the influence of British Gold—the deponent asked him if he meant the President of the United States; he replied No—Mr Genet declared he had very good letters which gave him this information. The deponent represented to Mr Genet that it would be impossible to subject the independent freemen of America to British or any other foreign power, & that the Executive Officers, the President, Mr Jefferson, Mr Hamilton, & Gen. Knox to be fools; to which Mr Genet replied, Mr Jefferson is no fool.

The deponent says further that in another conversation Mr Genet railed ag^t some of the measures of Congress & particularly ag^t the funding system, in very severe language. And further the Deponent says not. Dated at Hartford the twenty fifth day of September, 1793.

Noah Webster jun.

Hartford County Ss City of Hartford

Sepr 26; Anno Domini 1793

Personally appeared Noah Webster Esquire of said City the above named Deponent and made solemn Oath to the Truth of the facts contained in the foregoing & within Deposition

Before me

Chauncey Goodrich, prs. Pac.

No. 28

The United States were, at that time extremely agitated by the attempts of the French minister and his supporters among our own citizens, to draw their country into a war to support the French Revolution against Great Britain and other hostile powers.[36] While N.W. was in New York, the project of establishing a newspaper for the purpose of defending the measure of Gen. Washington, particularly his proclamation of neutrality, was formed, and it was suggested first by James Watson, Esq., to N.W. that he must undertake such an establishment.

To this proposition he agreed; but as he had not the necessary funds for the purpose, twelve gentlemen of the city and state agreed to furnish each one hundred and fifty dollars, for five years without interest. This money was advanced and was, at the end of the term, repaid.

N.W. knew the labor, difficulties and responsibilities of this undertaking would be great; but as he had then no better prospect of business, he engaged a printer, and in November 1793 he removed his family to New York. In December, he published the first paper, called the *Minerva*, a daily paper. In a few months afterward, he formed the plan of a paper for country subscribers, to be printed on a different form from the daily paper, but with the same columns, without the composition. This saving of labor enabled him to furnish a large paper at a small price. This mode of publishing newspapers for the country with the contents of the daily papers, in new forms, has since been extensively adopted.

The first semi-weekly paper for the country, called the *Herald*, was published in June 1794. The titles of the papers were afterward changed; and they are now published under the titles of the *Commercial Advertiser* (daily) and the *New York Spectator* (semi-weekly).

NO. 29

When these papers were first published the partisans of France, who took a warm interest in the Revolution, supposing it to be the commencement of a free government, and hailing it as a joyful era, were very numerous. The citizens of this country indeed were all friendly to the Revolution in France; but the President and a respectable portion of the citizens judged it impolitic to take any part in the contest. The French party or democratic party, consisting of American citizens, was numerous and violent; and to these were added great numbers of French refugees from France and from Haiti. When animated by the news of any strong democratic measure in the National Convention, or other favorable news, this party often assembled, and formed a procession which passed through the streets of N. York, singing *Ca ira* of the Marseillais hymn; and at times so violent were their proceedings, that N.W. was apprehensive for the safety of his printing office. But he steadfastly pursued his business without interruption.

The labor of selecting matter for the daily paper, of correcting proofs, and of keeping the accounts of the office, in which no clerk was employed, with the additional labor of writing or translating from French papers, very soon impaired his health. But his zeal was not limited to this course of business: in the winter of 1793–4 he increased his labors by writing matter for a pamphlet, which was published with the title of the *Revolution in France*, in which he described the changes and the horrors of the revolution; and predicted

the probable consequences. This pamphlet was read by the supporters of Gen. Washington with great satisfaction. (See Vol. of Pamphlets No. 23).

During this winter, his strength was exhausted; in two instances, his pulse was scarcely perceptible in the radial artery; but he
revived.

In 1796, the papers affording a handsome profit, N.W. gave the
immediate superintendance of them to a partner and a clerk and
took a house at Corlear's Hook, where he resided till he left New
York.

Here he kept a horse, and riding into the city daily, to attend to
his papers, in the hours of business, and returning in the afternoon,
he gradually recovered firmer health.

No. 30

In the year 1795, the premature publication of the principal articles of the treaty with Great Britain, negotiated by Mr. Jay, roused
into action all the opposition of the democratic party; and every
effort was made to prevent its ratification.[37] The twelfth article, was
deemed by the Senate objectionable and rejected. The others were
ratified. When the treaty was first published, many of the supporters
of Washington's administration were opposed to it, and so general
and violent was the opposition, that the president delayed, for a
considerable time, to affix to it his signature.

In this state of public agitation, N.W. undertook to vindicate
the treaty, and in a series of papers, to prove it to be as favorable to
the interests of this country, as we had any right to expect. The
principal papers written and published had the signature of *Curtius*.
These were twelve in number, of which N.W. wrote *ten* and Mr.
Kent,[38] afterward Chief Justice and Chancellor, wrote *two*, the *sixth*
and *seventh*. These were written in answer to the arguments of a
writer with the signature of *Decius*, which appeared in the morning
paper, the *Argus*. Curtius was published in the *Minerva* and *Herald*

between July 22 and Aug. 8, 1795; and republished with other papers in a pamphlet by Matthew Carey of Philadelphia (Document No. 11).

Within a few days after the first number of Curtius was published, Mr. Hamilton applied to N.W. to publish a series of papers which he had commenced writing with the signature of *Camillus*. Mr. Hamilton had entitled his papers *A Vindication of the Treaty*, the title which was prefixed to *Curtius*: but at the request of N.W., this was exchanged for *The Defense*. At the special request of Mr. Hamilton, N.W. consented that these papers should be first published in the *Argus*, the opposition papers, and be copied from that paper into the *Minerva* and *Herald*. *Camillus* was extended to thirty eight numbers, the last of which was not published till January 1796. This extended discussion probably prevented the papers from being generally read.

After the ratification of the treaty, when the public agitation had subsided and the minds of the people were satisfied or tranquilized, Mr. Rufus King[39] said to Gov. Jay, in the hearing and presence of N.W., that N. Webster's writings, had done more to quiet the public mind and reconcile people to the treaty, than the writings of Mr. Hamilton; stating as a reason, that his style and manner of treating the subject were better adapted to their understanding, than those of Mr. Hamilton.

No. 31

When the first number of Curtius fell into the hands of Mr. Jefferson he wrote a letter to Mr. Madison from which the following passages are extracted. "In the mean time, I send you post one of the pieces, [by] Curtius, but it should not have come to you otherwise. It is evidently written by Hamilton, giving a brief and general view of the subject, that the public mind might be kept a little in check till he could resume the subject more at large from the beginning, under the second signature of Camillus. The piece called

"The Features of the Treaty" I do not send, because you have seen it in the newspapers. It is said to be written by Cosee, but I should rather suspect by Beckley. The antidote is certainly not strong enough for the poison of Curtius. If I had not been informed the present came from Beckley, I should have suspected it from Jay or Hamilton. I gave a copy or two, by way of experiment, to honest, soundhearted men of common understanding, and many were not able to parry the sophistry of Curtius. I have ceased therefore to give them. Hamilton is really a Colossus to the anti-republican party. Without numbers he is a host within himself. We have only middling performances to oppose to him. In truth, when he comes forward, there is nobody but yourself who can meet him. For God's sake take up your pen and give a fundamental reply to Curtius and Camillus."

Life of Jefferson
Vol. 3 p. 315-316

No. 32

The Yellow Fever occurring frequently in our large cities, for several years, and physicians entertaining different opinions respecting its origin, whether from domestic causes, or from imported infection, N.W. took pains to collect facts, on the subject; in 1796 he published a *Collection of Papers*, in a pamphlet, containing accounts of the fever in New York and in various other places. (See Documents, No. 12, Miscellaneous papers.)

In 1797, N.W. wrote a series of papers, twenty five in number, as drafted to Dr. William Currie[40] of Philadelphia, on the subject of the Yellow Fever and in opposition to his opinions. The Doctor defended the opinion that the fever was foreign origin. (See *Minerva* and *Herald* from October to December 1796.)

In June 1796 Mr. Volney,[41] who was then in the United States, addressed a letter to the Editor of the Philadelphia *Gazette*, requesting facts respecting the winds in this country. (See *Herald* June 10, 1796.) This occasioned a letter from N.W. to Mr. Volney on that subject. Dated New York, July 10, 1796. (See Document, No. 13)

In 1797 N.W. determined to collect materials for a history of Epidemic and Pestilential diseases. For the purpose of obtaining authorities, he consulted books in a public library in New York: then visited the libraries in Yale College, and in the University of Cambridge, and afterward went to Philadelphia to examine books in the Loganian Library. This examination brought to his knowledge many valuable authors before unknown to him, and none did he more admire than that eminent writer, Thuanus, whose elegant and classical Latin gave him great delight.

Most medical gentlemen, from whom he requested information, most cheerfully complied with his wishes, and treated his design with respect. But making a request, one day, to the editor Dr. Bard, he received a very abrupt answer by way of rebuke for understanding to write on that subject, without professional attainments.

No. 33

Being weary of the drudgery of superintending the publications of a newspaper, he determined to remove his family to New Haven, where he could enjoy more leisure and have better advantages for educating his children than he could enjoy at Corlaer's hook. On the last day of March 1798, he left his residence with his family, embarked on board a ship commanded by Capt. John Miles and landed in the evening at New Haven. He took the house built by Benedict Arnold which had been forfeited and sold to a Mr. Sloan. This house, which was unfinished, he afterward purchased and completed.

During the summer of 1798, N.W. had occasion to visit New York in August, when the Yellow Fever was beginning to show itself; and on his return to New Haven, he was taken with a bilious fever, probably of the same kind. From this he recovered; but he had two or three relapses in which the disease took the form of a regular tertian. These left him in terrible health, which continued several months. This was the only instance of his being affected with severe disease, after the age of twenty years.

After being settled in New Haven, he continued for two or three years to write for his newspaper in New York, which had been left in the care of his nephew, Ebenezar Beldin.

Here he also proceeded to write the *History of Diseases*, which was published in Hartford in the Year 1799, in two volumes Octavo. A manuscript copy of it was sent to England, and published by the Robinson's in the year 1800. This work brought no profit to the author, and the publication in England did not indemnify the publishers. The work was little read, and excited little notice. One fact however is an exception, and deserves to be mentioned.

No. 34

In the year 1813 N.W. received a letter from Dr. Ennalls Martin of eastern Maryland, with the copy of a pamphlet published by the Doctor. This gentleman had to encounter insuperable difficulties in certain diseases which prevailed in his neighborhood in the year 1813 and 1814. He lost most of his patients; till he changed his course of treatment, in consequence of reading the *History of Epidemic* by N.W. and attending to facts furnished by that history. After changing his practice, he saved his patients; a fact which gave him great satisfaction. In consequence of these events, he wrote and published an account of his treatment of the diseases, in a pamphlet which he dedicated to N.W.

This history of diseases was however little noted for more than twenty years: when the remarkable phenomena of the hectic cholera called the attention of physicians to the work; and these phenomena most clearly verify the theory which the author has occurred from historical facts, and attempted to establish.

In June 1799 N.W. was elected a member of the Court of Common Council in New Haven. In the winter of the same year, he took an active part in establishing the Connecticut Academy of Arts and Sciences, and in the October following, he assisted in obtaining a charter for that institution.

In January 1800, N.W. wrote "Ten Letters to Dr. Priestly," on the subject of the French Revolution, and on various political topics. Some of the author's friends, who generally accorded with him in opinions, thought that in these letters, he had treated the Doctor[42] with too much severity. (Document No. 15)

In 1799, N.W. read before the Connecticut Academy, a dissertation on the supposed change of temperature or moderation of cold in Winter, in modern times, in consequence of the clearing and utilization of the earth in Northern latitudes. This dissertation was published with other papers of the Academy, in the year 1810.

No. 35

During the inveterate was between the combined powers and France, in the Revolution, Great Britain took vigorous measures to intercept the trade of neutral nations to that country, and at various times, orders in council were to take neutral vessels bound to France. In some instances, these orders were considered by neutral nations as grossly violating their rights. To counteract the effect of these orders violent and unwarrantable retaliatory orders were issued by the governing powers in France. These decrees operated mostly upon the trade of the United States, and occasioned frequent remonstrances from our government.

These controversies induced N.W. to examine the subject of neutral rights, and in 1802 he published an "Essay on the Rights of Neutral Nations," in which he traced the history of such rights from antiquity to the present period. Mr. Duponceau[43] of Philadelphia afterward told N.W. that he had read all the treatises on that subject, which he had formed in the English, French, Italian and German languages; and he gave it as his opinion that this essay of N.W. was the best he had seen. He said the same thing to others.

In the same pamphlet with this essay is a Brief account of the origin and condition of Banks and Insurance Companies, which the author took great pain to collect from the officers of those institutions. Among the accounts, that of the origin of the First National Bank, in 1781, is perhaps the most interesting; containing some facts not generally known or now wholly forgotten.

In April 1800, N.W. was elected by the citizens of New Haven to represent them in the General Assembly, and he continued to be elected for several years in jurisdiction.

About this time, the conduct of President Adams in dismissing from office the secretaries Pickering and McHenry⁺⁺ was the subject of much discussion, and occasioned no little ferment in the public mind. After much inquiry into the causes, N.W. thought it his duty to support the President, as far as his influence extended. This occasioned some difference between him and his Federal friends, who generally exposed the cause of the secretaries. But this difference was not of long continuance.

No. 36

In the year 1800 he began to write a series of books, intended as a system for the institution of youth, in various branches of learning. To these volumes he gave the title of "Elements of Useful Knowledge." The first volume was published in 1802; the second in 1804; the third in 1806; and the fourth in 1812. The three first contained geography and history of the United States and of the eastern continent; the fourth contained a history of animals. These books were much used for many years, in the schools in Connecticut. And they laid the plan of compilation by other persons, who profited by plagiarisms from these volumes.

In May 1801 N.W. was appointed a Justice of the Peace; in 1806, he was appointed a justice of the quorum; and second Alderman of the city. In these offices of the county and city courts, he continued till the year 1810.

In the year 1800, N.W. began to compile a dictionary for schools; but the plan not pleasing him, he destroyed the manuscript. In 1806 he published a "Comprehensive Dictionary of the English Language," which was an enlargement of Entick's English dictionary. This was generally well succeeded, and two editions of abridgments of it were afterward published; but the success of the latter was frustrated, chiefly by means of the popularity of Walker's dictionary, which had thus recently been published in the United States.

NO. 37

In May 1802, upon the report of the Controller of Public Accounts, representing to the General Assembly, the inconveniences experienced in vesting the public monies in the funded stock of the United States, N.W. and Elizur Goodrich Esq.,[45] then clerk of the House of Representatives, had a conversation on the subject of making some permanent provision for securing and rendering productive the money in the treasury. It was agreed by them that it would be expedient to vest the monies in bank stocks as fast as they were received into the treasury; but as the state had not the privilege of submitting to any of the banks in Connecticut, it was suggested to establish a state bank, of which should receive the stocks of the state; and it was agreed that N.W. should introduce a motion for a committee to consider the subject. This was done, and Gov. Treadwell of the Council was chairman of the committee. The committee reported in favor of appointing a committee by the legislature to confer with the president and director of the several banks, with a view to induce them to receive the monies of the state. The Treasurer and Controller were appointed for this purpose, and a confer-

ence between them, and committees of all the banks took place the
following summer. But the banks utterly declined to take the monies of the state, without a premium; as the stock of the bankers was
then from 20 percent to 25 percent above par.

During the October Session of the legislature, in the same year,
certain gentlemen in New Haven petitioned for the charter of the
banks, and offered to take all the monies of the state, as part of the
stock. This proposition excited an alarm among the stockholders of
the banks, who appointed committees to oppose the project. These
committees thus offered to take two hundred thousand dollars of
the money of the state, in installments payable in twelve or fifteen
years, for which they would pay the state six percent, per annum;
but the offer was not accepted; and nothing was effected at the session. At the same time, the sum of about fifty thousand dollars was
lying in the treasury unproductive.

No. 38

At the session of the legislature in May 1803 N.W. determined
to make one more effort to establish a state bank or induce the several banks then existing to receive the public money at par; being
confident that they could use it to advantage, he therefore formed a
bill for a state bank, and that he might not appear to be too officious
and ardent in the measure, he persuaded Mr. Canfield of Sharon
and Mr. Norton of Gorham to copy and introduce it into the House
of Representatives. The bill was printed by order of the House. This
alarmed the banks, and the directors of the Hartford banks met the
next evening and authorized their President, Mr. Caldwell, then a
member of the House, to offer to the General Assembly to receive
all the public money, as new stocks, at par. This step was followed
soon after by the New Haven and the Middletown banks; but the
New London and Norwich banks did not then unite in the proposition. The offer of three banks, after much consideration and some

differences by the legislature, were accepted by the committee of the two houses, and a bill was passed for the purpose.

In May 1803, when N.W. was not a member of the legislature, a petition for a state bank was presented by James Hillhouse,[46] Elias Shipman, John Morgan, and others: this was advocated before both houses, but it failed in the House of Representatives. At the next session in October, when N.W. was a member, the petition was again presented, and advocated before both houses. On this occasion the directors of the New Haven banks had a hearing to prove or show that they were able to accommodate the merchants with the necessary loans. The petition for a state bank was violently opposed by committees of the bankers and by some of the most respectable members of legislature; but it was granted by the house, and negated by the Council. The same petition was presented and heard again in May 1806, but too late in the session for action upon it, and it was continued.

NO. 39

At the next October Session, N.W. with the aid and concurrence of Lincoln Baldwin, James Hillhouse, and others, formed the project of a state bank, which was to unite all the banks in the state, by authorizing them to subscribe the amount of their whole stocks. The object was, by a friendly coalition, to blend them all into one bank, consisting of a mother bank and branches in the principal cities; and then to invest a clause in the Charter to restrain the legislature from ever establishing any other institution of the kind. A clause was invested in the bill giving to the banks a capacity of being enlarged by subscription of new stocks, whenever the dividends rose beyond a certain amount. This project was intended to prevent the use which has since occurred, in the multiplication of banking institutions; an evil which was clearly foreseen at that time. But the influence of all the banks was expected to oppose this scheme, and with success. An application was then pending for the Charter of a bank at Bridgeport and to defeat the project of a state bank, the friends of the bankers then existing, united with the petitioners for a bank at Bridgeport, and a charter was obtained. After the application for a bank in Derby, the opposers of the state bank discovered their mistake, and some of them expressed to N.W. their regret that his project had not been adopted.

In 1783, N.W. compiled a grammar, on the principles of Dr. Lowth, with various modifications. This passed through several editions. But in the course of his subsequent researches, into the history & principles of language, he became satisfied that some of his grammar, which was published in 1808, with the title of "A Philosophical and Practical Grammar of the English Language." This with alteration and improvements now bears the title of "An Improved Grammar of the English Language."

NO. 40

In the year 1803, N.W. wrote a letter to a number of respectable mechanics and seamen in New Haven, proposing the formation of a society for the relief of unfortunate families, on the same principles of those of the Charitable Society in Hartford, before mentioned. The following is the substance of the letter:

"The wise and humane policy of our ancestors has incorporated into our system of goverment a general provision for the poor of all descriptions, and the taxes necessary to carry the laws on this subject into effect, constitute no small part of our public burdens. But it is well known that the means of subsistence furnished to the poor by public bodies are often scanty, and the poor are under the necessity of taking their lodgings with persons whose habits are very different from their own; and many persons of sober habits and good character will rather suffer want in private dwellings, than submit to become associates with such persons as must often compose a large part of the residents in an alms-house.

In the vicissitudes of life, no man or family however prosperous and wealthy can calculate, with certainty, upon continuing in easy circumstances. Sudden losses at sea, or by fire; the death, sickness or inability of the head of a family, and various other misfortunes often reduce families from comfortable circumstances to real distress and compel then to solicit the charitable aid of their friends.

The poor of this class seem to stand on different ground from those who, by their vices or their laziness, fall into indigence and contempt; nor can it be reconciled to humanity, that merchants, seamen, salary-men and their families, and other persons, who, by their daily industry and services, have lived in comfortable or in affluent circumstances, and who, without a fault, are reduced to want by losses, sickness, the death of the head of a family or the like misfortunes should be placed on the footing with the outreach of society.

NO. 41

To make a more liberal provision for unfortunate people of this description, it appears to be commendable, that, while we are in prosperous circumstances, we should establish permanent and increasing funds, the interest of which may be appropriated for their relief. For this purpose, let a society be formed with such officers and under such regulations, as the subscribers shall direct each subscriber engaging to pay, towards the common fund, an annual sum, according to his choice; and the interest to be used for the relief of such as may be in want, especially the families of subscribers. In this way, they may be saved from the mortification of depending on the town.

For the purpose of encouraging an institution of this kind I will bind myself, my heirs, executors and administrators, and I do by this writing, thus obligate myself and them, to pay annually the sum of ten dollars, for the term of ten years, to such person as the society shall authorize to receive the same, to form a part of the funds of the society: on this condition however that a society shall be formed for the charitable purposes herein mentioned, within three months from this date."
New Haven   NW

June 7, 1803

No answer was returned to this communication. But not long after the mechanics formed a society for promoting their mutual

interest, which, it is believed, still subsists. Another class of gentlemen formed a charitable society, which with President Day for their
head, collected a considerable sum of money. After N.W. removed
to Amherst, the meetings of this society were discontinued; but the
treasurer of the society loaned the money, and saved it with interest
until the hospital was founded; when the money was appropriated
to that institution.

No. 42

While resident in New Haven, before his removal to Amherst
N.W. was often called on to use his pen in various writings. He
assisted in founding two schools, and provided their charters. He
drew a remonstrance for the merchants, and resolutions of the city,
in opposition to the restrictions on the trade of the country, by the
embargo and non-intercourse.[47]

At what particular time, N.W. began to think seriously of attempting the compilation of a complete dictionary of the English
Language, is not known. But it appears that soon after leaving New
York in 1798, he began to enter particular works and authorities on
the margin of *Johnson's Dictionary*, to be used, if occasion should
offer. As early as in February 1807 he issued a Circular informing the
public of his design and of the general plan of the work; accompanied with commendations from the faculty of Yale College, of Nassau Hall in New Jersey and of Williams College in Massachusetts
and of President Wheelock[48] of Dartmouth College. In August of
that year he issued a paper to obtain subscriptions for the proposed
dictionary, in *advance*, as his own resources were not deemed adequate to the object; but the success was inconsiderable. Indeed his
plan was not fully digested at that time; but was afterward much
enlarged.

No. 43

In the year 1808 the religious views of N.W. were materially changed. Information of this fact coming to the knowledge of his brother-in-law, Judge Dawes of Boston, the judge sent him a letter with a pamphlet containing sentiments not in accordance with those which N.W. had embraced. This called forth a reply from N.W. in which he gave a succinct relation of the manners in which his views had been changed. The following is the substance of the letter, but with some additions and commendations, made by his own hand in 1832, stating some facts which he deemed it inexpedient to communicate at the time the letter was written.

New Haven December 20, 1800

Dear Brother,

I have received your letter of Oct. 25, with a copy of *Review of Hints on Evangelical Preaching* enclosed. I have read both the letter and the pamphlet with attention, and I trust with a sincere desire to learn the truth. The subjects of them are important; but as I differ from you and the writer of the pamphlet on several points, which may be among the fundamental and essential doctrines of christianity, I will take the liberty of communicating to you, at some length the grounds of my own faith; being "ready to give an answer to every man that asketh me a reason of the hope that is in me, and (I trust) with meekness and fear."

You inform me that "you give me the pamphlet as a text only, on which you request my opinion, that you may know whether it is true, that I have lately received [No. 44] some impressions from above, not in the ordinary way of ratiocination—that you are no disbeliever, though you have many doubts, that you could never believe satisfactorily in the conversion by a ray of light—that the case of Col. Gardener, which you read when young, though the facts seem to be admitted, forms no ground of a general rule, and that you have thought to exercise our talents, such as we have to obtain knowledge, and honestly to abide by its dictates, is all that can be expected by our maker."

This candid avowal of your own opinions demands from me a faithful and applied exposition of mine, and the reasons on which they are founded. Errors are always mischievous, but never so much so, as in the concerns of our immortal souls, and in the relations which exist between God and ourselves.

Being educated in a religious family, under pious parents, I had, in early life, some religious impressions; but being too young to understand fully the doctrines of the Christian religion, and falling into vicious company in college, I lost those impressions, and contracted a habit of using profane language. This practice however was not of long duration; I relinquished it, considering the vice as, without an apology, and as unbecoming a gentleman as it is improper for a Christian.

At the time I took my final degree, Sept. 1778, the country was impoverished by the war, and little encouragement was presented to a young man for entering into any professional employment. Having neither property nor powerful friends to aid me and being little acquainted with mankind, I knew not what business to attempt, nor by what means I could obtain subsistence. [No. 45] Being set afloat in the world at the age of twenty, without experience and without a father's aid, my mind was embarrassed with solicitudes, and almost overwhelmed with gloomy apprehensions. In this state of mind, I read Johnson's Rambler with unusual interest, and with considerable effect on my opinions; for when I closed the last volume, I formed a firm resolution to pursue a course of virtue through life and to perform moral and social duties with scrupulous exactness—a resolution to which I have adhered though doubtless with many failures. I now perceive that I ought to have read my Bible first; but I followed the usual course of young men, and attended more to the duties which man owes to man, than to the duties which man owes to his creator and redeemer.

For a number of years past, I have been more impressed with the importance of regulating my conduct by the precepts of christianity. Of the being and attributes of God I have never entertained a doubt; and my studies and frequent contemplations on the works of nature have led my mind to most sublime views of his character and perfection. These views produced their natural affect of inspiring my mind with the highest admiration, and reverence of that Being, mingled with gratitude for his favors; and for some years last past, I have rarely cast my eyes to heaven, or plucked the fruit of my garden, without feeling emotions of gratitude and admiration.

Still I had doubts respecting some of the doctrines of the Christian faith, such as regeneration, election, salvation by free grace, the atonement and the divinity of Christ. These doubts served as apologies for my forebearing to make a profession of religion; yet I could not read, without some [No. 46] compunction and alarm, the declarations of Christ "that whoever shall confess me before men, him will I confess before my father who is in heaven; but whoever shall deny me before men, him will I also before my father who is in heaven." I could not however bring my mind to assent to the confession of faith required in the calvinistic churches, as the condition of admission to their communion. The truth is, I fortified myself as well as I could from the rebukes of conscience, by a species of skepticism, and endeavored to satisfy my mind that a profession of religion is not absolutely necessary to salvation. I placed great reliance on good works, so called, or the performance of moral and social duties, as the means of salvation, although I cannot affirm that I wholly abandoned all dependence on the merits of the redeemer. You may readily suppose that, in this state of fluctuation and indecision of mind, I neglected many duties of piety.

About a year ago, an unusual revival of religion commenced in New Haven, and frequent conferences of private meetings for religious purposes were held by pious and well disposed persons in the congregational societies. I felt an opposition to these meetings, being apprehensive, that by affecting the passions too powerfully, they would introduce enthusiasm or fanaticism which might be mistaken for religion. I expressed these fears to some friends and particularly to my family, including in them the importance of a rational religion and the danger of being misled by the passions.

My wife was however friendly to these meetings, and she was joined by my two eldest daughters who were among the first subjects of serious impressions. I did not forbid, but I rather discouraged their attendance on private religious meetings.

No. 47

Finding the feelings of my family wounded by my opposition and believing I could not conscientiously unite with them in a profession of the calvinistic faith, I made some attempts to persuade them to join with me in attending the episcopal service and ordinances. To this they

"Memoir of Noah Webster, LL.D."

were opposed. At some times, I also determined to separate from my family, leaving them to attend the congregational society.

In this situation my mind was extremely uneasy. A real desire to unite myself with some church by a profession of faith; a determination not to subscribe to all the articles of the Calvinistic creed; and an extreme reluctance against a separation from my dear family in public worship, filled my mind with unusual solitude. On examining the creeds of the two churches however, and the conditions of admission to church communion, I found less difference than I had before supposed as to the essential doctrines of Christianity; and a conversation with our pastor, Mr. Stuart, removed some of my objections to our own confession of faith.

During this time, my mind continued to be more and more agitated as in a manner unusual, and to me new and unaccountable. Frequently every day, and in the midst of occupations and business I was suddenly seized with impressions which called my mind irresistibly to religious concerns and the awakening. These impressions induced a degree of remorse for my conduct, not of that disrupting kind which often attends convictions; but something which operated as rebuke or reproof.

These impressions I attempted to stifle or remove by reasoning [No. 48] with myself and endeavoring to quiet my mind by a persuasion that my opposition to the wishes of my family and to the awakening, was not a real opposition to rational religion, but to enthusiasm or false religion. I continued for some weeks, in this situation, utterly unable to quiet my mind, and without any effort to provide peace and consolation from the only true source. Instead of obtaining peace, my mind was more and more disturbed; the impressions and rebuke of conscience grew stronger and stronger, till they interrupted my studies.

One morning, I entered my study and seated myself for writing or reading, when a sudden impulse upon my mind arrested me, and subdued my will. I instantly fell on my knees confessed my sins to God, implored his pardon, and made my vows to him that from that time I would live in entire obedience to his commands, and be devoted to his service.

From that time I enjoyed perfect tranquility of mind; my views of religion were wholly changed; all my opposition to the doctrines of God's sovereignty, election, the agenda of the spirit in regeneration, the atonement, and the divinity of Christ, was completely vanquished; I was surprised that I could ever have had any enmity to doctrines

which I could then cordially embrace, which indeed seemed to constitute all that is excellent in the Christian system.

You will perceive first, that this change of my views cannot be
ascribed to any efforts of my own reasoning, on the subject of religion.
It was a change independent of volition, for my will was struggling
against it, till the moment when I yielded to an impulse, which, if not
irresistible was sufficient to subdue my opposition.

NO. 49

I now began to understand and to relish many passages of the
scriptures, which were before not intelligible; or at least which appeared mysterious. The first time, I read the following passage, after
my change of views—"But the comforter who is the Holy Spirit,
whom the father will send in my name, he will teach you all things, and
bring all things to your remembrance, whatever I have said to you," I
was struck with surprise that I had read the passage a hundred times
before, without realizing the truth of the promise and without any def-
inite views of the subject.

This is a brief statement of faith, and I cannot reflect without
trembling what would have been my condition had I been left, as I
might justly have been to pursue my open course of opposition to the
revival and to the humbling doctrines of your holy religion. But my
reconciliation to those doctrines is cordial, and I trust will be durable.
Indeed from comparing my own preferred views of the religion of
Christ, with the history of the old testament saints, and that of good
men under the Christian dispensation, I am convinced that the calvinistic doctrines as now generally received, are not only true, but that they
are the only genuine religion of the Bible.

In the month of April last, I made a profession of faith and joined
myself to God's visible church. In this most solemn and affecting trans-
action of my life, I was attended by my two eldest daughters. I felt
some compunction that I had not sooner dedicated myself to the service of God, but it was with heartfelt satisfaction that I could then
present myself before my maker and say "Here am I and the children
which thou hast given me." (Thus far the letter.)

No. 50

The following fact is remarkable. Not long after I had become reconciled to the doctrines of scriptures, I was for sometime afflicted with a local pain. I used various remedies for it without success. After being disappointed repeatedly I resolved to supplicate ease from the only Being who is able to deliver us from troubles. I rose in the morning, retired to my study, and falling on my knees, I earnestly prayed God for relief. No sooner were my words heard, than the pain ceased, and never returned. That this was a supernatural interposition of divine power, I do not know; but the fact I know; respecting this there can have been no deception and the frequent recollection of this fact has had no small influence in confirming my faith through life. And it deserves to be considered, whether modern Christians, on the ground that miracles have ceased, do not go too far in denying or disbelieving the special interposition of divine power, in the ordinary course of God's moral government; and whether this is not a material difference between the Old testament saints, and modern Christians.

(Here may follow my letter to Judge Dawes in Manuscript and the copy printed in the *Panoplist*, July 1809.)

No. 51

In June 1810, N.W. declined a re-election to the office of Alderman, and that of Justice of the Peace and quorum with a view to devote his attention to the compilation of a dictionary. For this undertaking he was very ill provided with the proper books; but he imported some rare books, which could not be found in this country; and with these and some borrowed books he determined to prosecute the work.

At this period, he had to encounter great obstacles. His family was large and apprehensive, and for a period, his income was not sufficient to furnish subsistence for them in New Haven. He had foreseen this deficiency in his income and made attempts to sell his house, with a view of retiring into the country; but without success. He then attempted to obtain funds by subscription, but his proposals did not meet with adequate success. In addition to these discouragements, his undertaking was not countenanced by many influential men, on whose opinion he had reliance. On the contrary it was opposed by many, and particularly by gentlemen in South Carolina, whom his friend, Dr. Ramsay, considered. He was also assailed, with great virulence, through the press: and few men, even among his friends, had confidence enough in the success of the undertaking to wish either property or a favorable opinion, upon the issue. In this situation, he was doomed to pass a long time in great solitude. A few friends made liberal advances to aid him for a time; but he was compelled at last to yield to circumstances. In July 1812, he sold his house in New Haven, and purchased one in Amherst in Massachusetts, which was new and unfinished, but which he finished in a few weeks. To this he removed his family, the first week in September following; and here he resided for the ten succeeding years. He had a few acres of land, the cultivation of which contributed both to his health, and to gratify his love of agricultural employments most of his time he devoted to study and writing; and the interruption of his sedentary labors, by his attention to his land, and by an attendance, during the sessions of the legislature for three years, 1814, 1815, 1819, was probably favorable to his health.

While resident in Amherst, N.W. assisted in forming the Bible Society in Hampshire County, and a society for the promotion of agriculture. Before the latter, he delivered an oration in October 1818. He was present at the first meeting of the gentlemen in Northampton, in which a circular to the three near counties was prepared, suggesting to the citizens to convene in town-meetings, and address memorials to the legislature on the subject of public grievances, and of proposing a convention of delegates from all the northern and commercial states, to consult on measures in concert, for procuring alterations in the constitution for giving to them a due proportion of representation, and secure them from the exercise of powers injurious to their commercial interests. He was a member of the House of Representatives, when the proposal for a convention was made, and advocated the measure. His speech on the occasion was published in two newspapers: the *Weekly Messenger* in Boston, Nov. 4, and the *Dedham Gazette,* Nov. 4, 1814. He attempted also to induce the legislature to raise a fund for the support of common schools, by a sale of lands in Maine, introduced a bill for the purpose, but the project failed. Being one of the Committee on banking in 1815, aware of the pernicious tendency to the multiplication of banks, he used his influence to prevent the granting of any charter for a bank, one only was granted, which was to a bank whose charter had expired (in New Bedford).

No. 52

The principal event which took place while N.W. resided in Amherst, and in which he was concerned, as an actor, was the establishment of a college in that town. The circumstances which attended the origin and final accomplishement of this important event, were very extraordinary, and well deserve a distinct narration. See the *History of Amherst College.*

No. [53]

In August 1822, N.W. removed his family to New Haven, and erected a house, with a view to complete and publish his dictionary. But he could not execute the work to his mind, without some books which could not be procured in New Haven. He therefore determined before its publication, to visit Europe, partly with a view to gain access to rare books, and partly with a view to ascertain more accurately the state of the English language in England; also to sell the copyright of the work in England, and promise it to be published, if practicable. Accordingly, accompanied by his son, he sailed from New York, in the ship *Edward Quesnel,* Capt. Hawkins, June 15, 1824, and arrived at Havre de Grace July 10. He repaired to Paris, where he remained about two months, examined the more popular works on the physical sciences, to find the terms of recent origin which it might be proper to introduce into his dictionary. He then proceeded to England by the way of Dieppe and Brighton, crossing the channel in a steamboat September 17, in a warm calm day as pleasant as any weather in July. He proceeded from Brighton to London and then to Cambridge. There he remained till February 1825, having free access to several libraries, particularly the University library. There he became acquainted with Professor Lee[49] the celebrated oriental scholar, and several other gentlemen of literature, and there he finished writing his dictionary in January 1825.

From Cambridge, he went to London in February, where he remained till May. He offered his manuscript to certain booksellers, and one of them had a part of the manuscript in possession three or four weeks, and from circumstances, it was evident that this part of the manuscript was put into the hands of a gentleman then writing and publishing a dictionary. The booksellers declined publishing the *American Dictionary:* the great publishers being engaged in a new edition of Todd's *Johnson,* and in the new works of Richardson. N.W. then determined to return to his native country. He sailed from Cowes May 10 in the Ship Hudson, Capt. G. Champlain, and arriving in New York June 10, 1825, having been absent from that port a year and three days.

NOTES to Section III

1. George Wyllys (1710–96), grandson of Governor George Wyllys (1590–1645) was secretary of the colony and then of the state of Connecticut between 1730 and his death in 1796. His son Samuel (1738/9–1809) replaced him as secretary and held the office until his death in 1809. Samuel was captain of the First Regiment of Connecticut militia before and during the first months of the American Revolution and took part in the Siege of Boston. He was a notable attorney in Hartford.

2. John Webster (d. 1661) emigrated to Massachusetts Bay Colony in the early 1630s and moved to New Towne, now Hartford, in 1636.

3. Eleazar Mather (1637–69) gathered the First Church of Northampton.

4. For more on Webster's ancestry, see Noah Webster, *Webster Genealogy,* compiled and printed for preservation only by Noah Webster (New Haven: N.p., 1836), Brooklyn, N.Y. [Privately printed: 1876].

5. King Philip (1640–76), whose Indian name was Metacomet, was chief of the Wampanoags and son of the legendary Massasoit. The war was fought ferociously, ending with Philip's death in 1676.

6. Dr. Nathan Perkins (1727–1843), minister in West Hartford during Webster's youth, became a leading Connecticut evangelical in the 1790s.

7. Ezra Stiles (1727–95) scholar, clergyman, lawyer, astronomer. President of Yale, 1778–95.

8. On Yale during this period, see above, II. "Miscellaneous Letters and Essays," sec. 1, "Class Confession, 1778."

9. Samuel Johnson (1709–84), British lexicographer and essayist. The *Rambler's* didactic moralisms appeared in British newspapers in the 1750s and later in one volume.

10. Oliver Ellsworth (1745–1807), perhaps the best-known and most successful attorney in eighteenth-century Connecticut. Webster studied law with him in 1779. He was a member of the Contintental Congress, 1777–83, and held many political offices including U.S. senator from Connecticut, 1789–96, when he resigned to become chief justice of the Supreme Court. His son, William Wolcott Ellsworth, married Webster's oldest daughter, Emily.

11. Titus Hosmer (1737–80), member of the Continental Congress and lawyer in Middletown. He was also a poet and encouraged Joel Barlow to write the "Vision of Columbus."

12. Chauncey Goodrich (1759–1815), graduated from Yale in 1776 and became a successful lawyer in Hartford, became active in politics as a representative in the U.S. Congress (1793–1801) and senator (1807–13). A staunch Federalist and good friend of Webster, his son Chauncey A. Goodrich married Webster's daughter Julia and assisted in the publication of the second edition of the *American Dictionary* in 1841.

NOTES TO SECTION III

13. James Duane (1733–97), member of the Continental Congress, mayor of New York, successful lawyer and New York District Court judge, co-wrote the final draft of the Articles of Confederation.

14. Ezra L'Hommedieu (1734–1811), Yale graduate and perpetual public servant in New York; member of the Continental Congress.

15. William Livingston (1723–90), son of Patroon Philip Livingston, became the first governor of New Jersey (1776–90) and served as a delegate to the Constitutional Convention.

16. John Canfield, lawyer in Sharon and member of the Connecticut legislature.

17. John Trumbull (1750–1831), poet and member of the Hartford Wits; wrote *Progress of Dulness*(1772–73), a satire on formal education, and *McFingal* (1782), a comedy. He also collaborated with Joel Barlow and others on a social satire, *The Anarchiad* (1786–87).

18. Joel Barlow (1754–1812), Webster's best friend while they were undergraduates at Yale. Barlow wrote the democratic and patriotic poem "Vision of Columbus" (1787), but when he lived in France between 1788 and 1805 and became thoroughly enamored with French revolutionary principles (as seen in "Advice to the Priviliged Orders" of 1792), the friendship ended.

19. Webster's reading of Jean-Jacques Rousseau's (1712–82) *Contrat Social* (1762) heavily influenced his early political thought, and can be clearly seen in his *Sketches*. He adopted Rousseau's idealism, especially his ideas about individual and governmental rights, antislavery, and popular sovereignty. For a further analysis, see chap. 2 of Rollins, *Long Journey*.

20. For Webster's place in the events leading to the Constitution, see above, II. "Miscellaneous Letters and Essays," sec. 9, the letter to James Kent.

21. Webster played a key role in several states' adoption of copyright laws. For details of his efforts, see Warfel, *Webster*.

22. Dr. Henry Moyes performed numerous experiments, and wrote pamphlets on electricity and storage batteries.

23. Tobias Lear (1762–1816) served as Washington's private secretary between 1785 and 1792 and again in 1798-99. He married Washington's niece and held several diplomatic posts in the 1790s and after Washington died. Benjamin Lincoln (1733–1810), a member of the Massachusetts legislature in the 1770s rose to major general in the army and played a key role in the victory at Saratoga.

24. John Dickinson (1732–1808), wealthy and powerful conservative politician in Delaware and Pennsylvania, opposed the British Stamp and Sugar acts but also opposed the more radical patriot moves against them. His *Letters from A Farmer in Pennsylvania* ... summed up the opposition to the acts, but as a member of the Continental Congress he voted against independence. During the war he served in various military offices and served as a delegate to the Constitutional Convention.

25. Benjamin Rush (1745–1813), Philadelphia physician and friend of Franklin, Paine, and Jefferson; signer of the Declaration of Independence; ardent reformer dedicated to improving hospitals and prisons, abolishing slavery, and ending alcohol abuse.

NOTES TO SECTION III

26. David Rittenhouse (1732–96), highly respected astronomer and mathematician credited with many advances in both subjects. Friend of Rush, Franklin, and many of the revolutionary generation and member of the Royal Society of London.

27. David Ramsay (1749–1815), member of the Continental Congress from South Carolina, is best remembered as a prominent physician and author of one of the earliest histories of the United States.

28. Thomas Fitzsimmons (1741–1811), wealthy merchant who supplied the Continental Army with valuable war materials. Member of the Continental Congress, U.S. House of Representatives (1789–95), and supporter of a strong centralized government in the 1780s and 1790s.

29. John Fitch (1743–98). Born to poverty, Fitch became an itinerant clock-cleaner before the war and constructed a steamboat in 1785. It became his obsession: he spent the rest of his life trying to raise funds from benefactors to produce it commercially. He succeeded only in gaining a reputation of being insane, and died lonely and in poverty of an overdose of opium in Kentucky.

30. Ebenezer Hazard (1744–1817), postmaster general during the Confederation and publisher of newspapers. Also collected and published historical documents and inspired Jeremy Belknap to publish his histories of New Hampshire. He and Belknap made many negative remarks in their correspondence about Webster, describing him as a pompous egotist. Francis Childs was the publisher of the New York *Daily Advertiser* and became the printer of the Webster *American Magazine*.

31. Rebecca Greenleaf (1766–1847), daughter of wealthy Boston merchant William Greenleaf and sister of land speculator James Greenleaf (1769–1843); the latter went to debtors' prison along with Robert Morris.

32. John Winthrop, *A Journal of the Transactions and Occurrences in the Settlement of Massachusetts and Other New England Colonies from the Year 1630 to 1644*, edited by Noah Webster (Hartford: Elisha Babcock, 1790).

33. Joseph Dennie (1768–1812), often called the "American Addison" for his pithy essays on politics. As editor of the *Farmer's Weekly Museum* and the Philadelphia *Port-Folio* in the 1790s and early 1800s he took the side of the Jeffersonians and became one of Webster's harshest critics.

34. Edmund Charles Genet (1763–1834), a young, flamboyant French diplomat who attempted to influence the Washington administration into siding with France during the struggles with Britain in the 1790s by building and arming ships on American soil. Washington requested and accomplished his recall, but Genet decided to stay in America and settled in New York.

35. Timothy Phelps (1757–1812), a prosperous merchant in New Haven.

36. The French Revolution was originally hailed by Webster and nearly all Americans as an extension of their own efforts for independence from arbitrary authority. With the widespread use of the guillotine to behead almost anyone who fell out of immediate favor during the "Terror" of the early 1790s, many Americans became strongly critical, and in fact opposition to "French principles," or "Jacobinical terrorism," as many Federalists like Webster referred to it, became one of the primary divisive issues between Federalists and Republicans.

37. John Jay (1745–1829), one of the authors of *The Federalist* essays in behalf of the new Constitution in 1787, became chief justice of the Supreme Court and gover-

nor of New York. As chief justice he negotiated a treaty with England, called Jay's Treaty, that was the first with a world power for the new nation. In the Treaty of Paris (1783) ending the revolution, England had agreed to vacate several military installations in the Northwest Territories. They failed to follow through, and also seized many American ships in the Atlantic on their way to France. Jay negotiated a further agreement to vacate the forts and also the appointment of a bi-national commission to decide upon the proper boundaries and compensation for the ships. It was a controversial treaty and further exacerbated the divisions that led to the Federalist and Republican parties.

38. James Kent (1763–1847), an active Federalist who served three terms in the New York Assembly and a member of the New York Supreme Court.

39. Rufus King (1755–1827), delegate to the Massachusetts General Court in 1783–85 and to the Continental Congress in 1784–86, he was in favor of the Constitution in 1787. He played an important role in the development of American foreign policy as U.S. senator in 1789–96 and from 1813 to 1825 as well as minister to England in 1796–1803. He was one of Webster's biggest supporters in the early 1790s but parted ways with him with the divisions in Federalist ranks in the late 1790s.

40. William Currie (1754–1828), Philadelphia physician. His letter to Benjamin Wynkoop led to Webster's *Brief History*.

41. Constantin François Volney (1757–1820), French collector of antiquities and Egyptologist.

42. Joseph Priestley (1733–1804), English clergyman and natural philosopher, discoverer of oxygen. He arrived in Philadelphia in 1794 and wrote several essays supporting the French Revolution and in favor of the nascent Republican movement.

43. Peter Stephen Duponceau (1760–1844) came to America with Baron Von Steuben as his personal secretary in 1777, became an assistant to Robert R. Livingston, head of the Department of Foreign Affairs for the Confederation. He later became a lawyer and philologist of note.

44. James McHenry (1753–1816), secretary of war under Washington and Adams, was dismissed along with secretary of state Timothy Pickering because they took direction from Alexander Hamilton rather than Adams.

45. Elizur Goodrich (1761–1849), New Haven attorney, professor of law at Yale, mayor of New Haven, and member of the House of Representatives from 1799 to 1801.

46. James Hillhouse (1753–1832), officer in the Connecticut militia and in the Continental Army, member of the Connecticut legislature, U.S. Congress (1791–94), U.S. Senate (1794–1810), and treasurer of Yale.

47. "Memorial of the Inhabitants of the Town of New Haven [to President Jefferson]," *Connecticut Journal*, Sept. 1, 1808. See also several resolutions in opposition to the Embargo and Non-Intercourse measures in the *Connecticut Herald*, Jan. 3, 1809, written by Webster.

48. John Wheelock (1754–1817), president of Dartmouth for twenty-five years.

49. John Lee (1783–1866), collector of antiquities and founder of an important museum of artifacts. Member of the Royal Society of London, more widely known after 1828 as an astronomer and original member of the Royal Astronomical Society.

IV. The Diary of Noah Webster

First page of Noah Webster's diary.
Photograph courtesy of the New York Public Library.

A DOMESTIC JOURNAL
HARTFORD, JANUARY 1ST 1784.

There are five volumes of Webster's diary in the Papers of Noah Webster at the New York Public Library. The two major volumes are bound in buckram. Volume I runs from January 1, 1784, to July 1, 1786, and is 8 inches by 6½ inches by ½ inch. The first six pages are blank and seventeen pages have been cut out at the beginning of the volume. The remaining parts of the cut pages contain remnants of ink, indicating that they were used. The covers are worn, the binding is broken and the pages hang together in three groupings.

The second large volume begins on July 2, 1786, and ends on September 18, 1820 (the entry marked September 3, 1821, is misdated). It is bound in buckram, worn but intact, and is 8 inches by 6 inches by 1 5/16 inch, and all entries are in ink. On the flyleaf is written:

A Diary
Vol 2d
July 2—1786
Hartford

Three smaller volumes also exist in the collection. They are bound in paper and all are 3¾ inches by 6 inches by ½ inch, and were obviously travel diaries Webster carried with him. He copied all or part of the entries into the larger volumes at a convenient time. One volume contains entries from from November 1 to November 4, 1785; March 27 to 30, 1787; May 1 to 5, 1787; and July 6, 1786, to March 26, 1787. A second contains entries from May 2, 1785, to October 1, 1785, and the third from November 4, 1785, to July 3, 1786. Entries are in ink and pencil.

In cases where Webster copied only part of the travel diary notation into the larger volume, I have included the remainder in a footnote. Italicized words were added by Webster at a later time than the original entry.

NOAH WEBSTER JUN.
A DIARY—*from 1784.*
Lodgings—Capt John Skinners Hartford.

January 1st 1784. Thursday, at home.

2.   rode to West division; returned, and at evening danced at Mr. Collier's.

3.   P.M. rode in company with Mr Church Mr J Pratt and Mr W Coit as far as Dr MLeans seat.

Sunday 4th.   At Church; heard Mr Strong A.M. and Mr. Boardman P.M.

5.   Attended town-meeting Convened to deliberate upon the proposed act for incorporating the Town with City Priveleges. Meeting adjourned.

6.   Attended Town-meeting—a committee was appointed to fix the limits of the proposed City. Adjourned till Friday, the 9th.

7.   At home.

8.   do. [Ed. Note: An abbreviation of "ditto."] Assembly convenes at N Haven.

9.   Attended Town meeting, where it was unanimously voted to prefer a Petition to the Assembly for incorporating a part of the town.

10.   At home.

Sunday 11th.   Attended meeting at Hartford, A.M. and at Weathersfield P.M.

12.   At home. Death of Mrs Keith Et 88.

13.   do.

14.   do

15.   do. S Smith married and Dr M Lean died.

16.   do.

17.   do.

Sunday 18.   At Church, as usual.

19.   At home.

20.   do. At evening discovered a Comet.

21.   do. saw the comet in the evening and danced at Dr Butler's.

22.   PM. rode to Weathersfield.

23.   At home. A great rain, which sweeps away Mr Kneeland's Fulling Mill.

24. At home.

Sunday 25. At church.

26. At home.

27. do.

28. do.

29. Rode to Norwich in a sleigh, with Mr Coit.

30. Visited my friend Sh'–Breed, rode from the landing to town and danced at evening, lost my hat.

31. returned to Hartford. dined at Col Trumbulls, at Lebanon.

Sunday February 1st. At Church.

2. At home. PM. rode to Rocky Hill, to join a large company of Gentlemen and Ladies from Weathersfield and Middletown. No sooner had we arrived there, than it began to rain and the snow melted; returned to Hartford the same night, but most of the company tarried and returned next-day in wheel carriages.

3. At home. Three men belonging to Weathersfield drowned at Woods River on the north road to West division.

4. At home.

5. Rode to West division. The bodies of the three men are found.

6. At Westdivision, detained by a storm of snow.

7. Returned to town.

Sunday 8th. At Church, dined with Mr Coit and Mr Charles Hopkins at Wm Colliers.

9.
10.
11. } At home.
12.
13.

14. do. (one would think me a steady man)

15th. Sunday. At Church accordingly.

16.

17. At home, (too cold to be abroad).

18. do. At evening rode to Weathersfield with the Ladies, who reminded us of the mile-stones and bridges.

19. P.M. rode to E. Windsor, had a clergyman with us, who sang an excellent song. Mile stones and bridges almost totally neglected.

20.

21. At home.

Sunday 22d. As usual.

23. At home.
24. set out for N Haven, lodged at Middletown.
25. Arrived in the City; attended a philosophical Lecture delivered by President Stiles in the Chapel.
26. Came to Weathersfield. Lodged at Col Chesters.
27. Arrived at Hartford.
28. At home.
Sunday 29th. At Church, extremely cold.
March 1st. At home.
2. Do. Superior Court at Hartford.
3. do.
4. do.
5. Rode to Westdivision.
6. Returned.
7. Sunday. At Church of course.
8. At home.
9. do, and at court. Heard the verdict of the Jury in a case of C. Wells vs. S. Belding. The P^{lf} brought an action of trespass against the d^t for cutting and carrying hay from the p^{ts} land. The case was this: The P^f had an execution against one Eb^r Belding and levied it upon a piece of land which J. Belding, son of the said E. Belding, had conveyed to the D^t without the authority of his father who was yet living. The D^t entered and took the profits of the land under this false title, while the p^l entered also and cut grass by virtue of the title acquired by the execution. The verdict of the jury was, *not guilty;* but 3 Judges—Griswold, Pitkin and Huntington, were of the opinion that the Plain and whose right was indisputable had acquired such a possession by virtue of the execution that he might bring an action of trespass. The Jury were ordered to reconsider the verdict and found for the P^f his damages.
10. At home and Court.
11. do, do, received a letter from Genl. O Wolcott, giving me liberty to prefix his name to the recommendation published in the Institute.
12. do, do, PM. sick enough.
13. At home very unwell. The little indispositions of life are essential to happiness. Uninterrupted felicity never fails to cloy, indeed there is very little pleasure without preceding pain. The author of the universe seems to have framed it with a view to give his

creatures an opportunity to exert virtues, which could not exist without natural and moral evil. If it were impossible for mankind to sin, there would be no virtue in preserving their rectitude. If there were no pain, misery, misfortune or danger to which they could be exposed, patience, humanity, fortitude and prudence would be but empty names. The result of this doctrine is to teach us a peaceable submission to the evils of life and calm acquiescence in the disposition of divine providence which suffers no more evils to take place in the system than are necessary to produce the greatest possible good.

Sunday 14th.   Though better in health, yet too much indisposed to attend public worship.

15.   Still unwell. When a cold takes fast hold, it is no easy matter to disengage it.

16.   do do. Middletown Convention meets the fourth time.

17.   much better. First Meeting of the Cincinnati at Hartford.

18.   Almost well. My good Ol. Wolcott very sick.

19th.   do. Mr Wolcott better.

20th.   I am Nearly recovered. Finished the second reading of Vertot's Revolutions,—a valuable History.

Sunday 21st.   At Church. Mr Wolcott's disorder, which is inflammatory increased. Capt Skinner rides to Litchfield to inform his Parents. What an anxious suspense a person experiences when a friend is in danger!

22.
23. } At home
24.

25.   do. very dull, watched last evening with Mr Wolcott. In the evening saw a multitude of pretty faces. But my heart is my own.

26.   Rode up meadow to view the ravages of the water, which was driven out of its channel by the ice.

27.   At home. Saturday is a dull day.

Sunday 28th.   At church, heard an excellent sermon. It is much easier to hear than to remember and practise.

29.   At home. Busy in combating the Convention, a nest of vipers, disturbing the tranquillity of government, to answer selfish purposes.

30.   At home, finished my address to the Convention.

31.   do.

April 1. At home, a small fall of snow.
  2. do.
  3. do, a storm of snow.
Sunday 4th. At church, a small congregation. Bad weather is a common and often a very trifling excuse for neglect of public worship, but bad traveling on a pleasant day is a more trifling excuse.
  5. At home, took a short ride.
  6. do. drank tea at Mr Pomeroy's.
  7. do.
  8. At home. read a little, loitered some, had some company, and visited the Ladies in the evening as usual. If there were but one pretty Girl in town, a man could make a choice—but among so many! one's heart is pulled twenty ways at once. The greatest difficulty, however, is that after a man has made *his* choice, it remains for the Lady to make *hers*.
  9. At home, a fall of snow.
  10. At home, took a short ride.
  11. Sunday. At church. a fall of snow.
  12. Attended Freemen's meeting; chose Col Jesse Root and Capt John Ball to represent this town, a hard struggle to keep out Col. Seymour a convention man. PM. at town meeting. dismissed the members of convention—a fortunate event.

The following page was left blank and filled December 17th 1784. *N Webster jun*.

The Conduct of Connecticut in this affair furnishes a singular epoch in the History of the State. The grant, made by Congress in 1778 to the Officers of the army of half-pay for life, had given much uneasiness to the northern States, which had made early provision for making good the depreciation of Continental Currency to the army. This induced the Officers to offer to relinquish their claim of half-pay for life, for a certain sum in gross, or full pay for a term of years. Congress consented to make the exchange and gave 5 years full pay in lieu of half pay for life. This was accepted by the Army; and it happened just before the army was disbanded. As soon as the dangers of war were past, some individuals in these northern States, particularly in Connecticut, began to declaim against Congress, but principally against this grant to the Officers. These were very suspicious characters—men who had been very silent in the contest, or known to be opposed to the revolution. But they had the address to make themselves believed for a time, by the body of the people. They had their Emissaries, who were duped into their schemes, spreading unfavourable reports of Congress, and defaming these illustrious men in this State, who had been leaders of the revolution. Town-meetings were called and the public papers were filled with their spirited or rather *mad* resolves, as well as with inflammatory publications of individuals. Congress and the bold patriots of this state were represented as Tyrants, and the people as in danger of slavery. A Committee from a number of towns met at Convention in Middletown—with the ostensible view of procuring redress of grievances; but *really*, to change the Council. A nomination of theirs secretly handed about, in which the best men in the State were left out and doubtful characters put in. This however did not Succeed. Convention met three times by adjournment and after passing some feeble resolves, dwindled away.

13. ⎫
14. ⎭   At home.

15.   Fast Day. At Church, very rainy.

16. ⎫
17. ⎭   At home.

Sunday 18th.   At Church, suo modo.

19th.   AM at home; P.M. do.

20th.   Rode to West-division. Hail.

21.   At home, and court. Hail and cold.

22.   At home. this is the first pleasant day.

23.   do.

24.   do. dined at Mr Colts with Sir Peyton.

Sunday 25th.   In Loco usitato. Mr Strongs church abolish the half way Covenant, and all persons who renew the covenant of *[illegible]* are considered as members in full communion. But many churches in Connecticut practice still upon this absurd institution. Into what inconsistencies are mankind led by rigid, illiberal tenets! A *half member* of Christ's church is an *oddity* in religion. Scripture knows no such thing, and common sense rejects the idea, as the creature of superstition.

26th. ⎫
27. ⎪
28. ⎬   At home.
29. ⎪
30. ⎭

May 1.   At home. cold, cloudy, disagreeable weather. Such a Winter and Spring are seldom known in this climate.

Sunday 2.   At church.

3.   At home.

4.   [At home.]
5.   Mr Benjn Boardman, late Minister at E Haddam, installed to
      the Pastoral care of the South Society, Hartford. Prayer by Mr
      Perkins; Sermon and prayer before the installation by Dr
      Goodrich; Right Hand of fellowship by Mr Strong.
6.   At home.
7.   Rode to Lebanon.
8.   Returned to Hartford.
Sunday 9th.   very pleasant and warm, at church.
10. ⎫
11. ⎬   At home
12. ⎭
13.   General Election. No choice of Governor by the freeman.
      Matthew Griswold Esq. chosen by the Assembly. Samuel
      Huntington Esq. Dep Governor by the Freeman. Attended the
      Ball at Evening.
14.   Rode to Windsor PM, with the Ladies.
15.   At home.
Sunday 16th.   Heard Mr Plumb preach, at the North Church.
17.   At home.
18.   At home. PM rode to Weathersfield.
19.   At home. P.M heard the Debates in the Lr house of Assembly
      upon the Subject of the Impost. About 5 oclock the Question
      was put and it passed in the Affirmative—93 against 42. A
      happy event! The speakers against the General Impost were
      Genl Erastus Wolcott, Col Dyer Throop and Mr Tisdal—for it,
      Mr Root, Mr Wm Hillhouse, Genl Parsons, Mr Edwards &c.
20th. Rode to Westdivision.
21.   Attended his Excellency Governor Trumbull to East Hartford,
      on his way to Lebanon retiring from public life.
22.   At home
23.   Sunday, At Church.
24.   At home.
25.   do. commercial bill passed the Lower house
26.   do. Attended Assembly. Debates before both houses respecting
      the propriety of incorporating a part of Hartford. Col Seymour
      and Chauncey Goodrich Esq. agents for the town; Mr
      Chandler and Genl Newbury, Attorneys for the opposition.
      Under Capt George Smith and Mr Saml Wadsworth, two
      perverse souls.

27.　The incorporation of a part of Hartford, voted in the House of Representatives, by a great majority. Just at evening I suffered my horse to run, poor Diversion for a Philosopher!

28.　Rode to West division with Mr Beach and Lady who were bound for Litchfield. Incorporation Bill passed in the Council, to the great satisfaction of liberal minds.

29th.　At home. Part of Middletown Incorporated.

30.　Sunday. At church. Heard Mr Strong AM and Mr Boardman PM.

31.　At home.

June 1.　Set off on a journey through N England. Rode to Canterbury.

2.　Arrived at Providence

3.　Saild to Newport.

4.　Returned to Providence.

5.　Rode to Boston.

6.　Sunday. Very much fatigued. Lodged at Col Ingersol's, Corner of Queen Street Boston.

8.　Dined with Mr Battelle, and drank tea with Mr Bowdoin.

9.　dined with Mr Babcock. Rode to Cambridge and drank tea with President Willard.

10.　Rode in the Stage Coach to Newbury Port.

11.　Took a view of the town.

12.　Rode to Portsmouth.

13.　Sunday. Attended Mr Buckminster's meeting

14.　Took a view of the town. Drank tea at Dr Bracketts. At evening attended a ball and was agreeably entertained; had a fine Partner, but she is engaged.

15.　Sleepy; dull enough to visit.

16.　Drank tea at Col Langdon's. Mrs Langdon is a most beautiful Woman, 20 years younger than her husband.

17.　Rode to Exeter. Dined with Mr Woodbridge. Drank tea with Mr MClintock—Grantard?

18.　Dined with Mr Dearborn, an Ingenious man; took tea with Mr Pickering.

19.　Dined at Mr Robert's; drank tea at Mrs Bracketts.

20.　Sunday. Heard Mr Stephens preach.

21.　Drank tea at Deacon Penhallon's (Penhallow's).

22.　Left Portsmouth with Mr Penhallon (Penhallow). Lodged at Newbury Port.

23.　Arrived in Boston.

24.   Did little.
25.   Dined with Mr Battelle.
26.   too hot for business.
27.   Sunday. went to the Old Church; heard Mr Parsons preach.
28.   Rode to Dorchester, drank tea at Mr Bird's.
29.   Dined with Mr Gore, Majr Sedgwick, Dr Kilham.
30.   Attended Dr Moyse's Lecture on Electricity, in which he exhibited several experiments curious and instructive.

July 1.   Set off for Hartford. Lodged at Shrewsbury.
2.   Lodged at Palmer, &
3.   Arrived in Hartford.
4.   Sunday. Went to meeting, one half day.
5.   did very little.
6.   Went to Westdivision.
7.   Returned.
8.   Removed Lodgings from Capt Skinners to Dr Fish's, with a view to study Law under the instruction of Mr Trumbull.
9.   At home.
10.   Rode to Westdivision.
11.   Sunday. At church.
12.   did no great.
13.   Rode to Rocky Hill and brought up a number of books purchased in Boston.
14.   In Statu quo. Mrs Smith died suddenly of the small pox at 11 PM.
15.   Mrs Smith buried at 10 AM. Saw a small vessel Launched at 4 P.M.
16.   Put some boxes of books aboard Capt Moses Williams to carry to Boston.
17.   At home.
18.   Heard two excellent discourses of Mr Strong. He strongly enforced the necessity of resignation to the dispensation of Divine providence from this consideration, that not only the events which we call blessings, but all the evils of life are designed to answer some valuable purpose.
19.   modo quo.
20.   Attended City meeting, where several by-Laws were passed, Inspectors, &c. chosen.
21.   Very steady, over books and paper.
22.   Writing an answer to Dilworth's Ghost.

23.   At Books
24.   do. a dull day.
25.   Sunday. At Church. Heard Mr Strong, A.M. and Dr Goodrich P.M.
26.   Engaged with books.
27.   Rode to West division with Mrs Barlow, &c. Drank tea with Mrs Gay.
28th.   At books.
29th.   Drank tea at Dr Hopkins.
30.   Sober as a Judge.
31.   Do. Walked to Col. Talcotts with Mr Wolcott. Heard of the Bankruptcy of Parker, Hopkins & MacLean, Compny of Auctioneers, New York.

Sunday. August 1.   At Church. Singing performed AM wretchedly; PM We did better.
2.   First ate Watermelons. Received the Coat of Arms of our Family engraved on Copper Plate, &c. 270 copies struck off by Benjn Hanks, Litchfield.
3.   Very warm. At evening attended the Serenade.
4.   Too warm to stir.
5.   Finished reading Dr Blairs Lectures. Excellent Criticism!
6.   Received a Letter from Mr Law.
7.   Did nothing worthy of particular notice.
8.   Sunday. Ad Ecclesiam, profectus fui.
9.   Returned Mr Bliss his hat which he left in place of mine at Norwich 30th January.
10.   Amusing myself with books and with a flute. What an infinite variety of methods have mankind invented to render life agreeable! And what a wise and happy design in the organization of the human frame that the sound of a little hollow tube of wood should dispel in a few moments, or at least alleviate, the heaviest cares of life!
11.   My eyes are too weak to study constantly, at least one of them. I will favour them early, for it is much easier to prevent, than to cure a disorder.
12.   Read a little Law and some poetry, if a man lays up a few ideas every day and arranges them, it is enough.
13.   Ibidem.
14.   Capt. Israel Seymour of this City killed by Lightning, as he was standing near the front door of his own house. Several

persons were near him. Mr Alderman Wyllys was in the room, but not touched. Mr Alderman Bull was struck, but received a slight injury. Mr J. Root son of Mr Alderman Root was affected, and also Mrs Wattles. The house was considerably damaged.

Sunday. 15. Attended meeting. PM both Congregations met and Mr Boardman delivered a sermon suitable to the occasion and a great concourse attended funeral.

16. Mortified to find my eyes too weak to study. But if I cannot devote my time to books, I can to the Ladies. A Remarkable hurricane at Southington.

17.

18.

19.

20. I do little; but better than nothing.

21. Settled an action between Mr J Caldwell and Mr Thoms Bird of Salisbury.

22. Sunday. Mr Strong is unwell. Heard Mr Boardman in the fornoon.

23.

24. Study as much as I can.

25. Walk to West Division

26. Saw my Friend Coit from N York.

27. Walked to the New Bridge.

28. Get Grapes in the North Meadow.

29. Sunday. At church AM, but Mr Strong was too ill to preach a Sermon. At 2 o'clock had a heavy Storm of wind, rain and hail.

30. Saw an object of charity, a cripple, born in Dartmouth, Massachusetts, Trip, by name. His arms are small and without much strength, and so confined to his body that he can move his hand only; his legs are bent under and grow to the thighs, several inches from his knees; they are wholly useless. His body is nearly perfect; his health and his speech good; he is 48 years of age and lives by begging; he rides in a horse-cart, where he sits upright upon his legs and he guides the horse with a small cord which he handles with his fingers. He was carried from his native place in youth, and lost his residence—there being no record of his birth. On such an object it is a virtue to bestow charity. Mrs Silliman, of Fairfield, and two sons, arrive and Lodge at Dr Fishes.

31. Extremely hot. Mrs Silliman proceeds on her journey to the Eastward. Mrs Fish sets off for Killingworth. Miss Polly Alsop arrived to spend a few days at Dr Fishes.

Sept. 1.

2.

3. Warm and Rainy weather.

4. No news.

Sunday 5th. Heard Mr Strong AM and Mr Boardman PM. Attended public singing in the evening.

6. Divide my time between the Ladies and books.

7. Superior Court begin their Sessions.

8. Attended Court. Had a long dish of Discourse in the evening Mr Lyman concerning slander. In the evening too wrote a letter to Mr Buckminster, by Mr Langdon.

9.
10. } At Court.
11.

12. Sunday. At church. In the evening sang at the State house and had a large collection of people. Some from Rhode Island, &c.

13. At Court, heard the arguments in the famous case of Benton, on a Petition of John Thomas for a new Trial.

14. Heard the case of Genl Erastus Wolcott *vs.* Loomis for raising the water of a pond and flooding the Plaintiffs Land, on proof that the water was raised no higher than it had been used to be raised time out of mind, verdict for the Defent.

15. Walk to Westdivision. Procured my Brother's horse to ride to Salisbury.

16. Set off for Litchfield, at 11 oclock, in Company with Miss Rachel Stone and Mr Wm Marsh and his Sister, arrived at 8 oclock.

17.

18.

19. remained at Litchfield, detained by rain, hospitably entertained by Dr Sheldon. Dined With Mr Kirby.

20. Proceeded to Salisbury.

21. To Egremont by the way of Shelffield. Lodged at my Uncle Steele's.

22. Returned to Salisbury.

23. Detained by rain.

24. Set off for home, with Miss Sally Norton in company. Lodged in Litchfield.

25. Arrived in Hartford, 8 oclock at evening.

26. Sunday. Mr Strong too unwell to preach and his wife dangerous. I attended Mr Boardman's meeting.

27. Attended City meeting at the State House, where Laws respecting swine & the Highways were passed, & City Sisters appointed.

28. Rode to Westdivision.

29. Rode to Westdivision with Mrs Fish for Peaches, returned and dined at Mr Pratts on Sea-Turtle, passed the Afternoon in jovial mirth. Heard of the death of Governor Griswold, and also of that of Ezra Stiles at Portsmouth in Virginia.

30. Introduced to Miss Jennett MCurdy. Dr Sheldon arrived with his Lady from Litchfield.

October 1. Finished Reading Betsey Thoughtless. Novels will not bear reading but once. It would be well if people would not permit children to read romances, till they were arrived to maturity of Judgement.

2. Made a collection of books to be purchased in London. The Report of Govr Griswold's death proved to be premature.

Sunday 3. Heard Mr Strongs brother preach. Mr J Y Seymour married this evening to Miss Bull, Sister of Mr Amos Bull.

4. Passed the day in reading, writing and visiting, at Mr Alderman Wyllys's.

5. do.

6. do.

7. do. Col Wadsworth arrived in Hartford from Europe. Introduced to Miss McCurdy.

8. Learnt a song of the Ladies, a Sweet Country life. Drank tea with Miss Polly Sheldon.

9. Rode out with the Ladies. Miss McCurdy, Miss Field and Miss Stoughton, Majr Wyllys and Mr Wolcott.

10. Sunday. Went to Mr Boardmans meeting.

11. The Marquis Le Fayette arrived in this City, from Albany. Curiosity had led him to attend a treaty with the Indians. But Govr Clinton who attempted to treat with the savages for the State of N. York, when a treaty under Congress was on the carpet, failed of success. The Marquis is entertained by Col. Wadsworth.

12. The Marquis dined with a number of gentlemen at L Bulls. Money is so scarce that I cannot borrow 30 L for a few weeks, giving 12 pr cen t interest and good security; finished reading the Mirror.

13. The Marquis left this City on his way to Boston.

14. Nothing material.

15. Heard of the death of Olivia, the only child of my Sister Lord at Salisbury. A child not three years old, the third or fourth she has lost. I wrote a Consolatory letter and shed a tear.

16. My birthday. 26 years of my life are past. I have lived long enough to be good and of some importance. Introduced to Miss S Dwight of Springfield, a fine Lady.

Sunday, 17. Mrs Strong died, after having dragged out a life of 25 years in perpetual pain. Attended meeting at the South.

18. Nothing Material.

19. Attended Mrs Strong's funeral at the meeting house.

20. Miss Sally Hunt arrived in town. A Lady of Merit. Wethersfield Fair begins.

21. Miss J. MCurdy leaves town the regret and tears of her friends show how much she is loved. And surely no person on earth deserves more. Such sweetness, delicacy, and beauty are rarely united. May I ever love her; for heaven is her friend.

22. Walked to Westdivision. Saw my Uncle Eliphl Steele, and Cousin Amanda.

23. Returned and found Mr Law in town. My Uncle dined with me.

24. Sunday. Mr Boardman preached PM for Mr Strong.

25. Started the idea of dancing to-morrow.

26. Invited the Company, had a brilliant Assembly and an agreeable evening.

27. Much fatigued.

28. Read Belisarius, a work that deserves to be engraven on the heart of ever Legislator.

29. Finished my remarks on Domestic happiness and the character of Emilia, Institute 3d part.

30. Was invited too late to dine at Mr Barlows.

Sunday, 31. Accepted the invitation of yesterday, heard Mr McClewer preach AM., and Mr Boardman P.M.

November 1. Writing the character of Juliana. PM very sick with the head-ach.

2. A fine morning—Never were six weeks of finer weather in the autumn, than the last.

3. Rode to New-Haven.

4. to Fairfield and Greenfield. Obtained Liberty of Mr Dwight to insert a number of extracts from his Conquest of Canaan, in 3d Part of ye Institute.

5. Returned to New Haven, in Company with Mr Dudley Baldwin.

6. Rode to North Killingsworth, a terrible road for a Sulkey.

Sunday, 7th.   I arrived with my classmate Mr Ely Minister of the Parish.

8. Rode to Saybrook and Lyme; passed the evening at Mr MCurdys.

9. Returned to Hartford over Haddam-Hills, very glad to arrive safe. County Court sits.

10. Attended to a few domestic concerns. PM. went to Court. My friend Tracey stayed with me at night.

11. Had a family dance at Mr Barlow's in the evening.

12. Drank tea at Mr Trumbulls. In the evening walked to Capt John Olcotts, where I was introduced to Genl Hazen and his Lady.

13. Engaged in a Suit of Ebr Webster vs Medad Webster brothers—both my fathers cousins: a rainy day, bought me a winter hat.

14. Sunday. Mr. Strong preached—welcome event after so long an interruption.

15. I rode to Westdivision to see my sister Lord; returned.

16. Attended Court.

17. do. Saw Mr Dwight of Springfield. Mr Frothingham applied to me for instruction in the English Language &c to qualify himself for teaching a school at Middletown. (*This man was killed in the West with Major Wyllys.*)

18. At Court. A Case of Mr Lyman tried in Court. He was sued as an executor of his own wrong on his fathers estate, but the cause ended in his favour.

19. At Court.

20. Do. Mr. Langdon arrived from Portsmouth.

21. Sunday. At church.

22 & 23d.   At Court, heard the Case of the State against John Benton for lascivious carriage. Mr Tisdale admitted as a witness, when Ben-

ton had an action of defamation depending against him for prop-
agating the report of his behaviour, found Not Guilty.

24.   At Court—In the evening plead the cause of a Mr Brown,
before Col. Seymour. Caleb Bull versus Brown—Book debt.

25.   PM. Plead for Mr Bidwell vs Abiel Wilson before My Father.
Over ruled the defts plea of abatement. Court adjourned, till.

26.   Very rainy. Attended Court.

27.   Introduced to Dr Skinner of Colchester.

Sunday 28th.   At Church.

29.   Finished reading Mr Barlow's Columbus.

30.   Making extracts from papers respecting Susquehannah;
preparing to write a brief account of the settlement of that
country and the treatment of the Settlers by Pensylvania.

December 1st.   Finished the extracts. Walk to Westdivision to keep
Thanksgiving.

2.   Spent Thanksgiving at My Fathers as usual, with my Brother
Charles and Sisters. Heard Mr Parmale. My classmate is dead
at the southward.

3.   Rode home.

4.   Water in the River rises fast. Mr A Will lost, last night, 40
barrels of cider, washed away from the banks.

5.   Sunday. As great a freshet in the River as is Common in the
Spring.

6.   River still higher. Attended a Ball in the evening at Mr
Collyers. 25 Gentlemen and 53 Ladies. Col. Wadsworth, Mr
Colt, &c. were Present.

7.   Very dull.

8.   Hear a rumour that the Revd Mr Mather is dead, and also that
Mr Ol Lewis is dead, both in the Southern States; and Mr
Williams and Mr Fuller. The weather is remarkably warm.
Little or no ice has yet been made in the river.

9.   Drank Tea at Capt Hopkins.

10.   Went to Westdivision and plead Mr Bidwells cause. Judgment
for the Plaintiff. About 10 oclock this evening, it begins to
snow for the first time this year. Genl Green and Lady in town
on his way to New York.

11.   Pleasant weather, with 3 inches of snow.

12.   Sunday. At Church.

13.   At evening met for the purpose of establishing a literary club.
Had a family dance at Mr Wm Bull's. A Meteor seen at half

past 7 oclock, passing rapidly from SE to NW and followed by a loud report.

14. Cold; ice makes in the river.

15. Made a contract with Mr Theodore Pitkin for 42 reams of paper, large Demi. More moderate weather.

16. Received the Paper. Attended town meeting, for Choosing town-officers—adjourned till the first Tuesday in January. Spent the evening at Dr Hopkins with Mr Talmadge, &c.

17. The Printers begin the 3d part of the Institute. (*The weather is so warm that there is little or no ice in the River.*)

18. At home.

Sunday 19th. Heard Mr Boardman in the forenoon. Mr. Wm Patten preached for Mr Strong PM, but I was at home. Cold and some Snow.

20. Cold weather. A meeting of ye Common Council.

21. Superior Court began the adjourned Sessions, could not attend.

22. PM, attended Court.

23d. Very cold. Connecticut River first closed with ice.

24. At Court heard the Quaker Case. The Plaintiff brought an action against the Defendant, a *Shaking Quaker*, vulgarly so called,—one Mechum of Enfield—for harbouring his 2 daughters, who had been persuaded to embrace that curious religion. On evidence it appeared that they were convinced that this new fanaticism was the *way of God*, (to use their own expression) and had left their fathers house, merely to enjoy their worship unmolested. Judgement for the Defendant.

25. Christmas. Dined at Mr Morgans.

Sunday 26. At Church.

27th. At Court.

28. Attending to various small matters; at evening met and chose managers for the Assembly; also formed regulations for the Literary club.

29. Miss Belcher Came to board with Dr Fish. I read my writings on Susquehannah to Genl Parsons and Mr Judd. Received Tickets for the Assembly.

30. At evening attended the first Assembly, which consisted of about 60 Ladies and 40 Gentlemen.

31. Feel exceedingly well after dancing; close the year.

1785

January 1st 1785. Reward New Year's wishes with Presents.

Sunday 2. Hear Mr Strong preach a good Sermon.

3.   Invited to dine with Capt Skinner to morrow.

4.   Dine with him accordingly; attended town meeting. Appointed
        a committee to apply to the General Court for liberty to build
        a Poor-House; town charges are high; grant a /9 tax.

5.   I finish writing the stories of La Roche & of Edward &
        Louisa, from the Mirror and for the 3d part of the Institute.

6.

7.

8.   Read a little, oversee the Press, & do a thousand little things
        that are important. Send a box of books to Dr Truman & Co,
        Providence.

9.   Sunday. Attend meeting.

10.   Send a writ to Mr Abraham Bliss, Lebanon for selling my hat,
        which he took at Norwich in January, 1784.

11.   Disappointed of a sleigh-rid—no matter, it is a trifle.

12.   Settled with Mr Bliss for selling the hat which he took at
        Norwich on the 30th of January, 1784. He gave me a note for
        50/ on demand.

13.   Send 300 books in Sheets to Mr Thomas at Worcester, pr
        Stage. Write an Answer to the second Ghost, who has attacked
        the Institute.

14.

15.   Do little remarkable.

Sunday 16.   PM, Hear Mr Williams preach.

17.   Speak for a sleigh to ride into Windsor.

18.   Disappointed of my ride, obliged to correct the press, at
        evening went to Mr Strong's, but it rained & the members did
        not generally attend—adjourned.

19.   Write another answer to the Ghost. I have exposed myself to
        malice, envy, criticism &c. by my publications. I knew I should
        when I began and I am prepared for an attack on all sides. Mr
        Morgan & his Lady dined with us.

20.   At evening attend the 2d Assembly—about 80 Ladies and 50
        Gentlemen.

21.   Very dull.

22. More lively—read Dr Price's excellent remarks on the American Revolution.

23. Sunday. AM at meeting.

24. Went to Wethersfield to plead a case for Mr Isaac Mix before Saml Wm Williams Esq. Book debt of 28 years standing, judgement for debt, but I saved the interest.

25. Adjourned County Court. Hartford. At evening attend Club; converse upon the great question What are the means of improving & establishing the Union of the States?

26. At Court.

27.

28.

29. nothing Special.

30. Sunday, hear Parson Perkins.

31. A very cold day.

February 1. Pleaded my first cause before the Jury—Ebenezer Webster vs Medad Webster, my fathers Cousins; action of debt against the administrator. The Deft pleaded in bar that the Plf had not exhibited his accounts within the 6 months limited by Ct of Probate. Judgement for Plaintiff, I recovered in the first cause.

2. Cold attending upon court. My Brother Charles has an heir born. (*Charles Webster.*)

3. At evening attend Assembly, very agreeable indeed. Saw Miss Becca Fish dance a Minuet for the first time; of 3 Ladies, she did best.

4. Correct the last half Sheet of the 3d part of the Institute. Mrs Chorgh, Mrs Jones, Mrs Romons, Mrs Morgan visit this after at Dr Fishes.

5. The third part of the Institute finished.

Sunday 6. A little unwell, at home.

8. At evening attend club, question, whether Polygamy is prohibited by the Law of nature.

9. Court breaks up, I pass the evening at Mr Marsh's.

10. Walk to Westdivision.

11. Pass the afternoon at Mr Perkin's, with my uncle Steele and Mr N H Whiting.

12. Return to town.

13. Sunday. At meeting. Dl Smith and S Bull published.

14.   Nothing material of my own. Court of Common Council
        admit the Marquis de la Fayette and Mr St John and his Sons,
        to the freedom of the City. Enact laws respecting fire &c.
15.   Attend Club. Converse on this subject, 'Whether the being 3
        attributes of a God are discoverable by the light of nature.'
16.   Writing Politics. Govr Merrill married.
17.   Do. At evening Gallant the Ladies to the Assembly.
18.   Receive a Letter from Dr Leavenworth at Charleston, And Mr
        Coit—New York
19.   write politics. (*Sketches of American Policy.*)
20.   Sunday. Go to meeting.
21.   Get out an execution against A Bliss.
22.   Attend city meeting, pass laws with respect to fire. Grant the
        Freedom of the City to the Marquis Le Fayette and the Consul
        Mon St John.
23.   Write.
24.   Thursday night died Mr Arnold Jones, (*Grandfather of Rev.
        Henry Jones.*)
25.   Finish the Sketches of American Policy, and give it to the
        Printers.
26.   Mr Jones buried. The Masons walk in procession.
27.   Sunday. At church, that is meeting. Daniel Smith married to
        Miss Sally Bull.
28.   A very Pleasant day, prepare for a journey. Attend Society
        meeting to grant Mr Strong his last year's Salary, which ought
        to have been paid the first of January. We are always behind
        hand in Connecticut. At evening receive a letter & a Guinea
        from Mr Jedediah Strong of Litchfield.
March 1st. Set off for Providence, rode to Dorrance's, Voluntown.
2.   dined at Mr Dexters, Providence.
3.   Wait on Mr Robin, Tutor of College, have an invitation to the
        Assembly, refuse & sorry for it.
4.   Settle accts with Dr Truman & Co, wait on President
        Manning. Take tea with the Miss Browns.
5.   Sail to Newport. Lodge at Mr Fry's; take tea at Mr Ellery's.
6.   Sunday. Take tea with Majr Lyman.
7.   Ship what books remain unsold to Baltimore by Mr Hopkins,
        take tea with the celebrated Miss Vernon.
8.   Disappointed of a passage to Providence, take tea with Miss
        Arnold and Miss Cornwall.

210

MARCH 9, 1785

9.	Again disappointed of a passage.
10.	Sail at 9 oclock & arrive at Providence at 12, & dine & ride to Voluntown.
11.	Proceed to New London. Lodge at Mr Allen's Coffee House, take tea & sup with Mr Nathl Richards, pass the last of the evening with Mr Seton of New York.
12.	Ride to Lyme.
13.	Sunday. At meeting; hear Mr Johnson, dine at Mr MCurdy's.
14.	A stormy day; pass the day with the Ladies.
15.	Ride to New Haven, lodge at Smith's Coffee house.
16.	Take tea with Mr D Austin, attend the *Sans Souci* at Mr Meigs's. This is a company which meets for cards and social mirth.
17.	Ride to Hartford, attend the Assembly at evening.
18.	Ride to Westdivision.
19th	Return home.
20.	Sunday. At meeting.
21.	
22.	
23.	
24.	Almost sick with a cold; do little.
25.	meeting house seated.
26.	Sell the third part of the Institute to Mr D Jones. Quite sick with a cold, rare indeed for me!
27.	Sunday. At home, but better.
28.	City meeting, reduced the number of common councilmen from 20 to 12 & elected them, meeting adjourned till to morrow. Mr Seymour loses a pair of horses & sleigh in the river.
29.	Employed in business. Cannot attend meeting. Mr Jos Drake takes tea with me.
30.	A snow storm, the snow on the mountains is now from 2 to four feet deep; the river is still closed with ice. Very uncommon!
31.	This evening the Assemblies close.
April 1st	Write a statement of the dispute between Capt J Skinner and Mr J L De Koven.
2.	At evening sup on salmon at Collier's.
3.	Sunday. At meeting.
4th	River gets quite clear of ice.

5.   County Court.

6.
7.   } Attend Court.

8.   A storm of hail & rain.

9.   Nothing remarkable.

10.   Sunday. Several vessels arrive, heard Parson Marsh preach.

11.   Freemen's meeting. Mr Strong preached. Col Wadsworth & Col Seymour chosen to represent this town in Assembly.

12.
13.   } At Court.

14.   Attorneys give the Court a Dinner at Dl Bulls—Mr (*Stephen*) Titus Hosmer and Mr Saml Woodruff examined and (*Note: Judge Hosmer*)

15.   admitted to the Bar.

17th Sunday. At meeting.

18th   At Court.

19th   Cold weather. Snow two feet deep in the western towns. A Fall of hail and snow 3 inches deep.

20.   Fast day. We must fast regularly every year, whether we are plunged in calamities or overwhelmed with the blessings of heaven! Strange superstition! the effect of custom.

21.
22.   } At Court.
23.

24.   Sunday. At meeting.

25.   At Court.

26.   Rode to West division, returned, invited to dine with Mr Morgan.

27.   Court finish their Session. Fair at Wethersfield.

28.   Hear of the death of my good Friend Mr Wm Coit. His loss is to be regretted by every honest man. An Amiable character just rising upon the stage, but he is gone! Hapless youth! Such is the end of earthly prospects!

29.   A very great freshet in the River. Ride to Weathersfield Fair, take tea at Col Chesters & return.

30.   Make preparations for a tour to the Southern States.

May 1. Sunday. River very high & rising.

2.   Set out for South Carolina, arrive at New Haven. See a Balloon ascend—ingenuity of Mr Meigs. It rises several

Hundred feet. Contract with Mr Fitch to print an edition of the 2d part of the Institute.

3. Sail for New York, small wind, put into Rock Harbor, Fairfield; sleep on shore, at Mr Squires.

4th Sail at 4 0 clock and arrive in New York at 7. Lodge at Mrs Sheldons.

5. Take tea at Col Burr's[1].

6. Dine with Mr Law at Nortons. Mr Barnard's Sloop arrives with my baggage, which I put on board the sloop Liberty, Capt Woodger for Charleston. Take tea at Mr Alexr Stewart's.

7. A rainy day, take tea at Dr Coggswells.

8. Sunday. At Dr Rogers' meeting; dine at Dr Coggeswells; attend evening lecture.

9. Pass over to Elizabeth Town, lodge at Smith's where I see Mr Wade.

10. Ride at 3 oclock, breakfast at Drakes in Brunswick, 20 miles; dine at Trenton, arrive at Philadelphia at 6. Lodge at Nicholas's.

11. Dine with Mr S Austin. Take out Certificates for security of Copyright of Institute; of Mr Smith, Prothonotary.

12. Dine with Mr Pelh Webster.[2] Take tea at Mr Austin's.

13. Breakfast with Mr Webster, set off for Baltimore at 2 o'clock; pass thro' Chester, 15 miles, Wilmington 12; arrive at Newport 4 miles; lodge there.

14. Breakfast at the Head of Elk. 18 miles, dine in Bush Town, arrive in Baltimore at 10 oclock;[3] lodge at Grant's.

15. Sunday. Wait on Mr Blakeley; dine with him and take a walk over Col Howard farm. Introduced to Dr Moyes, the celebrated Scotch Lecturer or Natural Philosopher, blind, but sensible. Introd to Dr J. Mann from Massachusetts.

16. Dine at Mrs Sandersons, with Dr Mann, Mr Faulkner Mr Frasier, scotchman, the latter Dr Moyes's assistant; attend his Lecture on light; After having viewed Mr Ridgeley's burying ground enclosed with a brick wall 6 feet high, 2 feet thick, 30 yards in length & 40 in breadth.

17. Get lodgings at Mrs Sandersons attend Dr Moyes Lecture on Phosphorus.

18. Set out for Alexandria; stage waggon breaks down; return to town & hire a horse.[4]

19.   Meet with Mr Brown from Norwich; write a letter home; set
       out for Alexandria arrive at 8 oclock—50 miles.
20.   Visit Dr David Stuart, a member of the legislature; lay before
       him my wishes for a copy-right law; he promises his assistance;
       he introduces me to Col. Symms, another member from
       Alexandria. Afternoon I proceed to Genl Washington's seat, 9
       miles from Alexandria, down the River Potowmack, an elegant
       situation on the bank of the river; treated with great attention;
       continue with him the night. Play whist with the Genl and his
       Lady, who is very social.[5]
21.   Breakfast & return to Alexandria, cross the Potowmack; dine at
       Bladensburg, 12 miles. In proceeding as in haste, I beat a dull
       horse & break my cane—a little vexatious matter; hindered by
       a shower. Ride to Rose's and lodge.
22.   Sunday. Dine at Spurrier's and proceed to Baltimore.
23.   Attend Dr Moyes's Lecture on sounds.
24.   Rainy; attend lecture on electricity; the Dr has 190 hearers
       generally.
25.   at Lecture. Wait on Judge Mools
26.   Take tea at Mrs Clemmons.
27.   Take tea at Mr J. West's, and go to lecture; wait on Parson
       West.
28.   Make provision for a voyage to Charleston, cold weather, want
       a fire at noon.
29.   Sunday. At Mr West's church—horrible singing! P.M. take a
       walk with Dr Mann, Mr Blakeley & Mr Snow.
30.   Go on board the George for Charleston, wind a head, sleep on
       board.
31.   Sail at 5 oclock, with a gentle breeze at NE. Off Annapolis 30
       miles at 10 oclock. Off the southern point of Kent Island at 12,
       in 38° 46^m. A fresh breeze; Lie too at 12 oclock at night!
June 1.   Set sail, arrive at Norfolk at 1 oclock, go on shore. This town is
       low in situation at the bottom of Chesapeak, opposite the mouth
       of Elizabeth River. It consisted of about 300 houses before the
       war, but was burnt, & is not wholly rebuilt.[6] Opposite to it, on
       Elizabeth river is Portsmouth, a small pleasant town.
2.   Go on shore also, eat cherries. This is a place of business.[7]
3.   Sail at 5 oclock, a small breeze, tide carries us aground, wait for
       flood, sail at half after 3 PM. Not venturing to double Cape
       Henry in the night, we cast anchor.

4. Sail, clear the cape, but wind ahead, speak the sloop *Three Sisters* Capt Parkison, in 3 days from Charleston.

5. Sunday. Head wind. In 36°. 37.[8]

6. Head wind, in 36°. 15.

7. Calm, very disagreeable.[9]

8. Several sail in sight, speak a sloop from New York bound to Newburn; head wind, make Hatteras.[10]

9. A squall, succeeded by a calm, rough sea off Hatteras; we pass the cape 6 leagues distant in sight of breakers, water from 6 to 10 fathom.[11]

10. A pilot comes along side to know if we are bound to Ocracock (a passage so called, leading in to North Carolina,) calm till 11 oclock, head wind.[12]

11. Wind contrary, & calm.

12. Sunday. Strong breeze ahead.

13. Wind ahead, at noon in 34° 44.[13]

14. do. in 34°. 33.

15. Calm till 10 o'clock. Discover the shoals of Cape Lookout, take a dolphin, & eat, having first boild him with silver to prove him not poisonous. Fish on copper banks are poisonous. Harpoon a porpoise, but lose him.[14]

16. Head wind, in 34° 7.

17. do in 34° 15, carried backward by a current. Currents run every way on this coast, between the Gulph stream & land.

18. Head wind. A squall, then calm.

19. Sunday. Take a young shark—fresh provision expended![15]

20. Wish to go on shore, but there is no landing here; it is a double shore.

21. Begin to think of allowancing the water. Lat 34°. 3. cast anchor & send a boat on shore; get a little wood but no water, sail.

22. Go on allowance of water—2 quarts pr man,[16] is enough for me.

23. calm, wind still a head.

24. A favorable breeze, Good news!

25. breeze continues favorable. Take 2 young Dolphin for dinner. We Pass the Rattle Snake, a shoal, much frightened, at 10 feet water. Pilot comes on board; cast anchor off the Bar, 12 miles from Charleston, in sight.

26. Sunday—arive in harbor at 8 oclock. Go on Shore & get lodgings at Wilch's in King Street. Pleased with the appearance

of the town. Go to St. Michael's Church & hear Parson Smith. Miss Storer sings Part of Handel's Oratorio—Very odd indeed! A woman sings in Public after church for her own benefit! I do not like the modern taste in singing! P.M. I go to the White meeting & hear a little New England singing. In the evening hear a methodist. The people in Charles town are very polite. They behave with great decency in church. The slaves are kept in good order, they are remarkably attentive at church.[17]

27. Introd to Mr Cazeneau. Open my books at Mr Timothy's & advertise them.

28. Rain, breakfast with Mr MLean; take tea at Mrs Timothy's.[18]

29. Cool. Wait on Genl Gaddesden, an old & honorable Gentleman. Wait on Mr Nott & Mr Palmer, introdd to Mr Badger, teacher of Music.

30. Introd to Mr Richard Hutson Intendant of the City. I register the Institute in the Secretary's Office & get a Certificate.[19]

July 1 and 2. Nothing particular, the weather is hot & the Musketo's troublesome.

3. Sunday. Read Beattie's Theory of Language, lent me by Mr Sam Baldwin.

4. Independence Celebrated with Cannon, musquetry, fire works &c. a balloon set off, takes fire, falls on the market, but the fire extinguished. I ascend the steeple to take a view of the town from the steeple; Charleston is very regular; the most regular of any in America, except Philadel & New Haven. They have a good chime of bells.

5. Wait on Mr Hutson with a note, presenting the Mount Sion Society zoo first part of 100 2d part of the Institute; for the benefit of Winnsborough College. Read a little book called *Kisses*. Walk to Genl Gaddesden. A duel fought between Dr Apedaile & a Mr Taylor.[20]

6. Send letters to Connecticut. Prepare to sail for Baltimore. Dine with Mr MLean. Go on Board.

7. Detained by our anchor's being foul.[21]

8. Weigh anchor, and get under way.

9. A light breeze.

10. Sunday. Take a shark.

11. A squall; a fine 8 knot breeze.

12. Double Hatteras.

13. Good wind, make land—Currituck.

14. Enter the Capes, at 2 oclock A.M.
15. A fair breeze. A gust at N W obliges us to cast anchor, just below Baltimore. Weigh anchor again & reach Baltimore.
16. Lodge at Mrs Sanderson's, with my N England friends.[22] Wait on Dr Allison—who offers me his church for the use of a singing school.
17. Sunday. At home, which is very uncommon. PM Introd to Mrs Blanchard, Miss Blanchard, Mr Johonnot, Dr Mills &c; take tea at Mr Blanchard's & a walk.
18. Arrange some private matters. Procure Telemachus in French & English & a master to teach me.
19. Write letters to Hartford. Meet a number of Gentlemen at Dr Allison's church to agree upon a singing school. Take tea at Mr Wests.
20. Breakfast with Dr Allison.
21. Take a walk with Mr Blakeley. Have a second meeting.[23]
22. Take tea at Mr Blanchard's.
23. Send letters to Hartford.
24. Sunday. At Dr Allison's Church.
25. Meet for singing in the evening; people pleased.
26. Receive a letter from Mr Law, N Y.
27. Begin French.
28. Walk to Fell's Point.
29. Introd to Mr Merrymans. Give the Misses Smith their music Lesson.
30. Move my books from Mr Snows to Miss Goddards.
31. Sunday. At church.
August 1. Teaching Music & learning French.
2. Take tea at Mr Merryman's with the Misses Dorse, Miss Young, Mr Leve.
3. Take tea with Miss Goddard & Mr Snow.
4. Breakfast with Mr Allison.[24]
5. Nothing particular.
6. Take tea with Mrs Clemmons.
7. Sunday. At meeting.
8. Drank tea with Miss Boyd. Introd to Dr Morgan of New Haven. This is my first news from Connecticut.
9. Sail to the fort, meet the East India ship.
10. *Dans mes affaires.*
11. Pass the evening at Mr Merrymans.

12. In statu quo.
13. Walk to Howard's Spring with the Ladies. Breakfast at Mr Merryman's. Receid a letter from Genl Washington. Drink tea at Mrs Clemmons.
14. Sunday. At church.
15. Leave Mrs Sanderson's & take lodgings at Mrs Coxes.
16. Ne rien des Nouvelles.
17. Mr Donneville calls on me—a Dutch Gentleman.
19. Take tea with Miss Goddard.
20. Nothing new.
21. Sunday. At church.
22. Receive Letters from Charleston & Hartford & answer them. Hear my friend Wolcott is married.
23.
24. Writing.
25, 26 and 27. Do little. Go on board the Ballos the ship from China; she was navigated by 3 chinese and a number of Malayans, &c. Begin my remarks on the English language.[25]
28. Sunday. At church; introd to Mr Saml Snow & Mr Mannen Bull.
29. Statu quo.
30. Statu quo.
31. Two Ladies from St Kitts arrive & lodge at Mrs Coxes.
September 1. visit Mr West. Rain.
2. Bad weather.
3. Finish my first Dissertation.
4. Sunday. Begin to sing in church; astonish all Baltimore with ten scholars. Dine at Mr Merrymans.
5. Receive a Psalm book from Mr Barlow.
6. Wait on Parson West.
7 & 8. Great additions to my school; this is the effect produced (by) last Sunday.
9. 10. } Little.
11. Sunday. Church.
12. finishing 2d dissertation.[26]
13. la—la.[27]
14. Settle acct with Mr Snow.
16. Mr. Burgher killed by a fall from his horse.
18. Sunday. At church; tea at Mr Wests.

19.   Take tea at Mr Blanchard's. Introd to Mr John Gardner.
20.   a letter from Mr Babcock.
21.   Finish my 3d dissertation.
22.   Rain. Mrs Courtney buried.
23.   Rain.
24.   A terrible Storm: many vessels lost. Miss Becca Coxes loses her clothes in a sloop from New York.
25.   Sunday. Fill the churches with Music.
26.
27.   In company with Mr Gardner & Mr Blakeley, number the houses in Baltimore—find 1950 Dwelling houses[28] one half of which have been built in 3 years.
28.   Drink tea with Mr Cursons—a respectable character.
29.   At Mrs Callister's with the Ladies.
30.   Finish a 4th Dissertation.
October 1. Very little.
2.   Sunday. Where I ought to be.
3.   Election of Sherriffs; parties run high & some bloody noses.
4.   A miff between Mr Hall—a singer & myself[29]—People in Baltimore have not been accustomed to my rigid discipline.
5.   The Headach hard enough.[30]
6.   Complete my fifth & last Dissertation.
7 and 8. Little.
9.   Sunday. Music at Churches.
10.   Wait on Dr Allison.
11.   Take tea with him, & read my Remarks to him.
12.   Breakfast with him again; he concludes to permit me to read them as Lectures in his church.
13.   Rain.
14.   The Nabob ODonnel married to Miss Elliot;[31] altho' he has an India lass on board.
15.   Sing, in school, in public.[32]
16.   Sunday. My birthday. 27 etatis the revolution of a few years sweeps us away![33]
17.   Drink tea at Mr Blanchards.
18.   Walk on board Capt Palmer, from Portsmouth.
19.   Read my first Lecture, to a small audience, the weather very bad.
20.   Take tea at Mr Cursons.
21.   Read my 2d Lecture.

22.   Read my 3d to a larger audience.

23.   Sunday. Go to the Roman Chapel.³⁴

24.   Read my fourth Lecture.

25.   Repeat my first.

26.   Read my fifth & last Lecture & close my school. The Lectures have recd so much applause that I am induced to revise & continue reading them in other towns.

27.   Attend the Races. Horse-Races in these States, every spring & autumn, are holidays; like the Election & Thanksgiving in Connecticut. 7 horses enter the lists, 5 run 3 four mile heats. The Brilliant wins the purse £ 75.

28.   Nothing.

29.   I ride 20 miles into the Country, with Mr Gittings. Pass Sunday with Mrs Croxalls family.

30.   Sunday. As above.

31.   Return to Baltimore; visit prepare for Virginia.

November 1.   Mr White arrives from New England, offers to take a school. I endeavor to assist him, he obtains some prospects.

2.   It rains.

3.   Get read for a journey.

4.   Set out for Richmond, Virginia, arrive in Alexandria.

5.   Visit Genl Washington. He gives me Letters to the Govr & both Speakers.

6.   Sunday. Return to Alexandria with Major George Washington & Lady, & Mr Shaw, secretary. Go to Church, hear Parson Griffiths. Dine at Mr Herberts.

7.   Dine with Mr MWhir, an Irish literary Gentleman, who keeps the Academy; pass the evening with him & Dr Swift.

8.   Ride from Alexr to Fredericksburg, about 70 miles.

9.   To Richmond, 70 miles.

10.   Lodge at Mrs Allegre's. Wait on Dr Stewart on Mr Moses Austin; take tea with him. Introd to Mr Mumford, to Mr Clarkson from new Jersey.

11.   Wait on Mr Maddison.

12.   Walk over to Manchester, a village west of James River; visit Mr Frisbie.

13.   Sunday. At Church. Dine & walk to Mr Duvals; take tea.

14.   Dine with Mr Saml Hopkins—a very clever fellow.

15.   Dine with the late Govr Benjn Harrison Esq. speaker of the House of Delegates; eat green peas.

16.   Nothing singular.

17.   Dine with Dr Furchee; read my first Lecture to about 30 respectable Gentlemen in the Capitol, where the House of Delegates sit.

18.   Dine with Mr Hopkins; read my second Lecture.

19.   So–so.

20.   Sunday. At home.

21.   A fall of snow.

22.   Read the 3d Lecture.

23.   Walk to Manchester.

24.   Read 4 and 5th Lectures to a small audience & finish.

25.   Dine with Mr Hopkins.

26.   Ride to Petersburg, about 27 miles, settled on a branch of James River; the Indian Queen was formerly called Pokohuntus. The Randolph family descended on one side from this Queen.

27th   Sunday. Take a view of the city; find about 300 houses;[35] an unhealthy place. Dine with Mr Eustis.

28.   Procure Mason Hall to read a Lecture in, to morrow evening.

29.   Disappointed.

30.   At home with my friend Mr Monen Bull.

December 1.   Return to Richmond. Wait on Parson Blagrove.

2.   Ride to Williamsburg, 60 miles. This is a pleasant City, containing about 230 houses. It decays since Government was removed to Richmond.[36]

3.   Wait on Mr Andrews, professor of Moral Philosophy, a sensible polite man. He introd me to Mr Wythe, professor of Law, a good man, one of the Chancery Judges.

4.   Sunday. Dine with Mr Andrews. Walk to the Capitol with Mr Simeon Deane, view Lord Botetourt's Statue, erected 1771 by the Legislature to the honor of that excellent Govr Pass evening with some Law Students.

5.   Procure a room in College for reading Lectures.[37]

6.   Begin with 6 gentlemen only.

7.   Dine with Mr Carter; read my 2d Lect. The Virginians have much pride, little money on hand, Great contempt for Northern people, & amazing fondness for Dissipation.[38]

8.   Read Lectures.[39]

9.   finish them. Two of Genl Washington's nephews attended thro' the whole, & one Mr Harrison.

10.   Return to Richmond.

11.   Sunday. Breakfast & dine with Mr Austin.

12.   Dine with Mr Hopkins.

13.   Troubled with a boil on my cheek.

14.   Set out for the Northward; streams are high and we troubled to ford them, but arrive at the Bowling Green.[40]

15.   Proceed and reach Mr Daniels in Dumfres, a small village. Meet Mr Kirby.

16.   Proceed, breakfast at Mr Kirby's, reach Alexandria.

17.   Deliver Letters to Mr Swift; bad weather.

18.   Sunday. Receive a Letter from Genl Washington & answer it.

19.   Advertise to read Lectures. Invited to a ball of Mr Washington,[41] Genl Nephew, a young imprudent Lad; he prepares supper & liquors to the value of 18 pounds; no persons come & he cannot pay the bill. Virginia hospitality!

20.   Writing.

21.   Number houses—300. Read my first Lecture to 10.

22.   Postpone reading this evening.[42] Mr Wm Hunter is very polite.

23.   Read Lectures to a larger audience. Introduced to the Count Castiglioni, an Italian Nobleman, who attends the Lect.

24.   Dine with Mr Jonn Swift—very polite. Mrs Swift, daughter of Gen. Roberdeau, very agreeable.

25.   Sunday. Christmas Dine with Mr Mure in company with Mr Wilson & Mr Ramsey; take tea with Mrs Swift.

26.   Proceed to Bladensburg, & lodge.

27.   Dine at Spurriers, arrive in Baltimore.

28.   Write Letters & visit friends.

29.   Prepare for Annapolis.

30.   Disappointed. Dine with Mr Blakeley.

31.   Sail for Annapolis, arrive precisely at 12 oclock PM. Enter Annapolis & the New Year, at the same minute.

1786

January 1.   Sunday. Lodge at Mr Mann's. Wait on Dr Shuttleworth with a letter.

2.   Breakfast with him, introduced to Mr Quin.

3.   Introd to Govr Smallwood, a very good kind of Character. Number houses, 260; a pleasant city & more elegant houses in proportion than in any town in America; the earth is covered with verdure. Introd to Majr Lynch, an Irishman.

4.   Write, go to the Assembly, dance with Mrs Davison, wife of an honest Scotchman. Assembly brilliant.[43]

5.   Obtain permission to read Lectures in the State House by vote of the House of Delegates. Begin to read—to about 30 respectable people.[44]

6.   Dine with Mr White, Commissioner from Connecticut, with Mr Richmond, Mr Hamilton, Mr Hollingsworth of Elks, Mr Johnson. Read a Lecture to 14; converse with Mr Loyd,[45] man from the Eastern Shore.

7.   Finish my lectures on the language.

8.   Sunday. No church. I dine in Company with Govr & the Senators.

9.   Breakfast with my friend White. Read a lecture on America.

10.   Return to Baltimore.

11.   Dine with Mr Johonnot, &c. Visit the Ladies; tell them pretty stories.

12.   Set out for Fredericks Town, arrive at Hobbs, 35 miles, lodge.

13.   Proceed to Frederick 15 miles. Introduced to Baker Johnson Esq, to Col. Symm, to Dr Nelson, to Dr Philip Thomas—one of the best of men—to Mr Murdock, no great to Mr Young, to Dr Tiler, to Mr Runcles, the German Parson. Lodge at Capt. Morris'.

14.   Breakfast with Mr Benjn Ogle. Read a lecture to a small company.

15.   Sunday. Hear Parson Beard. Dine with Mrs Long and Mr Neil, with Parson Beard. I should have mentioned I breakfast with Dr Thomas & Dr Ridgeley.

16.   Read Lectures to a more numerous audience.

17.   Breakfast with Mr Ogle; take tea with Mr Beard & finish my Lectures.

18.   Set off for Baltimore. Horse takes a fright, falls & hurts my leg; very cold.

19.   Arrive at Baltimore.

20.   Receive Letters from home & Virginia. Quite lame.[46]

21.   Write Letters.

22.   Sunday. Lame & go not to church.

23.   Visit Parson West, pass the evening with the Ladies.

24.   An event takes place[47]

25.   Dine with Mr Blakeley.

26. Dine with Mr Curson; take tea with Miss Rush & Miss McCubin.
27. Mr Usher buried.
28. Dine with Mr Johonnet &c.
29. Sunday. Dine at Mr Rush's.
30. Take leave of Baltimore; lodge at Charlestown, near the Head of Elk.
31. Proceed to the Head of Elk. Take a horse & set out for Dover to attend the Assembly of Delaware. Lodge at Middletown 16 miles below.
February 1. Arrive at Dover, 40 miles from Elk; present a petition for a copyright Law; granted, but it being the last day of the Session, a committee is appointed to bring in a bill in form for the next Session.
2. Set out for Elk; lodge at Duck Creek, 12 miles from Dover, a great flour market.
3. Proceed to Elk. Lodge at Majr Brown's.
4. Proceed to Wilmington. Lodge at Capt O Flinns.
5. Sunday. A bad day; at home.
6. Wait on Dr Way, & Mr Jacob Broom, Trustees of the Academy. get leave to use it for Lecturing; advertise.
7. View the Academy. Introd to Mr Lake a scotch Lawyer, Mr Winder, commissioner. Take tea with Mr Lake & attend a literary society.
8. Dine with Dr Way, Mr Lake, Mr Rumsey, Mr O'Flin &c. Read a Lecture to about 15.
9. Number the houses—400; more than half the people quakers. Disappointed of a Ball, by not knowing the rules.
10. Read Lectures to a large audience.
11. Dine with Mr Geddes & drink tea; intro to Mr Dickinson the Amern Farmer, a very sensible man acquainted with the States. Read my 4 and 5 Lectures to a crouded audience.
12. Sunday. Attend Mr Smith's meeting. Dine with Col. Weemes—a bon companion & three Daughters. Capt Jaquette &c, converse with the sensible Miss Vining.
13. Dine with Mr Lake. Read my last Lecture to a crouded audience, whose applause is flattering. More taste for science in these States than below.
14. Breakfast with Mr Windar. Ride to Philadelphia. Lodge at Mrs Fords in Walnut Street.

15. Dine with Col Pickering—one of the best of men; take tea at Mr Austin's.
16. Wait on Dr Ewing, President of University & Dr White; take tea with Mrs Mears at Mr Gibbs. Attend Dr Sproats Lecture; hear Mr Hollingshead's first sermon.
17. Receive letters from Hartford. Wait on Dr Franklin as president of the Trustees for permission to use a Room in the University for Lecturing. Wait on Mr Bradford, the attorney Genl, Mr Sargent & Mr Biddle. Dine with Mr Blanchard, Mr Mears, Mr Gibbs, take tea at Mr Austin's.
18. Wait on Mr Cist, printer. Dine with Mr Gibbs, with Mr Blanchard, Mr J. Lockwood, Mr Sproat, Mr Meers &c; take tea with Mr Pickering. Sing with Mr Adgate.
19. Sunday. Dine with Mr Austin, & Mr Sitgreaves &c, tea at Mr Bradford with Mr Boudinot, Dr Moyes &c.
20. Very little.
21. Wait on Dr Moyes: hear him & Dr Rush converse of *harmony of tastes*. Wait on Mr (*Pelatiah Webster*) Pass the evening at Mr Pickerings, with Mr Horton & Dr Smith.
22. Take tea with Dr Sproat, attend Dr Moyes first benefit Lecture, on air.
23. Go to the Assembly; the Ladies will not dance with strangers, if they can avoid it—polite indeed![48]
24. Take tea at Mr Blanchard's; attend Dr Moyes last benefit Lecture—200 hearers. Dr had 1000 hearers in his first course, last winter; this course he had but about 100 generally. This is the little end of the horn.[49]
25. Dine with Mr Pickering, Dr Andrews, Dr Smith &c.
26. Sunday. At Mr Sproats meeting. Dine at Mr Conollys with Mr Ely & Adgate; take tea & pass the evening at Mr Gibb's.
27. Introduced to Mr T. Paine, Common Sense; examine his plan of a bridge, supported by angles solely, executed in miniature, with success. Introd to Mr Rittenhouse, a plain, modest man.
28. Read my first Lecture to an audience of about 100 reputable characters.[50]
March 1. I dine with Dr Sproat Mr Spencer &c.
2. Read my 2d Lecture to a small audiences, the weather is bad.
3. At home.
4. Dine with Dr Andrews, Dr White, Mr Blackwell &c, read my 3d Lecture to a larger audience.

5. Sunday. At Christ's Church. Dine with Mr Austin.
6. Mr Hewes & Mr Keen, a Committee of Hospital managers wait on me with a request for a benefit Lecture.
7. Dine with Mr Anthony, an agreeable man, with Mr Hillegas & read my 4th Lecture to a larger audience than usual.
8. Wait on Dr Moyes. Attend Mr Adgate's Vocal Concert—150 performers, very agreeable.
9. Take tea at Mr Austins. Read my 5th Lecture.
10. Dine at Mr Pickerings; tea at Mr Spencers.
11. Walk to the hospital.[51] Dine with Dr White. Read my last lecture to 150 with great applause, closed with an anthem from Sunday Songs, tune by Mr Adgate's school.
12. Sunday. At meeting. Dine with Dr Rush; at Mr Filmore's meeting in the evening.
13. Take tea at Mr Blanchards.
14. Take tea at Mr Gallaudets; attend Mr Peale.
15. Read my benefit Lecture for Pennsylvania Hospital; evening bad, about 300 hearers.
16. Dine with Mr Pickering, examine the museum & library, evening at Mr Anthony's.
17. Dine with Mr Hewes.
18. Dine with Pickering. Take tea at Mr Blanchards.
19. Sunday. Dine at home *by invitation,* bid my friends adieux.
20. Set out for the Eastward, arrive at Trenton. Wait on Mr Read, clerk of council, & record the Institute, according to act of Assembly.
21. Proceed to Princeton, pass the evening at Dr Smiths, with Mrs Stocton & Ladies.
22. Dine with Dr Smith. Take a view of College library almost ruined by the soldiers, 48 rooms in College,[52] 70 students, Presidents salary £400. Professor of moral philosophy £200, Tutors £150 currency. Take tea Parson Armstrongs, introd to Mr Snowden, Mr Dean & Lady, Mr Todd & Lady.
23. At home writing.
24. Move on to New York.
25. Arrive & lodge at Mrs Ferrari's in Maiden Lane. Wait on Col. Burr's family, at Capt Watson's in the evening.
26. Sunday. At Dr Rogers meeting.

27. Wait on Judge Hobart & Mr Duane, Mayor, to get the use of City Hall. Dine with Col Carrington, Col Grayson & Mr Arthur Lee, of Virginia.

28. Pass evening with Judge Platt, member of Congress for New York.

29. Read Conquest of Canaan, go to the play; the provoked husband was acted. Mr Henry, Mr Wagnell, Mrs Morris, Mrs Harper support their parts well, but some low scenes and indelicate ideas interspersed here & there are very exceptionable. Every exhibition of vice weakens our aversion for it.

30. Attend some exhibitions in College, take tea with Dr Crosby.

31. Dine with Mr Craigge & Theodore Hopkins.

April 1. A severe snow storm. Dine at Mr Newtons.

2. Sunday. Storm continues. I dine with Capt Watson.

3. Introd to Dr Rogers & family; Mr Mason; take tea at Mr Nichols & introd to Parson Scovil of Waterbury.

4. In study.

5. See my Cousin Josiah Steele. Introd to Misses Depeisters & Miss McEwin.

6. Begin my lectures before an audience of 70 or 80, among whom was Dr Ramsay, chairman & many other members of Congress.

7. Wait on Mr Mitchell.

8. Wait on Judge Platt; take tea with Miss McEwin.

9. Sunday. At meeting. Dine with M Nichols; take tea at Capt Watsons.

10. Attend the legislative Debates, take tea at Judge Tredwell's.

11. At Commencement in St Pauls; hear 8 dull speakers[33] read 2d Lecture to a very polite audience of 100.

12. Attend Senate, obtain a copyright Law.

13. Hear the Debates in Legislature on Impost. Dine with Capt Watson. Read my 3d Lecture to a numerous audience.

14. Take a walk to Bunker Hill out of the city. Visit the wax works.

15. Repeat my first Lecture.

16. Sunday. Hear Parson Wilson. Dine with Mr Currie. PM Hear Dr Livingston.

17. Dull, writing, attend the exhibitions of Miss Kip's school, very pretty, take tea at Mrs Vandervoorts.

18. Write, read newspaper remarks on myself, read my 4th Lecture.
19. Take tea at Mr Newton's.
20. Dine with Dr Ramsay & several other members of Congress. Read my 5th Lecture.
21. Take tea at Mr Loudons. A duel fought between Mr Burling & Mr Curson; the latter wounded, & afterwards dies.[54]
22. Rain.
23. Sunday. Dine with Mr Pierce with Col Talmadge.
24. Take tea at Mr Malcolm's.
25. Dine with Mr Childs. Take tea at Mr Beach's Episcopal Clergyman. Read my 6th Lecture.
26. Mr Curson buried. Take tea at Mr Nichols.
27. Breakfast with Dr Ramsay, in company with O'beal & five other Indians.[55] Read my last lecture to about 200 Ladies & Gentlemen with much applause.
28. Take the number of houses—3500 nearly. Take tea at Mr Vandervoorts.
29. Read a Lecture on the American States.
30. Sunday. At Dr Livingston's. Dine with Capt Watson.
May 1. Set out for Albany, dine at Peeks Kill, at Mandevilles. Lodge at Fish Kill.
2. Arrive at Claverack, walk 4 miles to Hudson city, take tea at Mr Gilberts.
3. View Hudson—160 houses.
4. Ride to Claverack with Dr Hamilton. Receive a right of Land in the Susquehannah Company of the Dr. Proceed to Albany.[56]
5. Visit Mr Sill &c.
6. Ride to Schenectady, 16 miles, on the Mohawk, nearly 300 houses, with Mr Goodrich.
7. Sunday. Return to Albany, take tea with Mr Goodrich at Mr Henry's.
8. Ride to New City, or Lansingburg. Lodge at Mr Coggswell's.
9. Cross the Hudson at half moon; view the Cohos[57] or falls of the mohawk, 30 feet; lodge at Mr Jane's.
10. Ride to Albany.
11. Begin my lectures to a few friends.[58]
12. Dull. 2d Lecture.
13. 3d
14. Sunday. Hear the Dutch Parson Westils—understand not a word. PM Hear Parson McDonald, fresh from Scotland. Dine

at Mr Philip Rensselaer's, Introd to Miss Yates; take tea with Miss Ray—a ten thousand pounder, Miss Ten Broeck. Walk, introd to Misses Metcalf, Miss Schyler, &c.

15. Walk the fields.

16. Read 4th Lecture. Tea at Mr Rensselaer's.

17. 5th Lecture.

18. Tea at Judge Yates. read the last lecture to about 30, cross the River.

19. Proceed towards New York, lodge at Fish Kill, find my Mr Ker.

20. At New York Lodge at Mrs Wheaton's.

21. Sunday. Take tea at Capt Watsons, Introd to Miss Woodbridge, of Stonington.

22. In business.

23. Breakfast at Mrs Sebrings with President Wheelock and Mr Law.

24. Visit, and drink tea at Parson Mason's with Miss Loudon.

25. Form a plan of a new Alphabet & send to Dr Franklin at the request of Dr Ramsay.

26. Leave New York for Connecticut, in company with Genl Webb and Col Humphreys. Lodge at Fairfield.

27. Arrive at Hartford, having been absent about 13 months.

28. At meeting.

29. Dine at Mr Barlow's.

30. Ride to West division.⁵⁹

31. Visit.

June 1. Return.⁶⁰

2. Visit.

3. Col Humphreys takes tea with me.

4. Sunday. At meeting.

5. Make arrangements for lecturing.

6. Begin—read to the Genl Assembly in the North meeting house; windows broken.⁶¹

7. Read Lectures at Mr Colliers in dancing Room.⁶²

8. Ride to West division. Return & read lecture.

9. To about 30.

10. Ride to Windsor with Miss M Wolcott.

11. Sunday. As usual.

12. Lecture.

13. Finish.⁶³

229

14. Ride to New Haven; attend Quarterly exercises in College.[64]
15. Visit.
16. Take tea at Mr Goodrich.
17. Number the houses in New Haven nearly 400.
18. Sunday. In Chapel, take tea at Mr Meigs.[65]
19. Read a lecture to about 40, in the State House.
20. Take tea at Mr Thompson's.
21. A scholar expelled from College, & 3 suspended.[66] 2d Lecture to 60.
22. Repeat my first Lecture—after tea at Mr Burr's.[67]
23. 3d Lecture to about 80; after, tea at Dr Wales.
24. Ride to Milford with the Misses Stiles; dine at Mr Lockwood's; return.
25. Sunday.[68] In College Chappel.
26. 4th Lecture to about 70.
27. Tea at Mr Parmeles.
28. Read my 5th after tea at Dr Stiles.
29. Mrs Watson arrives at New Haven, read a lecture on politics, &c after tea at Mr Sherman's.
30. Finish my last Lecture *avec eclat*.

July 1. Return to Hartford.
July 2. Sunday. At meeting. Dine at Col Wadsworths with Mrs Watson.
3. Oppressed with *vis Inertia*.
4. Ride to Westdivision; return.
5. Set out for Boston with Mr Laurence, call on Mr Dwight at Springfield. Lodge at Spenser.
6. Proceed. Breakfast at Worcester & settle all accounts with Mr Thomas; arrive at Boston & get Lodgings at Mr Archibalds.
7. Wait on some friends. Hear the English have taken some vessels in Province of Main.
8. Ride to Watertown with Mrs Shattuck, Mr Flint, & Mrs Parker. Stop at Mr Lee's seat; dine at Col Hull's; return.
9. Sunday. AM at chapel, hear Mr Freeman, a sensible liberal man, not ordained. P.M. Hear Mr Clark.
10. Dine with Mr Flint at Mrs Loring's. Pass the evening at Mr Guild's. Introd to Mr Freeman & Dr Appleton.
11. Pass the evening & sup with Dr Appleton.
12. Pass the evening at Mr Elliots in club, a social meeting once a week, Composed of 3 Clergymen, 3 Lawyers, 3 Doctors & 3 Merchants.

13.   Dine at Mr Clark's. Begin my Lectures before 30, in Mr Hunts
        School House.
14.   Ride to Cambridge in a Hackney with Mr Laurence Drake &
        some Ladies. Dine with Govr Bowdoin, with Mrs Temple, the
        Consul's Lady from New York, the Govr Daughter, with Miss
        Temple, afterwards Mrs Winthrop, Miss Sears, Mr S. Adams,
        Dr Waterhouse, Mr Gill, Mr Thatcher, Mr Snowden of
        Philadel. Dr Williams &c. Take tea with Mr Bingham.
15.   Do business.
16.   Hear Mr Porter of Roxbury & Mr Thatcher, who has an
        excellent ariculation, but is a slovenly writer.
17   Ride to Roxbury. Read 2d Lectre to about 50, among whom
        was the Govr &c.
18.   Hear the examination of Mr Tichnors school. Dine at Parson
        White's. attend Mr Richard's school exhibition—not pleased;
        take tea with Mr Montague—a young church Clergyman at the
        North End.
19.   Attend Commencement at Cambridge; pleased with the
        exercises, except that they were too lengthy,[69] the students
        affected to smile in all their speeches, & their actions was too
        mechanical.
20.   Recive a letter from Dr Franklin. Dine at home with Mr Pitkin
        & Mr Dennison. Fish market burnt at 11 oclock P.M.
21.   Take tea with Dr Appleton; read my 3d Lecture.
22.   Dine with Mr Flint. Walk to Bunker Hill; take tea at Mr
        Hatch's. Introduced to Parson Stillman's family, & Mr Balsh's.
23.   Sunday. At Mr Stillman's meeting—see the ceremony of
        Baptism of adults. PM at Mr Lathrop's; take tea with him; pass
        the evening at Mr Balsh's.
24.   Dine with Mr Winthrop at Mrs Cottons. Introd to Mr
        Campbell, Mr Brewster; read a Lecture; take an evening stroll.
25.   Mr Winthrop married to Miss Temple. I ride to Cambridge,
        visit Mr Stillman at his seat. Take tea with Mr J Winthrop
        librarian, in Compy with Judge Dana, Mr President, Professor
        Williams &c Ladies &c.
26.   Read a Lecture.
27.   Dine with Dr Chauncey. Introd to Dr Haslet.
28.   Dine with Mr Elliot & Mr Minot. Take tea at the Govrs with a
        large concourse, on a wedding visit.[70]

29. Ride to Dorchester Point; cross over to the Castle, view the works & Prisoners condemned to labor. They make nails, to advantage.

30. Sunday—Hear Mr Parker. Dine with Mr Gore. PM hear Mr Elliot. Take tea with Mr Hunt.

31. Dine with Mr Lathrop, read a Lecture.

August 1. Ride to Salem—Lodge at Mr Robinson's.

2. Get Lodgings at Mrs Jeffry's; attend a lecture & hear Mr Barnard; take tea at Mr Prince's.

3. Get permission to read Lectures in Mr Noyes's school house. Introd to Mr Bentley, a very liberal clergyman; at club evening.

4. Take tea at Mr Goodale's; begin Lectures to 24.[71]

5. Dine at Mr F Cabots with Mr Barnard, Mr Prince &c. Walk to Gallows hill where formerly 17 witches were hung; the locust trees where they were hung are yet standing & the graves are visible.

6. Sunday. Hear Mr Prince, & Mr Bentley. Walk to Mr Cleveland's, & Mr Prince's.

7. Walk with Mr Goodale to see the Fish Flakes, south; visit Mr Bentley, take tea with Mr Noyes & Mr Hiller. Read 2d Lecture to 40 Ladies & Gentlemen.

8. Ride to Marblehead, so called from its being a Rocky point, just below Salem. Dine with Mr Hubbard & the association; take tea with Mr Sewall, return.

9. Number houses—730, take tea with Mr Macky, read 3 Lectures.

10. Read Abbe de Cadillac; at club at Mr Appleton's.[72]

11. Dine at Dr Holyoke's, take tea at Mr Prince's. Read 4th Lecture.

12. Dine at Mr Goodale's. Walk to Beverly with Mr Pulling; take tea at Mr George Cabot's, visit Mr Andrew Cabot's elegant seat; return.

13. Sunday. Hear Mr Parsons of Lynn. Take tea at Mr Appleton's.

14. Read 4th Lecture to 50; at club at Col Pickman's.

15. Dine at Mr Prince's; take tea at Dr Holyoke's.

16. Read my last Lecture. Take a glass of wine with Mr Pinchon, Attory.

17. Ride to Newbory with Mr Gardner. Wait on Mr Marquand; sup with him. Intr to the Misses Coombs, after taking tea at Col Cross's.

18.   Ride to Portsmouth, after having waited on Mr Murray Mr Cary & Dr Swett.

19.   Lodging, Mrs Purcell's; wait on Sheriff Parker; go to Mr J Langdon's.

20.   Sunday. AM at home. PM hear Mr MClintock at Dr Haven's. Mr Buckminster is not well.

21.   Dine at Mr Buckminster's with Mr Stephen's. Take tea at Mr Langdons. Read my first Lecture to 16.

22.   Take tea at Mr Woodbury Langdon's with Miss Hooker, Misses Simpson, Miss Tilton, from Exeter.

23.   Dine at Mr J Langdon's. Take tea at young Dr Haven's, pass evening at Dr Hills.

24.   Read 2d Lecture in the Assembly room after taking tea at Mr Cutts's.

25.   Dine at Mr W Langdon's, & tea; read 3d Lecture.

26.   Take tea at Mr Pickering's.

27.   Sunday. At meeting; take tea at Mr Hale's.

28.   Take tea at Dr Penhallows. Read 4th Lecture.

29.   Rain. I dine at Dr Hilles; take tea at Sheriff Parker's Read a Lecture to a small number.

30.   Dine at Mr Cutts's, take tea at Mr Langdon's; read last Lecture to 40.

31.   Ride to Newbury Port.

September 1.   Number houses.[73] Read first Lecture to 20.

2.   Ride to Haverhill, a handsome settd town 14 miles up the Merrimack; return.

3.   Sunday. Hear Mr Adoniram Judson in Mr Spring's church. Dine at Mr Murrays & hear him preach. Wait on Mr Judson.

4.   Dine with Mr Carey; visit Mr Whitefields remains under Mr Murray's pulpit. This is deposited here with the former Ministers, Mr Parson: father of the Genl Whitefields has been here 16 years, his breast is not fallen in, his surplice is consumed & his silk gloves crumble between my fingers like burnt paper; take tea at Mr Mycalls; read 2d Lecture.

5.   Take tea at Mr Marquand's; visit Miss Cross. Inrd to Miss Parson's.

6.   Read 3d Lecture.

7.   A muster day with militia; take tea with Mr Long; read last lecture to 27.

8.   Visit my friends.

9. Ride to Boston with Mr Grenough.
10. Sunday. At the Chapel. PM at Mr Clarkes, take tea with him.
11. Dine with Col Battelle; visit Parson White.
12. Rain. I dine with Mr Flint; evening at Mr Clarke's & Mr Balshs.
13. Dine at Mr Jackson's, with Mr N Tracey, Mr G Cabot, Mr Coxe of Philada Mr Lowell. Take tea at Dr Appleton's; at club at Dr Welshs.
14. Ride to Cambridge visit Mr Pearson. Wait on the President; view Mr Brattles Garden. Return; sup with Dr Appleton & Miss Greenleaf.
15. In the evening at Mr Stillman's, & Mr Newman's.
16. Take tea with a large company at the Castle.
17. Sunday. AM writing Letters. Dine at Mr Gore's; go to church. Introdud to the Misses Blanchard.
18. Preparing a Lecture.
19. Very rainy. Read a Lecture in Fanueil Hall to 80 or 90, who had subscribed for a repetition of it. Genl Lincoln attended, Mr S Adams, Mr T Russell &c.
20. Visit; dine with Mr Flint, at club.
21. Ride to Providence, with Mr Flagg of Charleston; lodge at Judge Bowler's.
22. Wait on Mr Hitchcock. Introd[d] to Mr Benson; hear Miss Talbot play on the Forte Piano beautifully.
23. Dine with Mr Hitchcock.
24 Sunday. Hear Mr Homer of Newtown in Mr Hitchcock's church.[74]
25. Number houses 560. Read my first Lecture to 20.
26. Take tea with Mr Welcome Arnold; read a lecture to 30.
27. Take tea with Mr S Snow, a lecture to 35.
28. Dine with Mr Hitchcock, a lecture to 25.
29. A lecture to about 40.
30. Sail to Newport. Lodge at Mr John Wanton's.
October 1. Sunday. At Quaker meeting—not a word said.[75] I wait on Mr Rogers. Introd to Dr Flagg, of Charleston.
2. Went to Quaker meeting, hear an English man exhort.[76]
3. Number houses, nearly 800.
4. Drink tea with Mr Rogers; my first Lecture to 20.
5. Attend the most villainous Assembly, that ever undertook to make laws. Wait on Mr Stephens & Miss Marchant.

234

OCTOBER 6, 1786

6.

7. At the Assembly.

8. Sunday. Hear Mr Patten—he speaks like a schoolboy, but his ideas are good & his style tolerable, except a little bombast; take a walk to the beach. Go to Singing school with the Misses Marchant.

9. Cross over to Connanicut, an Island, 8 miles long & 1 broad, 3 miles from Newport; view Mr Lyman's farm. Read a lecture.[77]

10. A Lecture.[78]

11. Dine with Mr Rogers, & tea; read my last Lecture to few. Newport people are poor.

12. Walk to *Purgatory,* 3 miles from town, an opening in the Rock on the bank—a Curiosity.

13. Sail for N London with Capt Niles; wind changes & we return.

14. Sail; reach New London. Lodge at Mr Miners; wait on Mr J Coit.

15. Sunday. Hear Mr Channing. Dine at Mr Dudley Saltonstall's PM at church hear the Bishop. Drink tea with Mr N Richards Introd to Mr Winthrop & family Peggy is handsome.

16. My birthday—another large portion of life gone forever!

17. Read a lecture to 14; sup with Mr Coit.

18. Reading Priestley & Price, lent me by Mr Rose.

19. Sail to Norwich; see my friend Breed & Drink tea with him. Ride to Town and lodge at Mr Azariah Lathrop's.

20. See some friends.

21. Visit Miss Fanny Rogers. Take tea with Mr Bushness and sisters at Mr Wetmores.

22. Sunday. Hear Mr Strong. Dine with Mr Leffingwell with Mr Broom & take tea there.

23. Walk to the Landing; see Mr Frisbie & return.

24. Read a Lecture to 24.

25. Dine at Mr Wetmore's. Walk to Col Roger's. Wait on Miss Rogers & Miss Woodbridge to Mr Lathrops, take tea there. Read lectures to a handsome audience.

26. Leave Norwich. Lodge in Lebanon. Pass the evening, Col Trumbulls with Miss Faithy & Miss E Banker.

27. Reach Hartford; find Mr Byard & Sister from Philad.

28. Visit; take tea at Mr Barlow.

29. Sunday. At meeting, take tea at Mr Morgans, dine at Capt Skinners. Pass evening at Col Wadsworths.
30. A snow Storm. I visit Mr Barlow; write.[79]
31. Visit; hear of Mr Canfields death—an immense loss to the State, as well as to his friends.

November 1. At home; assign the copy-right of the Institute to Messs Hudson & Goodwin.
2. Doing búsiness.
3. Settle all accounts with Barlow & Babcock. Take tea with Mr Moseley.
4. Ride to West division.
5. Sunday. A meeting. Dine with Mr Perkins. Pass the evening at Sister Belding's.
6. Visit Mr Whitney, Mr Wells, &c.
7. Return. Pass the evening with Miss Butler, Mr Beach Dr Butler &c.
8. Pass an agreeable evening at Capt Marsh's.
9. At court.
10. Pass the evening at Mr Laurence's.
11. At Court, arranging papers &c Pass the evening at Dr Lemuel Hopkins.
12. Sunday. At meeting. PM church in the State House; at Mr Moseley's.
13. At court; take tea at Mr Wolcotts; evening at Mr Lawrence's.
14. At Court.
15. Do Drink tea at Mr Barlows.
16. At home. Mr Perkins takes tea with me.
17. Mr Tracey visits us.
18. PM at Mr Moseley's.
19. Sunday. At home; visit Mr Trumbull.
20. It snows.
21. Ride to West division, & return
22. Prepare for the Southward.
23. Thanksgiving-day. I leave Hartford,[80] to seek a living. Ride to Durham in a coach & to New Haven in a sleigh. Lodge at Mr Brown's.
24. Wait on Mr Fitch & the President Dr Stiles. Take tea at Dr Wales.
25. Visit Mr Baldwins, & Mr Parmele.

26.   Sunday. In chapel; hear Mr Holme's, & Mr Austin, young
       preachers. Walk to Mr Broom's, take tea at Mr Meigs's &
       spend the evening at Dr Stiles.
27.   Take tea at Dr Stiles. Wait on Mrs King. Read my first Lecture
       to about 60 Students & some others.
28.   Wait on Mr Duane, Mr Smith, Mr Yates, & Mr Haring—
       Commiss⁣ʳˢ. from New York to Hartford to settle the western
       Boundary of New York on Massachusetts; to College Library.
29.   Take tea at Mr. Sherman's; read 2d Lecture to the same. Pass
       evening at Dr Stiles.⁣⁸¹
30.   Write to Dr Smith, Princeton. Read Chaucer, take tea at Dr
       Stiles, with the handsome Mrs Platt; read a Lecture.
December 1.   Dine at Mr Drake's; read a Lecture. Pass evening at Mr
       David Daggett's.
   2.   In parvis.
   3.   Sunday. At Chapel; evening at Dr Stiles.
   4.   Very cold. Dine at Dr Stiles. A violent snow-storm. Visit Dr
       Wales with the Ladies.
   5.   Snows violently; keep close.
   6.   Reading Bolinbroke on history; my last Lecture.
   7.   Prepare for the westward. Dine at Dr Wales's. Write Letters,
       instead of attending assembly.
   8.   Set off for N. York. Dine at Stratford; get into a snow-drift,
       break the sleigh, walk to Fairfield.
   9.   Turn out at 5 oclock in another snow storm; overset & get
       buried in snow; arrive at Wentworth's in Norwalk; dine
       proceed in snow drifts to Stamford. Lodge at Mrs Wells.
  10.   Sunday. Proceed—very cold. Walk much; dine at Horse Neck,
       arrive at Byram. Take Horses & proceed to Mrs Havilands.
  11.   Proceed to N York, arrive.
  12.   Lodge at Mr Pendleton's.
  13.   Visit; dine at Mr Fisher's with my friend Wetmore; take tea at
       Mr Davis's.
  14.   Dine with Mr Watson; get Lodgings at Mrs Vandervoorts, No
       55 Queen Street.
  15.   Write. Take tea with Mrs Smith & Miss Hunt.
  16.   Writing on manners.
  17.   Sunday. do. PM at. St Pauls-church, hear a miserable Irish
       preacher.
  18.   Mr Law sails for Charleston.

237

19. Finish a dissertation on manners & fashions. Read a Lecture.
20. Begin a Dissertation on Government. Pass evening at Mr Loudon's.
21. Writing. Walk to Mr Watson's, Dr Coggeswell's. Take tea with Mr Beach. Introduced to the Irish Preacher, Mr Wright.
22. Attend an exhibition in College of Mr Cochran's school. Master Muleghan performs admirably.
23. I wait on Judge Smith. Dine with Mr Watson.
24. Sunday. Dine with Mr Bowen.
25. Christmas Day. I set off for Philadelphia. Lodge at Elizabeth Town.
26. Ride to Philadelphia. Lodge at Mrs Fords.
27. Wait on friends. Go to church with the Masons.
28. Visit Mr Lockwood, Dr Sproat, Dr Franklin.
29. Take tea at Mr Blanchard's. Visit Mr Anthony.
30. Dine with Dr Franklin.
31. Sunday. Dine with Col Pickering.

1787

January 1st 1787. Read Horne's Diversions of Purley, a new & useful Theory of language.
2. Publish subscription papers for a course of Lectures. Wait on Dr Ewing.
3. Breakfast with Mr Brown, Master of the Ladies Academy. Pass the evening at Dr Sproats, obtain permission to use the University for lecturing.
4. Read Bishop Wilken's Real Character. Evening at Mr Austin's.
5. Write Grammar. pass evening at Mr Anthony's.
6. Take tea at Mr Lockwood's.
7. Sunday. At church, hear Mr Snoodgrass. Tea at Mr Blanchard's.
8. Tea at Mr Austin's.
9. Pass eve at Mr Gibb's.
10. Dine at Mr Gibb's, with Mr Waldo, from Bristol, England. take tea at Mr Roger's.
11. Take tea at Mr Anthony's. attend City Concert. Mr Julian on the violin, Mr Brown on the flute are inimitable. But I am not amused.
12. Evening at Mr Pelatiah Websters.[82] Talk politics, & drink wine.
13. Evening at Mr Blanchard's.

14.   Sunday. Mr Gibbs. evening Mr Austin's.

15.   At court. hear an important cause between the proprietors & a claimant of land by an old title. Tea at Mr Lockwood's. Attend Uranian society, for vocal music. See Mr Dibble.

16.   He visits me, a young man almost ruined by dissipation. Take tea at Mr Byards. Go to the Amateur Concert. Dance.

17.   Tea at Mr Lockwoods. attend Mr Adgate's Rehearsal for Vocal Concert.

18.   Dine at Mr Byards. at Court hear Mr Sargeant.

19.   At court. hear Mr Wilcox. evening at Mr Lockwoods with the Misses Sproats.

20.   At court hear Mr Bradford Atty Genl. pleased with him.[83]

21.   Sunday. Hear Mr Green. take tea at Mr Bradford's, with Mr Boudinot.

22.   Rain.

23.   Tea at Mr Pickerings. see Mr Saml Blanchard.

24.   Rain.

25.   tea at Mr Andrew Hodges.

26.   Rain.

27.   Read a lecture on manners, to a small audience.

28.   Sunday. Dine at Mr Lockwoods. go to church.

29.   Snow falls. visit Dr Rittenhouse.

30.   Visit Mr Du Ponceau, an Italian of great erudition. Wait on Dr Franklin. at Mr Ely's.

31.   Tea at Dr Sproats. attend Rehearsal of music.

February 1.   My Grammar 3d edition goes to press, in Philadelphia. I pass the eve at Dr Andrews.[84]

2.   Evening at Mr Montgomery's.

3.   Take tea at Mr Hodge's.

4.   Sunday. Breakfast with Mr Brown. Tea at Mr Lockwood's.

5.   Visit Mon Peter S Du Ponceau. Take tea at Mr Gibbs. attend Uranian Society.

6.   Visited by Mr Thomas Blanchard. Read my lecture on Government.[85]

7.   Visit Mr Browns school.

8.   At Mr Lockwoods.

9.   Wait on Mr Rush, Carver, for a Bust of Dr Franklin, for Mr Isaac Beers, N Haven. View Mr Fitch's Steam Boat.

10.   Dine at Mr Blanchard's. Tea at Mr Anthony's.

11.   Sunday. Pass evening at Mr Austins.

12. Attend to Mr Barlows affairs. Wait on Majr Jackson. Take tea at Mr Blackwell's with Dr Andrews, Dr Ruston & Lady.

13. Pass evening at Mr Blanchard's.

14. Rain.

15. Pleasant.

16. Call on Mr P Webster.

17. Take tea with Dr Sproat. In a scuffle with Mr Blanchard at Mr Lockwood, we break a chair. folly in men is inexcuseable![86]

18. Sunday. At church. take tea at Mr Lambs. Walk with Miss Caldwell to Evening Lecture. Return to Mrs Rhea's.[87] Introduced to Mr Blair, a worthy Clergyman.

19. at Col Pickerings, & Uranian.

20. Dine at Mr Lockwood's. Play whist at Mr Hodges.

21. Call on Mr Ely & Mr Lockwood. Take leave of Mr Thomas Blanchard, he's for France, an adventurer for a fortune, without a shilling.[88]

22. Take tea at Mr Brown's.

23. Dine with Mr Gibbs. Visit Mr Blanchard & Mr Lockwood.

24. Read a Lecture on Reforming the English Alphabet.

25. Sunday. Dine at Col Pickerings. at church hear Dr Smith, Princeton. Take tea at Col Byards.

26. At Mr Websters & Dr Sproats.

27. At Mr Spencer's.

28. Dine at Mr Austins with Mr Tench Coxe, Col Wadsworth, Mr Lea, Mr Campbell, Mr Chaloner, Mr Swanick, Mr Spicer, Mr Ingersoll. Attend in the evening the Annual Philosophical Oration. delivd by Dr Smith on the Colors of the Human race.[89]

March 1. Walk with Miss S Hopkins to visit Dr Sproat, Mr Ingraham's family, & Miss Greenleaf, Mr Newport & Dr Ewing.

2. Pass the evening at Mr Browns, with Mr Hopkins, Student of Law.

3. Pass the evening at Mr Lockwood. Wait on Some Printers.

4. Sunday. Bad Weather, dull, at evening go to Quaker meeting, & to see Miss Hopkins.

5. statu quo.

6. Dine with Col Pickering, & a Mr Pryor from Dover. Introduced to Mr Thomas, Student of Law under Col Tilghman.

7. Take tea with him. visit the sweet Miss Greenleaf.

8.	Open proposals with Messrs Spotswood & Seddon, for printing the Institute—never completed.
9.	Pass the evening with the agreeable Miss Greenleaf.
10.	Meet my good Friend Mr Blakely from Baltimore. Pass the evening at Col Pickering's.
11.	Sunday. at church. tea at Mr Blanchard's.
12.	Dine at Mr Logan's at Germantown. he has a good estate, but not an esteemable man. Count Castiglioni & Mr Vaughn dine there.
13.	Take tea at Mr Budd's.
14.	at Dr Andrews, after visiting College Library.
15.	At Mr Ingraham's. Dine with Col Pickering. see Dr Franklin.[90]
16.	Take tea at Mr Lockwoods. Write a Letter Govr Bowdoin.
17.	With Miss Greenleaf.
18.	Sunday. Mr Blakeley sets off for Baltimore. I dine at Mr Lockwoods.
19.	At Mr Ely's & Mr Gibbs.
20.	At Mrs Rhea's with some Ladies.
21.	At Mr Ingrahams.
22.	Take tea at Mr Ingrahams & attend Concert with the lovely Becca.
23.	
24.	Dine with Mr Hodge, tea at Mr Ingraham's.
25.	Sunday. at home.
26.	Dine at Mr Lockwood's with Mr Little. Take tea at Mr Ingrahams.
27.	do.
28.	dine at do. with Mr Little.
29.	Go to the Assembly—but 6 Ladies present.
30.	Take tea at Mr Nathl Ingrahams.
31.	Do.
April 1.	Sunday. at church hear Mr Grear, Dr Sproat & Mr Blair—the last is a cool, modest, sensible, systematic man.
2.	With Miss Greenleaf.
3.	Dine at Col Pickerings with Mr Logan.
4.	Attend Rehearsal for the Grand Concert.
5.	Dine at Mr Ingrahams with Mr Stillman from Boston. Walk to Schuylkil.
6.	Take tea with Mr Thomas.
7.	At Mr Ingraham's.

8.   Sunday. at Christ Church.
9.   Take tea at Mr Barton's. Evening at Mr Nathl Ingrahams.
10.   Ride to Chester with Mr Borger, Mr Coch, Mr Greenleaf & Mr Ingram & Ladies. Return. Wait on the Trustees of the Episl Academy, accept of a place there 6 months—@ 200 £ a year—Currency
11.   Take tea at Mr Austins.[91]
12.   The First Grand Uranian Concert, performed at the Reformed German Church in Race Street. about 300 performers & 400 Spectators.
13.   Enter the Episcopal Academy. take tea at Mr Vanuxems.
14.   Send to New York Dr Franklin's Bust, Some Grammars, &c.
15.   Sunday. Hear Mr Green, Mr Blair. at Mr Ingrahams.
16.   The Bishop of Pennsylvania in presence of the teachers & pupils of the Episcopal Academy, lays the first stone of the New Building in Chestnut Street, above fifth.
17.   Attend Mrs OConners Lecture. She is co-rect, but not original, dull, unanimated.
18.   Mr Barlows poem arrives. I am at my favorite place.
19.   Evening at Mr Browns.
20.   With my heart.
21.   At Mrs O Connor's Lecture, dull.
22.   Sunday. at Christs Church. Dine at Mr Ely's.
23.   Walk to Mr Blanchard. Return with Mr Vanuxem.
24.   Dine at Mr Lockwoods.
25.   Take tea with Miss Hopkins.
26.   School examined by the Bishop & Committee of Acady.
27.   Mr Duncan Ingraham returns from Europe.
28.   Take tea at Mr Sproats.
29.   Sunday. Breakfast at Mr Brown's.
30.   Busy enough with the Boys of the Academy. they have been managed, or rather not managed, by poor low Irish Masters. O habit! O Education! Of what Importance that our first examples be good, & our first impressions virtuous.[92]

May 1. Warm.
2.   Cool. Pass the evening at Col Pickerings.
3.   Red a Letter from Mr Eells.
4.   At my favorite place.
5.   Dine with Mr Brooke Smith at Mr Ingraham's.
6.   Mr Austin & Mr Greenleaf & Mr Mussi dine with me.

7.	Attend Uranian Concert.
8.	At Mr Lockwoods. See Mr Blakeley & his daughter.
9.	With the most lovely.
10.	At Mr Blanchards.
11.	At Mr Ingraham's.
12.	Mr Blakeley & Mr Gibbs dine with me.
13.	Sunday. dine with Mr Gibbs.
14.	Take tea with Mr Hitchcock at Mrs Clarke's.
15.	Attend ordination of Mr Green. Dine at Mr Ingraham's.
16.	Walk to Mr Rittenhouses.
17.	At Mr Lockwoods.
18.	trifles.
19.	At Mr Ingrahams.
20.	Sunday. at church. take tea at Mr Austin's.
21.	Walk with Mr Caper's.
22.	Walk with the Ladies to the Bettering House, or Work-House. the Gardens are elegant. take tea at Mr Donaldson's.
23.	Walk with Mr Caper & Mr Blakeley.
24.	Write on Domestic debt.
25.	Visit Mr Lockwood, Mr P Webster. talk on the Debt.
26.	Head-ach keeps me at home. Genl Washington calls on me.
27.	Sunday. Walk to the Gardens with Dr Judson, Mr Hopkins, &c.
28.	Visit Dr Franklin's with the Ladies.
29.	Wait on Mrs King with Miss Greenleaf. Mr Eells arrives.
30.	Rain.
31.	Visit Dr Sproats & Mr Ingrahams.
June 1.	Busy in accomodating Mr West.
2.	Dine at Mr Ingraham's with Mr Porter, Mr Donnevills, &c.
3.	Sunday. dine at Dr Andrews.
4.	Walk with Mr West.
5.	Mr Eells takes tea with us.
6.	Enter the English Department in the Academy. I before had the Mathematical. Mr Wests. visit Mr Webster.
7.	Visit the best of women.
8.	Walk with Mr Greenleaf.
9.	Dine with the Bishop, & Mr Willcox, Dr Johnson, &c. Walk to Bettering House with ye Ladies.
10.	Sunday. At home. evening See Mr A. Baldwin from Georgia.
11.	Walk to Dr Magaw's.

12. Walk with Mr West to Dr Rittenhouse.
13. Visit Mr Blanchards family.
14. Call on Dr Franklin, with Mr Greenleaf.
15. An agreeable evening at Mr Ingrahams. Interchanging friendly words—.
16. Take tea at Mr Pelatiah's, with Mr Bowen, a newly made Parson.
17. Sunday. at Church. take tea at Mr Gibbs.
18. Walk in the State House Gardens with Mr Eells.
19. Walk to Schuylkil with Mr West. Begin to Copy my Grammatical Lectures.
20. At my studies. Walk in the Gardens. Meet Mr Greenleaf. Visit Mr Ingraham's.
21. Walk in the Gardens in contemplation.
22. Visit my best friend.
23. Mr Montague from Boston arrives to take orders.
24. Sunday. I ride to Col. Thompson's, 12 miles. Go to church & dine there. return take leave of my favorite.
25. Call on Mrs Ingraham. See Mr Watson from N York.
26. My trunk arrives from N York.
27. Take tea at Mr Brown's. Walk.
28. Take tea at Mr Rogers, with Mr West, Mr Montague, Dr Rush.
29. At home.
30. Write on education. Take tea with Mrs Ingraham. visit Miss Donaldson. write to the best.
July 1st, Sunday. Write. Walk with Miss Donaldson from Mr Ingraham.
2. Hot. Mr Law arrives, takes tea with me.
3. As usual.
4. Anniversary of Independence. I call on Dr Johnson & Mr Baldwin. attend the Oration, spoken by Mr Campbell, could not hear, the appearance is indifferent. Meet my friend Dr Mann. Walk in the evening to the half way house, to see the fire works.
5. Carry to press my Remarks on Education.
6. Writing for the third part, Institute, third Edition.
7. Dine with Mr Vanuxem. Take a little money at the Academy. Call on Mr Ingraham.
8. Sunday. Write.
9. Settle all accounts with Mr Law & Mrs Timothy of Charleston.

10. Examination at the Academy.
11. Walk with Mr Law.
12. Stroll about for Exercise.
13. Walk with Mr West. Begin to copy my first Lecture.
14. Write. Paper money in Philadelphia dies.
15. Sunday. Write, take a walk.
16. ⎫
    ⎬ Writing, & correcting the last sheets of the first Part of the
    ⎪ Institute.
17. ⎭
18. Take tea at Dr Franklin's. take some extracts from the history of the grants & settlements in New Jersey.
19. First Part of Institute finished at Philad, 7th edition & first here.
20. Wait on Mr Swanwick, & pass the evening with Mr West at Mr Webster's.
21. Writing. Take tea at Mr Ingraham's.
22. Sunday. Writing.
23. In my usual course. purchase Livy & a German & Spanish Grammars of Mr Mussi.
24. Walk to Dr Sproats. Mr Ingrahams Take tea with Mr Law.
25. Mr Law sets out for Eastward.
26. Mr West Takes tea with me.
27. Nothing particular.
28. Hear Mr Brown's young Misses read Dr Rush's Dissertation on female education.
29. Sunday. At home. Evening take tea at Mr Gibbs' walk with Mr Lockwood & Mr Meers, go to Dr Sproats. walk to Mr Greens with the Ladies.
30. Take tea at Dr Sproats with the beautiful Miss Peggy Caldwell.
31. Pass evening at Mr Blanchards.
August 1. Cold as April.
2. Mr Morse dines with me.
3. Mr West. do.
4. Wait on Mr Maddison, Dr Franklin, Mr Hopkinson, who lends me Mr Jeffersons notes on Virginia. I pass the evening with Mr Sherman, Mr Ellsworth, Govr Livingston & Mr Chief Justice of N Jersey.
5. Extracting from Notes on Virginia. Sunday & warm.

6. Take tea at Mr Brown's. Walk to Mr Roger's. Send letters to Rhode Island by Mr Wetherhill. call on Mr Green.

7. Pass over the Delaware with Mr Randolph & Mr Morse. View the City from the Jersey shore. Return & take tea with Mr Randolph & his Daughter, Mrs Sleighter, an unhappy woman who married a foreigner for his supposed wealth & within 2 or 3 weeks stepped out her coach into indigence & dependence on her father.

8. nothing particular.

9. Meet my old Friend Dibble, bound to Charleston. Visit Mr Lockwood.

10. Take tea at Mr Blanchards.

11. Holydays commence. I walk to Parson Duffield's & chat with him. Mr Morse calls on me. I ride to Germantown. Take tea at Mr Logan's.

12. Sunday. Dine with Mr Ely. at church, hear Mr. Morse, a very good preacher. Walk to Mr Duffield's, & to Mr Austin's.

13. Visit Mr Meers at a Mr Brown's, & sup at Mr Ingrahams.

14. Take tea at Mr Vanuxem s & visit Miss Caldwell.

15. Pass evening with Mr Barton.

16. Visit Dr Sproat.

17. Call on Mr Gibbs, Mr Hillegas, Dr Franklin, &c Mr Ely in the evening.

18. at home.

19. At home. Sunday.

20. Writing as usual. rain.

21. Do.

22. Walk to Shuylkill. Pass evening at Mr Gibbs.

23. Pass evening at Mr Marshalls, with Convention Gentlemen.

24. Ride to Trenton. Call on Mr Armstrong.

25. Return to Bristol. cross the river to Burlington. Lodge at Col Hooglands with Mr Eells.

26. Sunday. At quaker meeting Walk in the evening to Mr Kisslemans & Mr Bloomfields, Atty Genl.

27. Breakfast with the Atty. Dine & sail to Philadelphia.

28. Call on Mr Barclay, for a pocket book I lost going to Trenton. Pass evening at Mr Ingraham's.

29. Write.

30. See Mrs Meers, who is very far gone with the dropsy.

31.   Mr Poor & Mr Ely call & take tea with me. I dined with Mr Lockwood.

September 1st.   Rain.

2.   Sunday. Writing. Call at evening on Mr Ely.

3.   Begin business in Academy after Holydays. Sick-almost.

4.   Mr West takes tea with me.

5.   I take tea at Mr Roger's: walk with Mr West.

6.   Pass the evening at Mr Rittenhouse's with Mr West.

7.   At Mr Rogers, the evening.

8.   Take tea at Mr Ely. Mr Le Coutaille & Lady dine with us. I sup at Mr Ingrahams. Miss Ross dies.

9.   Sunday. call on Mr Gibbs.

10.   as usual.

11.   Call on Dr Johnson & Mr Baldwin.

12.   Call on Mr Rogers.

13.   Pass evening with Mr Pelh. Webster & Col Dennison.

14.   A violent Thunder Gust cools the extreme heat.

15.   Receive a written request from Mr Fitzsimmons to use my pen in support of the New Federal System, which is almost finished. ride to Dr Logan's Germantown. see Mr Marsh from Hartford.

16.   Sunday. At home. Take tea at Mr Austin's.

17.   Attend Mrs Meers funeral as a mourner. Met some friends from Hartford. *The Great Convention* finish their business & offer to the public the *New Federal System.*

18.   Genl Washington leaves town. Dr Franklin presents the Speaker of the House of Assembly in Pennva with the Federal System which is read. Bells ring. All America waits anxiously for the Plan of Goverment.

19.   Take tea at Mr Lockwoods.

20.   Mr Wood sails for west Indies.

21.   Call at Mr Ingrahams.

22.   Call on Mr Brown. write an answer to Mr Kidd.

23.   Sunday. At home.

24.   Take tea at Mr Blanchards, & wait on the Ladies to Mrs Vanuxems.

25.   Take tea at home with some Quakers. Receive a Letter from Mr Barlow.

26.   Mr West & son take tea with me Dr Manning calls on us at the Academy. Mr Dwight Doctor died at Princeton.

27.   Mr Law arrives from the Eastward.

28.   Pass evening at Mr Ely's.

29.   Attend Mr Ely's school & pleased. Mr Davis calls on me.

30.   Sunday. At Arch Street meeting.

October 1.   Take tea at Mr Marshals, with Mr Law.

2.   Call on Dr Magaw, & Mr Hopkinson.

3.   Take tea at Mr Brown's with Mr Meers. Pass the evening at Mr Lockwoods.

4.   Dine with Dr Andrews, with Mr Blackwell, Mr Forster, Mr Swanwick. Quarter Day which releases me from the Episcopal Academy.

5.   Pass the evening with Mr Dennison Counsellor from Wiomeng.

6.   Take tea with Miss Ray & Miss Caldwell.

7.   Sunday. Rain. Mr Johnson dines with me.

8. ⎫
    ⎬ Write an Examination into the Leading principles of the New Federal Constitution.
9. ⎭

10.   Visit. Take tea at Mr Ely's & Pass the evening at Dr Rittenhouse's.

11.   Call on Mr Swanwick for pay.

12.   At home.

13.   Take tea at Mr Reeds.

14.   Sunday. Mr Fry dines with us & a Mr Clarke. I walk to Dr Sproats.

15.   Packing up for New York.

16.   My Birthday. 29 years of my life gone! I have been industrious—endeavored to do some good, & hope I shall be able to correct my faults & yet do more good. Put my trunk aboard for N York.

17.   My Examination in the Leading Principles of the Federal Constitution published.

18.

19.   Mr Law calls. Mr White arrives. I prepare to leave town.

20.   Dine with Mr Lockwood.

21.   Sunday. At home.

22.

23.   Settling accounts. Pass the evening with Dr Franklin.

24.   Prepare to leave Philadelphia.

25.   Leave the City. Lodge at Brunswick.

26.   Ride to New York.
27.   Lodge at Mrs Vandervoorts. dance on Long Island. Dine at Mr Morton's.
28.   Sunday. Dine at Mr Watson's.
29.   Breakfast with Mr Davis. Pass evening at Mr Loudon's.
30.   Take tea at Dr Coggeswells.
31.   Make a Contract with Mr Saml Campbell for five years printing the Spelling Book.
November 1.   Embark for New Haven, get aground at 6 o'clock off the Harbor.
2.   Land at day break at N Haven.
3.   Ride to Hartford. Have Mrs Philips, Mr Tracey & Col Wyllis for company.
4.   Sunday. at Colliers, & church.
5.   Purchase Mathers Magnalia, & the first code of Connecticut Laws. Take tea at Mr Moseley's.
6.   Dine with Dr Fish, Ride to West division.
7.   Visit my Sister.
8.   Ride to Litchfield. Lodge at Col Talmadge's.
9.   Ride to Cornwall to see my Quaker Uncle. NB I had previously called on the Miss Champions at 12 oclock & they treated me with New England Rum & apples!
10.   Ride to Salisbury.
11.   Sunday. at meeting.
12.   Proceed to Egremont.
13.   Return to Salisbury. Lodge at Mr Holly's.
14.   Visit Mr Nortons & Col Porters.
15.   Thanksgiving day. Rain detains me.
16.   Rain.
17.   Ride to Hartford, almost sick.
18.   Sunday. Unwell.
19.   Visit Mr Perkins.
20.   Mr Whiting & Mr Wells.
21.   Rain
22.   Visit my Sister. walk to town Lodge at Mr Butlers. Take tea at Dr Hopkins with Miss Stone.
23.   Dull Weather.
24.   Ride to Westdivision. Take leave of my friends.
25.   Sunday. At church. Dine with Mr Wolcott. Visit many friends.

26. Ride to New Haven.
27. Visit Dr. Stiles. &c.
28. Embark for New York.
29. Arrive at evening.
30. Take lodgings for the year at Mrs Vandervoorts at £ 80–0.0.

December 1. Take tea at Mrs Mortons. Write to Mr Wharton.
2. Sunday. at home. Dine at Mr Watsons.
3. Making a contract with Mr Loudon, where I take tea.
4. Make the bargain for printing the American Magazine & get the paper on Shore.
5. The work is begun.
6. Writing. Mr Lawrence passes the evening with me. Delaware Ratifies Constitution.
7. Rain.
8. Fair.
9. Sunday. Dr Mann calls upon me. We walk.
10.
11. } At home, writing.
12. Sup at Mr Watsons. Pennsylvania ratify New Constitution.
13. At home.
14. Mr Mat Steele calls on me.
15. At Mr Loudons in the evening.
16. Sunday. Pass evening at Mr Laurence's.
17. At home.
18. Mrs Otto buried. Mr Campbell arrived from Philadelphia.
19. Snow.
20. Mr Wharton from Phild. calls on me.
21. Pass the evening at Mr Laurences.
22. Visit Col Stephens & Mr Watson.
23. Sunday. A snow Storm, the first this Season.
24.
25. } Nothing singular, except a little romp at Mr Loudon's.
26. See my friend Mr Greenleaf from Boston.
27. Walk over town.
28. Busy answering the address of the dissenting members of Pensylvania.
29. Sunday. At home.
30. At home.
31. End of the year.

1788

January 1st. 1788   At home.

2.   Busy sending the first number of the Magazine to the Eastward.

3.   Cold.

4.
5.   } Very busy at home.

6.   Sunday. do.

7.

8.   Visit Parson Rogers.

9.   Parson Beach. Miss MEwen.

10.
11.   } Do little of consequence.
12.

13.   Sunday. At Dr Livingstones church. Take tea at Mr Stephens.

14.   Unwell.

15.   At a heelkicking at Mr Huletts Public.

16.

17.   at a Ball at Mr Beekmans.

18.   dance till fatigued

19.   Rain.

20.   Sunday. At home.

21.

22.   Visit Miss Morton.

23.   Mr Ingraham arrives. I call on Dr Livingstone.

24.   Call & take tea with Mrs Ingraham at Mr Elsworths.

25.   Call on Mr Mumford.

26.   Visit Mr Hitchcocks school.

27.   Sunday. At home.

28.   At evening I attend the theator—The Earl of Essex. tolerable.

29.

30.   Visit Mr McEwen & Miss Loudon introduced to Miss Panton & Miss Robertson.

31.   Take tea at Mr Rogers. introdd to Miss Woolsey. Mr Lawrence passes the evening here. Mr Blakeley arrives. it is good to see our old friends.

February 1.   Go to the Play—The Comedy the Busy Body. Farce, the Dissenter.

2.   At home.

3.	Sunday. Dine at Mr Watson's.
4.	Pass the evening at Mr Lawrences.
5.	At home. coldest day we have had these several years. Mercury at 6 below cypher.
6.	Take tea at Mr Broomes.
7.	
8.	At a dance.
9.	Dull.
10.	Sunday. At home.
11.	Mr Lynn calls on me.
12.	Sitting for my Miniature. taken by Mr Wm Verstille.
13.	Call at Mrs Ferari's. Go to Play.
14.	At 3 oclock AM. alarmed, with the cry of fire, which is soon extinguished.
15.	At Court.
16.	Snow.
17.	Sunday. At home.
18.	Mr Blakeley leaves town.
19.	
20.	Attend the theater.
21.	Go to Church. in the evening Mr Vandervoort dies.
22.	Go to Play. Hamlet not well performed.
23.	Hear from home.
Sunday 24.	Attend Mr Vandervoort to his grave.
25.	Do a little business for Mr Greenleaf. Go to Play. The *Heiress* acted for the first time with applause.
26.	Mr Barlow calls.
27.	
28.	Mr Barlow leaves town. I attend Assembly for the first time. 60 brilliant Ladies.
29.	Dr Post introduced to me.
March 1.	Dine with Mr Moses Rogers, & take tea there. Go to a singing.
2.	Sunday. very cold. Take tea with Miss Lowther.
3. 4. 5.	Nothing singular.
6.	Take tea at Mr J Watson with Mr Pierce & family.
7.	Call on Mr Alden. Pass evening at Mr Pierces.
8.	Dine at Mr Watson's.
9.	Sunday. At home. Take tea at Mr Roger's.

10.   Invited to a dance.

11.   Attend the Military dance. much pleased with the attention of the Mangers & the brilliancy of the Ladies.

12.   Visit.

13.   Introduced to Mrs Graham & Mr Henry & Miss Graham. Mr West dines with me.

14.   Mr Bull calls & passes the evening.

15.   Take tea at Mr Rogers.

16.   Sunday Write an address to the Ladies. See Mr Colt. Miss Wadsworth arrives in town.

17.   Admitted & take my seat as member of the Society for promoting a knowledge of the English Language.

18.   Take tea at Mr Loudons.

19.   Send away corrected copies of the 2d part Institute, to Hartford & Philadelphia.

20.   Wait on a number of friends Take tea at Mr Laurences.

21.

22.

23.   Sunday. Hear Mr Mason. dine at Mr Pierces. Go to St Pauls & hear the Bishop.

24.

25.   Take a long walk. Play at Nines at Mr Brandons. Very much indisposed.

26.   Call on Dr Beardsley at Dr Cogswell's.

27.   It is said the inhabitants of the western Counties are leagued to oppose the new Constitution.

28.   Drink tea with Miss Graham, or rather pass the evening.

29.   Take a few steps in dancing under Mr Hulet.

30.   Sunday. Dine with Mr Watson & drink tea at Mr Rogers's.

31.   Take tea at Mr Laurence's. Meet Mr Breed & Mr Leffingwell from Norwich.

April 1.   Take tea with Miss Lowry & attend some Ladies to Singing.

2.   Visit Mr Franklin.

3.

4.   Take tea at Mr Atkinson's. Meet Mr Steele at Mr Storys.

5.   Mr Hodgdon Dr Mitchill, Mr Griswold Mr Hoffman dine with us. I attend the Slack Wire Dancing.

6.   Sunday. Attend the Funeral of Mr Ripley.

7.   At Evening form a Constitution for the Philological Society.

8.   Attend Mr Campbell's school Exhibitions.

9. Walk & wait on Mr Morse.
10. Dr Craige dines with us, Mr John Pratt arrives from the western army. Attend Lecture in ye Episcopal Church.
11.
12.
13. Sunday. At St Paul's. After church, a mob collected at the Hospital, & destroyed all the anatomical preparations; amounting to several hundred pounds value. The cause was, the frequent digging up of dead bodies for dissection—the students of physic having been shamefully imprudent in taking up bodies of respectable people & without sufficient secrecy.
14. Mob collects to the number of a thousand or two, attacks the houses of Dr Kissam, Mr Knight, Bailey & break windows, enter & destroy furniture &c. They then attackd the jail where some physicians were lodged for safety, a small body of armed men defend it. The Governor & Mayor insulted. At evening about forty men armed with muskets & about as many with swords, by order of the Magistrates, march & take possession of the jail. the rioters attack them with brick bats &c. wound Mr Jay Baron Steuben &c, a few shot were fired at them & 3 persons were killed.
15th. Militia are ordered out, in New York, on L. Island & from West Chester A Company appears in arms. two pieces of artillery are prepared. The populace stand dispersed over Broad way, but dare not collect, & the riot ceased. A guard of men had kept possession of the prison, but the rioters broke the windows & doors, & wounded several men.
16. I take a ride on Long Island, with Mr Dusnicke. visit Miss Lowry.
17. Mr Hodgdon dines with us. I take tea with Mr Hazard. go to Play & return with Mrs Crosby & Miss Bedlow
18. Take tea at Mr Loudons. walk.
19. Walk to Brandon.
20. Sunday. Cold. at home.
21. Take tea at Mr Franklin's. Attend Philological Society. finish the Laws. Miss Sally Vandervoort elopes.
22. Rain: Mr Watson's calls & after some conversation, determined upon a connection with Mr James Greenleaf in trade. I have been the principal means of bringing about the partnership.
23. Take tea at Mr N Lawrence's.

24.   Mr Dusnicke leaves us. Mr Ingraham arrives.

25.   Pass the evening at Mrs Lowther's Introduced to Miss Eusticks.

26.   Pass the evening at Mr Currie's.

27.   Sunday. Dine at Mr Elsworth's with Mr Greenleaf.

28.   Sick, but at evening attend the philological Society, & read a Dissertation. ordered to be published.

29.   Mr Barlow arrives & Mr Blakeley Attend Singing school with Mr Franklin.

30.   I wait on Mrs Barlow.

May 1.   I move with Mrs Vandervoort to Maiden Lane Poll for electing Members of Convention & Assembly Closed. Walk with Mr Blakeley.

2.   Very pleasant.

3.   Prepare for a journey. rejoice that Maryland has acceded to the Constitution.

4.   Sunday.

5.   Set out for Hartford. arrive at Norwalk.

6.   Proceed to New Haven, dine & ride to Hartford.

7.   Visit my fathers family.

8.   Election day. I ride to Wethersfield.

9.   Rain.

10.   do.

11.   Sunday. Take tea at Dr Hopkins.

12.   Go to Westdivision. dine at Mrs Gay's.

13.   Return, to town.

14.   Visit several friends.

15.   Attend a ball.

16.   Set out for New York. embark at New Haven.

17.   Calm.

18.   Sunday. Calm till towards evening. arrive in New York.

19.   Meet Mr J Smith of Sharon.

20.   Dine at Mr Watsons, with Mr Barlow, Mr Benjn Reynolds of Carolina.

21.

22.

23. } Preparing my Miscellaneous Collection of papers for the press.

24.

25.   Sunday. Mr Barlow sails for France.

26.   Take tea at Mr Child's. Attend society.

27.

28. Call on Mrs Van wyck.
29. Dine at Mr Atkinson's with Mr Gore of Boston. Take tea at Mrs Lowther's.
30. Settle Mess Hudson & Goodwins account with Messr Campbells.
31.
June 1. Sunday—Reading Rieds Essays on the Intell powers of man. Go to Church, hear Mr Lynn. Take tea at Mr Watsons Introduced to Miss Hodgdon at Mr Stephens.
  2. Write to Mr Dwight, Read a Philological Dissertation before the Society. Take tea at Mr Stephens & walk with the Ladies.
  3. Unwell.
  4. Dine with Mr M Rogers. attend singing.
  5.
  6. *My Grand mother steele dies aged 87.*
  7. Official intelligence of the ratification of the Constitution in South Carolina. I write an address to the opposers of the Government.
  8th. Sunday. At church. at evening call on Majr Hodgdon at Col Stevens.
  9. Set out for Albany. Lodge at Peeks kill, at Mandevilles.
  10. Ride to Rhinebeck flats. Lodge at Trempers.
  11. Arrive at Albany.
  12. Proceed to Bennington. Lodge at Mr Freend's, Mr Smith's.
  13. Call on Mr Blodget, Mr Tichenor & Dr Shepard. Return to Lansingburg.
  14. Remain there & P M. ride to the Cohoes or Falls of the Mohawk. I measure the banks of the river, 100 feet, the falls more than half that distance.
  15. Sunday. Ride to Albany.
  16. To Claverack. Visit Mr Ludlow's family & Mr Chin's.
  17. Walk to Hudson & return.
  18. Take tea at Mr Chin's with Miss Ransalaer & Miss Governeur Sup at Mr Wm Ludlow's.
  19. Leave Claverak. ride to Rhinebeck.
  20. Proceed to Poughkeepsie. attend the debates in Convention. proceed to Peekskill.
  21. Arrive in New York.
  22. Sunday. P M at St Pauls.

23.   Very busy, Mr Ogden calls & gives me two Pamphlets—of Sermons.

24.   Take tea at Mr Loudon's. Hear of the death of my Grandmother Steele, aged 87. She died at my Father's house on the 6th Instant.

25.   Hear that New Hampshire has ratified the Constitution. Great joy at the Ninth.

26.   At evening read my 2d Lecture before the Philological society.

27.   Rain.

28.   Rain. It has rained almost every afternoon these two months.

29.   Sunday. at North Church. News of Virginia's ratifying the Constitution arrives. *Premature.*

30.   Ride out. Attend Philological Society. Hear Mr Dunlaps 'Love in New York' a new Comedy, read—it is ingenious.

July 1.

2.   Informed that Virginia has adopted the Constitution—89 to 79.

3.

4.   Mr Duer speaks an oration. Public rejoicings to celebrate the memorable aniversay of Independence.

5.   Writing.

6.   Sunday. Writing.

7.   At evening attend Philological Society. choose officers.

8.   Attend the same & read my 4th Lecture. Appointed one of the committee to arrange matters for the procession.

9.   Wait on the Federal Committee for the purpose.

10.   Assist in forming the arms of the Philological Society.

11.   Ride to Jamaica, Long Island, with Miss Loudon. at evening Read my 4th Lecture & finish it.

12.   Warm.

13.   Sunday.

14.   At evening attend Society.

15.   Writing for Mr Morse's Geography.

16.   Taking medicine for the removal of a bilious complaint.

17.   Meet the Committee of arrangement for the Philological Society, & order the Procession for the 23d Inst.

18.

19.

20.   Sunday. At home.

21.   Prepare for Procession. attend Society.

22.   Mr Dusnick arrives.

23. The Grand Procession in New York to celebrate the Adoption of the Constitution by 10 States. Very brilliant, but fatiguing. I formed a part of the Philological Society, whose flag & uniform black dress made a very respectable figure.

24.

25.

26. Employed in arranging a general account of the procession for the public. News of the Convention's adopting the Constitution received, & great joy testified. Mr Greenleaf's windows broken. (—*The printer opposed to the Constitution.*)

27. Sunday. Not very well.

28. Writing an account of the procession. Attend Society.

29. Sick.

30.

31.

August 1st.   Mr James Greenleaf & Mr Dusnick sail for Amsterdam. I ride on Long Island to the Narrows with Misses Loudons.

2. Mr West & Mr White arrive from Philad & Mr Ledyard from Groton.

3. Sunday. At home. Mr West Dines with me. Dr Johnson & Son call. Mr John Pierce *(of Litchfield)* buried—an irrepairable loss!

4. Sick.

5. Sick still.

6. Better.

7. Prepare for a journey to Boston.

8. Sail for Providence, in company with the Rhode Island Delegates, Mr Arnold & Mr Hazard, Mr Ingraham Mr Joy &c.

9. Arrive at Newport, & lodge.

10. Sunday. Sail to Providence.

11. Ride to Boston.

12. Wait on the dear Girl. deliver letters &c.

13. Dine at Mr Lambs. hear the Particulars of Miss Whitman's death at Danvers.

14. Dine at Mr Dawe's. Ride to Dorchester with Capt McGee. Ask consent of Mr Greenleaf & am happy in receiving it.

15. Dine with Dr Appleton. meet the booksellers, but do not agree upon the sale of the Institute.

16. Dine at Mr Wm Greenleafs.

17. Sunday. Dine with Capt M. Gee. Go to meeting.

18.	At home.
19.	Dine at Mr John Jay's.
20.	Dine at Mr Daniel Greenleaf's; ride to Cambridge. take tea at Mr Foxcrafts. examine the records of that town.
21.	Dine at Mr Thomas Lambs.
22.	Ride to Dorchester & play.
23.	Take tea at Mr Wm Greenleafs Walk in the Mall.
24.	Sunday. At meeting. dine at Mr Dawe's. take leave of friends.
25.	Set out for N York.
26.	Arrive at Hartford.
27.	At New Haven. sail for New York.
28.	
29.	Calm or contrary winds.
30.	Arrive at New York A West India Gentleman Mr Jansen dies in the family. I watch.
31.	Sunday. At home. writing letters to Europe.
Sept 1.	Write to Mr Greenleaf at Amsterdam.
2.	Take tea at Mr Watsons.
3.	At home, have company.
4.	Take tea at Miss Elberies.
5.	Hear of a singular death at Boston—Miss Fanny Apthorpe, by laudanum. Unhappy Girl.
6.	Dine with Mr Burrall.
7.	Sunday. rain.
8.	Set out for New Haven, with Mr Samuel Prisleau, a young Gentleman from S Carolina. Arrive at Fairfield at 12 oclock at night.
9.	Proceed to N Haven.
10.	Commencement. well conducted. Dine at Dr Stiles, Attend Ball—120 Ladies.
11.	Go to Hartford.
12.	Visit & do a little business. Take tea at Mr Seymours.
13.	Ride to Westdivision.
14.	Sunday. At meeting. hear Mr Saml Perkins.
15.	Sett out for New York. arrive at N Haven. Go aboard a sloop.
16.	Calm: or winds contrary all day. Take tea at Mr Hillhouses, with Miss Loudons.
17.	Sail for New York.
18.	Arrive at 3 o'clock A M.
19.	

259

20. Attend to business.
21. Sunday. At the Chapel.
22. The large India Ship burden about 650 tons, belonging to Mr Macomb &c. launched, in view of innumerable Spectators.
23.
24. Attend singing.
25.
26.
27.
28. Dr Barker dines with me.
29th. Have two teeth extracted, one by mistake—this is hard indeed— *(By Dr Coggswell)*.
30. A grand review of Militia.
October 1. Very Cold. Attend Publick Speaking in Columbia College, also Mr Cunningham's Examination. Mr Chaplin & Mr Stevens leave us.
2. cold. Mrs Simpson & family arrive from Manchester in England & take lodgings at Mrs Vandervoorts.
3. I walk to the Ship-Yards
4.
5. Sunday. Dine with Mr Gilman & Mr Kearny.
6. Attend the examination of the Students at Erasmus Hall in Flat Bush. The performances were generally good. Amend the Constitution of the Philological Society.
7. Easterly Storm.
8. Attend, Singing.
9. Walk with Miss Watson to the Battery.
10.
11.
12. Sunday, ride to Dr Ledyards, on Long Island.
13. Return, & attend Philol Society, where I am appointed an Examiner in Philology.
14.
15. Recite French to Mr Cunningham to perfect myself in the tongue.
16. Mr Wm Young calls on me. My birth-Day. 30 years of my life gone—a large portion of the ordinary age of man! I have read much, written much, & tried to do much good, but with little advantage to myself. I will now leave writing & do more lucrative business. My moral conduct stands fair with the

world, & what is more, with my own Conscience. But I am a bachelor & want the happiness of a friend whose interest & feelings should be mine.

17.
18.
19.   Sunday. Take tea at Mrs Morton's.
20.   Attend Society.
21.   Call on Mr Flint.
22.   Mr Allen of Litchfield calls. Mr Peter Vandervoort calls & settles the contract by which Mr James Greenleaf becomes possessed of Charles, a Negro boy, belonging to the Estate of Mr Peter Vandervoort of New York Deceased.
23.
24.   ne rien de nouvelles.
25.
26.   Sunday. Reading Bayley's Remarks on History, sacred & profane.
27.   Examine Mr Dunlaps accounts as Comtee of the Philo. Society. Receive Gillies History from N Haven.
28.
29.
30.   } nothing material.
31.
Novr 1.   Receive letters from Boston. Take tea at Mr Rogers.
2.   Sunday. Introduced to Miss Abbey Burr.
3.   Attend Philo. Society.
4.   Warm as summer.
5.   do . . .
6.   Wait on Mr Hazard, dine with Mr Childs, attend auction of books.
7.
8.   busy endeavoring to form a Society for publishing the American Magazine & Universal Register. succeed.
9.   Sunday. My friend Wm Capers sails for Carolina.
10.   A gale of wind begins.
11.   A violent Gale.
12.   Receive Letters from Hartford.
13.   Attend church in the evening, at Lecture on Music.
14.
15.

16.	Sunday. Correcting some writings.
17.	Sup at Mr Atkinson's.
18.	Dine at Mr Morton's.
19.	Mr Wilcox sails for Charleston with his lady. Mr Morse arrives.
20.	
21.	Receive pay of Messs Janes & Dole, for 100 Spelling books & Magn.
22.	Take tea at Mr Newtons. Receive a letter from Dr Appleton.
23.	Sunday, Write letters.
24.	Take tea at Mr Depeysters.
25.	Ship my trunk of books for Hartford.
26.	
27.	
28.	hear of Mr Greenleaf's arrival in Europe.
29.	
30.	Sunday. Sup at Mrs Morton's with Mr Abraham & Lady.

December 1.

2.	Take tea at Mr Watsons & go to singing.
3.	Sup at Mr Atkinsons.
4.	At Mr Stephens.
5.	
6.	Sign articles of agreement for the publishing of a Magazine & Register, with Mr F Child & Mr E Hazard.
7.	Sunday.
8.	Dine at Mr Burrals.
9.	Warm like May.
10.	Take tea at Mr Kings & sup at Mr Pintards.
11.	Go to Elizabeth Town. Sleep at Mr Austin's.
12.	Make an acquaintance with Mr Livingstone. Ride to Newark.
13.	Walk to New York.
14.	Sunday.
15.	Prepare to leave the City.
16.	do.
17.	Snow Storm.
18.	Set out
19.	and return.
20th.	Sail to New Haven. Happy to quit New York.
21.	Sunday. Cold. Wait on some friends.
22.	Proceed to Hartford.
23.	

24.   write.
25.   Walk to Westdivision.
26.
27.   Return to Town.
28.   Sunday. Dine at Col Wadsworth.
29.   Set out for Boston, lodge at Wilbraham.
30.   proceed to Worcestor. Take tea at Mr Thomas's, pay him some money ye advance for printing my Dissertation.
31.   Arrive in Boston, meet my Friends well.

1789

January 1st 1789.   Visit my very agreeable friends.
2.   do.
3.   Dine at Mr Dawes.
4.   Sunday. At home, dine with Mr Greenleaf. Do some business with Mr Thomas & form a plan of uniting the American & Massachusetts Magazine.
5.
6.   Writing—correcting my first Dissertation for the press.
7.   Dine at Mr Bell's, with Mr Thatcher.
8.   Pass the evening at Mr Dan Greenleafs.
9.   Dine at Dr Appleton's.
10.   At home.
11.   Sunday. Dine with Mr Dawes, go to church.
12.
13.   Dine with Mr Azor G Archibald.
14.   Dine with Mr Wm Greenleaf.
15.   with Mr Clarke. Pass evening at Mr Greens.
16.   At Mr Schollay's.
17.   At home.
18.   Sunday. At Mr Thatcher's meeting. At Mr Greenleafs at dinner. Go to hear Mr Clarke, & pass the evening at Mr Dawes.
19.   Take tea at Dr Appletons.
20.   At Mr Dawes Ball.
21.   at Club at Mr Eliots.
22.
23.   Call on Mr Lathrop.
24.   Dine at Mr Bullfinch's in a large Compy.
25.   Sunday. At home.
26.   Dine at Mr Danl Greenleafs.

27.   at home.

28.   Dine at Govr Bowdoins, the first time of seeing Dr John Adams, & Mr Parsons of Newbury Port.

29.   At home.

30.   Dine at Dr Appleton's.

31.   At Mr Freeman's with Mr Ames & Mr Nancrede.

Feby 1. Sunday.   At home. Take tea at Mr Dawes. Coldest evening.

2.   Dine at Mr Wm Greenleafs.

3.   at home.

4.   Dine at Mr Dawe's.

5.   Ride to Cambridge & pass the evening at Mr Professor Pearson's.

6.   Introduced to Mr Pope & Lady from Bedford.

7.   At home.

8.   Sunday. At Church. pass the evening at Mr Dawes.

9.   Dine with Mr Nancrede. Miss Scollay married. Introduced to the Miss Goldthwaites

10.   Dine with Mr D. Greenleaf.

11.
12.   } at home.
13.

14.   at home. Receive Letters from Mr James Greenleaf at Amsterdam informing of his Marriage with Miss Scholter.

15.   Sunday. Writing Letters.

16.
    } At home.
17.

18.

19.   Writing deposition in the Case of Hudson & Goodwin vs Patten for breach of Copy-right Law.

20.

21.   nothing material. Dine at Mr Greenleafs.

Sunday 22.   dine at Mr Dawes.

23.   Reading Selden.

24.

25.

26.   Attend Supreme Court, & read.

27.

28.

March 1.   Sunday. At Mr Clarke's Meeting.

2.   Take tea at Mr John Eliots.

3.
4.
5.   pass time at Court or in Reading Law.
6.
7.
Sunday 8.   At Mr Thatcher's.
  9.   Pass evening at Mr Dawe's.
 10.   Drawing of *Pope's Lottery* commences. Take tea at Mr Williams.
 11.   At Dr Appleton's, Club.
 12.   As usual.
 13.   at home.
 14.   do.
 15.   Sunday. Dine at Mr Greenleafs.
 16.   At Club.
 17.
 18.
 19.
 20.   Take tea at Dr Appletons.
 21.   Dine at Mr Lambs.
 22.   Sunday. Dine at Mr Dawes'.
 23.
 24.   Receive Manuscript of Winthrops History.
 25.   At Club. Introduced to Dr Tufts.
 26.
 27.
 28.   Dine at Mr Jay's with the Dutch Consul, Mr Berkel &c.
 29.   Sunday. At home, not well. Saml Belknap dies.
 30.
 31.
April 1. I hear the funding act in Pennsylvania repealed. I predicted this
        two years ago, & was abused in the paper for my opinions. Con-
        gress form house of Representatives.
  2.
  3.
  4.
  5.   Sunday. At Mr Clarke's, he christens his own child by the
        name of Charles Chauncey.
  6.   Senate in Congress formed.
  7.
  8.   Take tea at Mr Greenleafs with Miss Mason.

9.	
10.	
11.	Ride out. Hear from Mr J Greenleaf.
12.	Sunday. Dr Brownson, from Madras dines with us.
13.	Mr Adams, Vice President, sets out for N York.
14.	
15.	Mr Morse attends club.
16.	
17.	Walk to Cambridge. prepare a copy right bill for Congress.
18.	
19.	Sunday. Dine at Mr Greenleafs. hear Mr Morse preach at Mr Thatchers.
20.	
21.	Move from Court Street to Cornhill with Mr Archbalds family.
22.	
23.	Dr Appleton dines with me.
24.	Rain.
25.	
26.	Sunday.
27.	
28.	
29.	at club.
30.	
May 1.	
2.	
3.	Sunday, dine at Mr Dawes—five.
4.	Dine at Mr Wm Greenleafs. Walk to Maiden bridge, which is half a mile long.
5.	Set off for Bedford with Miss Greenleaf. Ride to Taunton, 36 miles, where we lodge.
6.	proceed to Bedford 26 miles, arrive about 2 o clock at Mr Pope's.
7.	
8.	
9.	
10.	Sunday. Ride to meeting at the head of the bay. 4 miles, hear Mr West. an odd, but learned candid man.
11.	Pass the day with Mr Saml West at Mr Popes.
12.	Set off for Boston. ride to Taunton.
13.	arrive.

14.	Rain. Dine with Dr Greenleaf.
15.	Visit Mr Coburn, Mr Eliot & introduced to Dr Hull.
16.	Rain. Several Gent. dine with me. prepare to leave town.
17.	Sunday. Dine at Mr Greenleafs.
18.	Set out for Hartford, settle with Mr Thomas of Worcester.
19.	Arrive at Hartford.
20.	
21.	Go to West division.
22.	Visit.
23.	Return. take lodgings at Mr Trumbulls at 10/ a week.
24.	Sunday. At Church.
25.	Attend assembly.
26.	do. hear Mr Gould's Memorial tried.
27.	do.
28.	do. Report of Auditors on Mr Lawrence's the treasurers account, great marks of fraud, appear.
29.	Mr Lewis visits Mr Trumbull.
30.	
31.	Sunday. at home.
June 1.	
2.	
3.	attend Assembly.
4.	
5.	
6.	M Tracy & Mr Cannon dine with us. at home with a lame wrist.
7.	Sunday receive letters from Boston.
8.	
9.	Rain confines me.
10.	
11.	Mr Trumbull sets out for Watertown.
12.	
13.	Receive Letters from Boston.
14.	Sunday.
15.	Walk to West division.
16.	Visit & dine with Mr Perkins. Return.
17.	Begin to bathe in the morning.
18.	Repeat it with benifit.
19.	do. Mr Trumbull returns.
20.	I ride to Windsor to visit Mr Wolcott.

21.   Sunday. Very hot. I visit Dr Hopkins.

22.   Mr Bingham calls on me with the acct of Phelps & Wheelock.

23.

24.   Dine at Col Wadsworths, with Miss St John & Miss Trumbull.

25.

26.

27.   Receive letters from Amsterdam.

28.   Sunday.

29.   Set out for Albany. Ride to West division.

30.   to Litchfield.

July 1.   to Salisbury.

2.   Stay & visit.

3.   to Poughkeepsie.

4.   to Ketchums where I remain, during the night a rain falls that injures the grass on Cloverak river.

5.   Sunday. Ride to Hudson. Visit Mr Gilbert. Mr Buttle, a Simsbury man, who trades with the indians, tells me there is a Webster among the Onandagoes, who was taken an infant the last French War (about 1758 probably) son of a Mr Webster of New London. Bred a savage, he will not leave that life, altho' his father brot him away at 13 years of age & put him to school, yet he staid but two years at Dartmouth College; he ran away, married & still lives among the natives. He must be of our family.

6.   Ride to Albany, on the West side of the Hudson, & to Lansingburg.

7.   Return to Albany.

8.   Breakfast with Mr Sill.

9.   bathe in the Spring. Visit the Shakers at the evening worship. Monsters of absurdity! But absurdity exists every where under different shapes.

10.   Ride to Pittsfield. Visit Mr Larned, then to Egremont.

11.   Ride to Salisbury.

12.   Sunday. Rain.

13.   Ride to Litchfield. Lodge at Mr Tracy's. Visit Miss Prince.

14.   Return to Hartford.

15.   Pass evening at Col Wadsworths.

16.   Write letters to Boston.

17.   Walk to East Hartford.

18.

19.   Sunday.
20.   Ride to Wethersfield. Call on Mr Simeon Belding for some papers.
21.
22.
23.   Draw a blister on my right hand.
24.   at home for several days.
25.   hear of the death of Mr John Ledyard.
26.   Sunday. Mr Sigourney calls on us.
27.
28.
29.   Cloudy weather.
30.
31.   Ride to West division.
August 1.   Return.
2.   Sunday.
3.
4.   Still cloudy. East winds.
5.   Lightning strikes a tree by Mr Saunders, near the South Meeting.
6.
7.   Set out for New York.
8.   Excessive Heat.
9.   Sunday. At New Haven
10.   Proceed.
11.   Arrive. Lodge at Capt Hardings.
12.   Attend debates of Congress.
13.
14.   heat extreme.
15.
16.   Sunday. dine at Mr Mortons.
17.   Set out for Newport.
18.   Headwind. Judge Leonard & Mr Gilman aboard.
19.   Put into New Haven.
20.   Sail at 12 at night, arrive at Newport.
21.   Proceed to Providence.
22.   At Boston Welcome.
23.   Sunday. At Mr Thatcher's with Mr Mullet & Lady.
24-29.   attend to visiting & business. Making preparation for keeping house.

30.	Sunday. at Meeting. Mr Dawes has a fit.
31.	
Sept 1	
2.	
3.	still employed in getting furniture.
4.	
5.	
6.	Sunday at Church.
7.	
8.	
9.	Set out for Hartford.
10.	Arrive.
11.	
12.	Draw writs against Dr Charles Mather & Bryan Dougherty.
13.	Sunday. No preaching!
14.	Dance.
15.	Visit at Col Wadsworth's.
16.	
17.	Walk to Westdivision.
18.	Return.
19.	Hear from Boston.
20.	Sunday. At home. Mr Morse in town & Dr Hartley from Carolina.
21.	
22.	
23.	Waggon overset with Mrs Green, Miss Dr Hartley &c going to N York.
24.	
25.	
26.	
27.	Sunday. At church. rain.
28.	
29.	
30.	
October 1-4	Sunday. At church. hear Mr Holmes from Georgia.
5.	
6.	
7.	Walk with Mr Strong. Sue Col Seymour for Mr Oothoudt.
8.	
9.	

10.   Ride to Westdivision.

11.   Sunday. At home.

12.   Mr Trumbull & wife go to New Haven.

13.

14.

15.

16.   My birthday. 31 years of my life gone! A material part of life.

17.   Prepare for Boston.

18.   Sunday.

19.   Set out for Boston on an important errand.

20.   Arrive.

21.

22.

23.   Taken with the Influenza.

24.   President Washington arrives in Boston, and all the world is collected to see him. I am almost confined with the Influenza. This differs from a common cold, by affecting the eyes & taking away all taste. The head appears to be fastened with chains, and the disorder is attended with a cough. The best remedy is hot liquors to produce perspiration, or a sweat brot on by violent exercise in a warm room. But if the stomach is disordered & refuses diet, a puke is necessary.

25.   Sunday. Confined, but my disorder has come to its crisis.

26.   Much better. This day I became a husband. I have lived a long time a bachelor, something more than thirty one years. But I had no person to form a plan for me in early life & direct me to a profession. I had an enterprising turn of mind, was bold, vain, inexperienced. I have made some unsuccessful attempts, but on the whole hav done as well as most men of my years. I begin a profession, at a late period of life, but have some advantages of traveling and observation. I am united to an amiable woman, & if I am not happy, shall be much disappointed.

27.   dress & wait on visitors.

28.

29.

30.

31.   See my new brother & Sisters.

November 1.   Sunday. Design to go to church, but my hairdresser defeats my plan & Mrs Webster goes with the family to attend Sacrament. To punish my hairdresser, I keep back part of his due. But I attend afternoon. Dine at brother Daniels.

2. Mrs Webster & her Sister Priscilla with myself set for Hartford. Lodge at Worcester.

3. proceed to Palmer. rain.

4. Arrive in Hartford. Lodge at Mr Trumbulls'.

5.

6. Set up furniture.

7. Begin housekeeping.

8. Sunday. Mrs Webster attacked severly by the Influenza.

9. very ill.

10. much better.

11.

12. attending to Domestic matters.

13.

14. Sister Priscy unwell.

15. Sunday. At home.

16.

17. Dr Hull & Lady dine with us.

18. Mr Eliot & Sister from Boston call.

19.

20. Mr Wadsworth passes the evening.

21.

22. Sunday. Sister Priscy & myself at Church.

23.

24. Mr Watson of N York calls on us.

25.

26. Thanksgiving Day. First federal one.

27. Mr Watson, Jude Root, Col Wadsworth &c dine with me, and Club meets at my house. Question. Whether a woman can be bound by warranty of land, made under coverture.

28.

29. Sunday. Mrs Webster goes to church for the first time.

30. The last day of a dull wethered month. Visited by Mrs Wadsworth & daughters & Mrs Colt.

December 1

2. Club at Mr Perkins. Quest. Whether the father can maintain an action of Trespass *per quod*, for seduction of the daughter, living with him & more than 21 years old. Generally agreed *not* for loss of service, but for expenses he may.

December 3, 1789

3.

4.

5.   Dr Cogswell arrives & passes evening with us.

6.   Sunday. Mr H Otis & Dr Cogswell take tea with us.

7.   Capt Conkling arrives from Boston with a trunk &c.

8.

9.   Club at Mr Trumbulls. Mr Trumbull Mr Goodrich, Mr Root, Mr Perkins & myself present. Quest. Whether the Excise of this State is consistent with the general government. Agreed it is, but bad policy to be so.

10.   At the first Assembly. Dance till 12. oclock.

11.

12.

13.   Sunday. at church.

14.

15.

16.   At Mr Root's. Club debate whether a note given by a minor, who, after age, acknowledges the note, is recoverable. agreed not on simple acknowledgement, but on *promise to pay*, recoverable.

17.

18.   Writing on excise.

19.

20.   Sunday at church, pass evening at Mr Colts.

21.   At Mr Goodrichs.

22.   Sign lease for the House with Col Wadsworth. have Dr Cogswell D Wadsworth & J Chenevard to dine. Ladies wait on Mrs Wadsworth.

23.   Have a large number of Ladies to wait on.

24.   Assembly, brilliant.

25.   Dine at Col Wadsworth, & Mrs Webster also.

26.

27.   Sunday. At church. Dr A Hopkins & Mr Perkins wait on me.

28.   Issue an attachment agt James Stanley.

29.   Snow.

30.   Mr Ames in town.

31.   Visit Mr Trumbull. An end of the Old Year. Good bye.

1790

January 1 1790.   Mild Wether.

2.   Col Wadsworth visits us.

3. Sunday. At church. Mr Strong visits me.
4. Meeting of Merchants on Excise, I call on our nabor Parsons.
5. Visit Mr Colt. Introduced to Mr John Trumbull. see his Gibralter.
6.
7. Hed-ache prevents my attending Assembly.
8. Better. Mrs Webster takes tea at Mr Parsons's; Miss Wadsworth & Miss Trumbull with us in eve.
9.
10. Sunday. At home.
11. Snow.
12. At City Court. Questions decided, that for neglect of serving an execution, Sheriff shall pay interest on the judgement from date of execution. That City Courts have jurisdiction of petitions in Equity. Mrs Webster visits Miss I. Hart.
13. Miss Hopkins visits us.
14.
15.
16. Father Greenleaf arrives to our great joy.
17. Sunday. At Church, hear Mr Perkins.
18. Walk about town with Mr Greenleaf. My brother Charles & Sister dine with us.
19. Visit the manufactory.
20. Dr Fish & Col Wyllys dine with us. My father vizits us.
21. Mr Greenleaf & Sister Priscy leave us for Boston. Attend a most brilliant Assembly.
22. At Court.
23. Do.
24. Sunday. At Church.
25. At Court.
26. do.
27. do.
28. do.
29. do.
30. Do. Hudson & Goodwin recover judgement agt N Patten for selling my books.
31. Sunday. At home. Writing. finish my Essays.
February 1. At Court.
2. Do. Mr H Seymour & Dr Cogswell pass evening. Town Meeting my brother declines Collectorship of Town tax.

3. Court adjourns. Take tea with Mrs Morgan.
4. Assembly.
5. Have company at evening.
6. At home.
7. Sunday. At Church, take possession of *my pew*.
8. Cold. at home.
9. City Court.
10. Dine at Capt Chenevards. Saffa comes to live with us.
11. Coldest week this winter.
12. Miss Watson & Miss Trumbull visit us.
13. Pleasant.
14. Sunday. at home.
15.
16.
17.
18.
19.
20.
Sunday 21. At Church
22.
23. Superior Court.
24.
25. M Nathl Tracy arrested at the suit of Caleb Gibbs
26. In Cowles Case, verdict for defend on plea of usury.
27.
28. Sunday. At Church. Mr Harbach calls on us.
March 1
2.
3. Mr C Gibbs arrives.
4. Mr N Tracy released & leaves town. Last Assembly night.
5. Take tea at Mr Goodrich's.
6. Supr Court calls their Session. Mr Pattens Complaint abated.
7. Sunday. At home, Mrs Tracy & Miss Watson with us.
8. Mrs Philips visits us.
9. Coldest day almost this Winter
10. Visit Col Seymour's.
11. Snow very deep. I hear of the intended publication of Barry Spelling book at Philadelphia.
12. My father visits us. At Col Wadsworths pass the evening happily.

13. Draw a writ. Mr Charles Webster of Albany calls on us & Mr Thoms Franklin. Col Wadsworth comes home.
14. Sunday. At home. Mr Marsh preaches.
15. At Mr Trumbulls.
16. Snow.
17. My Father, Mr Belding & brother dine here.
18.
19.
20. Mr Ingraham arrives. & passes
21. Sunday, with us. Church.
22.
23. Ship Rudiments for N York.
24. Col Wadsworth sets out for Congress
25. I go for Albany; lodge at New Hartford.
26. Ride to Canaan with Mr Saml Pitkin Lodge at Col Burrds.
27. Dine at Mr Elipht Steeles, my Uncle's at Egremont. Ride to Mesuks, near Clavarak.
28. Sunday. Arrive & pass the day at Hudson; at Church.
29. Ride towards Albany, lodge at Millers, 12 miles from the City.
30. Arrive & dine at Albany; proceed to Lansingburg with Mr Charles M Webster, printer & 2d Cousin. Lodge at Mr Doles's.
31. Return to Albany, but dine at Troy & take tea with Mr H Othoudt.
April 1. Finish my business, & set out for Hartford; ride to Millers.
2. Proceed towards home thro New Concord & New Canaan, ride in the Rain to Stocksbridge, lodge at Mrs Bingham's.
3. Proceed to Porters in the Woods, and lodge
4. Sunday. Ride early & get home before night. Never was the road so bad!
5. Make an offer to Yale College of 1 pr Cent on sales of my Institute.
6. County court opens.
7.
8. Fast Day. Mr Ingraham calls on us. Mrs Vandervoort sets out for N York. We have a good Sermon.
9.
10. Storm of rain, violent thunder, at 12 at night Mr Mitchels barn burnt by lightning (*Wethersfield*).
11. Sunday. At meeting. Mrs Webster bled.
12. Freemen's meeting.

13.	Influenza rages, attended with more inflammatory symtoms than last fall, a pain in the back, side of loins.
14.	My father sells his farm to Lemuel Hulburt & deed given.
15.	Sick with a cold.
16.	A little better; issue a writ for Dr Brownson agt Jo Burne jun
17.	Sick. Death of Dr Franklin.
18.	Sunday. Storm. Mrs S., no preaching.
19.	
20.	dull, east winds, influenza. Dr Franklin buried.
21.	
22.	Take out execution agt Judd.
24.	Attend Court, Col Wyllys—dispute
25.	Sunday. At home, Mr D Goodwin buried.
26.	Judgement rendered for Dr Brownson agt J Burne jun Inspector, 7/ damages
27.	I read acct of Pelew Islands, plant a few hills of corn
28.	Snow all the forenoon
29.	
30.	becoming Pleasant.
May 1.	I draw a plan for paving our Streets, or rather covering them with hard rock stone; which proves agreeable to many. P M. Ride to West division.
Sunday. 2d.	Daniel Smith buried.
3.	
4.	Supreme Court of errors sits.
5.	My Cistern put down.
6.	
7.	
8.	
9.	Sunday. At Meeting, hear Mr Campbel. Mr Allen dines with me.
11.	Plant potatoes, beets, carrots, parsnips, Cucumbers.
12.	Warm
13.	Election day, pleasant, Mr Flint Miles, Davenport & Taylor dine with me. Mr Strong's sermon very good, guards appeared well.
14.	Little business done.
15.	Mr Edwards, two Davenports & Tracy dine with me.
16.	Sunday. At home.
17.	At Assembly

18.   do. Mrs Goodwin arrives and Mr Hughes.
19.   Dr Stiles dines with me.
20.   Rain, issue several writs.
21.   Ride to Westdivision.
22.   Auditors in Oothoudt & Seymour's Case meet & adjourn
23.   Sunday. At home, at eve Mr Leonard Jarvis, Boston, calls on me.
24.   Have Lettuce at table. P M. House of Representatives on motion, suspend their rule, 'that on report of Comt^{ee} of conference, vote of concurrence shall be taken without debate,' in order to discuss the first & second amendments to federal Constitution & concur with the Council.
25.   Amendments 1st & 2d rejected.
26.   Have letters from Amsterdam, & receive a clock, a present from Mr Dawes of Boston.
27.   House of Representatives vote to exclude Senators & Representatives in Congress from a seat in our Legislature
28.
29.   Audit between Col Seymour & Henry Oothoudt Esq. decided in favor of Col Seymour. Col Pope & Lady arrive in town.
30.   Sunday. at meeting, Judge Jay in town.
31.   Rain.
June 1.   Ride with Mr & Mrs Pope.
2.   Miss Seymour & Miss Bull visit us, company
3.   Take tea at Dr Fish's.
4.   Take tea at Mr Colt's
5.
6.   Sunday—At home—no preeching—
7.   Rainy
8.   At Mr Perkins.
9.   At Mr Avery's. Eat Cucumbers sent us by Mrs Wadsworth.
10.
11.   Made district rates. Mr Chenevard & Mr Parsons take tea with us.
12.   Rain.
13.   Sunday Rain
14.   Writing Farmers Catekizm.
15.   Walk over the River.
16.   My coat turned.

17. Plant potatoes. 3d crop, in rows, 2 N rows, 7 or 8 inches apart in the others, the plants nearer.

18.

19. Mr Whitman's estate attached.

20. Sunday. Mr Strong Absent

21.

22.

23.

24. St Johns, Mr Mc Clure preaches; rode to West division.

25. Experiment, lay 3 square yards of mellow earth with seed potatoes about 8 inches apart, cover them with half rotten hay & straw, cover 1 yard with shoots broken off from the potatoes.

26.

27. Sunday. At church.

28.

29.

30.

July 1. Set out for Northhampton. Sleep at Westfield.

2. Ride to Northampton, view water works.

3. Ride to Springfield

4. Sunday. At church.

5. Return to Hartford.

6.

7. Cincinnati meet. Dr Dana preaches.

8.

9.

10.

11. Sunday.

12. Mr Gridley's Barn burnt by lightning.

13.

14.

15. First Cucumbers in our Garden

16. Mrs Watson calls on us.

17.

18. Sunday. Mr Boardman

19. Squashes, Jedh Strong's trial, bound to his good behavior by Mr Meeve.

20.

21.

22.
23.   Huccleberries. Mr Gallaudet's child dies.
24.   Father Greenleaf & Lady arrive.
25.   Sunday. At Church.
26.   Take tea at Judge Root's.
27.   Ride to Wethersfield
28.   Visit Mr Trumbull & Mr Colt
29.
30.   Winthrops Journal published.
31.
August 1.   Sunday at Church.
    2.   Mrs Webster taken ill. Women sent for.
    3.   Illness continues, her pains severe & her case difficult.
    4.   At half past 4 oclock P M. She is delivered of a daughter.
             whom we call *Emily Scholten*; the Scholten being added in
             honor of the family in Amsterdam into which our Brother
             James is married.
    5.
    6.
    7.
    8.   Sunday. At church. Papa & Mama attend.
    9.   They leave us for Boston.
10.   Mrs Symms arrives from Philad.
11.
12.
13.   Balloon ascends, takes fire & falls.
14.
15.   Sunday. At home.
16.
17.
18.
19.
20.
21.   Ride to East Windsor.
22.   Sunday. My daughter baptized by the name of *Emily Scholten.*
23.
24.
25.
26.   Draw on Mr West for 85 dollars.
27.

28.

29. Sunday.

30. Receive the money on the Draft on West. Mrs Webster dines below stairs.

31. Mr W rides out.

September 1. Nurse leaves us.

2.

3.

5. Sunday. Mr Murray preaches at South Church Universalist.

6. Purchase 10 cords of wood. Superior Court.

7. Mr Murray preaches again at the South Church, & afterwards he & Lady & Miss L Bull take tea at our house.

8. At Court

9.

10. Mr Van Berkel in town.

12. Sunday. Mrs Webster goes to Church

13. At Court.

14. Do.

15. Hear from brother Abram. Mr Webster attacked with Cholera Morbus.

16. Wm Steele of Berlin tried for procuring & giving cantharides, found guilty.

17. Fair Wether. Court adjourn. Winds S W. m.

18. Fair. Wind N W. moderate.

19. Sunday. Fair. moderate. at home, nursing

20. Fair, m. Wind. N. Write an agreement with Haswell & Russel.

21. Set out for Lenox, lodge at Colebrook, fair, warm

22. Proceed to Canaan. A sudden change of wind to N W. a squall, go to Salisbury

23. Ride to Lenox, cold high wind at N W

24. Ride to N Lebanon, fair, mild W wind.

25. Return from Lenox & arrive at Colebrook warm.

26. Arrive at Hartford, warm S W wind. Sunday.

27. Warm, but rainy. W S. & S W

28. Cold. Rain. W Strong at N.

29. ride to Westdivision, engage a boy for winter. Wind N E modrate cloudy. pick a bushel of squashes.

30. Prepare for Boston.

October 1. Set out for Boston, lodge at Spencer, fair.

2. Arrive in Boston, fair.

3.   Sunday. At Mr Thatcher's in morning & Mr Clarkes P M. rain.

4.   Visit.

5.   Dine at Dr Appleton's, visit Mr Binghams school, fair

6.   Take tea at Mr Dawe's, in company of Mr John Thayre *fair*

7.   Dine at Mr Cleland's, *fair*

8.   Set off for Hartford. fair

9.   Arrive. Rainy. W. N & N E.

10.   Sunday. Rain at home. Mr Graham of S Carolina & Capt Roach of Ireland take tea with me.

11.

12.   City Court, Col Seymour & J Pratte case tried, decided in favr of Defendant.

13.   Ride to Granby & take a note for Dr Thomas Greenleaf, of Dr Joseph Jewitt £ 45.19.0. Mr Trumbull & take tea with me

14.   Rain & high wind. N N E.

15.   On an audit, in the case of Wm Lawrence & John Seymour, decide for plff. & £ 4.6.4. awarded. Clears up. Wind S W. at eve.

16.   my birth day, 32 years old, pleasant, wind W. Ride to East Windsor to look after a farm of my father in Law.

17.   Sunday. Warm & Pleasant W. S W. At church.

18.   pleasant.

19.   part of the evening at Mr Perkins. pleasant.

20.   Mrs H. Wyllys visits. W N E. moderate

21.   Cloudy & calm

22.   Circuit Court sets in Hartford Justice Jay presides. pleasant

23.   Pleasant.

24.   Sunday. Mr M Leavenworth dines with me. Judge Cushing & Lady return our visit. Mrs W & myself.

25.   The Judges call on me, take some books. Winthrops Journal & Essays.

26.   Anniversary of our marriage, one year past & no quarrelling, of course the Flitch of bacon is won. Court adjourns. mild.

27.   Dine at Mr Colts. very cold. wind N & N W.

28.   Ride to East Windsor to look after Mr Greenleafs land. mild.

29.   Mild, calm.

30.   Mr Elisha Colt married. mild.

31.   Sunday. At Church. Hear Mr Noyes. mild.

November 1.   Mild, calm. Young Mr Brunson calls to converse on pur-
chasing Mr Greenleaf's land in E Windsor. Apples from Enfield
arrive for Winter.

2.   Court adjourned one week by Assembly. mild. Mr Wolcott
passes evening.

3.   At evening thunder Storm, violent from S. Wind high at S &
E. Mr S. Lawrence.

4.   Clear. W moderate at W.

5.

6.   Miss Elliot arrives from Fairfield.

7.   Sunday.

8.   Miss Elliot leaves us for Boston.

9.   County court meets.

10.   Court adjourned to Monday.

11.   Thanksgiving, hear of Govr Bowdoins death. Dine at Col
Wadsworth's. cold.

12.   At home. Dr Cogswell dines with me.

13.

14.   Sunday. At home, reading.

15.   Court sits. I argue a plea of abatement, N Seymour ye S. Mix.

16.   Rain. N. E Cold.

17.   Argu the case of Stephen Root agt Heirs of Joseph N Ensign,
action on Covenant of Warranty.

18.   Cold N E Storm.

19.   do.

20.   Storm abates. Mr F. Bull's house broke open, & 300 dollars
stolen

21.   Sunday. Hear Mr Flint.

22.   At Court. mild Wether.

23.   Mild.

24.

25.

26.   Very cold.

27.   Violent snow Storm.

28.   Sunday. Sleighing.

29.

30.

December 2.   First Assembly this night.

3.

4.

JANUARY 1, 1791

5. Sunday. Very cold.
6. Ride to New Haven, with Mr Leonard.
7. Purchase Law Books of Mr J Been. Thermometer at 16°. call on Dr Stiles.
8. Return to Middletown, colder.
9. Argue a Demurrer at Court in the Case Greenleaf vs Jewitts, then Return to Hartford.
10. Moderate. Mr Wadsworth & sister dine with us, & Miss Blakeley
11. Rain.
12. Sunday. Writing to Mr Jefferson & Mr Wetmore.
13. At home.
14. Not very well. Henry Seymour and Dr Cogswell here at eve.
15.
16. Freemen's & town meeting. Col Wadsworth had every vote to fill the vacant seat in Congress. P Edwards resigned. Snow.
17. Send Jairus to Say brook. cold.
18. At sunrise, Mercury 14° below Cypher. pay S Clark £ 15. for E Hoisington.
19. Sunday. At Church, cold. News of Majr Wyllys deth.
20.
21.
22.
23. Take tea at Dr L Hopkins.
24. Take tea at Mr Trumbulls.
25. Christmas. very cold.
26. Sunday. Snow; moderately cold. Wind N. In evening at Club, at Mr Strong's.
27.
28. Take at Dr Fish's.
29. Mr Moseley calls for bill of Cost in favr of Jewitts & paid £ 2.13.0
30. Assembly night, some altercation about wine, but a very brilliant.
31. Very cold; between 10 & 11 oclock at night Wm Hooker's barn was burnt. Dr Butlers nearly adjoining, hardly saved. Several persons hurt. Snow Storm.

1791

January 1st. 1791.   Snow. Begin to translate Plowden's Repts

2. Sunday. Plezant. No church N Side
3. Moderate
4. Take tea at Mrs Ledyards.
5.
6. Mrs Brunson, Miss Olcott.
7. Mrs Perkins & Miss Pitkens.
8. Cold.
9. Sunday. Snow.
10.
11.
12. Mr Anthony in town.
13. Assembly eve.
14.
15. Emily not well. Mr Anthony dines with me.
16. Sunday. No meeting, North Side.
17. Mr David Bull's house, tenanted by Ebr Clarke, Joiner, burnt; snow storm.
18.
19.
20. Cousin Steele here.
21. Mrs Fish, &c visit Mrs W.
22.
23. Sunday Mr Adams in town.
24.
25. County Court, by adjournment.
26. Rain a little.
27. Assembly. 12 Strangers attend.
28.
29.
30. Sunday. Snow.
31.
Feby. 1
2. at Court. Brother Abram arrives.
3.
4.
6. Sunday, at church.
7. Lottery commenced drawing, highest prize 1000, drawn by No 2069.
8. Champion & Wadsworth &c cause heard on plee of usury & decided in favr of Champion.

9.
10.   Assembly evening, about 11 oclock cry of fire disturbs the
        company. Stebbin Wilson's barn burnt.
11.
12.
13.   Sunday. Mr Perkins preached.
14.   Ride to Glastenbury with Mr Goodrich. Receive visits from W
        Division.
15.
16.
17.   Have much company, a very cold day.
18.
19.
20.   Sunday.
21.
22.   Superior Court.
23.
24.   Last dancing assembly.
25.
26.
27.   Sunday. At home, unwell.
28.
March 1. Weather moderates.
2.
3.
4.
5.   Ride to West division.
6.   Sunday. River not open.
7.   Not well.
8.   Bot. 3 Tickets in Hartford Woollen Manufactory Lottery, No.
        3969, 3990, 3971. I have in the Massachusetts Semi-annual
        Lottery. No 20.045.
9.   Rain. Writing, the Patriot, No. I.
10.   Rain
11.   Rain. Write on the Utility of banks in Connecticut Courant.
12.   do. Connecticut River cleard of ice. M Caldwell's brig driven
        ashore by ice.
13.   Sunday. Take my seat in South Church. Mr Marsh preaches.
14.   Pleasant.
15.   Rain. Col Wadsworth arrives from Congress

16.	cloudy.
17.	Pleasant, warm, very warm for season.
18.	Cloudy. Col Wadsworth passes eve with us. Mr D & Dr Cog.
19.	Snow. half the day.
20.	Sunday. River high in consequence of the warm weather the 17th. at Church.
21.	At home.
22.	Busy with clients.
23.	At home. Cow calves at night.
24.	Moved to a Room under the Controllers Office. This evening three very heavy peals of thunder.
25.	Rainy.
26.	Pleasant. Dine at Mr Trumbulls.
27.	Sunday. Pleasant, at church.
28.	City meeting. Donegani performs feats before the Court house.
29.	Ride to Litchfield; rain.
30.	Lodge at Mr Tracy's. Wait on Govr Wolcott &c.
31.	Return to Hartford; pleasant.
April 1.	Streets dry.
2.	Rain.
3.	Sunday, Eclipse of the sun, the whole body of the moon immersed in the sun's disk, left a circular ring of light, bright day turned into half night. Mr Apthorp brings letters from Boston.
4.	
5.	Court.
6.	Cold chilling Northerly winds, dry.
7.	A Little Snow.
8.	Cold.
9.	do Mr Thayer *(My class mate, Catholic.)* arrives & lodges with me.
10.	Sunday. I attend high Mass in his room. Go to church.
11.	Freeman's meeting. Receive a horse from Mr Holly & Cotton.
12.	At Court.
13.	Purchase 69 lb. salmon a /3° for winter.
14.	Ride part of the way to Westdivision.
15.	At audit at Mr Heath's between Dr Hooker & Aaron Cadwell.
16.	Warm. Meet Dr Hitchcock.
17.	Sunday. Dr H in the morning preaches & Mr Maxey P M.
18.	At Court.

19.   Court rise
20.   Revd Mr Abel Flint ordained over the 2d Parish. A ball at evening.
21.   Set out for Fairfield. Lodge at Wallingford.
22.   Ride to Fairfield, lodge at Dr Hull's
23.   Ride to Rye, at Mrs Havilands.
24.   Sunday. Reach New York, put up at Mr Watson's.
25.   Very busy.
26.
27.   Set out for home. Ride to Stamford, lodge at Mr Davenports.
28.   Ride to Greenfield, attend Dr Dwights exhibition. Lodge at Mr Eliots.
29.   Ride to New Haven & to Wallingford
30.   Arrive at home.

May 1. Sunday.   At church.
2.   Draw a petition to the Assembly for Arnel Allen.
3.   Ride to West division to see Wm Sedgwick.
4.   Circulate a petition for a lottery to build a Court House.
5.   At Court.
6.   At Court. Ride to West division with Mrs Webster
7.
8.   Sunday. At Church.
9.   Pass evening at Geo' Bull's.
10.   Warm.
11.   Warm.
12.   Election. Mr Wm Lockwood & Miss Sturgis, Mr Eliot & his daughter, dine with us. Dr Dwight preached excellently. Mr Zephh Swift delivered an oration before the Abolition Society, of which I am chosen a member. Mrs Blackleach arrives; a ball.
13.   Rain; ball at Wethersfield
14.   M John Trumbull arrives in town.
15.   Sunday. At church. Mr Perkins preached. Mr Trumbull, Mr Eliot, tea.
16.   Attend Assembly. An Earthquake at half past 10 o'clock at night.
17.
18.   Warm.
19.
20.
21.

22.	Sunday.
23.	Argue a plea of Abatement in Mrs Blackleach cause agt J Blackleach her husband, on petition of divorce before Gen Assembly.
24.	Warm
25.	
26.	
27.	
28.	Mrs Blackleach's cause tried, obtains.
29.	Sunday. Very warm.
30.	Set off for Boston with Mrs Webster & little Emma, in a chaise; cloudy; lodge at Springfield.
June 1.	Proceed to Brookfield, slight rain.
2.	Proceed to Shrewsbury.
3.	Arrive at Boston; fatigued.
4.	See our friends.
5.	Sunday. At church.
6.	Artillery Election. Dr Parker preached the sermon, at the old Brick. An Episcopalian in a Dissenting Church.
7.	
8.	
9.	
10.	Nothing remarkable.
11.	
12.	Sunday. Hear Mr Bently of Salem preach.
13.	
14.	At Mr Dawes; at evening at Mr Gore's.
15.	at Dr Appleton's.
16.	
17.	
18.	Dine at Mr Bonds with Mr Flint
19.	Sunday. At Mr Dl Greenleaf's.
20.	Set out for Hartford; arrive at Attleboro.
21.	Pass Providence & find a horrid road. Lodge at Coventry in R. Island.
22.	Proceed with difficulty & danger to Norwich.
23.	Proceed to Lebanon; dine at Col Trumbull's. Borrow his horse & arrive within 6 miles of home.
24.	Get home safe.

25. Find great multitudes of black worms devouring fields of grass & corn.
26. Sunday. At church.
27. Send for a Cow to North Bolton, purchased of Alexr MLean.
28. Begin to write Lessons for the Husbandman.
29. Warm.
30. Plant peas of this years growth.
July 1. Dry season.
2. A shower from the east.
3. Sunday. At church. Mr John Gardner from S Carolina, calls. Pick the first cucumbers in my garden.
4. Ride to Mr Parsons.
5. Visit Dr Fish's.
6.
7. Have company
8. Visit the Miss Patten's
9. Mrs Tisdale & Mrs Isaac Sanford visit here.
10. Sunday. Mr Carey with me.
11. Superlative heat. Miss Wadsworth & Miss Delia Dwight visit here
12. Heat extreme. 98°. blood heat, a shower
13. Ride to Westdivision & pass the day with Mrs W, & little Emma
14. Rain, violent thunder. Mr Riley's barn struck.
15. Ride to Norwich at request of some persons, to get appointed Notary Public. Wait on the Govr.
16. Breakfast with the Govr & receive my commission; set off for Hartford, & Ride to Whites; a shower detains me all day.
17. Return to Hartford. Sunday.
18.
19.
20. Set Out for Vermont.
21.
22.
23. Arrive at Windsor; lodge at Mr Jacobs.
24. Sunday.
25. Proceed over the mountains thro Cavendish to Otter Creek
26.
27. Arrive at Bennington.
28. Proceed to Lansingburg.

29.   Lie by.

30.   Ride thro Albany to New Lebanon

31.   Sunday. Proceed thro Stockbridge to Sheffield.

Augt 1.   Get home, having post 370 miles; left my horse at pasture in Colebrook at Heydon's. Rain.

2.   Hot.

3.   Ride to Westdivision, & P M visit Mr Marsh of Wethersfield.

4.   Emma's birth day; takes tea at Mrs Olcotts

5.   Very rainy.

6.   Dismiss Jairus Kibbe from my service.

7.   Sunday. At church.

8.

9.   Rain; at City Court; trover by Luke Diggins for 1/4 of a sloop tried; verdict for deft.

10.   Hot.

11.   A party for watermelons at William's; rain.

12.   Mr W. visits Mrs Goodrich. Mr Jedh Strong in town; engages me to negotiate with his wife for a release of all claim to her dower; she declines.

13.   Ride to Williams by the lower ferry to lay out a bowling green.

14.   Sunday. Mr McClure preaches, Mr Seaman of New York calls on me. Mr Fredk Wolcott.

15.   Ride to Wethersfield; visit Mrs Belding.

16.   Rain.

17.

18.   Ride to Westdivision; break one spring of my carriage.

19.   Rain.

20.   Ride to Williams.

21.   Sunday. At church.

22.

23.   An agreeable party to Williams.

24.

25.   Thunder; hear of the attempt of the French king to escape.

26.   Settle accounts with Capt Alexander McLean of North Bolton, & receive a balance by his due bill for 5 reams of paper.

27.   Eliphl & Mother Steele call on me.

28th.   Sunday. At Church.

29.   At Col Wylly's at tea.

30.   Very hot.

31.   Wind suddenly changes from S to N. cold.

September 1. Rain.

2. Cold. A Dance at Mr D Bull's.

3. Cold.

4. Sunday. Rain; at church. Mrs Skinner dies.

5. Mrs S. is buried. Rain.

6. Superior Court. Saffa's birthday.

7. Little Misses take tea here. Grand Jury sit on the Windsor man charged with the murder of his child.

8. At Court.

9. do.

10. Ride to East Windsor.

11. Sunday. At church. Rain.

12. At Court. McLean & Barnard the great cause respecting D Goodwins will, begun.

13. The cause continued & argued. Take tea at Col Seymour's.

14. Rain. Commencement N Haven Selah Sheldon tried for his life & acquitted on the ground of insanity.

15. Rain. S Laurence's Case tried & verdict for him. Hear of Riots in England at Birmingham and at Cape Francois.

16. Clear. Wind at N W. Court adjourn.

17. Mr Cutting (Leonard M) in town. Mrs Hopkins dies at half pt 12. Powder Mill blown up, 3 persons killed.

18. Sunday. At meeting.

19. Ride to E Hartford to see the ruins of the Powder Mill; attend Mrs H. funeral.

20. Hear Mon. read:

21. Begin to wean Emma. Accept Paul Richardson for debt. Go to Wethersfield. Take tea at Col Chesters.

22.

23. Mrs W. taken ill. Wait on Mr Channing.

24. Cloudy.

25. Sunday. Rain.

26. Cloudy, but 5 fair days yet in September.

27. Clear at noon. M Mais a French Gentleman drinks tea with us.

28. Ride to Westdivision; cool.

29.

30. Sup at Avery's on turtle.

October 1. Warm.

2. Sunday. At home.

3.

4.
5.
6.
7.　Company from Wethersfield. Mr Webb.
8.　Company. Miss Wads & Miss Seymour
9.　Sunday. Last night first frost to injure vegetables. Col War & Mr Bond in town with their wives.
10.
11.　Set on foot subscription for Court house.
12.　Mr Russell & Mary, friends from Bedford, arrive.
13.
14.　Kill a hog. Mr Belding brings 6 barrels of cider.
15.
16.　Sunday. Col Stephens takes tea with me, go to Church.
17.
18.　Take tea at Mrs Ledyards.
19.　Ride to New Haven with Mr Hudson; lodge at Isaac Jones.
20.　A most disagreeable day.
21.　Take tea at Dr Stiles. Visit Mr Blackleach; become acquainted with Mr Maxwell & Mr Hazard N York.
22.　Return to Hartford; find my niece ill with plurisy.
23.　Sunday; wind at N W. violent a hurricane almost.
24.　More pleasant. Sapha very ill.
25.　Circuit Court.
26.　Pleasant. Sapha better.
27.
28.
29.
30.　Sunday.
31.　Wait on Judge Jay &c
November 1.　Prompter first published.
2.
3.　A cold day. First Snow falls.
4.　Preparing the Elsworth house.
5.　do.
6.　Sunday. At Church.
7.
8.　Friend Russell & Mary arrive.
9.
10.　Mr Bond calls, from Philad.

11.   Try the Petition of West Lane people, for a highway.
12.   Move from Col Wadsworth's house to Mr Elsworths.
13.   Sunday.
14.   Warm like summer.
15.   Argued the Cause of Nathl Hoisington vs Elisha allen & Aaron Cadwell, false imprisonment, recovered £ 15 & cost. Cause appealed.
16.
17.   At Court.
18.
19.
20.   Sunday. At Church. Mr Chenevard & Dr Hopkins pass the evening here.
21.
22.
23.   Court adjourns to 3d tuesday of Jany. Settled acct. with Hudson & Goodwin.
24.   Thanksgiving. Dr Cogswell, Mr Dwight & Mr Waterman dine here. Receive 2 casks of apples from Col Pope.
25.
26.
27.   Sunday. At meeting.
28.   Ride to Westdivision; rain.
29.   A Tragedy & Comedy acted by a number of Gentlemen & Ladies, at Coolittle's.
30.   Becca Allyn leaves us. I ride to Bristol; engage a Girl for help; lodge at Thompson's.

December 1.   Return home; weather moderate. Ordination at Wintonbury.
2.
3.   Sold my horse to Mr Davenport.
4.   Sunday. P M. at church. Julia Seymour visits in the evening.
5.   Brother Abraham arrives; a small fall of snow at night.
6.   Rachel Griswold comes. Mr Flint & Mr Laurence pass evening here.
7.   Purchase a cow of Mr Ebr Crosby, price £ 3.15. Miss Lucy Bull calls on us.
8.
9.   Very cold; ice makes in the river.
10.   Mrs Webster indisposed.

11. Sunday. At home.
12. Mr Johnson Calls on me with Mr Benjamin. Northerly rain.
13. Snow. City Court.
14. Pay Mr Prosper Wetmores Acct to E Benjamin. Hear of the defeat of the western army under Gen Sinclair.
15. Town meeting.
16. Pay a small bill to Mr Morgen for Curtain tassels &c.
17. Alter my office Chimney. Pay Mr Geo Seymour for the hay I had of Capt Skinner, & the first payment for Frank.
18. Sunday. Rain. Pass evening at Capt Chenevards.
19. Paid to Ebr Bernard jun the interest on My fathers note due the Estate of Daniel Goodwin £ 7.14.3 3/4. Writing dialogues out of Cecilia.
20. Mrs Webster visits Col Wadsworth.
21. Very cold. Ice stopd in the river last night—first time this season—at Hartford.
22. Snow last night to make the first sleighing.
23.
24. Charles & wife visit us. Very cold, horses cross the river on ice.
25. Sunday. At Mr Strong's church. Mr Flint calls on me.
26. My father in town. Mrs W visits Miss Seymour. Pleasant.
27. St John, with Masons; warm.
28. Altered my keeping-room Chimney.
29. Cold. Betsy Colton comes to live with us. Town Meeting by adjournment.
30th. Brother Abram arrives. Visit at Mr Perkins.
31. Mild weather. Thus ends the year 1791.

1792

January 1. 1792.   Sunday. Attend Mr Strong's church. Begins to snow.
2. Rain.
3. Cloudy & warm.
4.
5.
6. High wind. Cold. Capt Heath & Geo' Webster call on me
7. Very Cold.
8. Sunday. Very cold, attend church.
9. At evening Mr & Mrs Colt & Mrs Perkins visit us.

10.	Very cold. City court.
11.	Very cold, no sleighing.
12.	Very cold. Mrs Colt drinks tea with us.
13.	Snow—a good supply & the first this winter of consequence.
14.	Ride to West division; plead J Goodwins cause before Justice Whiting.
15.	Sunday. At home, Emma not well.
16.	Still Cold.
17.	County Court.
18.	At night a great fall of snow.
19.	Stormy. Snow two feet deep.
20.	Cold.
21.	do.
22.	Sunday. At church P M
23.	This morning extreme of cold. Mercury 12° below o.
24.	A little more moderate.
25.	Much the same.
26.	Coldest morning. Mercury 13° below o.
27.	Still cold.
28.	do.
29.	Sunday. At Church; a little more pleasant.
30.	Cold.
31.	Rain.
Feby 1.	Clear & cool.
2.	
3.	Mr Tho. Merril Mr Root of Shefield & wives arrive on a visit.
4.	
5.	Sunday. Warm.
6.	Cooler.
7.	Write to Mr Greenleaf at Amsterdam; finish the Patriot, No 7; a fall of snow.
8.	Good weather.
9.	
10.	Fine sleighing.
11.	Receive Letters from Boston. Miss Wadsworth & Miss Trumbull take tea with Mrs W.
12.	Sunday. light snow. Dr Hopkins & Lady visit us.
13.	My friends from Westdivision visit us.
14.	Light snow.
15.	Mild.

16.
17. Brother Abram & wife visit us; write Letters to Amsterdam.
18. Cool. Mr Sam Burr dies suddenly at Wethersfield of an Apoplectic fit, so called, the effect of cold.
19. Sunday. At home.
20. At Court.
21.
22. Mr Royal Flint calls on me.
23.
24. Mr Burr buried.
25. Court rises.
26. Sunday. At Church. Mr Brown preaches.
27. Uncle Elijah Steele arrives
28.
29. Mr Emery passes an evening with us.
March 1. Fine pleasant weather.
2.
3.
4. Sunday. Mild & pleasant.
5. Snow, hail & rain.
6. Pleasant. Meeting of Gentlemen for forming a bank in this City.
7.
8.
9.
10. Great Rain. Between 9 & 10 oclock at night very heavy thunder.
11. Sunday. Clear; at Church.
12. Mild.
13.
14. Mr Horbach calls, issue for Roberts.
15. fair. get bass from Norwich
16. River breaking up. Snow.
17. Pleasant, with deep mud.
18. Sunday. Cloudy. At home.
19. Cloudy.
20. Pleasant. Settled Mr Hildness bill.
21. Pleasant. Settled Mr J Hosmers bills.
22. Very pleasant. Eclipse of Sun.
23. Rain.

24.	Rain.
25.	Sunday. Pleasant. At church.
26.	Choice of City Officers. My first election to be of the Common Council
27.	Rainy.
28.	
29.	
30.	Court of Common Council & city meeting.
April 1.	Very pleasant Sunday.
2.	Very warm.
3.	County Court.
4.	Very warm Wm Segdwick bound to Col Talcott for 15 months.
5.	Cloudy.
6.	Rain.
7.	Ride to Westdivision, to plead the cause of Mullikin. Receive letters from Amsterdam.
8.	Pleasant Sunday. At Church.
9.	Freemen's meeting. M J Trumbull first chosen to represent the town in Legislature. Connecticut river at its height, & a flood.
10.	My cause with Kibbe tried & judgt in his favr 30/.
11.	Mrs Webster taken very ill suddenly.
12.	Fast day.
13.	Mrs W. better; very disagreeable weather.
14.	
15.	Sunday. Cold. Frost.
16.	Attend Court at Mr Bull's.
17.	Pay & satisfy the Judgement agt me in Kibbe's case.
18.	Mr W. rides out. Court rises.
19.	Meeting of Physicians.
20.	Engage in L. Chester's affairs'.
21.	Do. Receive Letters from Boston.
Sunday 22.	Cool.
23.	There has been a light frost these many nights pass. Last night I suffered with pain in my head &c owing to a violent cold.
24.	Called up in the morning to attach Col Leffingwell.
25.	Mrs Olcott dies this morning of the small pox. Circuit Court at New Haven. Mrs Olcott buried this eveg. at 9 oclock.
26.	Rain.
27.	Issuing writs for L. Chester. Pleasant.
28.	Dull weather.

29.   Sunday. At church.

30.   Last day of suing of old debts. Emma sick. Pleasant.

May 1.   Supreme Court of Errors sits. Very warm.

2.   Ride to East Windsor. Jude Wolcott gives me some idea of the defects of our present mode of taxation. Attend district meeting.

3.   Rain. First deposit made of five per cent on bank shares in this city.

4.   Cloudy. Court rises. Attend court at Wethersfield for some blacks, at request of Comtᵉᵉ of Abolition Society.

5.   Cloudy.

6.   Sunday. At church.

7.   Attend court at Col Wyllys for L. Chester.

8.   do. Mr Appleton arrives from Boston.

9.   Govr arrives.

10.   Genl Election. Mr Stone preaches. Horse guards commanded by Maj. Seymour & infantry by Capt Hopkins. I am appointed to deliver the annual oration before the Society for promoting Freedom & Mr Dwight my second. Dr Appleton arrives from Boston. Warm, fair.

11.   Warm. Take tea at Mr Colts.

12.   Ride to Wethersfield; little Rain, Very warm. Turn my Cow to pasture.

13.   Sunday. Very warm. Mr Thatcher takes tea with us.

14.   Cool N West wind. Dr Appleton & Lady with Mrs Webster set out for Boston.

15.   More pleasant.

16.   Violent rain. House of Representatives debate on making up the losses of those whose houses were burnt by the enemy during the war.

17.   House vote to give them 500.000 acres of land on the West end of Connecticut reserved lands.

18.   Petition for Hartford & New London bank heard & advocated.

19.   This morning a white frost covers the buildings & fences. Trees killed.

20.   Sunday. At meeting. Mr Tracy dines with me.

21.   Pleasant.

22.   Attend Assembly.

23.

24.

25. Bank Charter passed. Petition for a Court House heard; very warm.

26. Very warm. Ride out with Mr Halsey, Mr Fanning &

27. Sunday. Rain. Attend worship.

28. Cool. Court House petition rejected. Mr Huntington taken by execution of federal Court, & imprisoned, while under protection of the Legislature. I assist in copying the bill in form on the grant to the sufferers in New London &c.

29. Fine weather. Mr Huntington brot. before the legislature by Habeas Corpus, sum causa, & discharged.

30. Set off for Boston.

31. Very hot. thermometer at 92°. Arrive at Boston.

June 1. Change of weather, wind at N E.

2.

3. Sunday. Dine with brother Daniel.

4.

5.

6. Rain. Cold North East Wind. We sit by a fire most of this week.

7.

8.

9. clear weather.

10. Sunday. Cool; we use a fire

11. Dine at Dawes, use a fire.

12. Set off with Mrs Webster for Providence; cool, N E wind. Lodge at Dixons.

13. Proceed to Norwich.

14. Arrive at Hartford in Company with Dr Wainwright. grows warm.

15. Warm fine weather.

16. Mow my grass.

17. Sunday. Mrs Webster unwell.

18. Very warm.

19. hot weather. Farenheite 90°

20. Farenheite 93°.

21. More cool & agreeable.

22. Warm. Ride to West division. At night Daniel Merrill dies in a fit.

23. Episcopal Church raised. Violent shower of Rain.

24. Sunday. Col Pickering & Dr Haven call on me.

25.   Cloudy. Mr Flint preaches at St Johns.

26.   Very pleasant. Cool.

27.   Not well myself. Mrs W takes tea at Mr Colts. Ordination at Glastenbury

28.   Pleasant. Receive a Letter from Amsterdam. Dated April 20.

29.   Cloudy. Ride to Westdivision.

30.

July 1—Sunday.   Very warm; thunder at evening. Hurricane at Philadelphia & New York.

2.   Cooler.

3.   Employed in searching Town Records respecting the Public Landing Place.

4.   Anniversary of Independence. Mr Theodore Dwight delivers a well written oration.

5.   Cool. Take tea at Col Wyllys.

6.   Searching Records.

7.   Writing a Report on the Landing place in this city.

8.   Sunday. Cool. Hear Mr Rowland.

9.   Warm. Violent thunder.

10.   Cool.

11.   Ride to West division & visit Mr Perkins.

12.   Fine weather. Visit Mr Flint.

13.   at home.

14.   do. Take a load of hay of Mr Thomas

15.   Sunday. At church.

16.   Set off for Norwalk. Rain.

17.   Meet Saml Franklin &c at Norwalk at Tho Benedicts.

18.   Adjusting estate of Benedict among his creditors. Breakfast with Mr Burnett.

19.   Return to Hartford. Mr Law calls on me.

20.   Mr Law calls.

21.   Call at Mr Trumbull's who is absent.

22.   Sunday. At church. Reading Millar's Hist View.

23.

24.   Rain. Cold North East Storm. Mr Blakeley & daughter arrive.

25.   Reading Vaillants Travels.

26.   Mr Blakeley dines with us. Judge Wolcott calls on me

27.   Warm. Reading Valney's Travels.

28.   Cool.

29.   Sunday. A Baptist preaches.

30. Col Pickering calls on me. Unwell; take a puke.

31.

Augt 1. Ride to Westdivision. Caught in a shower.

2. Cool.

3.

4. Ride to Westdivision.

5. Sunday. At Church.

6. Levi Pease establishes a line of Stages from Springfield to Dartmouth College.

7–8. Set out for Albany. Lodge at Litchfield.

9. Ride to Cornwall.

10. To Salisbury.

11. To Hudson. Extreme heat.

12. Sunday. Very hot.

13. Ride to Albany.

14. Go to Lansingburg, & return 12 miles.

15. Proceed to New Lebanon & from thence to Stockbridge.

16. Proceed to Norfolk.

17. Get home.

Augt. 18. Warm. Mr Wolcott comes to town.

19. Sunday. At Mr Strong's.

20.

21. Ride to West Mountain, on a party of *fatigue*. My mower mowed.

22. Mr Watson & Lady arrive in town

23. Col Chester & Lady take tea with us. Get in my hay.

24.

25.

26. Sunday. At Church

27. Mrs Dubois of St Domingo buried. Common Council held & a Report respecting the Public Landing Read.

28. Take tea at Mr P Colts. Mrs J Watson & Lady pass the evening with us.

29. Mr Trumbull's Black girl buried.

30. Purchased with Mr J Bull a Ticket in Fairfield Lottery No. 2307, Signd J Davenport Jun.

31. Ride to West division. Dr Strong spends afternoon with me.

September 1. Mr Michl Bull moves into M Elsworth's house.

2. Sunday. Mr Saml Millar preaches & takes tea with me.

3.

302

4.	Superior Court. Very dry weather.
5.	
6.	Ride to Weathersfield & visit Mr Webb's family
7.	
8.	Common Council lay out the North End of Front Street.
9.	Sunday. Mr Chapman, a clerk of Mr Imlay died. Rain. N E Storm begins at 3 oclock P M. This night Lavinia Morgan died.
10.	Sell to Mr P Sanford Col Dawes's funded Stock.
11.	Ride to New Haven to Commencement with J Pitkin
12.	Commencement. First under the enlarged Corporation & very brilliant.
13.	Meeting of Abolition Society. Mr Hart preaches. New Constitution adopted. Mr Pitkin speaks an oration before the Phi Beta Kappa Society.
14.	Return home, in Company with Govr Huntington & Judge Marchant. Mr James Bunce killed by the falling of earth in a trench.
15.	City Council meet, concerning Landing place.
16.	Sunday. Mr Emmerson preaches. Takes tea with me. Rain.
17.	Great Rain after the severe drouth. Freemen's & town meeting.
18.	Mrs Watson visits Mrs Webster.
19.	Attend to fixing the bounds of highways in the city, according to survey Review at Wethersfield.
20.	do. First Considerable frost this night.
21.	Setting up Mear Stones in highways.
22.	do.
23.	Sunday.
24.	Ride to Wethersfield to attend the suit of Robins agt Law for Society.
25.	Circuit Court sits. Judge Wilson, Judge Iredell, Judge Law. Visit Mr Geo Bull.
26.	Warm. Visit Col Wadsworth's family.
27.	Rain.
28.	The Judges take tea with us.
29.	Pleasant.
30.	Sunday. Pleasant.
October 1.	Cloudy.
2.	do. We dance at David Bull's. Judge Iredell attends.
3.	Procure pensions for E Easton. Wm Weare & Ebenezer Bevins.

4.	do for Jonn Bowers & John Watson.
5.	Posting books.
6.	
7.	Sunday. At Church; death of Wm Burr jun.
8.	
9.	Sick.
10.	Extreme drouth.
11.	Reference between Israel Williams of Hatfield & Christ. Leffingwell of Norwich, decided in favor of Mr Leffingwell.
12.	At night rain.
13.	Begin to examine town Records respecting public lands on banks &c.
14.	Sunday. Pleasant.
15.	
16.	My Birthday. 34 years of my life past. one year more will make half the *three score years & ten.*
17.	Warm.
18.	Rain. Paid George Burnham all account.
19.	Warm
20.	Ride to Westdivision.
21.	Sunday. Rain. Stay at home.
22.	Cool.
23.	
24.	Warm. Making extracts from Records
25.	Mr Morgan's ship in launching falls on one side, by the giving away of the ways.
27.	Warm enough to sit with doors & windows open.
28.	Sunday. Mr Geo Thatcher & Mr Gore in town
29.	The weather warm enough to sit with windows open.
30.	
31.	Ride to Berlin for Mr Elisha Colt.

November 1.   Rain.

2.	
3.	warm enough to keep open windows.
4.	Sunday. Pleasant. At Church.
5.	Warm. Windows open. Mrs Dwight visits Mrs Webster
6.	Warm. do. Saml Andrus calls for his Certificate. Write an answer to S Campbell.
7.	Warm. Mrs Trumbull visits us.
8.	Forming a Constitution for a Charitable Society.

9.   Violent Rain.
10.
11.   Sunday. Pleasant.
12.
13.   County Court.
14.
15.
16.   Rain.
17.   Walk down S Meadow to Little Landing
18.   Sunday. pleasant.
19.   Rain. From oppressive heat weather changes to cold & wind
      veers from S W to N E.
20.   Cold.
21.   Very Cold.
22.   Cold.
23.   Considerable fall of Snow & *first fall*.
24.   Snow 18 inches deep. Very uncommon!
25.   Sunday. Pleasant.
26.   Dr Cogswell sets out for New York, on hearing his brother is
      very ill.
27.   Court Rise. Warm.
28.   Very bad travelling. A South East Rain at night which melts
      great part of the Snow. Receive a letter from Dr Appleton with
      Mr Belknap's Discourse.
29.   Thanksgiving Day. At evening a number of Gentlemen
      convened at the Court House & formed themselves into a
      'Charitable Society.' I ought to be recorded that Col. Seymour
      opposed the plan. (*Jonn Bull & Wm Mosely.*)
30.   Clear & cold.
December 1.   Pleasant.
2.   Sunday. Very Cold.
3.   Cold. A number of Gentlemen meet at my house for the
      purpose of forming a social Club. It is agreed to form one.
4.   Buy wood.
5.   Mrs Wadsworth & family visit us.
6.   Meeting of Charitable Society, adjourned.
7.   First Assembly night.
8.   Receive Letters from Boston by Nathan Webb.
9.   Sunday. At Church. Mr Flint's first child baptized. At evening
      the Charitable Society meet & elect their Officers.

10.   Club at Mr Colts. Ice in the River stops this night. Very cold.
11.
12.   Fair & Cold.
13.   Cloudy. Assist in surveying the town Landings on Connecticut & Little River.
14.
15.
16.   Sunday. Very Cold.
17.   Town meeting.
18.   Very Cold. Snow.
19.   Dr Cogswell arrives from N York.
20.
21.   Go to Wintonbury for Jonn Butler.
22.   Receive news from Mr & Miss Wadsworth at Bermuda.
23.   Sunday. Receive a Letter from Mr Meigs of Bermuda.
24.   Town meeting by adjournment.
25.   Christmas Day. Cold.
26.   Cold.
27.   St Johns. I draw a petition for Mr Morgan.
28.   Cold.
29.   Pleasant.
30.   Sunday. At meeting.
31.   Town meeting, my report respecting the landing places banks &c read. My expense for wood this year £ 20.9.3 About 40 Cord.

1793

January 1. 1793.   Cold.
2.   Cold.
3.   Cold.
4.   Attend a Court before Justice Bull for A Hopkins; a fall of Rain which freezes.
5.
6.   Sunday. At home; no Church.
7.   Writing. Attend Club at Dr Hopkins.
8.   City Court.
9.   Rain.
10.   Clear.

11.

12.   Receive letter from Amsterdam.

13.   Sunday. Very Cold. Mr Wolcott sets off for Philadela in Stage.

14.   Cold, this morning.

15.   Milder wether. Court sits.

16.   Rain.

17.   Rain. Mrs Hosmer visits us.

18.   Cool & Clear.

19.   Warm. Snow gone.

20.   Sunday. Cool.

21.   Meeting of Charitable Society.

22.   A little fall of Snow.

23.   Clear & Cold. Argue the Cause of Skinner & Hatch.

24.   Cold.

25.

26.   Ride to Windsor in a Chaise. Very Cold

27.   Sunday. Cold.

28.   Rain.

29.   Clear & Cold. No snow this winter yet.

30.   Cold; a Snow that bids fair to make some sledding.

31.   Cold; about a foot of snow this morning.

February 1. Cold.

2.   Cold.

3.   Sunday. First Charity Sermon preached for the Charitable Society & 100 dollars collected.

4.   Cold.

5.   My second daughter Julia born.

6.   Warm, & Rain.

7.   Very Cold.

8.   Cold.

9.   Warm.

10.   Sunday. Very Cold; at Church.

11.   Cold. This evening my second daughter very ill.

12.   Very cold, & a violent storm of Snow. Superior Court Sits.

13.   Snow Storm continues.

14.   Cold. Snow two feet deep nearly.

15.   Cold.

16.   do. Attend Court at Mr Moseleys for J Mullikin vs Aaron Cadwell.

17.   Sunday. Rain all day; at home.

18.   Warm; deep snow & water. My 2d daughter baptized at home by the name of Frances Juliana.
19.   A great rain at Night.
20.   Rain. Ice in Mill River breaks up.
21.   Warm.
22.   Very Cold.
23.   Wether moderates. Superior Court rises. At night rain & Violent thunder.
Sunday, 24.   A violent Gale from S West; rain.
Monday. 25.   Cold. N West wind.
26.   Snow, hail & Rain.
27.   Warm. Wet.
28.   One of the Coldest days of the winter. Such a winter is rare!— A Ball at David Bulls.
March 1.   Milder wether.
2.   Mild. Some loads of wood fall into the River in attempting to cross, tho some get over. Rain.
3.   Sunday. Very warm. Ice in the River breaks up!
4.   Warm, but cloudy. At night rain
5.   Warm, rain, fog, deep mud.
6.   Cool, pleasant.
7.   Cool. Cloudy.
8.   Rain, at night snow. Violent wind.
9.   Violent Wind. Mrs Bull dies
10.   Sunday. Mild weather.
11.   Rain.
12.   Mrs Bull buried. Cloudy & chilly.
13.   A flight of snow.
14.   Pleasant
15.   Cool.
16.   Very Warm; sell a parcel of highway to Mr John Caldwell.
17.   Sunday. Very warm. A Stranger buried, who died in the Street yesterday.
18.   I visit the Indian chiefs, from the Wabash, Under the command of my old friend A Prior.
19.   Lay out side walks in Main Street. Warm
20.   Pleasant. Water in Connecticut River high. Mrs Emery arrives, on way to Boston
21.   Rain & Snow
22.   Cold, clear.

23. Buy a boat load of wood, fair.

24. Sunday. Pleasant, Cold.

25. Annual City Meeting.

26. Ledyard Seymour & Mr Timons tried on a Complaint for firing a gun in the night near S School. District Meeting, on Highways.

27. Ride to West division.

28. Attend in viewing the Little Landing. Very Cold.

29. Cool. On Committee for settling with persons in possession of Town property.

30. Audit between Hezl & George Merrill.

31. Sunday. Pleasant.

April 1. Mrs Wells dies this morning. Court of Common Council held. Law for inspecting of wood passed &c.

2. County Court opened. District meeting for highways very clamorous. Tax/3d

3. Very warm. Mrs Wells buried. School District meeting; vote to set up public schools, which have been long neglected; choose me Clerk & Committee Man.

4. Public Singing at Westdivision. Music very good.

5. Warm.

6. Rain. Employed in examining the records of the State & taking copies for the Susquehanna settlers, to be used in trials for their claims in Circuit Court, Philadelphia.

7. Sunday. At Church. Wabash Indians in Town. Capt Webster dies aged 70.

8. Freemen's meeting, & Town meeting.

9. Capt Medad Webster buried.

10. I am preparing for N York. Flood in Connecticut River at the highest.

11. Cooler.

12. Set out for New York. Rain. Lodge at

13. Proceed, to Norwalk.

14. Sunday. Arrive at N York.

15. Visit.

16. Breakfast with Mr M Rogers. Dine with Mr Cotton.

17. Dine with Mr Blakeley.

18. do. Set out for Hartford at 3 oclock P M. Ride to Rye.

19. Ride to Stratford.

20. Rain. Dine with Mr Lockwood at Milford. Lodge at New Haven.
21. Sunday. Reach home.
22. Cold.
23. More pleasant.
24. Pleasant. Julia very sick.
25. do.
27. Dry N E Wind.
28. Cool; Sunday. Hear Mr Bradford.
29. Cool.
30. Pleasant. Court of Errors sit.
May 1. Pleasant. Hear of the death of Harriet Wadsworth at Bermuda April 10th.
2. Meeting of Common Council We hear of the Arrival of Mr James Greenleaf from Amsterdam.
3. Cloudy.
4. Very Warm. Mr Dawes arrives on a Visit.
5. Sunday. Cool & Wet.
6.
7. Mr Dawes leaves Town.
8. Warm. Govr escorted into Town.
9. Genl Election. Col Seymour, Mr Miller, Mr Grosvenor, elected members of the Council. I pronounce an Oration before the Society for Promotion of freedom.
10. Pleasant.
11.
12. Sunday. Pleasant. Emma sick. At Mansfield a man killed with lightning.
13. Very warm.
14. Very warm. Change in Superior Court.
15. Cool N Wind. Excessively dry.
16. Cool. Slavery debated in house of Representatives.
17.
18.
19. Sunday. A little Rain.
20. Warm.
21.
22. Very Warm.
23. A Public Singing at South Church. Mrs Emery passe to N York & Philad.

24.	Cooler.
25.	Cool.
26.	Sunday. Some Rain; at Church. Mr Porter preaches.
27.	At night rain.
28.	Warm.
29.	Cloudy. Mr J Greenleaf arrives.
30.	Cool N E Wind.
31.	Mr G. departs with Mr Lagarenne.
June 1.	Rain. Take a view of Col Seymour's Farm.
2.	Sunday. At Church.
3.	Prepare for Boston.
4.	Set out for Boston. Cool. Unwell
5.	Cold. Arrive at Boston
6.	Dine at Bro. Daniels.
7.	Dine at Dr Appleton's.
8.	Dine at Mr W Greenleafs.
9.	Sunday. At Church. Dine at Judge Dawes.
10.	Dine at Dr Appleton's.
11.	Set out for Hartford. Excessively hot.
12.	Very hot; get home.
13.	Brother Greenleaf arrives from Boston.
14.	Ride to Wethersfield, to Col Chester's
15.	Warm. Mr Greenleaf and Mr Charles Nicholas. Mareth de Lagarenne leave us for N York.
16.	At Church. Sunday.
17.	Copious Showers, great heat.
18.	Ride to Westdivision with Mrs W.
19.	Extreme heat.
20.	Sultry. Mrs Knox drowns herself.
21.	Cool.
22.	Cool. Cape Francois burnt on 23d
23.	Sunday. At Church.
24.	Receive letters from Mr Greenleaf.
25.	St John's Day. A sermon preached by Mr Strong. At Night great Rain.
26.	Cloudy.
27.	Mrs Webster at Amos Bulls.
28.	Mrs Flint &c visit here. Elijah Steele here from Cornwall. Very warm.
29.	Very hot.

30.   Sunday. Extreme heat. Mr Flint indisposed. Harriet Trumbull dies.

July 1.   Very hot.

2.   Extreme heat.

3.   a little Cooler.

4.   hot.

5.   Reading Young's Tour in France.

7.   Sunday. At Church.

8.   Cooler.

9.   City Court.

10.   Ride to Windham; pass eve'ng with Col Dyer.

11.   Return to Hartford. Dine at Mr Cotton's at Bolton.

12.

13.

14.   Sunday. At Church.

15.

16.   A violent shower.

17.

18.   Ride to Mr Bull's farm house.

19.   Rain.

20.   Weak eyes prevent my reading

21.   Sunday. At home

22.   Warm.

23.   Very warm.

24.   We have squashes from our garden & Watermelons in markets. A shower

25.   We hear of the death of Judge Sherman on Tuesday evening last; cooler.

26.   Cool. Martin's tumbling feats draw half the town.

27.   Cool. Dine at the Mulberry trees on a fishing party.

28.   Sunday. At Church; draw up Resolutions respecting neutrality of U States.

29.   Meeting of Common Council. Very hot.

30.   Meeting of the Gentlemen in Hartford to consider the propriety of addressing the President.

31.   Hot. Some rain.

August 1.   Cooler. Action betwen the Ambuscade & Boston.

2.   Meeting of Citizens to hear the address to the President; agreed upon.

3.   Cool.

4.	Sunday. At Church, very hot.
5.	Very hot. De Wit & Benjamin stop payment
6.	Rain, fair. Mrs Fish, Morgan & Roots at our house.
7.	Cooler.
8.	Ride to Durham on a journey to New York.
9.	to New Haven. Wait on the Tutors & President Stiles.
10.	Procceed to Norwalk. Lodge at Marvins Col Wadsworth & Mr Sandford in company.
11.	Sunday. Proceed towards N York. Major Davenport stops the Driver. Walk to Knaps on foot. Very hot. Proceed to Kingsbridge. Lodge at Hyatts.
12.	Arrive in New York. Lodge at Mr Bradley's with Mr Genet.
13.	Dine at.
14.	At home.
15.	Dine with Dr Rogers.
16.	Dine at Chief Justice Jays.
17.	At home. Ride to Newark.
18.	Sunday. Ride to Patterson. Return to New York.
19.	Dine with Mr Abrahams.
20.	Dine with Mr Blakeley.
21.	Dine at Mr Watson's
22.	at Mr Hammonds
23.	Go on board the Ambuscade.
24.	Dine at Mr King's; prepare to set out for home.
25.	Sunday. Rain, wind a head.
26.	Dine with Mesrs Johnson's.
27.	Go on board; set sail for N Haven.
28.	Arrive; proceed to Middletown in Company with Mr Borie & Lady.
29.	Get home.
30.	Forming a partnership with G. Bunce to carry on the Printing business in N York.
31.	Ride to Westdivision.
Sept 1.	Sunday. At Church Miss Williams dines with us
2.	Cool
3.	Superior Court. Sell my Law Library to D Wadsworth, & J Lathrop.
4.	
5.	
6.	Sick with Influenza.

7.   do
8.   Sunday. Influenza at its hight in my head.
9.   Rain, violent Rain.
10. Cold. Cloudy. Trial of E Case for murder.
11. Trial finished. Case acquitted on ground of insanity
12.
13. Visit Mr Talcott.
14. Mr Wm Wilcox in Town.
15. Sunday. Dr Dwight preaches in town
16. Very Warm. Meeting of the freemen. Chauncey Goodrich first
     Chosen Representative of the Town
17. Common Council of the City.
18. The first frost appears this morning. Which, after the hottest
     summer ever known, is very agreeable. The plague rages in
     Philadelphia, or a disorder like it. The dysentery & influensa
     common all over the country, but not formidable.
19.
20. Mrs Austin arrives from Phild, by water
22. Sunday. Mr Green preaches, from Pensylvania.
23. Warm. Regimental Review, in this town.
25. Circuit Court. Judges Wilson and Blair take tea with us.
26. Send on my deposition respecting Mr Genet to O. Wolcott,
     Philad.
27. Ride to Springfield to see Brother Dawes.
28. Return to Hartford.
29. Sunday. Public prayers ordered every afternoon on acct of the
     fatal sickness in Philadelphia.
30.
October 1. Ride to Westdivision with Sophy who leaves us for her fa-
     ther's.
2.   Attend Court; hear the argument in the great Case whether a
     Protection granted by the Genl Assembly is valid agt.
     Execution from Courts of United States, Deblois agt. Chester.
3.   Do.
4.   Rain. Circuit Court rise.
5.   Cool. Vines first killed by frost.
6.   Sunday. Pleasant. Cool.
7.   do. No favorable news from Philada as to the fever. it still
     rages.
8.   City Court. Pleasant.

9. Pleasant. Very warm.

10. Very warm like June.

11. do. fever in Philad carries off 159 in a day

12. Cloudy.

13. Sunday.

14. Annual meeting of the Charitable Society.

15. Wind changes, cool.

16. My birthday, completing 35 years, half the life of man. Very cold.

17. Cold; disorder in Philad: abates.

18. Ride to Westdivision.

19. Cloudy. Mr Strong's mother dies; a Shower & thunder this evening.

20. Sunday.

21.

22. Warmer.

23. Settling accts.

24. Pleasant.

25. Gave my note to E Barnard jun for 400 dollars payable in 60 days.

26. Begin to pack furniture for N York.

27. Sunday.

28. Begin to put my goods on board.

29. Snow.

30. At Mrs Colts.

31. Leave Hartford with my family in a carriage. Stop at Middletown.

Novr. 1. At Middletown, waiting for the vessel.

2. do. Take tea at Mr Alsop's.

3. Sunday.

4. Go on board.

5.

6. A Gale from S E.

7.

8. Still in the River at Saybrook.

9. Leave the river, anchor off Killingworth.

10. Sunday. A fine Easterly breeze in the morning. P M. wind at S W, rises to a Gale; we put in to Horseneck, or Greenwich.

11. At anchor all day, wind a head.

12. Proceed & anchor near Hell Gate.

13.   Arrive in New York. Lodge at Mr Watson's, this rainy day.
14.   Move our goods.
15.   Take lodgings in our own hired house. No. 168 Q Street.
16.   Very busy.
17.   Sunday. A rain. Terrible Fire in Albany.
18.   A Storm of Rain.
19.   Cold. Mr. Lagarenne & James Greenleaf take lodgings with us.
20.
21.   Inoculated my two little Girls.
22.   Paid for Elizabeth Town Printing press. At evening company.
23.   Mr Cornillon calls on us.
24.   Sunday. Capt. Armour dines with us.
25.   Anniversary of Evacuation of this City by British troops.
26.   Begin Printing with the Prompter. Fire at Norwich.
28.   Mrs Colt arrives.

December 1.   Sunday.
2.
3.   Issue proposals for the Minerva.
4.
5.   Very ill with sick headache, obliged to leave Mr Rogers at Dinner.
6.
7.
8.   Sunday.
9.   Begin a Daily Paper.
10.   Meeting of the Merchants on Greenleaf publication.
11.
12.   Call on Mr Bogert.
13.
14.   Purchase a share in N York Library.
15.   Sunday.
16.
17.
18.
19.
20.   Dine at Mr Watsons. Hear from Hartford.
21.   Very Cold. Call on Mr Wilcox & Mr M Rogers.
22.   Sunday. Cold.
23.
24.

25.	Christmas.
26.	Dine at Mr Mortons.
27.	
28.	
29.	Sunday. At Church: hear Mr Millar.
30.	
31.	Rain.

1794

January 1st 1794.   Cool, W. NW. clear.

2.	Warm, fair.
3.	Warm, (rain at night) fair
4.	Warm, fair
5.	Sunday. Warm, fair.
6.	At night to the Theater. Belles Strategem—Cymon & Sylvia.
7.	
8.	
9.	Cloudy.
10.	do.
11.	Dr Appleton arrives.
12.	Sunday. Cold.
13.	Cloudy, rain.
14.	Snow Storm, fair.
15.	Mr Greenleaf & Mr Lagarenne arrive
16.	I had a tooth drawn, face much swelled. News that Duke of York is taken.
17.	
18.	Very ill with an inflamed throat.
19.	My throat ulcerated, confined. Sunday.
20.	Pleasant Wether, am better.
21.	Rain. I am still confined.
22.	Cloudy, very little better.
23.	Still confined.
24.	Dr Appleton sets out for Philad.
25.	Dr Returns. unable to pass ferries.
26.	Sunday. At home.
27.	
28.	
29.	
30.	

31.   Dine at Dr Nichols.
Feby. 1. Attend tragedy of Carmelite. Mrs Morgan, King &c take tea.
2.   Sunday.
3.   Mr Morris & Wadsworth dine here.
4.   Warmer, after a long cold turn.
5.   Cold.
6.
7.   Mr Morgan leaves town.
8.   Col Wadsworth in town.
9.   Sunday.
10.
11.
12.
13.   Visit Mrs Watson.
14.
15.
16.   Sunday. Mr Morton & Sisters call on us.
17.   English Mail arrives. Take tea at Mrs Kings.
18.
19.   Miss Mortons visit.
20.
21.
22.
23.   Sunday.
24.
25.
26.
27.   Meeting of Democrats at City Hall
28.
March 1. Col Wadsworth & Sister arrive.
2.   Sunday.
3.   Fog & rain.
4.
5.   Very cold.
6.
7.
8.
9.   Sunday. Mr Greenleaf sets out for Boston
10.
11.

MARCH 12, 1794

12.
13.
14.
15.
16.   Sunday. Very Warm, dine at Mr Watkins.
17.
18.   Warm
19.   warm
20.   Meeting of the Citizens to petition Legislature to grant money to fortify this port.
21.   Rain.
22.   fog.
23.   Sunday. Warm.
24.
25.
26.   Mr Greenleaf returns from Boston.
27.
28.
29.
30.   Thunder.
31.   Thunder.
April 1.
2.
3.
4.
5.
6.   Sunday. Gaol in Hartford burnt.
7.
8.   News favorable from W Indies.
9.
10.
11.
12.
13.   Sunday. Ride out.
14.
15.   Mr Swaine arrives in town.
16.
17.   Mr Burral calls upon me from Phil.
18.
19.

20.   Sunday. At Church.
21.   Ship Ohio from England.
22.   Rain. Rochambeaus Secretary arrives
23.   Rain. It is too much trouble to make *particular* remarks every
        day, & genl ones are of little use.
May 12th.   Mr Jay, Envoy Extraordinary sailed for England. The Citizens
        showed him great respect at embarking.
15.   S & Mrs W. set out for Poughkeepsie. I go as far as Albany &
        Bennington & return on the 25. On the night of the 17th Inst
        there was the severest frost ever known at the same season.
        Some Wheat, much flax & oats, all the fruit & garden
        vegetables together with oak, hickory chestnut, butternut, were
        killed from Clavarack to Bennington; to the southward of
        Columbia County less damage was done.

1798

April 1. 1798. Removed with my family to New Haven. My attachment to
        the State of Connecticut, my acquaintances, my habits, which are
        literary & do not correspond with the bustl of commerce & the
        taste of people perpetually inquiring for news & making bar-
        gains; together with the cheapness of living, are among my mo-
        tives for this change of Residence. Take Mrs Sloan's House, near
        the water.

April 10. Begin to write my History of Epidemic diseases, from materials
        which I have been three months collecting.

May 20. 1798. Purchase the House of Mrs Sloane for 2666 dol 66/100—(*The
        Benedict Arnold House.*) The month of May was dry beyond exam-
        ple, no easterly rains, all garden & pastures parched up. About
        the last of the month & beginning of June commenced excessive
        rains, great flood in Connecticut River, as also in the Delaware.
        The rains continue more than usual through the month, &
        weather rather cool. The 2d & 3d Days of July hot in extreme. In
        the coolest situations, mercury was at 93° & 95°, in some towns,
        higher. Then cooler than usual & almost as cool as April, till the

last week of July. On the 27th began great & excessive heat, Mercury for some days rose to 92, & in some places to 97°.

1798 (August) Weather rather rainy the first week in August. The two or three days of July & first of Augt. I was in New York. Melancthon Smith died of Yellow Fever in New York July 29th the day of the month that Dr Treat died in 1795. Some coughs & croup among children & whooping cough in some places, some dysenteries beginning at Augt in Farmington, Berlin, New York &c. Yellow fever in Philadelphia & Boston.

Augt 7th 8 & 9, very hot, on the 9th the mercury in my garden rose to 93° in a situation where on July 3d it rose only to 90°. In the sun it rose to 104, & in the sand in the highway to 118°. The whole month of Augt. & most of Sept. unusually hot, no cool northerly winds, part of Augt rainy, moist & southerly weather. Yellow fever spreads in NYork about the 20th of Augt. City alarmed a few days after & the eastern Streets abandoned. The disease assumes, this year, in Philadl & New York more of the characteristics of the plague, is contagious & fatal beyond what has been known in America for a Century. It breaks out suddenly at New London without contagion, & is greatly mortal, also in Wilmington, State of Delaware. In Boston, the same disease appeared & prevailed in the low parts of the town. In Portsmouth, a few die of the same disease. In N York & Philadl. it raged till the begining of November; a severe frost from Oct. 30th to Novr 2d & snow put a stop to it.

Number of deaths in Phil.—3436		
do in N York—about	2000	
do in Boston—	200	
do in Wilmington—	252	
do in New London—	80	

I was in New York Augt 20th for four or five days, after I returned, I was taken ill of symptoms of bilious fever, & as it was but five days after leaving that city, it is not improbable, I received some of the poison from that atmosphere. Some men I saw in the city were seized & dead in a week after I left the city, & some men from Connecticut who visited the city about the time I did, were soon after seized with the fever & died. My disease was of a lighter kind. It was soon reduced to a remittent, & after a it took the form of an intermittent. I was ill about 10 weeks. Weather continues warm or rather hot till the 26th Sept. Then suddenly changes to cool, producing cholera morbus, on the morning of the 30th frost kills the vines & tender plants.

No cool rains, but dry cold northerly winds. The public prints mention that an epidemic of a malignant kind broke out in Italy in June, in Consequence of dearth of Corn, also the eruption of a Volcano in Teneriffe, in June which lasted till Augt, at least. At Amuskeeg falls in New Hampshire a number of men were lately seized suddenly with violent sickness of which two died, supposed in Consequence of drinking the water of a well that had for a long time been disused. Two men at Alexandria killed by attempting to descend a well. The third discovered at 30 feet depth a column or stratum of smoke or vapor, issuing from the sides of the well, which was the noxious cause.

We hear from Europe, that the plague rages in the Turkish dominions. Belgrade is abandoned. Yellow fever prevailed in autumn in New Milford, with considerable mortality, also in Royalton in Vermont on White River, on the Grand Isles, in Lake Champlain. Bilious complaints prevail in many other places more than usual. The weather in November temperate, till the 17th, then cold easterly rain & snow.

Sunday, 18th. Very warm & cloudy, in the evening much thunder, wind changed to east.

Monday, 19th. Cold N E wind & rain, at night it began to snow & continued through the 20th a most violent gale, snow fell on the earth when not frozen, about a foot deep, cold weather on wednesday 21, & on the morning of 22d thermometer at 12°. Very cold for the Season, then the weather moderated. I was in New York from the 14th to the 18th Int, returning home detained at Greenwich two days, by the snow. The weather of December generally cold with frequent snows.

1799

Beginning of January 1799 excessively cold; then moderate for the rest of
the month. The Close of February & beginning of March extreme cold weather. On the morning of the 5th of March, Thermometer at 6° below Cypher in New Haven; at 1 oclock P M. 10°
above, after which the cold abated. On the whole the winter has
been longer & Colder than usual. Snow, hail & severe frost on
the 15th March. About the 20th. the Snow began to thaw, & at
New Haven was generally gone on the first of April. On the 2d of
April, a deluging rain, with violent winds from N E, & on the 3d
a Hurricane, the whole day, from the W, with squally clouds;
very cold, ice an inch thick. April then dry, with cold N W winds
mostly till the last week. Severe frost about the 20th mostly cold
till May, planted peas & sowed lettuce & turnips on the first of
April. Cut & eat lettuce & turnips on the first of April. Cut & eat
sparrograss on the 2d May for the first time. Trees begin to ger-
minate in April but no leaves or flowers on May 1.

On the 2d of May a fall of snow with rain. On the morning of the 4th & 5
frost at New Haven, that made ice as thick as glass. On the night
after the 10th or morning of the 11th of April a considerable earthquake in South Carolina. On the morning of May 8th a fall of
snow, cold freezing weather, trees begin to have small leaves, but
no blossoms, except the Apricot. Peaches blossomed about the 12
or 15, & Apples were not in full bloom till the 23d. April was dry.
May had rain enough. On the 30th of May, thunder & rain. On
the 31st Rain from the N E all day. On the 1st of June high cold
winds at N W, & a fire very comfortable. Moon in apogee on the
30th. & N Moon on the 3d of June following. On the 15th eat
green peas for the first time. May dukes & early English Cherries
begin to be ripe on the 20. Tuesday 18th. very hot. Thermr. 82 in
my entry, 88° at College, followed by severe thunder, & cool,
north winds. We have yet had but 2 or 3 hot days. Eat my last
pippin of the last year on the 22d of June.

July in General temperate, some hot days. Eat green corn on the 21st. Early
apples eatable on the 20th.
I have been twice to New York, this Summer, & in both instances, the air of the city produced universal debility & inflam-

mation in the throat. July 29th. I set out on a Long tour through the Northern States, & did not return till Sept 1. Every where the drouth extreme. Maise cut short by it. Caterpillars in July & Augt innumerable, also Grasshoppers. Great rains commence in Sept. The Heat of this season not extreme, but Yellow fever appears at Phila. N York & Hartford. In North & South Carolina, the fever mortal.

Sept. & Oct. rather cool & Wet, but nothing extraordinary occurred. November mostly warm & very fine wether. The first snow, a light squall, on the 26th. Singular fall of shooting Stars Novr 12, followed by a gale wind, at New Providence. Great mortality among fish in the Ocean between Cape Fear & Cape Look out.

Winter began in December. Connecticut River closed by ice about the 12th & snow fell for sledding, at Albany, Hartford &c about that time; the earth well frozen, but the first considerable snow at New Haven fell on the 17th. December.
Note—The ice in the River Neva, at St. Petersburgh in Russia, did not break up last Spring, till May 21st the latest day for that event, known since registers of the weather have been kept, London Paper.

My History of Pestilential Diseases was published in December 1799. On the 14th of December 1799 died the Great & Good Washington in the 68th year of his age, of a Cynaneche Tonsillaris, after 24 hours illness. All America Mourns.

1800

Jany. 1800, mostly fine weather, at New Haven & along the Sea Coast, no snow, the ground bare, dry & hard as in Summer, in the interior, some snow. On the 10th. & 11th an unusual tide at the Full moon & Moon at mean distance, explained afterwards by hearing of a Snow Storm on the 10th in Carolina, supposed with an easterly wind, but no storm in New England; pleasant, moderate weather, wind westerly. In Carolina & Georgia the snow was two feet deep, as report stated. Mild weather in New England, till January 28th when the cold increased & the thermometer on the morning of the 29th stood at 2°. the next day at 5. & on the 31. at 13. Before this it had been twice at 10° but for a single day, & generally for 2 months at about 30.

Feby 1. A fall of snow of about 6 or 7 inches. The whole month has been as cold as common winter months. On the last day, a fall of Snow, with a violent gale of Wind at N N E.

March was not distinguished for anything uncommon, unless I may except a single violent clap of thunder, in a rain near the close of the month.

On the morning of April 6th. at three o clock we had an unusual storm of rain, thunder & lightning with some hail, the thunder was as violent as in the midst of summer, planted early peas March 24, they appeared above ground April 6. On the night of Saturday 12th April, 1800, a violent thunder shower at New York, & the water that fell was accompanied with a substance like sulphur, in smell & taste, which formed a scum on the surface. Supposed to be the pollen of flowers. Apl. 7. Planted peas again. Apl. 24. First eat Sparrograss. Saturday. 19th Put in grafts.

May was mostly cool & wet.

First eat peas June 10, first Strawberries ripe at the same time, cut grass June 11th.

Early apples ripe July. 15.

Eat green corn. July 21.

The second week in July unusually hot.

July 20. Very hot Sunday, much thunder & rain. The close of July & August were cool with the exception of a few days, in general dry, till the Equinox, when an unusually long eastly wind, with heavy rains succeeded. The bilious plague severe in Norfolk & Baltimore, among strangers in Charleston as usual, a few cases in New York & Providence. Dysentery prevalent & Mortal in Springfield & adjacent towns, in Hanover, (Dartmouth) Bilious fevers prevailed in Guilford & Chester, Connecticut.

More rain than usual in October, & Gales of wind from the S E. One on the night of Oct. 5. brot in a high tide & did some damage to the Wharf in New Haven, a Still more severe on Oct 18th just after an

JANUARY, 1801

Eclipse of the Sun, & the highest tides the following night & day, that had been known for many years. Thermometer at 64°. Sunday. Oct. 19. President Adams in Town, on his way to Washington to open the first Session in Congress in that City. Oct. 30. 1800. weighed a beet from my garden & found it 1b. 11.5 oz, another weighed upwards of 6 1b. November as mild as usual, till the 20th On the 21st a violent Snow Storm, & a fall of snow again on the 23d, good slaying. Several shocks of earthquake were felt at Lancaster (Penn) on the morning of the 19th & 20th., at 5 & 6 oclock. Moon in perigee. Snow in North Carolina at this time. The beginning of December some rain & sleet. On the 12th a gale of Wind at East with rain. The month remarkable for mild wether, snow dissolved with great freshlets, the ground bare, so warm at Christmas as scarcely to want fire. Thermometer for some days between 45 & 60°, grass started & many buds. A little Snow fell on the last day or two of the year, & Thus ends the Century. A violent tempest or hurricane in the north of Europe Novr. 9. 1800, during which a shock of earthquake at Brussels, 2000 trees blown down in one district.

1801

Jany. 3. 1801. Thermometer fell last night from 30°. to 2°. Very sudden Change, but cold continues only 2 days. Mild wether, no snow. On the 15th. Calm, clouds like April, heavy thunder, the highest perigee tide I ever saw without wind, high water about 11 o clock A M.

Jany. 23. 24 & 25. severe cold from 20°. to 7° by Farenheit, the harbor of New Haven closed with ice a mile before the pier. Then mild wether till Feby 10th. when it became cold & in two or three days, the thermometer was at cypher in the morning; a considerable fall of snow & good sledding. This lasted but three or four days, then mild; on the last of Feby the thermometer at 60. I planted peas & turnips. On the 6th of March a great fall of snow of 8 or 10 inches, but the wether moderate & it soon dissolved. Spring flights of Wild Geese March 11th. On the 18th a great rain which lasted two or three days, a gale of wind, at east; the great-

est flood in the Connecticut known since 1692, also in Farmington, Chickopee & others. Great damage done on that & all our
rivers—bridges, mills, fences, houses swept away. This was occasioned by heavy rains.

March 25. Peas & turnips planted Feby. 27. begin to appear, but cold &
frost check their growth.

29th. Storm of rain at E N E.
Cut first Sparrowgrass April 20th, put in grafts, April 19th.

April 22d. Hail storm. 24th. Violent Easterly gale, & great rain. Incessant
East Winds, till the 27th. then southerly & pleasant.
Visited the schools in New Haven in 1801. number of schools.

Public,	15
Private,	5
	21 [*sic*]

Scholars, 787.
Inhabitants in the town 5757.

May 8. Unusual of the tide in New Haven, the water running many rods as
fast as a man would walk and then returning suddenly, on the
ebb. It appears that in April, probably the 22d. the snow fell a
foot deep in Pennsylvania. And the winter has been colder than
usual in the West Indies, & heavy gales of wind frequent.
In March & April slight Influenza.
In May, much thunder & severe hail storms, in various parts of the country.
White frost in Litchfield County in the night of the 26th; great
changes from heat to cold.
My peas fit to pick May 31; eat the first June 3, being absent in Litchfield
County till the 2d.
First Strawberries June 5.
Mowed my garden June 2d & 3; a large crop.

June 6th. Morning cold, a fire would be comfortable. Thermometer in the
house 55°. My Uncle Josiah Steele died March 12th. aged in
Hinesburg, Vermont.
Temperate, till after the 25th of June. Then very hot; some showers, but
mostly very dry.
My pippins continued good till July 10. Eat the last apple July. 13th.
Picked my first Indian Corn July 12th. & Genneting apple ripe.

MARCH, 1802

Much injury from drouth, till July 22, then rain from S E. beginning of
August rainy. Thermometer, down to 50 twice, in midst of sum-
mer. (July & Augt Pears ripened together, both lasted till Augt.
14.) At Nassau, New Providence, July 22d. a violent & destructive
Hurricane
My pound pear fully ripe, Augt 20th.
The Vergaloo was ripe Sept. 1st.
The first week in Sept very warm, Thermometer, several days at
81°; rather wet since July 22d.
The hot weather in Sept. continued till the 10th at night. Ther-
mometer for some days at 90° in the shade, a rare instance!
The whole of September warm as Augt a thing without example.
Yellow fever appeared in New York the last week in Sept. &
drove people from the east river side by the 10 of Oct.
October warm & dry.
Dysentery, remitting, intermitting & yellow fever prevalent; a
sickly autumn, in many places.

1802

January 1. 1802.
  Very mild weather, little frost as yet, & no snow, except a little
  fall of two or three inches in November, & about as much last
  week.

Jany. 2d. is like the middle of April. We have had some rains, but springs
  are lower than ever known, or at least, remembered.

Feby. 22. The weather continued very mild, till this day; no snow & during
  January great rains; in January violets blossomed, the tulips ger-
  minated in my garden, & grass started. Alternate frosts & mild
  weather in Feby till this day, but we have now a violent Snow
  Storm at N E.

March 2d. The Snow storm on the 22d Ult. was as violent as had been
  known in 20 years; for 24 hours, the snow fell at N Haven 18
  inches. Wind violent. On Thursday it began to Rain, with strong
  wind at N E. & latter with rain, snow, sleet & hail for four days
  incessantly. In the interior Country, this last storm also was snow

& hail, which accumulated to the depth of three or four feet.
Latter part of the month, I planted early corn & peas.
April, with the exception of a day or two, was cold, till the 24,
with many frosts, & very dry.
Cut Sparrograss April 25.
Mr Peleg Sanford died on his passage from Charleston, April,
17th.
Mrs Phelps, April. 25., both of the consumption!
Peaches blossomed April 30th
Apples May from 10 to 15.
(*May 10, put my Cow to pasture.*)
The Measles appeared in New York &c early in winter, & in the
course of the winter prevailed over most parts of the U States. In
April the disease became very severe, highly inflammatory, & attended or followed with peripneumonic affections. Three of my
daughters, Julia, Harriet & Mary, severely affected. May was a
continuation of heavy rain & east winds, from the 12th to the first
of June, & very cool so as to retard vegetation, about ten or
twelve days. Eat peas for the first time June 15, about a fortnight
later than usual, the same is true of my grass, a fortnight later.
Last year strawberries fit to eat June 5, but this year not till the
20th.
Severe cold & catarrhal complaints frequent in May, & Epidemic
Catarrhal fever prevailed from June to August & Sept.
June mostly wet & cool. The vegetation so much retarded, that
cherries not ripe till June 20th, & the honey-hearts & black cherries & Strawberries all ripe at the same time.
In the evening of July 1. was a *Lumen Boreale*. The first considerable light of this kind, which has appeared for many years—I believe about twelve or thirteen years!

July. 7th. Rozberries ripe. 20th. the jenneting apple begin to be ripe, &
early pear.

July 20. Gathered the first green corn.
(A great earthquake in Italy May 9 at 40 minutes past ten A M
the town of Crema demolished, & Menquin swallowed up.
Moon in Apogee, Com. Adv. Augt 17. 1802) Great rains & very
wet southerly weather all July & Augt, & Sept. The wettest Season known in many years.

Augt 15th. Great earthquake in South America, at Cumana. Moon,
    Perigee. Spectator. Oct. 2. 1802.
Sept. from 12th to 24. excessively hot, much rain, & severe thunder! I set
    out for Boston Sept. 14. & returned Oct. 1. Dysentery very fatal in
    the towns above Springfield, especially on the west of the Con-
    necticut, as at Northampton, Blanford, Chesterfield, Greenfield,
    in some other places. a few fatal cases in New Haven. Some cases
    of nervous fever, & malignant sore throat in Rhode Island &
    Massachusetts. Malignant fever in a small part of Boston at the
    bottom of Summer & Purchas Street; almost every one seized has
    died!, about 40 or 50, the rest of the town very healthy.
    The same fever more malignant than usual in Baltimore & Philad.
    but cases not very numerous. Crops good in general, but flax
    blasted, a black spot on the Stalk where it breaks off, & the seed
    falls short. Wheat good along the Atlantic & for a hundred miles
    or more in the inland country, above which it is shrunk & light.
    Wheat very good in southern States.
    Autumn in general warm or mild, especially November. No
    snow, except a slight fall, nor any considerable Cold till Decr 16.
    when severe wether began but lasted only three or four days.
    Earthquake in all the Eastern part of Europe Oct. 27th.

1803

January. 1803. Mild, till after the middle of the month. Much rain & change-
    able weather, the last Ten days cold, & a light Snow fell. On the
    28th, a slight earthquake at Salem & another, Wednesday Evg
    following. Eruption of Etna this winter. Sudden changes from
    Cold to warm & wet to dry.
    On the 3d of Feby, a violent thunder Storm, at N York & N
    Jersey. Several vessels struck at the hook, & two men killed. The
    Episcopal Church in N Brunswick set on fire, by lightning, but
    saved.

Feby. 26. The brewery belonging to Mess Bakewells in this City burnt.
    All Feby & March, very variable. Cold, warm, wet & dry in ex-
    tremes, little snow.

In Carolina, Snow 18 inches deep in Feby, but none in New England. For the two or three last winters, the most snow has fallen in the Southern States.
Planted my first peas March 19th.
In the middle of April, a storm of snow & hail, & severe frost, the snow lay in drifts for a week, the month in general cool. Cut a small parcel of asparagus April 23. for the first time.
Set out for New York on the 19th & returned the 29. of April.

May 8. Sunday. A fall of snow to the depth of two or three inches, & had the ground been frozen, the depth would probably have been 6 inches, the cherries in blossom, as also the pears, the peaches are past the blossom, & the apples not yet blown, followed by a frost, which produced ice one fourth of an inch thick! In Litchfield the ice was half an inch thick; but the trees not forward enough to suffer any injury. May dry & Cold, fruits backward & late.
The beginning of June wet along the Sea Shore, but by means of showers of limited extent only. In the interior country, very dry from April to July, especially at the westward & Northward in New York, Pennsylvania & Vermont. Then three weeks of great rain at the Northward in harvest by which means wheat grows in the ear. Then mostly a dry autumn.
Diseases, Scarlet fever very general in Spring & summer, dysentery appeared in June, became more general than usual, & in some places, concurrent with Scarlet fever. Malignant fever in New York & Alexandria, & lightly in Philadelphia. Crops generally good, maiz better than usual.

October more rainy.

Novr 1. A clear day, a gale of Wind at N E. & the highest tide known in fifteen years—several inches higher than Oct. 18. 1800.
In general, November & December were remarkably warm, the latter rainy, little snow. Connecticut River not closed, till the middle of January. In Novr & December I was in Philadelphia, procuring types for the revised Spelling Book.

1804

January. 1804. Moderate weather till the 8 or 10th. then some snow, sleet & very cold, for a few days.

From January to late in March, generally cold winter wether, & frequent snows, which accumulated to 4 feet depth. The first week in March fell a great snow, & until late in March the snow was three feet deep in the country generally. More snow than since 1780, fodder scarce by reason of the drouth of last summer, & in the interior, many cattle died.

April colder than usual. Cut my first shoots of Asparagus on the 26. & but little till May 2.

Peaches in blossom May 5.

May, June & July, with the exception of a few days, unusually cool. By reason of a cool July, maiz did not thrive well, & a very dry season at the same time & in August, assisted to cut short the crop. Other crops mostly good, & abundance of fruit.

The month of august not so hot as usual, the heat of the beginning of September very great, & then commenced a general gale of Wind as violent as a hurricane. This Gale was felt by Capt Lines in the latitude of Barbadoes at the Windward, on the first of Sept, but was not general among the islands till the 4th. On the 4 & 5th it was tremendous & drove ashore almost every vessel in the harbors. On the 7th 8th & 9th it was equally violent on the southern shore of the U States. The inundation of all the low grounds & islands of S Carolina & Georgia, with terrible loss was the consequence. On the 11th & 12th it was severe in New England, but nothing unusual. On the night of Oct. 8th, commenced, with a clear sky, a smart Southerly wind, in the morning of the 9th. rain with thunder, before noon the wind veared suddenly to N N E & or N E. & blew a hurricane till the next day, great damage done on the Eastern shore of New England.

Oct. 15. 16. & 17. I was viewing the ground between Fairfield & Stamford for a new road, with a view to State the condition of it to the Genl Assembly.

Note. During the storm of the 9th Oct, which was accompanied with rain at N Haven, & generally on the sea-bord, the snow fell in the country back, from four inches to eighteen inches deep. It appeared in small quantities on the highlands in Wood bridge, at

Litchfield, several inches, & in Vermont, was from 12 to 18 inches deep, & so drifted as to be 3 & four feet deep, travelling was obstructed, & sleys used. Such an event is very remarkable—the only one I have found recorded.

October mostly cold & tempestuous.

November 15th. A gale of wind at E.N E. & S E. which brought in the highest tide known in more than 20 years, a few inches higher than on the first of November last, the wharf was covered; after this more pleasant wether.

1805

January, 1805. Winter commenced about the middle of December, & was severe by the 20th with good sleying. It continued with severe & steddy cold, through January & most of February. The harbor of New Haven was covered with ice about 10 weeks, & a part of the time men travilled on foot from the light house to town. Naviga-tion was also obstructed at New York. The Snow in January 1805 was about 3 feet deep. This was the severest winter since 1780. But the snow left the earth in March in good season & Spring was early. I cut asparagus on the 14th of April, 9 days earlier than last year.

It appears that violent earthquakes convulsed Spain last autumn during the terrible plague. Crops failed, a dearth ensued. Tuscany also infected with pestilence.

Vesuvius began to throw out fire in August, a little before the great Tempest in September, 1804.

The Month of May 1805, & the first part of June, wet & cold; then commenced a summer of great heat, & drouth, over the Northern part of the United States, but the first crops were good. In some places, were great showers with much thunder. In gen-eral the drouth has been the severest known in many years, & extreme heat continued from early in June to the Equinox. Then the weather became cool & wet. Lumen borealis appeared Sept 21, & some following nights.

In July some cases of Malignant fever in New Haven, but in three weeks the disease disappeared. Late in August & Beginning of

Sept. the same disease appeared in Philad. & N York. In Philadelphia, the fever was most severe in Southwark, but cases occurred here & there in the City. The eastern streets in N York were deserted, & the disease, tho unusually fatal, was not accompanied with a great mortality.

July 26. At the change of the moon, a terrible earthquake shook Naples & the country, with the loss of many lives.

Augt. 12. following, at 10 o clock P M. was a great eruption of Vesuvius, a stream of lava run near Terre del Greco to the sea.
October was rainy. November very pleasant.
December was also very mild wether, no snow & little frost.

1806

January 1806. Winter set in with a light snow, & severe cold on the 9th but of short duration.
February was unusually mild, & the peach blossomed in Maryland.
March & April were colder than February, & the frost killed the peach in some places. The Spring was later than usual, by 12 or 14 days. I cut my first asparagus May 4th.
Several snow storms in April on the mountains in Connecticut & Massachusetts. One in Berkshire the last week in April, which detained me half a day at New Lebanon. The hills in Patridgefield covered with snow for two days.
May was unusually dry; no easterly rains. Springs were as low as is common in autumn.
June & beginning of July equally dry, and we were alarmed with a prospect of loss of crops, but in the latter part of July, August & September, great rains. The summer in General cool, with much northerly wind. Flax & oats rather short. Wheat & rye excellent. Great Eruption of Vesuvius in May & June.
Sunday Augt. 24. Violent gale of Wind at N E with great rain, many vessels lost. Genl McPherson of S. Carolina & 20 others lost off Barnegate by the upsetting of the ship *Rose in Bloom*. Yet this gale was at sea & on the Atlantic coast only, for 100 miles in the country,

the weather was fair & calm. It began on the Coast of North Carolina on Thursday the 21, & ceased on Saturday, before it began at New Haven. On the Second of September, another gale in the same latitudes, these were most violent between the 20th & 40th degrees of latitude, & most severe on the Carolina coast. Shipwrecks more numerous than for many years before.
September mostly cool & wet.
Autumn in general cool.
Much snow in Massachusetts at Boston, where I was Sunday Novemr. 26. First snow at New Haven December 3d. Severe cold & a few days of good sledding, then a thaw.

1807

January 1. 1807.

Very cold this morning—Mercury at 3° below Cypher at Sunrise—Two or three weeks of good sleying, then no more snow of consequence, & this dissolved before the great rain.

On Saturday 31st of January, a great rain. The severe frost of 3 weeks had made very thick ice in the rivers, & the ground. The rain was sudden, the ground hard, no snow to detain it, & the whole being poured into the rivers, broke up the ice, & swelling beyond the banks all the streams, swept away most of the bridges in the State of Connecticut, especially on the large streams.

On Saturday, Feby 14. a still greater rain, after severe frost had again made thick ice, & the few bridges which remained were swept away, with many mill-dams & mills.

On the last of February, a third flood nearly as great as the first, from rain & melted snow.

In March a considerable Snow, the month unusually Cold.

On the 31st March, a violent gale from the east with snow, hail & rain. Then for the first time I saw a *common tide* in the harbor at *low water*, that is, the violence of the wind kept the water from ebbing—time of low water, a little before noon; at three oclock, the tide was as high as ever known, then the wind having abated, the ebb began at half flood; no moderate weather & no peas planted till about April 6 or 7th.

April & May cold. Apple trees not in blossom till May 20th.
Cut my first Asparagus May. 2d.
      Several earthquakes in March & April. One at Richmond April.
30. One in Maine some time before, & in Canada Great snows in
the interior country; the first week in April snow three feet deep
on a level in the western counties of New York, and at Marietta
much snow; the Ohio froze a month so as to bear loaded carriages. High flood in the Connecticut for two or three weeks in
April & May.

May & June, wet & cold; with the exception of three or four days of great
heat—8th & 9th & 10th of June—the month remarkably cool. On
Monday, June 22d cut the grass in my garden. Wednesday a cold
N E rain, & Thursday I was obliged for comfort to make a fire in
my study.

July & August, warm, but extremely wet; continual rains & damp southerly
wind, in short the wetest season known by the present generation; in most of New England, grain short & got in in a bad
state—as is grass.
      A severe earthquake at Lisbon &c June 6, at change of the moon.
Influenza epidemic in August over the northern States.

Sept. 25. or about that time appeared a Comet in the west—about 30 or 35
degrees from the sun. It was of the bearded kind, the beard extending a few degrees. It disappeared in November. Some cold
weather the latter part of November, then moderate through December. Snow very little in Connecticut. Saturday, Decr. 5. a violent gale from the east & a very high tide.
      Monday morning December 14th a meteor fell or burst, & large
masses of stony substances fell in Fairfield County.

1808

Winter generally mild; little ice; navigation in N Haven harbor not ob-
    structed. Weather variable, alternate frost, snow & rain.

April pleasant; first week in May warm, then very wet & cold till June 22.
    The falls of rain extraordinary; a flood in June, that did injury to

crops on the meadows on Connecticut. We sat by a fire June 20 &
21. Then commenced hot weather.

July very rainy, with an almost constant southeasterly wind—a humid atmosphere, when it did not rain. Farmers put to great difficulty to
make their hay, & the grain somewhat injured.

The petechial fever prevailed in Farmington, Bristol, Canton & some adjoining towns, also in Wethersfield, from early in the Spring to
midsummer, but the country in general healthy.

Early frost Sept. 21. but nothing remarkable in the Autumn. December
rather colder than last year, but no snow in New Haven. Near the
last of the month, snow in the country, and a light fall in N Haven.

On May 1. 1808. a great eruption of fire, or Volcano, on St Georges, one of
the Azores, which continued till June, sweeping away the town of
Ursulina, & greatly destroying improvements. Connect Herald
Feby. 28. 1809. Letter from Mr Daubney. American Counsel.

1809–1811 [sic]

January 1809. First week, cold, but no snow at New Haven. The cold continued without much abatement through January, till the last
week in February. Harbor at New Haven closed a few weeks; the
snow in January & Feby. fell to the depth of two feet nearly in
New Haven & in the country, three or four feet. A severe winter,
but not of the first degree. The harbor of N Haven was closed to
Black rock for some time, & about the pier & wharf 8 or 10
weeks; it was not wholly clear of ice till March 22.

The Spring Cold & late. Martins first appeared May 5. & that day I cut my
first asparagus. Appletrees in blossom about the 20 to 25.

May 25. about 10. o clock in the Morning a slight shock of earth quake was
felt at New Haven, attended with a rumbling sound. I did not
feel it, as I was on the water, just entering the harbor on my return from New York.

[JUNE, 1810]

June & July, as well as May wet & cool; a few warm days excepted. In July, two long N E rains—the last 17. 18 & 19th, & this day. the 19th. I am writing by a fire. I do not recollect such a July. August also wet & cool. At Portsmouth, in New Hampshire, I sat by the fire at the Revd Mr Buckminsters August 26—On the 27. great rain, then the rain ceased, & six weeks of dry weather succeeded; the beginning of October was warmer than August.

March 26. [1810] a great eruption of Mount Etna, as the papers inform us. Spectator Feb. 21. 1810—Spect. Oct 1809. Latter part of August & beginning of September, great eruptions of Vesuvious. Spectator. Nov. 4. 1809.

Novr 20. the first snow at New Haven, two or three inches, but not cold.

21. More snow

24. A violent Snow Storm, & about a foot of Snow.

In December, a violent storm of Snow, & extremely cold; then moderate weather with repeated rains & fogs, till Jany' 18th. A D. 1810, when the wind suddenly sprung up from the N West, with a squall of snow, followed by extreme cold through Friday 19th. Saturday & Sunday following. The mercury in Farenheit fell in New Haven to 7°. below zero, & the harbor closed to Morris' Cove below the fort, & continued covered with Ice till Feby. 20. A cold month. A slight earthquake in Virginia on the evening of Saturday, Jany. 19th. (& another in Vermont, as I have heard). Changes of wind have been surprisingly great & rapid. No snow since December, in this State & generally east of the Hudson, but in the beginning of February a great snow, of a foot depth, fell in Pennsylvania, Maryland & Virginia.

May has been a very dry month—& the beginning of the month cold. Cut my Asparagus first. April 23.
Picked my first peas June 9th.
June 5th. received a visit from my father, now 88 years of age.
June 8th. a violent tempest at N East with abundant rain.

European accounts state that in Hungary, between January 14 & Feby 14, there were 1000 shocks of Earth quake. This was the time of the great change of weather in America. About the same time there was an earthquake at the Cape of Good Hope.

July & August were mostly very rainy, hot & moist, with Southerly winds.

September less rainy, but a long Equinoctial storm.

My daughter Harriet was seized with a bilious fever the beginning of August, & confined about 4 weeks, & did not go to Church in 8 weeks. But a merciful God preserved her.

Oct 31. a light snow at night.

Novr 2. A snow storm at N E. the snow fell the preceding night & all day—about a foot in depth—but the ground not froze. I have never known such a snowstorm & such severe cold, so early by a fortnight. & I am now 52 years old.

A few weeks ago, there were two eruptions of fire of the Volcanic kind in Strafford, Connecticut.

The snow soon disolved, & the middle of the month was moderate with great rains, violent wind & high tides. Such a tide in Raritan River never before known. The lower rooms of the houses on its borders, in New Brunswick, were half filled.

At the close of this great Rain, after 8 days rain or cloudy weather, a considerable earth quake was felt in Massachusetts from Charlestown to Portland—at least. This was on Friday night the 16th. at 9 o clock. On the 10th of September Vesuvius began to throw out fire & lava, & an astonishing eruption suceeded for several days. Courant. March. 1811.

Great storms this autumn & immense losses at sea.

[1811]

January 1811.

Generally moderate weather but wet with very frequent changes. Late in January commenced a series of cold weather with snow, & the beginning of February & indeed most of the month we had good winter weather. Snow about 15 or 18 inches. The harbor of New Haven was closed a week or two only.

March was warmer than usual.

[DECEMBER, 1811]

April was a temperate month.

May was dry & cool, June was dry, & cool till about the 20th. when summer weather began. The first week in July was dry, & excessively hot, So that our garden plants withered, even the leaves of maize, in my garden, turned white. But on the 9th we had a copious rain; grass is very light, but wheat & rye, remarkably good.

August was temperate, except a few days of great heat, rain sufficient.

The first week in September very hot. On Tuesday Sept. 10, a most violent Tornado, in Charleston, S Carolina, which blew down houses, killed several persons, & did immense damage. The first week in Sept. appeared a Comet, it sets in the N N W & rises in N N E. nearly. It was seen at the Cape of Good Hope in May.

Sept. 17, a great eclipse of the Sun. In Virginia, it is annular. Weather very warm.

In July, a hurricane in the West Indies. In May or June, a great erruption of fire at the Western isles, & an island thrown up.

In the East Indies, at the Cape of Good Hope & in the Atlantic, the Gales of wind have been violent the year past. Spectator. Sept. 21. 1811.

October was remarkable for heat & for gales of wind, for many days about the middle of the month, the heat was very oppressive, & followed by frequent & tremendous winds. On Thursday the 31st. a violent tempest from the E & E S E. brought in the highest tide, which had been seen for many years. See Nov. 1. 1803.

Novr was moderate, & December, till the 24th. when we had a most violent tempest of wind, with snow, & very cold. Before this, there was little frost or snow. In this storm fell about a foot of snow at N Haven, but the wind at North was a hurricane, & accompanied with unusual cold, the thermometer being at 6 above cypher in the middle of the day, & at 2 at night. A great number of vessels driven ashore on Long Island, & many persons perished. The decks & rigging of vessels were covered with ice. This was the day before Christmas. Decr. 26. the theater at Richmond burnt & 75 persons suffocated & burnt.

[1812]

January 1812. Generally Cold. On the 19th, a cold storm, the wind not so high on the 24th Ult, nor so much Snow, but it was colder; the thermometer sunk to 7 below cypher.

On the 23 of the month, at about a quarter past nine A M. the weather being calm, an earthquake was felt in New York, on Long Island & in New Haven. It was a gentle waving motion, without any preceding sound or any jar or concussion. I reeled as I sat in my chair, & at first ascribed it to dizziness. On the 16th of December, there was a violent earthquake which extended from the State of Ohio, to North & South Carolina, & Georgia, in a south-eastern direction. It was between 2 & 3 o clock A M. An apothecary in New Haven being in his shop, at the time, perceived a little vibration of the vial sticks suspended by strings from the ceiling.

On the 23. of January, another shock was felt in the Southern States, & to Connecticut. It happened at a little after nine o clock A M. I felt dizzy, & reeled sensibly, no noise attended or preceeded.

Feb. 7. at 3 or 4 oclock another shock was felt, preceeded by a rumbling sound. It awoke me & others of the family.

February & March were cold, & in the country much snow.

April 13. it Snowed all day, at New Haven. Most of the month cold, & spring late.

May 3. I cut my first Asparagus.
The 4th It snowed all day.
May was cold & mostly wet.
Apple-trees were not in full blossom, till June 1., a fact I never before knew!

June was generally cooler than usual: as was July, with frequent Showers.

August was mostly cool & very rainy.

July 2. 1812 I sold my house in New Haven & on the 13th purchased a house & six acres of land in Amherst, Massachusetts. The principal motive of this change of residence, was to enable me to subsist my

[JANUARY, 1814]

family at a less expense. I removed the first week in September. July & August were rainy, & cool.

September was cold but dry. October was cold & dry, so cool a summer is rare; maize did not ripen, & in the country at large there was not half a crop, in high cold land, little or none came to maturity before the frost in September killed it.

November was as cool as usual, & from the first week in September, we had fire in our chimneys almost every day.

December was cold & dry, & we had little snow till Jany 15th 1813.

[1813]

January 1813. Cold & dry, the dust flying, till the 15th when a snow fell, sufficient for sledding till middle of March.

April & May rather cooler than usual. Appletrees not in full blossom till May 25, rain sufficient.

June. a few warm days, but mostly cooler than usual.

July. as warm as usual, with plenty of rain.

August & Sept. warm & dry, springs very low.

Oct. Rainy & colder than usual. Crops good. Maize ripened well.

Novr. pleasant, as usual.

December. Dry & cold as usual. Connecticut river closed with ice, 24th. but no snow for sleds till the 29th. of the month.

[1814]

January 1814. Winter moderate. Little snow along the Atlantic coast, but in Amherst, good sledding till March.

[APRIL, 1814]

The last week in April very hot, so the latter part of May, full summer heat at the Election in Boston, where I was attending the general Court. But a long period of cloudy weather, easterly wind & cool weather succeeded. In the country generally great rains in May & June, & violent winds, hail storms, tornadoes unusually violent.

July more wet than usual, but on the whole a good month for hay & harvest, grass good, rye tolerably good, a little blasted, wheat good.

August, & September rainy. A flood in Connecticut river injured the Crops in many places.
Maise ripened well, a tolerably good crop, not so good as last year.

Oct. 5. Extra Session of the Genl Court. The month unusually pleasant. dry & warm.

Nov. Wet & cold, I rode in a sley to Church in Amherst on the 20th. but the snow light. & no frost.
Monday Nov 28. 1814. at 10 minutes after 7 oclock P M, in a Calm, moon light evening, there was a slight shock of Earthquake, Persons who were occupied or moving did not perceive it, I was writing in my chamber, & no noise interrupted my observations. The joints of the timber in my house cracked, & there was a shaking for about 5 or 6 seconds.
November & December in general moderate & little snow.

[1815]

Jany. 1815 Moderate till the 17th then began to be tempestuous, & several storms of snow followed. The last week very cold, & on the last day the Thermometer fell to 12 below cypher in Boston. It continued to be very cold in Feby, & our harbors were closed with ice. Some very warm weather early in March dissolved the snow, then followed a cold wet spring. Apple trees in Amherst began to blossom about May 23. I finished planting corn May 24, in fine weather.

June was colder than usual. July was remarkably hot, & August was as unusually cold, heavy gales of wind Augt 8. at sea, & on the American Coast. Sept. 1. severe gales damaged shipping. On Saturday
Sept 23. a severe storm of wind & rain from the N E. from 8 o
clock A M to 11. The spire & vane of the Steeple in Amherst
blown off, & some trees blown down, and some timber & fruit
trees, but the principal damage in Hampshire county was the loss
of bridges & mills swept away by the water. The destruction of
property was immense on the sea shore. The wind was most violent from Connecticut to the District of Maine, & the great destruction of trees shows the utmost vehemence of the wind to be
limited to about 70 miles into the interior country. The storm
was a proper hurricane, like those experienced in the West Indies—This was succeeded by warm, calm, clear weather.
Autumn was as mild as usual, & crops good.

[1816]

Jany. 1816. The winter was open, a snow in January, which was sufficient for
sledding was swept away in a few days. the ground was uncov-
ered most of the winter.

In May & June the degree of Cold was unusual. We had repeated frosts in
May, & after a warm day June 5. & a shower, the wind blew
violently from the N W, so cold as to kill the leaves of vine plants.
It continued 5 or 6 days, with frost every night, till the 11th day, &
on the hills 30 or 40 miles north & West, snow fell several hours.
Tender plants were all killed. The maiz in low ground was killed,
& on high ground much injured, in Hampshire County.

July very dry, with cold Northerly winds, frost the eighth day, rain the 26th.
to wet tilled land a few inches.

August cool & dry, no rain, except a sprinkling, springs & streams very low.
frost. 21. & 28.

[SEPTEMBER, 1816]

Sept. dry till the 12th, no second crop of grass. Great rain & flood in southern states, sufficient here to water the plants, but not to fill the
Springs, & none in Vermont
Sept. 27. Severe frost, all the Corn killed & so little of the corn
hard or ripe, that it is doubtful whether there will be seed for the
next year.

Oct. very warm & pleasant till the 17th., then a light rain, followed by
squalls of snow, which lies on the hills on the 18th. No rain yet to
fill the springs.

Novr & December. Mild & little snow, Cattle grazed till January.

[1817]

January 1817. Mild the first week or two, on the 17th a squall with thunder &
lightning & rain. In the north, New Hampshire &c the thunder
very heavy, & snow at the same time, a church burnt by
lightning.
23d. Snow sufficient for sledding, a very cold season succeeds.

Feby 5. The mercury in Farenheit, fell to 20° below Zero. On the 15th to 25°
in Northampton. On the 24th a great tempest with snow. The
first week in March, snow two feet deep or more. The season was
dry till June, when the earth was suyplied abundantly for the first
time since Sept. 23d. 1815. during the hurricane. Weather cool.
grass thin & late. Worms of various kinds did much injury, in
May & June.

July & August hot. Great rains in August, during harvest & grain injured
by growing, but crops good.

Sept. & October warm, as usual. First frost in Hampshire. Oct 1. Maiz ripened well, though late.

Oct. 5. Sunday at noon, a slight earthquake, or trembling, without report,
in Hampshire County.

Novem. & December, moderate.

[JANUARY, 1820]

[1818]

January 1818, The first part of the month moderate. The latter part & most of February very cold, & good sledding.

March. Early in March warm & a great & sudden flood destroyed a multitude of bridges, among which were those of Sunderland, Springfield & part of that at Hartford, over the Connecticut.

April & May, unusually cold & wet. Spring later than I have ever known. My black cherry blossomed, May 22. 23. & appletrees, May 26. 27. I planted corn May 25. Then commenced a very hot summer, & extremely dry. The *first* crop of grass was unusually abundant, the second failed. Wheat, rye, oats & barley—were a light crop. Maiz tolerably good, unless in very dry land. Apples very scarce, & other fruits, except pears. The first frost, a light hoar-frost, on the morning of Sept. 24th.

[1819]

Jany. 1819. Winter moderate. Little snow.

Summer very hot & long continued. Crops good, but great drouth in the Southern & western States. A comet. Yellow fever very fatal at Charleston, New Orleans, Natchez. Mobile &c

[1820]

January 1820.
  Winter began rather earlier than for some years past. Two or three violent storms. In January & February the snow in New England was from three to four feet deep. A few days of severe cold, & the cold was continued for about five weeks with little intermission.

[AUGUST, 1820]

August 9. 1820. The Corner Stone of the Collegiate Institution in Amherst was laid by Dr Parsons. president of the Board of Trustees of the Academy, & it fell to me to make a short address standing on the Stone.

Sept. 3. 1821. A violent hurricane from the S East. commenced at evening. It prostrated trees & overset some sheds & houses. It was violent at Amherst & as far north as Brattleborough &c but more violent on the Sea Shore from Rhode Island to Norfolk in Virginia. Immense damage done to shipping.

Sept. 18. 1820. Was dedicated the Collegiate Institution in Amherst. First prayer by Rev' Joshua Crosby of Enfield. Sermon by Rev Dr Aaron W Leland of Charlestown S Carolina, a native of Peru, in this State. At the same time President Moore & Professor Estabrook were inducted into Office; the Ceremony performed by myself, as president of the Board of Trustees. The last Prayer by the Revd Thomas Snell of North Brookfield. The business of founding this Institution has been very laborious & perplexing, as we had no funds for erecting the building, & every thing almost was to be collected by begging Contributions. As soon as I was satisfied the Institution was well established by the Induction of Officers, I resigned my seat in the Board of Trustees Sept. 19. 1820, & Dr Moore was elected into the Board & made President.

NOTES to Section IV

1. Take tea with Mrs Burr. Find many friends that I have not seen a long time.
2. A very sensible man. Take tea at Mr Austin's.
3. terrible roads.
4. I curse all stage Waggons and return to town. Loiter about & do little, but hire a horse.
5. Visit Dr D Stewart upon business of procuring a law for copyright in Virginia; he promises his patronage; introduces me to Col Symms. Afternoon I visit Genl Washington 10 miles from Alexandria, agreeable entertained by him and family, Major Washington &c. continue with him will next day.
6. It consisted of two or three hundred houses well built of brick; but it was burnt by the British troops and has not recovered its former elegance. Portsmouth lies opposite Norfolk, and is a pleasant town, smaller than Norfolk.
7. Go on shore and walk the streets of Norfolk. Eat cherries for the first time. The country here is level & the soil good. Considerable business is done here: but little

Notes to Section IV

attention is paid to religion, education or morals. Gentlemen are obliged to send their children to the Northward for education. A shame to Virginia! I leave 3 dozens of the Institute with Mr Benn Pollard &c to be sold. Green Peas are plentiful.

8. Continue beating on & off the land, small breeze a head, weather fair, out of sight of land in 36°37.

9. Becalmed from morning till 2 oclock PM. A calm is very disagreeable, the vessel constantly rolling, at 2 o'clock we pursue our course with wind contrary.

10. Breeze continues. Several sail of vessel in sight, beating to windward. Spoke a sloop from N York, bound to Newburn. Two men offer to come on board for Charlston, but will not give the price. Cape Hatteras in sight.

11. A squall, succeeded by a calm, rough seas off Hatteras; we roll our waist under water.

12. Got under way with a small breeze, which continues all day. We sing and dance on quarter deck.

13. Wind continues contrary. O how disagreeable! We make but 10 or 12 miles in a day. at noon we are in 34°44^m.

14. Becalmed from 4 to 10 oclock. Set sail with a light breeze. Discover from mast head the shoals of Cape Lookout. Take a Dolphin with a harpoon. Boil a piece of him with silver to know whether he is poisonous or not, as this fish often possesses poisonous qualities, especially when he lives on Copper banks. He proves free from this quality. We make an excellent dinner of him. PM harpoon a porpoise; but in a hurry & confusion, lose both the harpoon & the porpoise. He must have weighed 200 lb as one man could not lift him into the sloop & a large rope was broken in the attempt.

15. Beat to pieces with the rolling of the sloop, take a young shark with a hook, set sail at 12 oclock with wind at South. Fresh provisions expended.

16. Pr day

17. Sunday—Get under way early & arrive in Charleston at 8 oclock—lodge at Mr Welsh's at the sign of the Cross Keys in King Street. Happy to find shore & good provision. Go to St Michael's Church; hear Parson Smith & Miss Storrer sing. She sung a part of the Oratorio of the Messiah; the organ joined. An odd affair this, for a woman to sing for benefit; but I put a quarter of a dollar into the plate. She sung *well* in the modern taste, but I cannot admire it. I went to the White meeting P.M. & heard the New England method of psalm singing. Heard part of a Methodist Sermon in the evening. The people in Charleston are very civil & polite. They behave with great decency at church, & the slaves attend in greater numbers & behave with more decorum than I have seen in America.

18. I hear his school and am much pleased at seeing his New England method adopted here.

19. Introduced to Mr Hutson, Mayor of the City & Intendent in this state. He approves of the first & second part of the Institute. I get a certificate for entering the title of the Institute in the Secretary's office, agreeably to act of Assembly.

20. Genl Gadeson & Capt. Gadeson call at my lodgings; unhappy that I was absent.

Notes to Section IV

21. of 3 others & obliged to weigh all. Get clear.
22. Mr Blakeley, Dr Mann & my other friends
23. for collecting a singing school.
24. & had a dish of discourse upon my grammar
25. Lament that I am in Baltimore.
26. Wait on the Miss Donelly's.
27. Ne rien de nouvelles.
28. beside 150 stores & public buildings.
29. offended at Mr Hall, & offended him.
30. Endure, with christian patience, a severe paroxysm of the head ach.
31. Tho' his Chinese miss is pregnant by him.
32. Sing bad this evening.
33. & a few revolutions more with accelerated motion, wil turn me off the stage.
34. AM & to meeting PM.
35. Nearly the same number as in Richmond. The Church here as well as in Richmond are built at a distance from town; it seems to be the taste of the Virginian to fix their churches as far as possible from town & their play houses in the center. There is not any free school in Virginia at present, Novr 1785. The College at Williamsborough is well endowed & pretty respectable; one Academy at Prince Edward & one at Alexandria are most of the schools in the State. The education is very indifferent. Plays, horse-races & games are almost the sole objects of pursuit.
36. This is the most beautiful city in Virginia. It is situated on a sandy plain about 4 miles from James River & about   from Hampton on the Bay. It consists of 230 Houses well built & regular. The College of William & Mary is large and elegant as also the Church & Capitol; but they are decaying, & so is the city, by reason of a removal of the seat of Government to Richmond. Here is the only public clock & bell of consequence in Virginia.
37. & advertise to begin tomorrow evening.
38. Dine with Mr Carter. Read my second lecture to the same number. Several causes may be assigned for this inattention. I am a stranger, & a Yankee, tho well introduced; the Virginians have little money & great pride, contempt of Northern men & great fondness for dissipated life. They do not understand grammar.
39. Proceed with my Lectures. Pass a few hours with Mr Wythe—a great man for Virginia, & a sensible man anywhere.
40. Set off for the Northward, the streams are high, we are turned from our road & yet hardly able to ford the streams that form York River. We escape all dangers & lodge at the Bowling Green.
41. Ladies would—not come
42. Mr Hunter informed me that people had not been made acquainted with my design & many wished me to begin them again.
43. A brilliant circle of Ladies.
44. Mostly member of Assembly.
45. Converse with Mr Lloyd, a senator—a sensible man from the Eastern Shore. He informs me that, great numbers of men, who acknowledge deeds before him

Notes to Section IV

cannot write their names. This is the case in Maryland & Virginia. An eminent merchant in Alexandria informed me that of 50 planters in Virginia, who sold him Tobacco, 4 or 5 only could write their names but make a mark on the receipts. O New England! how Superior are thy inhabitants in morals literature, civility & industry. A small fall of snow & cold weather.

46. A weak head.

47. An event takes place that will materially affect my future situation in life, & render me more happy or more wretched.

48. People in high life suppose they have a right to dispense with the rules of civility.

49. But he is become unpopular by his parsimony.

50. Mostly literary characters. They express their applause by silence & attention & clapping.

51. An institution founded by subscribers, a large fund & donations support it. Before the war the funds amounted to £ 17,000. Now diminished.

52. Besides the cellar rooms. Funds not 150 pr Ann.

53. The first exhibition does not great humour to Columbia College.

54. Mr Curson dies this day.

55. P. Bail the Seneca chief & five others who came on business to Congress. They behave with great civility, & took tea & coffee with decency & some appearance of breeding. When they left the house they shook hands with men & women, without any bow, wearing strong marks of native independence & dignity. Read my last Lecture to about 200 Ladies & Gentlemen, who express the warmest approbation. The evening is closed with music by Mr Laws school.

56. Receive a present from him of a Right of land in Susquehannah. Proceed to Albany. Lodge at City Tavern 160 miles from N York—2 days travel.

57. Kahoze.

58. The Dutch have no taste for the English language.

59. And meet my friends with joy.

60. Return to the City. Hear the debates of Assembly respecting the requisition of Congress—rejected.

61. Begin my lectures in the North meeting House; disturbed by a mob. Let it be remembered that in the year 1786, there are people in Hartford so illiberal, that they will not permit public lectures to be read in a church because they cannot be admitted without paying two shillings! The General Assembly to whom I presented tickets, attended. They ought at least to have been secured from the insults of wealthy farmers.

62. Read my 2d Lecture at Mr Collier's. I obtained permission of the Govr & Upper House to read in the State House, but it was judged not prudent.

63. Finish my Lectures in Hartford.

64. Ride to New Haven and have for company Miss Ruth & Polly Stiles. Arrive at half after 1 oclock. Attend Quarter Day in the Chapel. Take tea at Mr Thompson's.

65. Sunday. At Chapel AM. hear Dr Bellamy PM hear Mr Edwards, take tea at Mr Meigs. Walk to Dr Goodrich's, walk west of the town, return & walk with Mr Kenny.

66. One scholar expelled from College & 3 rusticated, for breaking the Tutors windows &c. Read my 2d Lecture to about 60 hearers.

67. To nearly the same number, take tea at Mr Burr's with a knot of Ladies.

68. Sunday. At College Chapel hear Mr Pitkin. In the absence of Dr Wales, Professor, who is gone to Europe for his health, the neighboring clergymen supply his place.

69. which were six hours.

70. Read my 6th Lecture to 60.

71. Attend Club—a number of literary men collected for sociability.

72. 4 1/2 miles situated on a point of land or rather of rock, consisting of about 300 houses, two Presbᵃ Churches. M Hubbard & Mʳ Storer; an Episcopal Church. The people live by fishing.

73. 560

74. A young man of genius

75. Not a word spoken, all day, a whisper or two among the Ladies excepted, I was very attentive, to the silent exhortations of a pretty of sixteen. Such blushes, such lips made one feel devotion.

76. Went to Quaker meeting heard an Englishman Exhort. Saw a sweet girl.

77. To about 14

78. To about 20

79. Visit Mr Barlow; a snow storm. I write an assignment of the copy-right of the Institute in New England to Messrs Hudson & Goodwin for the whole term granted me by the laws of the several States.

80. perhaps for life

81. an earthquake

82. a long head

83. Adjourn lecture for bad weather.

84. Put my 3d edition of 2d Institute to press—Young & M'Culloch—first in Pennsylvania.

85. to a small audience

86. In a boyish scuffle with Mr Blanchard, Tho' against my will, a chair is broke, folly in little boys is excuseable, but in great boys it is odious.

87. Miss Sally Rhea, a sweet girl.

88. God bless him

89. upon the causes of the Varieties in the Complexions and figures of men—very ingenious.

90. Visit Miss Greenleaf, the black-eyed beauty.

91. with the pretty Miss Hopkins.

92. Pass the evening agreeably.

BIBLIOGRAPHY

Manuscript Collections

The largest collection of letters, the Papers of Noah Webster housed in the Rare Books and Manuscripts Division of the New York Public Library, fills ten large boxes. It also includes the diaries and many other documents, such as honorary degrees and Webster's collection of clippings of newspaper articles he wrote and that were written about him.

The second largest collection, the Webster Family Papers at the Sterling Memorial Library at Yale University, contains letters from all members of the Webster family.

Other collections include those at the American Philosophical Library, Philadelphia; Bienecke Rare Book and Manuscript Library, New Haven, Connecticut; Connecticut Historical Society, Hartford; Burton Collection of the Detroit Public Library; Spahr Library Archives, Dickinson College Library, Carlisle, Pennsylvania; Henry E. Huntington Library, San Marino, California; Historical Society of Pennsylvania; Jervis Public Library, Rome, New York; Archives of the Maryland Historical Society, Baltimore; Rufus King Papers, New-York Historical Society, New York, and the following special collections of the Library of Congress: Henry Clay Papers; William Cranch Papers; Jeremiah Evarts Papers; Benjamin Franklin Papers; Thomas Jefferson Papers; James Madison Papers; Miscellaneous Manuscripts; Henry E. Schoolcraft Papers, and George Washington Papers.

Selected Works by Noah Webster

An American Dictionary of the English Language. 2 vols. New Haven: Hezekiah Howe, 1828.

An American Dictionary of the English Language: First Edition in Octavo. 2 vols. New Haven: By the Author, 1841.

Bibliography

Biography, for the Use of Schools. New Haven: Hezekiah Howe, 1830.

A Brief History of Epidemic and Pestilential Diseases: With the Principal Phenomena of the Physical World; Which Preceed and Accompany Them, and Observations Deduced from the Facts Stated. 2 vols. Hartford: Hudson and Goodwin, 1799.

A Brief View of Errors and Obscurities in the Common Version of the Scriptures. Addressed to the Bible Societies, Clergymen and Other Friends of Religion. [New Haven: N.p., 1834?].

A Collection of Fugitiv Writings on Moral, Historical, Political and Literary Subjects. Boston: J. Thomas and E. T. Andrews, 1790.

A Collection of Papers on Political, Literary, and Moral Subjects. Boston: Webster and Clark, 1843.

A Collection of Papers on the Subject of Bilious Fevers, Prevalent in the United States for a Few Years Past Compiled by Noah Webster, Jun. New York: Hopkins, Webb and Company, 1796.

A Compendious Dictionary of the English Language. New Haven: Sidney's Press, 1806.

A Grammatical Institute of the English Language . . . Part I. Hartford: Hudson and Goodwin, 1783.

History of the United States: To Which Is Prefixed a Brief Historical of Our English Ancestors, from the Dispersion of Babel, to Their Migration to America; and of the Conquest of South America. New Haven: Durrie and Peck, 1832.

The Holy Bible, Containing the Old and New Testaments, in the Common Version. With Amendments of the Language. Ed. Noah Webster. New Haven: Durrie and Peck, 1833.

Instruction and Entertaining Lessons for Youth: With Rules for Reading with Propriety, Illustrated by Examples. New Haven: S. Babcock & Durrie and Peck, 1835.

A Manual of Useful Studies: For the Instruction of Young Persons of Both Sexes, in Families and Schools. New Haven: S. Babcock, 1839.

"Memoir of Noah Webster, LL.D." Webster Family Papers. Sterling Memorial Library, Yale University.

An Oration, Pronounced before the Knox and Warren Branches of the Washington Benevolent Society, at Amherst, on the Celebration of the Declaration of Independence, July 4, 1814. Northampton, Mass.: William Butler, 1814.

The Peculiar Doctrines of the Gospel, Explained and Defended. [New York: J. Seymour, 1809].

A Plea for a Miserable World. . . . Ed. Noah Webster. Boston: Ezra Lincoln, 1820.

The Prompter: or a Commentary on Common Sayings and Subjects, Which Are Full of Common Sense, the Best Sense in the World. Hartford: Hudson and Goodwin, 1791.

The Revolution in France Considered in Respect to Its Progress and Effects. By an American. New York: George Bunce and Company, 1794.

A Rod for a Fool's Back. New York: Read and Morse, [1800].

Value of the Bible and Excellence of the Christian Religion: For the Use of Families and Schools. New Haven: Durrie and Peck, 1834.

"A Voice of Wisdom." [New York] *Commercial Advertiser*, Nov. 20, 1837.

"Will of Noah Webster," June 7, 1843. Webster Family Papers, Yale University.

Secondary Works on Noah Webster

Carpenter, Edwin H., Jr., ed. *A Bibliography of the Writings of Noah Webster.* New York: New York Public Library, 1958.

Ellis, Joseph J. *After the Revolution: Profiles of Early American Culture.* New York: W. W. Norton, 1979.

Ford, Emily Ellsworth Fowler. *Notes on the Life of Noah Webster.* 2 vols. New York: Privately printed, 1912.

Friedman, Lawrence J. *Inventors of the Promised Land.* New York: Knopf, 1975.

Monaghan, E. Jennifer. *A Common Heritage: Noah Webster's Blue-Backed Speller.* Hamden, Conn.: Archon Books, 1983.

Rollins, Richard M. *The Long Journey of Noah Webster.* Philadelphia: University of Pennsylvania Press, 1980.

Scudder, Horace E. *Noah Webster.* Introduction by Richard M. Rollins. New York: Chelsea House, 1981.

Shoemaker, Ervin C. *Noah Webster: Pioneer of Learning.* New York: Columbia University Press, 1936.

Warfel, Harry R. *Letters of Noah Webster.* New York: Library Publishers, 1953.

———. *Noah Webster: Schoolmaster to America.* New York: Macmillan Company, 1936.

Secondary Works on Autobiography

Allport, Gordon. *The Use of Personal Documents in Psychological Science*. New York: Social Science Research Council, 1942.

Begos, Jane DuPree, comp. *Annotated Bibliography of Published Women's Diaries*. Pound Ridge, N.Y.: Begos, 1977.

Bercovitch, Sacvan. *The Puritan Origins of the American Self*. New Haven: Yale University Press, 1975.

Bitton, Davis. *Guide to Mormon Diaries and Autobiographies*. Provo, Utah: Brigham Young University Press, 1977.

Blasing, Mutlu Kanuk. *The Art of Life: Studies in American Autobiographical Literature*. Austin: University of Texas Press, 1977.

Bontemps, Arna. "The Slave Narrative: An American Genre." In *Great Slave Narratives*. Ed. Arna Bontemps. Boston: Beacon Press, 1969.

Buckley, Jerome Hamilton. *The Turning Key: Autobiography of the Subjective Impulse since 1800*. Cambridge: Harvard University Press, 1984.

Carlock, Mary. "American Autobiographies, 1840–1870: A Bibliography." *Bulletin of Bibliography* 23 (May–August 1961).

Couser, G. Thomas. *American Autobiography: The Prophetic Mode*. Amherst: University of Massachusetts Press, 1979.

Cox, James M. "Autobiography and America." In *Aspects of Narrative*, ed. J. H. Miller. New York: Columbia University Press, 1971.

———. "Jefferson's Autobiography: Recovering Literature's Lost Ground." *Southern Review* 14 (1978).

Cronin, James M., ed. *The Diary of Elihu Hubbard Smith*. Philadelphia: American Philosophical Society, 1973.

Eakin, John Paul. *Fictions in Autobiography: Studies in the Art of Self-Invention*. Princeton: Princeton University Press, 1985.

Earle, William. *The Autobiographical Consciousness: A Philosophical Inquiry into Experience*. Chicago: Quadrangle Books, 1972.

Egan, Susanna. *Patterns of Experience in Autobiography*. Chapel Hill: University of North Carolina Press, 1984.

Erikson, Erik. "Ghandi's Autobiography: The Leader as Child." In *Life History and the Historical Moment*. New York: W .W. Norton, 1966.

Fiering, Norman S. "Will and Intellect in the New England Mind." *William and Mary Quarterly*, 3rd series, 29 (1972): 515–58.

Forbes, Harriette Merrifield, comp. *New England Diaries, 1602–1800: A Descriptive Catalogue of Diaries, Orderly Books, and Sea Journals*. Topsfield, Mass.: Perkins Press, 1923.

BIBLIOGRAPHY

Garraty, John A. *The Nature of Biography.* New York: Knopf, 1957.

Gilman, Richard. *Confusion of Realms.* New York: Random House, 1976.

Howarth, William L. "Some Principles of Autobiography." *New Literary History* (Winter 1974): 365–69.

Jackson, Donald, ed. *The Diaries of George Washington.* Vol. I. Charlottesville: University Press of Virginia, 1976.

Jay, Paul. "What's the Use? Critical Theory and the Study of Autobiography." *Biography* 10 (Spring 1987): 39–54.

Kaplan, Louis. *A Bibliography of American Autobiographies.* Madison: University of Wisconsin Press, 1961.

Labaree, L. W., et al., eds. *The Autobiography of Benjamin Franklin.* New Haven: Yale University Press, 1964.

Langness, Lewis. *The Life History in Anthropological Science.* New York: Holt, Rinehart and Winston, 1965.

Lerner, E. D. "Puritanism and Spiritual Autobiography." *Hibbert Journal* 55 (1957).

Levin, David. "The Autobiography of Benjamin Franklin: The Puritan Experimenter in Life and Art." In *Defense of Historical Literature: Essays on American History, Autobiography, Drama and Fiction.* Ed. David Levin. New York: Hill and Wang, 1967.

Lillerd, Richard G. *American Life in Autobiography: A Descriptive Guide.* Stanford: Stanford University Press, 1956.

Lokken, Roy N. "The Case of the Mysterious Diary." In *The Historian as Detective: Essays on Evidence,* ed. Robin Winks. New York: Harper Colophon Books, 1970.

Mandel, Barrett John. "The Autobiographer's Art." *Journal of Aesthetics and Art Criticism.* (Winter 1968): 215–16.

Matthews, William, comp. *American Diaries: An Annotated Bibliography of American Diaries Written Prior to the Year 1861.* Berkeley: University of California Press, 1945.

McGiffert, Michael G., ed. *God's Plot: The Paradoxes of Puritan Piety, Being the Autobiography and Journal of Thomas Shepard.* Amherst: University of Massachusetts Press, 1972.

McLoughlin, William G., ed. *The Diary of Isaac Backus.*Vol. I. Providence: Brown University Press, 1979.

Morgan, Edmund S., ed. "The Diary of Michael Wigglesworth." Colonial Society of Massachusetts *Publications,* no. 35. Boston, 1951.

Murphy, Murray G. "An Approach to the Historical Study of National Character." In *Context and Meaning in Cultural Anthropology,* ed. Melford E. Spiro. New York: Free Press, 1965.

356

BIBLIOGRAPHY

Olney, James. "Autobiography and the Cultural Moment: A Thematical, Historical, and Bibliographical Introduction." In *Autobiography: Essays Theoretical and Critical,* ed. James Olney. Princeton: Princeton University Press, 1980.

———. *Metaphors of Self: The Meaning of Autobiography.* Princeton: Princeton University Press, 1972.

Pascal, Roy. *Design and Truth in Autobiography.* Cambridge: Harvard University Press, 1960.

Sayre, Robert F. "Autobiography and the Making of America." In *Autobiography: Essays Theoretical and Critical,* ed. James Olney. Princeton: Princeton University Press, 1980.

———. *The Examined Self: Benjamin Franklin, Henry Adams, Henry James.* Princeton: Princeton University Press, 1964.

———. "The Proper Study—Autobiography in American Studies." *American Quarterly* 29 (1977): 335–351.

Shea, Daniel B., Jr. *Spiritual Awakening in Early America.* Princeton: Princeton University Press, 1968.

Spacks, Patricia. "Women's Stories, Women's Selves." *Hudson Review* 30 (1977).

Spengemann, William. *The Forms of Autobiography: Episodes in the History of a Literary Genre.* New Haven: Yale University Press, 1980.

———. and L. R. Lunquist, "Autobiography and the American Myth." *American Quarterly* 17 (Fall 1965): 117–135.

Stone, Albert E. "Autobiography and American Culture." *American Studies: An International Newsletter* (Winter 1972).

Ward, John William. "Who Was Benjamin Franklin?" *American Scholar* 32 (Autumn 1963).

Watkins, Owen C. *The Puritan Experience: Studies in Spiritual Autobiography.* New York: Schocken Books, 1972.

Weintraub, Karl. "Autobiography and Historical Consciousness." *Critical Inquiry* 1 (June 1979): 821–48.

———. *The Value of the Individual: Self and Circumstance in Autobiography.* Chicago: University of Chicago Press, 1978.

Wilner, Eleanor. *Gathering the Winds: Visionary Imagination and Radical Transformation of Self and Society.* Baltimore: Johns Hopkins University Press, 1975.

Wolf, Cynthia G. "Literary Reflections of the Puritan Character." *Journal of the History of Ideas* (1967): 99–121.

Zuckerman, Michael. "The Fabrication of Identity in Early America." *William and Mary Quarterly,* 3rd series, 24 (1977): 183–214.

BIBLIOGRAPHY

Additional Selected Secondary Sources

Adams, Henry. *The Education of Henry Adams*. Introduction by James Truslow Adams. New York: Modern Library, 1931.

Bercovitch, Sacvan. *The American Jeremiad*. Madison: University of Wisconsin Press, 1978.

Buel, Lawrence. *New England Literary Culture: From the Revolution through
Renaissance*. Cambridge: Cambridge University Press, 1986.

Fliegelman, Jay. *Prodigals and Pilgrams: The American Revolution against
Patriarchal Authority, 1759–1800*. Cambridge: Cambridge University Press,
1982.

Greven, Phillip J. *The Protestant Temperament: Patterns of Child-Rearing,
Religious Experience, and Self in Early America*. New York: New American
Library, 1977.

Schulz, Constance B. "Children and Childhood in the Eighteenth Century." In *American Childhood: A Research Guide and Historical Handbook*,
ed. Joseph M. Hawes and N. Ray Hiner. Westport, Conn.: Greenwood
Press, 1985.

Tuveson, Ernest R. *Reedemer Nation: The Idea of America's Millennial Role*.
Chicago: University of Chicago Press, 1968.

Walzer, John F. "A Period of Ambivalence: Eighteenth-Century American
Childhood." In *The History of Childhood*, ed. Lloyd deMause. New York:
Harper & Row, 1975, pp. 351–82.

359

Oil Portrait.
Samuel F. B. Morse, 1823. *Henry Ford Museum and Greenfield Village. (Possibly a copy of the original.)*

INDEX

Index

Index

Index

Index

Index

Index

Index

Index

Index

Index